STUDIES IN SLAVE AND POST-SLAVE SOCIETIES AND CULTURES

Series Editors: Gad Heuman and James Walvin

SLAVERY AND COLONIAL RULE IN AFRICA

STUDIES IN SLAVE AND POST-SLAVE SOCIETIES AND CULTURES

Series Editors: Gad Heuman and James Walvin

ISSN 1462-1770

Other Titles in the Series

Unfree Labour in the Development of the Atlantic World
edited by Paul E. Lovejoy and Nicholas Rogers

Small Islands, Large Questions
Society, Culture and Resistance in the Post-Emancipation Caribbean
edited by Karen Fog Olwig

Reconstructing the Black Past
Blacks in Britain 1780–1830
by Norma Myers

Against the Odds
Free Blacks in the Slave Societies of the Americas
edited by Jane G. Landers

Routes to Slavery
Direction, Ethnicity and Mortality in the Atlantic Slave Trade
edited by David Eltis and David Richardson

Popular Politics and British Anti-Slavery
The Mobilisation of Public Opinion against the Slave Trade, 1787–1807
by J.R. Oldfield

Classical Slavery
by M.I. Finley

SLAVERY AND COLONIAL RULE IN AFRICA

Edited by
SUZANNE MIERS
Ohio University

and

MARTIN KLEIN
University of Toronto

LONDON AND NEW YORK

First published in 1999 in Great Britain by
FRANK CASS PUBLISHERS
Reprinted 2004
By Routledge
2 Park Square, Milton Park,
Abingdon, Oxon, OX14 4RN

Transferred to Digital Printing 2004

Copyright © 1999 Frank Cass Publishers

British Library Cataloguing in Publication Data

Slavery and colonial rule in Africa. – Studies in slave
and post-slave societies and cultures ; v. 8)
1. Slavery – Africa – Case studies
I. Miers, Suzanne II. Klein, Martin A. (Martin Allen), 1934–
326'.096

ISBN 0714644366

ISBN 0-7146-4884-1 (cloth)
ISBN 0-7146-4436-6 (paper)
ISSN 1462-1770

Library of Congress Cataloging-in-Publication Data

Slavery and colonial rule in Africa / edited by Suzanne Miers and
Martin Klein.
p. cm. – (Studies in slave and post-slave societies and
cultures, ISSN 1462–1770)
"This group of studies first appeared as a special issue of
Slavery and abolition, vol. 19, no. 2, August 1998" – T.p. verso.
Includes bibliographical references and index.
ISBN 0-7146-4884-1 (cloth). – ISBN 0-7146-4436-6 (paper)
1. Slavery–Africa–History. 2. Africa–Colonization–History.
I. Miers, Suzanne. II. Klein, Martin A. III. Series.
HT1321.S555 1998
306.3'62'096^{a}dc21

98-27601
CIP

This group of studies first appeared as a special issue of *Slavery and Abolition*, Vol.19,
No.2, August 1998 (ISSN 0144-039 X), published by Frank Cass.

*All rights reserved. No part of this publication may be reproduced, stored or introduced into a
retrieval system or transmitted, in any form or by any means, electronic, mechanical,
photocopying, recording, or otherwise, without the prior written permission of the
publisher of this book.*

Printed and bound by Antony Rowe Ltd, Eastbourne

Contents

List of Maps   vi

Introduction   **Suzanne Miers and Martin A. Klein**   1

THE INTERNATIONAL CONTEXT

Slavery and the Slave Trade as International Issues, 1890–1939   **Suzanne Miers**   16

FRENCH AFRICA

No Liberty, Not Much Equality, and Very Little Fraternity: The Mirage of Manumission in the Algerian Sahara in the Second Half of the Nineteenth Century   **Dennis Cordell**   38

Slavery and Muslim Jurisprudence in Morocco   **Ahmad Sikainga**   57

Slavery and French Rule in the Sahara   **Martin A. Klein**   73

'The Ties that Bind': Servility and Dependency among the Fulbe of Bundu (Senegambia), c.1930s to 1980s   **Andrew F. Clark**   91

GERMAN AFRICA

The 'Freeing' of the Slaves in German East Africa: The Statistical Record, 1890–1914   **Jan-Georg Deutsch**   109

Slavery in Colonial Cameroon, 1880s to 1930s   **Andreas Eckert**   133

BRITISH AFRICA

The Administration of the Abolition Laws, African Responses and Post-Proclamation Slavery in the Gold Coast, 1874–1940   **Kwabena Opare-Akurang**   149

'Amana' and 'Asiri': Royal Slave Culture and
the Colonial Regime in Kano, 1903–26   **Sean Stilwell**   167

'When the Slaves Left, Owners Wept':
Entrepreneurs and Emancipation among
the Igbo People   **Don C. Ohadike**   189

'Do Dady nor Lef me Make dem Carry me':
Slave Resistance and Emancipation in
Sierra Leone, 1894–1928   **Ismail Rashid**   208

The End of Slavery among the Yoruba   **Toyin Falola**   232

Festina Lente: Slavery Policy and Practice
in the Anglo-Egyptian Sudan   **Taj Hargey**   250

Notes on Contributors   273

Bibliography   276

Index   293

List of Maps

1. Societies discussed in this volume   vii

2. Morocco, Algeria and Sahara   viii

3. Southern Sahara and Sahel   ix

4. Nigeria and Cameroon   x

5. North East Africa, circa 1930   17

6. North East Africa and Arabia   18

7. German East Africa   110

8. Sierra Leone and Guinea   209

Maps 1 to 5 were prepared by Carolyn King of the York University Cartography
Laboratory.

MAP 1
SOCIETIES DISCUSSED IN THIS VOLUME

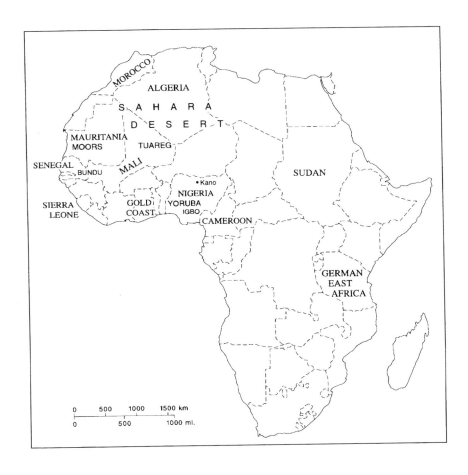

MAP 2
MOROCCO, ALGERIA AND SAHARA

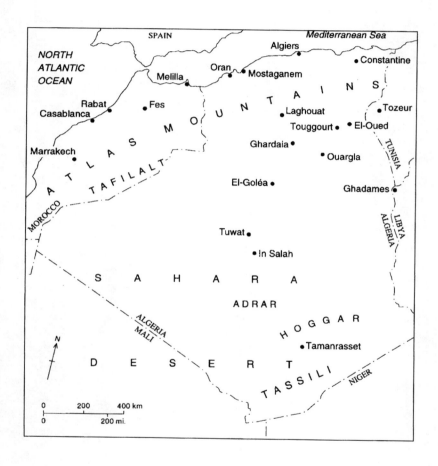

MAP 3

SOUTHERN SAHARA AND SAHEL

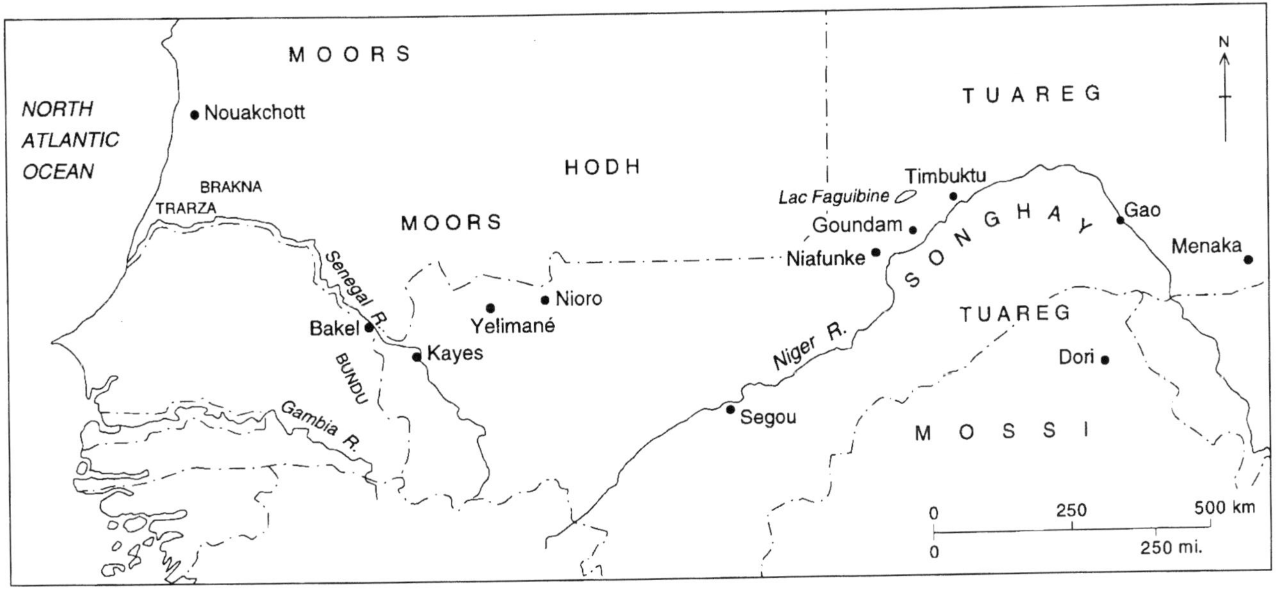

MAP 4
NIGERIA AND CAMEROON

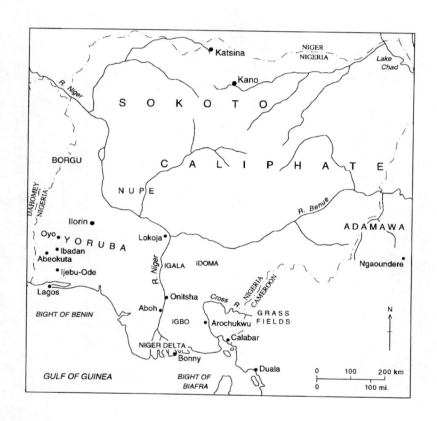

Introduction

SUZANNE MIERS and MARTIN A. KLEIN

Slavery in Africa attracted a great deal of attention in the Western world on the eve of the colonial partition of the continent in the last decades of the nineteenth century. From press and pulpit came heartrending descriptions of the horrors of slave raids and the suffering of thousands of hapless victims brutally torn from their homes and marched off to a lifetime of bondage. The public was led to believe that colonial rule would end this scourge – and indeed this was one of the moral justifications for the conquest of Africa. These expectations, however, were only partially fulfilled. Certainly, as they gained control, the new rulers hastened to end warfare and slave raiding, although it often continued in the more remote areas. They also attacked the slave trade so that it eventually ceased to be a large scale operation, although clandestine petty dealing continued to the end of colonial rule. Slavery, however, was quite another matter. Not only were the colonial rulers reluctant to attack it, but in many cases, they actually supported it.

In spite of all the propaganda at the time of the 'scramble', both slavery and its fate under colonial rule attracted little academic attention until the 1960s and early 1970s when a new generation of scholars was struck by the fact that little was known about its demise, in spite of its role in pre-colonial history and the importance of abolition on the agendas of the colonial conquerors. Their initial research focussed on Africa's role as a supplier for the export slave trade and on the nature of slavery within Africa. This resulted in the publication of important collections of articles beginning with Claude Meillassoux (ed.), *Esclavage en Afrique Pré-Coloniale,*[1] and Suzanne Miers and Igor Kopytoff (eds.), *Slavery in Africa: Historical and Anthropological Perspectives.*[2] Then came Paul Lovejoy (ed.), *The Ideology of Slavery in Africa.*[3] Claire Robertson and Martin Klein (eds.) opened the discussion of gender and slavery with *Women and Slavery in Africa,*[4] and J.R. Willis edited *Slaves and Slavery in Muslim Africa.*[5] There were also a number of studies of slavery in particular societies as well as general works, some of which covered the colonial period.[6] The first collection to focus on slavery under colonial rule, however, was Suzanne Miers and Richard Roberts (eds.), *The End of Slavery in Africa,* which appeared in 1988.[7]

These books made it clear that the colonial powers, especially in the early decades, depended heavily on slave-holding elites to administer their empires. Administrators were convinced that freeing the slaves would lead to a decline in economic productivity and a rise in lawlessness. Experience in the plantation colonies, particularly in the Caribbean, had led them to believe that the newly liberated would desert their masters and work only to provide for themselves, and that their erstwhile owners would not engage in manual labour. Hence most colonial governments limited their efforts to ending slave raiding and trading in the hope that slavery would decline gradually without causing economic and social disruption. They attacked only the worst cruelties of the institution – the brutalities inherent in the acquisition and sale of slaves. This policy appeared to have been so successful that many later observers felt that slavery had simply faded away without serious repercussions. The new studies, however, showed that its decline and eventual demise had not been a simple progression. In some cases it ended abruptly with the departure of the slaves. In others it faded out quietly, causing little disturbance to the overall economic and social order, but bringing great changes in the lives of individuals. Moreover, its demise was not complete. Almost everywhere traces of it could still be found.

Research on slavery in the colonial period was, and often still is, bedevilled by silence. Colonial regimes were reluctant to reveal the truth. The missionaries, once on the cutting edge of the humanitarian crusade against the African slave trade, turned, with a few notable exceptions, to other questions once the caravans of weary slaves no longer trudged along the paths of Africa. Worse still, former slaves and their descendants frequently even now prefer not to discuss what is still seen as a dishonourable status, and researchers themselves are wary of breaking the confidences of informants unwilling to reveal their ancestry. Scholars also face the very real danger that, if they publish all they have discovered, they may not be welcomed back to continue their work. However, the research that has been done has cast more light on the flaws and hypocrisies of colonial policies as well as on the subtleties and the infinite variations in the legacy of slavery.

In order to encourage this research, we organized panels at the annual meetings of the African Studies Association of the United States from 1994 to 1997. Their aim was to foster the exchange of ideas between scholars working on slavery-linked subjects and particularly to call attention to doctoral research and other works in progress. These panels focussed on entrepreneurs and their use of slaves, on the policies of selected colonial governments, on the international dimensions of African slavery, and on contemporary forms of slavery. The chapters in this volume by Clark, Cordell, Hargey, Klein, Miers, Ohadike, Rashid and Stilwell were all originally presented at these meetings. Some of the other papers have

INTRODUCTION 3

already been or will be published elsewhere, while some came from books in press or in progress, and others from ongoing research, including doctoral dissertations.[8]

Parallel to our endeavour there have been important publications by other scholars. In *Slow Death for Slavery*, Paul Lovejoy and Jan Hogendorn detailed British efforts to control the process of emancipation and gain the collaboration of elites in the Sokoto Caliphate of Northern Nigeria.[9] Fred Morton's *Children of Ham: Freed Slaves and Fugitive Slaves on the Kenya Coast, 1873 to 1907* argued that most slaves on the Kenya coast escaped, established their own settlements or sought refuge in European missions, rather than squatting on their former owners' estates.[10] Carolyn Brown, writing on the Igbo in southeastern Nigeria, showed how the legal abolition of slavery did little to break the power of slave owners over their former slaves, and provided new opportunities for exploitation by masters, even as it opened new avenues to freedom.[11]

Several authors have explored the emergence of new social groups. Thus Ahmad Sikainga's *Slaves into Workers* chronicled the transformation of slaves into a modern working class in the Sudan, showing how British recruitment of former slaves shaped the later development of the wage labour force.[12] Ann O'Hear's *Power Relations in Nigeria: Ilorin Slaves and Their Successors* discussed the slave system in Ilorin and linked the decline of slavery with the emergence of small peasant producers.[13] Ibrahim Sundiata in *From Slavery to Neoslavery: The Bight of Biafra and Fernando Po in the Era of Abolition, 1827–1930* explained the shift on the Spanish island of Fernando Po from slavery to contract labour – complementing his earlier work on Liberia.[14] The long continuance of slave raiding on the frontiers of Ethiopia is covered in articles in D. Donham and Wendy James' *The Southern Marches of Imperial Ethiopia*.[15] In 'The Suppression of Slavery in Ethiopia', Miers discussed the antislavery policies of the Ethiopian government between 1912 and 1936.[16] Jay Spaulding analysed the traffic from western Ethiopia into Sudan in 'The Business of Slavery in the Central Anglo-Egyptian Sudan, 1910–30'.[17] On South Africa, Robert Shell's massive study of slavery, Pamela Scully's perceptive analysis of emancipation and gender relations, Watson's study of emancipation, and collections published by Elizabeth Eldridge and Fred Morton (eds.) and by Nigel Worden and Clifton Crais, and have enhanced our understanding of Cape society, the Cape frontier and the emergence of a racist social order.[18] Martin Klein (ed.), *Breaking the Chains*, compared emancipation in Asia and Africa,[19] following on from James Watson's ground-breaking collection *Asian and African Systems of Slavery*.[20]

The new works on Africa, including the chapters in this book, have confirmed some of the conclusions of Miers and Roberts, modified others,

4 SLAVERY AND COLONIAL RULE IN AFRICA

and opened new lines of inquiry. All of our authors provide examples of the reluctance of colonial regimes to deal with slavery. They show how, short of European manpower and reluctant to spend more than minimal sums on their colonies, they depended largely on slave-holding elites to administer their empires. They were convinced that without slave labour, economic activity would decline dramatically and the colonies would be a drain on metropolitan taxpayers. However, to appease humanitarian groups at home, they often clothed their actions in anti-slavery rhetoric and issued pronouncements or proclaimed laws which were all too often merely cosmetic or simply unenforceable.

Even before the 'scramble for Africa,' when most colonies were tiny coastal entrepots, colonial rulers feared that if they freed the slaves of their residents and the fugitives from neighbouring peoples, they would drive away the trade on which they depended. As their empires expanded, therefore, they sought an approach to slavery that would neither antagonize African elites nor draw fire from humanitarian groups at home. Under British law slavery had to be outlawed in colonies. To avoid this, as new areas were conquered, they were designated 'protectorates'. In these they could use the model of abolition worked out by the British in India. Under this model slavery lost its legal status, but did not become illegal.[21] This meant, in theory, that the colonial regime did not recognize rights over slaves in colonial courts, nor – again in theory – did it return runaways or permit slave-owners to use force to retrieve or retain their slaves. This was acceptable to many colonial policy-makers, and even to some humanitarians because they believed that slaves in Africa were in general well treated. The hope was that this model would enable the seriously oppressed to leave, but would keep most slaves in place and at work, until eventually they were replaced by a free wage labour force – the ultimate aim. This solution was cheap. Owners did not need to be compensated. Its impact could be delayed by not informing slaves of their rights and large numbers would not be suddenly freed with no means of support. This solution was so successful that variations of it were adopted by the British, French and Germans. In other colonies, not dealt with in this volume, various legal niceties were tried. For instance, the Portuguese declared slaves free in 1878 but did nothing to make the laws a reality.[22] Thus the results were always the same – real emancipation came only slowly.

Sometimes abolitionist agendas prevailed for a while. Cordell describes a conflict in Algeria between civilian and military agendas. Opare-Akurang writing on the Gold Coast in the 1880s, Falola on the Yoruba in western Nigeria and Rashid on Sierra Leone in the 1890s describe genuine efforts to liberate slaves, but this was unusual. Hargey records blatant British collaboration with slave-holding elites in the Sudan. Klein shows how the

INTRODUCTION 5

French in the Sahara could not operate in the desert without the support of the slave owners. Moreover servile groups in the oases and on the desert edge were reluctant to sever ties with their owners since they could not count on French protection and had no desire to work for the French – which was the price of cooperation. Deutsch, writing on German East Africa, where large plantations were worked by slaves, shows how the Germans eroded slavery by allowing redemptions and official manumissions. In contrast, Eckert tells us that in Cameroon, where slavery was widespread but had not attracted much attention from the German public, they passed laws against it but only occasionally enforced them and even allowed slave trading for many years. Thus in very different situations and in colonial possessions remote from each other the same general trends can be observed. The authors in this volume stress the reluctance or outright aversion to sudden abolition on the part of the colonial rulers. Moreover, when they took action against slavery, it was often selective – a tool to reduce the power of those owners who opposed colonial rule. Otherwise they supported slavery as a means of retaining the loyalty of the elites, maintaining social control and avoiding any disruption of the economy.

The fact that colonial administrations countenanced slavery for so long does not mean that all officials accepted the institution. They came from nations which had long rejected slavery and doubtless most would have liked to end it, but the fragility of colonial power, the sparsity of European officials in Africa, combined with the need to turn their possessions into viable assets to the mother country, led them to compromise with their principles. However, there were dissenting voices even among administrators, as Hogendorn and Lovejoy made clear in *Slow Death for Slavery*. Hargey's chapter on the Sudan here shows that these dissenters could sometimes force a change in government policy, although not without cost to themselves.

The impact and pace of abolition varied dramatically, depending on the number of European officials, the actual strength of the administration, the economic changes which came in the wake of colonial rule, the degree of interest taken in the metropole, and the need, as Miers and Rashid demonstrate, by the 1920 and 1930s to send reports to the League of Nations. In some societies, particularly decentralized ones, slavery ceased rapidly to be meaningful. These were, however, societies that rapidly integrated outsiders, servile or other. The Igbo were a notable exception. Both Ohadike in this volume, and Brown in the article cited above, show that Igbo slave owners were tenacious in their efforts to retain control over their slaves. Even when forced to allow them to leave, they denied them full social and ritual equality. In fact, in most societies change was slow. Even where large numbers of slaves left, either to return to their earlier homes or to seek new lives, most remained where they were and slowly renegotiated relations with their owners. Colonial policies – not laws which were so often not enforced – established the context within which slavery operated. They could make it theoretically possible for slaves to leave, but they usually did not govern the actual pace of emancipation.

This depended on whether or not freed slaves had access to land and jobs. Colonial rule frequently opened up a struggle for control of land and labour. Official fears that freed slaves would not enter the labour market but would become subsistence farmers, vagrants or criminals were in general totally unjustified. As Falola and Ohadike show, when jobs were available they provided a reserve of migrant labourers oscillating between rural and industrial areas, as well as a large part of the small but steadily increasing permanent labour force. Hargey emphasizes that given access to land, credit and livestock, many soon became self-supporting peasant producers. If anything, freeing the slaves was a way to create the very reservoir of labour the colonial regimes needed. Colonial proconsuls, however, rarely foresaw this and often resorted to new forms of coercion. Thus during the early colonial period all colonies relied heavily on forced labour – often carried out by slaves supplied by chiefs and other owners. In time the colonial rulers came to use less direct devices to drive people into the labour force, such as land alienation, regressive taxation, compulsory crop growing and conscription into the military or into labour battalions.

At the same time they devised various ways of forcing slaves to remain with their masters. In Northern Nigeria, as Lovejoy and Hogendorn have shown, the British made it difficult for runaway slaves to get land and they worked out a system to make the discontented ransom themselves. Schemes for redemption as well as self-redemption operated in areas as different as Sierra Leone, Yorubaland, the Sudan and German East Africa, where the Germans also allowed European planters to ransom slaves, who then had to work off the cost of their redemption. In Southern Nigeria, slaves were freed only to be bound to their owners as 'apprentices' until the system was ended in 1914 after an outcry in Britain. Opare-Akurang cites cases of slaves in the Gold Coast actually freed by the courts and then handed back to their owners as 'apprentices' – thereby nullifying their liberation. Clark, Hargey, and Rashid, writing respectively on Senegal, Sudan and Sierra Leone, all describe instances of forcible – and quite illegal – return of fugitives, a widespread practice often noted by other scholars.

Several writers demonstrate how indirect rule and the use of Muslim or customary law shielded slave-owners from colonial legislation. Sikainga shows how Shari'a courts in Morocco enabled former masters to maintain a measure of control over freed slaves. Hargey discusses British attempts to end abuses by Islamic courts in Sudan, particularly in cases involving

INTRODUCTION 7

marriage or the custody of the children of slave concubines. In Northern Nigeria, slave cases were handed over to Muslim courts which could enforce claims against slaves or make their liberation more palatable. They could, for instance, award compensation to masters whose female slaves left under the guise of damages for matrimonial disputes. In non-Muslim areas Native Courts were set up to deal with cases according to 'customary law' but in the early colonial period European administrators hardly knew what such law was, and elders were often able to manipulate it to suit themselves, particularly as these courts were controlled by chiefs. Thus in Cameroon African courts enforced owners' claims over their slaves once German courts were prohibited from doing so, and among the Yoruba they were used to force slaves to ransom themselves. In the Gold Coast, on the other hand, chiefs were not allowed to try slavery cases for fear they would favour the owners, but the result was the same because there were so few colonial courts and European officials were so scarce that slaves had trouble securing a hearing. For the same reason, in Sierra Leone the chiefs who were supposed to oversee the treatment of slaves were able to prevent them from bringing their cases to court. The few who did succeed, however, showed ingenuity in gathering evidence to gain their freedom.

In fact slaves themselves were usually important actors in their own liberation. In many parts of Africa, they took the initiative and fled in massive numbers. They took advantage of the disruptions of the conquest period to test the antislavery rhetoric of the conquerors. In Northern Nigeria, Lovejoy and Hogendorn reported over 60,000 departures during this time. Sometimes, however, departures took place long after the establishment of colonial rule. The most massive exodus of this sort seems to have been in French West Africa, where up to a million slaves picked up and left between 1906 and 1912.[23] Slaves usually fled singly or in small groups, but numbers could still be considerable. Falola and Ohadike respectively record numerous departures in southern Nigeria. Rashid notes that defection was so serious in Sierra Leone that the government passed legislation to prevent it, and British and French officials collaborated to stop cross-border flights and to return fugitives. Cordell describes how slaves within Algeria and from nearby countries took advantage of French law. Hargey describes slave flights in the Sudan and the large scale exodus of fugitives from Ethiopia in the 1930s. In German East Africa, where slaves took advantage of German manumission policies in increasing numbers from year to year, only 60,000 were officially freed, but many more must simply have left as the overall number of slaves declined from an estimated 500,000 in 1890 to less than 160,000 in 1914. Former slaves played a significant part in helping others to gain their freedom. Falola and Rashid call attention to the role of ex-slave soldiers in provoking slave flight in Yorubaland and Sierra Leone. Hargey

8   SLAVERY AND COLONIAL RULE IN AFRICA

points to similar actions by ex-slave soldiers in the Sudan, although in this case they may actually have been appropriating slaves for themselves under pretext of reuniting families. He shows, however, that the success of freed slaves in establishing themselves as free labour or as independent farmers attracted others to emulate them.

Many first generation slaves simply wanted to return home. Others fled to escape harsh treatment. Departures were sometimes unwittingly stimulated by colonial policies. Thus Clark has shown that defection in eastern Senegal accelerated after the First World War, when slave soldiers refused to return to servitude after having served in the trenches. In the West African Sahel departures were caused by disastrous droughts and the famine of 1913–14, when owners could no longer support their dependants, rather than by any official measures.[24] Conversely, the same drought led to widespread sales of both slaves and free children.[25] Similarly, Klein notes that the famine years from 1968 to 1983 loosened ties between the slave owners of Mauritania and their servile dependants. In Sierra Leone, Rashid notes that the hardships of the First World War and the Depression, which followed it, on the one hand aggravated slave discontent and on the other caused the British to conclude that slavery was unproductive.

Slave initiative was important even when slaves stayed with or near their owners. Many stayed because they lacked a viable alternative, or, as in the case of those in the Sahara, because flight was too dangerous. But in most instances, their position was probably tolerable, particularly if they had been born in the community and were linked to other members of the society by ties of kinship, marriage and friendship. To maintain control, however, masters often had to concede change. Slaves struggled hardest for the right to choose their own spouses, pay their own bride price, and keep control of their own children, as well as to achieve personal autonomy and the right to work for their own benefit.[26] Masters struggled to maintain their claims over labour and over slave children. They often succeeded in keeping former slaves dependant on them for land and livestock, and sometimes for access to migratory networks. Some ex-slaves, however, were able to turn their inferior status to advantage by doing well paid jobs scorned by the freeborn. The availability of wage labour was an important factor in liberation, enabling slaves to ransom themselves or to make a living on their own.

One group of slaves struggled not to end their bondage but to preserve it. In a chapter that breaks new ground, Stilwell considers the royal slaves of Kano in Northern Nigeria. Such slaves have not been the subject of much inquiry, probably because they were not among the wretched of the earth. They were, however, very much slaves, and their privileges were rooted in their dependence on state power. Here slave initiative was exerted, not to

INTRODUCTION   9

end or ameliorate their status, but to protect the privileges that depended on it. The long continuation of a slave bureaucracy in northern Nigeria made these slaves more visible than their counterparts elsewhere, but royal slaves existed in many societies, and in general their descendants are more willing to talk than those of humble agricultural slaves.

Another field in which further investigation is required is the fate of slave-owners under colonial rule. Opare-Akurang cites the ingenuity of owners in the Gold Coast in procuring and keeping slaves in spite of colonial efforts to end the trade. For instance, they bought children without facial scarification who could not be readily identified as slaves, and were young enough to learn local dialects. They exerted pressure which made it difficult to get evidence against dealers and against owners who ill-treated slaves. Both Opare-Akurang, writing on the Gold Coast, and Klein discussing the Sahara, point out that owners also intimidated slaves by threatening to use supernatural powers. Rashid stresses the entrenched opposition of owners in Sierra Leone to emancipation and their demands for compensation. In contrast, more realistic owners in German East Africa, as slavery eroded, often allowed slaves to redeem themselves, as a means of salvaging something from the institution before it ceased to exist. Ohadike's chapter specifically examines the fate of Igbo slave-owners under colonial rule. Slave owning and trading had been a factor in their unparalleled prosperity in the later nineteenth century and they were among the Africans who resisted the imposition of colonial rule most fiercely; but finally abolition and competition from European firms wiped out their predominant position and large fortunes. Their decline was irreversible and they were eventually replaced by a new and more flexible group of entrepreneurs. Similarly research among the Giryama on the Kenya coast has shown that the descendants of nineteenth-century slave-owning entrepreneurs have not maintained their dominant place in society.[27] In both these cases, descendants of slaves who were the first to receive Western education have fared better than the descendants of owners who were reluctant to have their children attend mission schools.

In other cases, however, owners kept control. Brown, writing on a different Igbo society, shows that owners long retained their dominance through control of land and rituals and through their position as colonial chiefs.[28] Mbodj has argued that nineteenth-century entrepreneurs in St. Louis used their control over land and jobs to maintain their power over labour until the end of the nineteenth century.[29] Roberts and Klein focussed attention on the Maraka of Banamba, whose harsh exploitation of slave labour led to a massive exodus after 1906.[30] Although immediately after this exodus the French found, to their surprise, that the Maraka of Banamba were working their own fields, three quarters of a century later, many of

10 SLAVERY AND COLONIAL RULE IN AFRICA

their descendants were rich merchants or influential clerics. In Botswana, the descendants of the Tswana cattle owners who, in the late nineteenth century, reduced hunter-gatherer families to servile labour on their cattle posts and in their homes, have retained their dominance.[31] In general our knowledge of the fate of slave owners is incomplete. We know that emancipation frequently wiped out large accumulations of capital. Even where entrepreneurial classes survived, we often do not know whether they were the same people who surfaced a generation later as merchants and transporters.

Eventually, in all areas, even in the heart of the Sahara, change did take place. Ohadike and Falola both point to the crucial role of changes attendant on colonial rule. With time, wage labour increased so that by the 1930s, in most parts of Africa, the problem was not finding workers, but finding work. Slave porters were replaced by free men working for wages, and then by railways and trucks. Ohadike cites figures demonstrating the importance of these changes in transport. With the end of warfare, slave armies were not needed. Slave soldiers in colonial armies were replaced by free professionals, though often recruited from former slave communities. Royal slaves gave way to a paid civil service. In time, Western education and good business sense, rather than control over people, became the avenues to power and wealth. The pre-colonial status symbols – large numbers of dependants (children, wives and slaves) – became expensive burdens and were replaced by new, and less demanding possessions such as cars, real estate, cocoa farms, even bicycles and watches. These and various money-making projects became more economic and productive, hence more desirable, investments than large holdings of slaves.

However, even today, slavery has not completely disappeared from Africa. In these final decades of the twentieth century it is illegal everywhere, and in many areas it has vanished without trace. But in others it remains as a social status carrying various forms of disability. The historian's task is often not so much describing when or whether slavery ceased to exist, but analysing changes in the relationshps between former slaves and former masters. It is rarely possible to record the process of renegotiation. It seems, however, that in cases in which owners have lost their economic advantange, they have often succeeded in maintaining the social distance between temselves and former slaves by preserving their monopoly of status symbols and control over rituals. Clark gives a particularly vivid picture of the results in a Fulbe community in eastern Senegal. Here a decade ago he found there was no longer significant economic exploitation, but the descendants of slaves and free did not intermarry. Persons of slave descent could not lead prayers in mosques or hold local official positions. They performed menial tasks such as cooking

INTRODUCTION

11

at festivals for the descendants of former owners. They maintained the servile connection so that they could call on the descendants of their former owners for help in hard times. Social distinctions of the same kind are maintained in many societites. Among the Igbo persons of slave descent often cannot officiate at religious ceremonies or purchase the higher titles, and intermarriage with descendants of the free is discouraged. In Cameroon, it is offensive to call anyone a slave or refer to servile origins – clear evidence that such origins remain a social problem. This is also true elsewhere.

If these cases seem relatively innocuous, Ohadike remainds us that *osu*, the descendants of cult-slaves among the Igbo, are still a despised caste. Although their status is not legally recognized and they may never see the shrines to which they or their ancestors were dedicated, they cannot intermarry with the free or change their status, which is hereditary. Among the most exploitative forms of cult slavery is the *trokosi* (*tro*, fetish; *kosi*, slave) system practiced by the Ewe in the Volta region of southern Ghana. Here girls as young as five or six may be dedicated for life to the service of a deity to atone for the offences of their male relations. They become virtual slaves of the priest, working for him and bound to respond to his sexual desires. Their children, whether by the priest or by marriage to an outsider, which may be allowed as they become older, inherit their status.[32]

In Mauritania, as late as 1980, chattel slavery itself persisted. There Klein shows that slavery had enjoyed the support of the colonial regime although it was outlawed. It was also declared illegal under the constitution promulgated at independence in 1960. In 1980, however, Mauritania suddenly announced its abolition – thus confirming that earlier laws had been ineffective or not applied. Since then, Mauritania has had to deal with the agitation of former slaves called Haratin, who are now organized to fight for their rights, and have succeeded in securing the attention of the United Nations, the world press and various humanitarian organizations. However, in recent years, in Mauritania and among the Tuareg in the Sahara, the increase in wage labour and the decimation of herds by drought have eroded the remaining manifestations of slavery more than government policies.

In Sudan, as Hargey shows, there has actually been a resurgence of chattel slavery as the result of two generations of civil war. Women and children have been captured in raids or kidnapped by militias in the south and taken north to serve as unpaid domestic or agricultural labour. The government of Sudan maintains that it does not recognize slavery and that these are merely manifestations of customary raiding between pastoral groups.

This volume still leaves many areas unexplored. Constraints of time and space precluded our soliciting articles on Portuguese, Italian, Belgian and

12 SLAVERY AND COLONIAL RULE IN AFRICA

Spanish colonies as well as South Africa, which has been the subject of such exciting research over the last decade. However, Deutsch and Eckert have provided us with studies of German Africa, hitherto a little explored field of research.[33] Cordell and Klein open up key questions on the Sahara. Sikainga summarises concisely the question of Islamic law and slavery in French Morocco.[34] Miers' chapter breaks new ground with a discussion of the British international antislavery campaign, focusing on the League of Nations. Stilwell's work on royal slaves and Ohadike's on slave owners both suggest new fields for research. Rashid's discussion of changes in the moral economy of slavery takes up a theme already pioneered by other scholars and applies it to Sierra Leone. Opare-Akurang and Hargey provide valuable new information on Gold Coast and Sudan.

Our panels at the African Studies Association opened new lines of inquiry only partially reflected in this volume, such as the relationship between African entrepreneurship and slavery, and, of considerable importance, the metamorphosis of slavery into different types of coerced labour, now designated 'contemporary forms of slavery'. Since the emancipation of slaves did not end the demand for controllable cheap workers, slavery was soon replaced by other forms of exploitable labour, some of which also have a long history. Thus under colonial rule in many areas there was an increase in pawning, particularly, as Falola and Opare-Akurang point out, during the interwar period.[35] Pawning was the pledging of a person, usually a young girl, who lived and worked for the creditor, in return for a loan. Colonial regimes correctly did not regard this as slavery, but took measures against it because it involved the involuntary grant of a person's labour and often exposed young women to sexual exploitation. The Second World War and the prosperous period that followed it decreased the demand for pawns, and as patriarchal authority broke down the control that men could exert over their children and other dependants weakened and with it their ability to pawn them. However, other forms of coerced labour continue to this day, including, as Miers shows, child labour supported by a traffic in children.

The most necessary task to be undertaken is the recovery of the slave voice. This is particularly difficult, as people often do not care to admit that they are of slave descent. Some scholars, however, have been successful. Among our contributors, Cordell writing on Algeria shows how cases coming before colonial administrators can be used to picture the grievances and strategies of slaves. Sikainga demonstrates the value of court records in giving us a picture of the strivings of slaves and former slaves. Here Morocco is a particularly rich source because colonial conquest did not disrupt the continuity of the judicial system. Court records are valuable in the recent periods, particularly for cases involving inheritance, marriage and

INTRODUCTION

13

kinship relations.[36] Rashid, using such records in Sierra Leone together with the proceedings of the Legislative Council, reconstructs the problems facing slaves and the recalcitrance of many masters.

Marcia Wright and Edward Alpers have reminded us that missionary publications also often preserve slave biographies, particularly of those who became Christian. Wright teases from these accounts a subtle analysis of the strategies of slave women in seeking protection in the harsh world of the late nineteenth century.[37] Life histories can also be valuable here. Joseph Ki Zerbo has written a biography of his father, who escaped after being kidnapped and sold into slavery in the Sahara. Life histories have been used to particularly good effect by historians of women. Robertson has demonstrated that with patience, they can be used to recover the lives of slave women.[38] The way emancipation worked for women often got entangled with the patriarchal notions of Muslim clerics, Christian missionaries and European administrators. Slave owners learned that if they claimed female slaves as wives, the colonial administrators were less likely to let them go, and when they did leave, these women often found themselves subject to other men. Rashid and Deutsch make the point, however, that slave women were not less eager to 'break the chains' than men, but that their options were more limited, particularly if they had children. The impact of abolition on free women remains an important field for research not touched on here, since wives and children often replaced slaves in the fields and other occupations.[39] Gender remains, like other fields mentioned above, a priority for future research.

NOTES

1. (Paris, 1975).
2. (Madison, Wisconsin, 1977).
3. (Beverly Hills and London, 1981).
4. (Madison, Wisconsin, 1983).
5. (2 volumes, London and Totowa, 1985).
6. John Grace, *Domestic Slavery in West Africa: with Particular Reference to the Sierra Leone Protectorate, 1896–1927* (London, 1975); Frederick Cooper, *Slaves to Squatters: Plantation Labor and Agriculture in Zanzibar and Coastal Kenya 1890–1925* (New Haven, Connecticut, 1980); Paul Lovejoy, *Transformations in Slavery: A History of Slavery in Africa* (Cambridge, London, New York, New Rochelle, Melbourne, Sydney, 1983).
7. (Madison, Wisconsin, 1988).
8. An earlier version of Ohadike's chapter was presented at our panel in 1994, together with Andreas Eckert's 'African Enterpreneurs and Labor in the Cameroon Literal, 1880–1960s', *Journal of African History*, forthcoming, and Justin Willis and Suzanne Miers, 'Becoming a Child of the House: Incorporation, Authority and Resistance in Giryama Society', *Journal of African History*, XXXVIII, 3 (1997), pp.479–96. Clark, Deutsch, Hargey, and Miers presented papers in 1995, Rashid in 1996, and Clark, Cordell, Stilwell and Klein in 1997. Books by our contributors in press include: Martin Klein, *Slavery and Colonial Rule in French West Africa* (Cambridge, 1998) and T. Hargey, *Days of Freedom: The Suppression of*

14 SLAVERY AND COLONIAL RULE IN AFRICA

Slavery in the Anglo-Eygptian Sudan (London, 1999). Jan-Georg Deutsch and Suzanne Miers both have books in preparation.

9. *Slow Death for Slavery: The Course of Abolition in Northern Nigeria, 1897–1936* (Cambridge, 1993).
10. (Boulder, Colorado, San Francisco, Oxford, 1990).
11. Emancipation Struggles in Nkanu, Northern Igboland, 1920–29', *Journal of African History*, 37 (1996), pp.51–80.
12. (Austin, Texas, 1996).
13. Rochester, New York, Wisconsin 1997.
14. Madison, 1996. See also *Black Scandal: The United States and the Liberian Labor Crisis 1929–36* (Philadelphia, 1980).
15. (Cambridge, 1986).
16. In *Slavery and Abolition*, 18, 3 (December 1997), pp.257–88.
17. *African Economic History*, 17 (1988), pp.23–44.
18. Elizabeth Eldridge and Fred Morton (eds.), *Slavery in South Africa: Captive Labor on the Dutch Frontier* (Boulder, Colorado, 1994); Nigel Worden and Clifton Crais (eds.), *Breaking the Chains: Slavery and its Legacy in the Nineteenth-Century Cape Colony* (Johannesburg, 1994); R.L. Watson, *The Slave Question: Liberty and Property in South Africa* (Hanover, New Hampshire, 1990); Robert Shell, *Children of Bondage: A Social History of Slave Society at the Cape of Good Hope, 1652–1838* (Hanover, New Hampshire, 1994); Pamela Scully, *Liberating the Family? Gender and British Slave Emancipation in the Rural Western Cape, South Africa, 1823–1853* (Portsmouth, New Hampshire, 1997). There is also an important forthcoming work on South Africa by John Edwin Mason.
19. (Madison, Wisconsin, 1993).
20. (Oxford, 1980).
21. See Miers 1975, and Miers and Roberts, pp.12–13.
22. For this and other examples see *inter alia* Miers and Roberts.
23. Klein, *Slavery and Colonial Rule*, ch.10.
24. Andrew F. Clark, 'Internal Migrations and Population Movements in the Upper Senegal Valley (West Africa) 1890–1920', *Canadian Journal of African Studies*, 28, 3 (1994), pp.399–420.
25. Andrew F. Clark, 'Environmental Decline and Ecological Response in the Upper Senegal Valley, West Africa, From the Late Nineteenth Century to World War I', *Journal of African History*, 36 (1995), pp.197–218.
26. Klein, *Slavery and Colonial Rule*, chs.10–14.
27. Miers and Willis, 'Becoming a Child of the House'.
28. Brown, 'Testing the Boundaries'.
29. Mohammed Mbodj, 'The Abolition of Slavery in Senegal, 1829–1890: Crisis or the Rise of a New Entrepreneurial Class?', in Klein, *Breaking the Chains*, pp.197–211.
30. Richard Roberts and Martin Klein, 'The Banamba Slave Exodus of 1905 and the Decline of Slavery in the Western Sudan', *Journal of African History*, 21 (1980), pp.375–94.
31. Suzanne Miers and Michael Crowder, 'The Politics of Slavery in Bechuanaland: Power Struggles and the Plight of the Basarwa in the Bamangwato Reserve, 1926–1940', in Miers and Roberts, pp.172–200.
32. Report by Anti-Slavery International to the United Nations Working Group on Contemporary Forms of Slavery, 20th Session, April 19–28 1995.
33. See also Donna J.E. Maier, 'Slave Labour and Wage Labour in German Togo, 1995–1914', in Arthur Knoll and Lewis Gann (eds.), *Germans in the Tropics. Essays in German Colonial History* (New York, 1987); Thaddeus Sunseri, 'Slave Ransoming in German East Africa, 1885–1922', *International Journal of African Historical Studies*, 16, 1993, pp.1–18; W.G. Clarence-Smith, 'Cocoa Plantations and Coerced Labour in the Gulf of Guinea, 1870–1914', in Klein, *Breaking the Chains*, pp.150–170; Ralph Austen and Jonathan Derrick, *Middlemen of the Cameroons Rivers: The Duala and their Hinterland, c.1600–c.1960* (Cambridge, forthcoming).
34. On Morocco, see also Mohammed Ennaji, *Soldats, Domestiques at Concubines: L'esclavage au Maroc au XIXe siècle* (Casablanca, 1994).

INTRODUCTION

35. Paul Lovejoy and Toyin Falola (eds.), *Pawnship in Africa: Debt Bondage in Historical Perspective* (Boulder, Colorado, 1994).
36. See Allen Christelow, *Thus Ruled Emir Abbas* (East Lansing, Michigan, 1994) for Kano court cases.
37. Marcia Wright, *Strategies of Slaves and Women: Life Stories from East Central Africa* (New York, London, 1993); Marcia Wright, 'Bwanika: Consciousness and Protest among Slave Women in Central Africa, 1886–1911', and Edward A. Alpers, 'The Story of Swema: Female Vulnerability in Nineteenth Century East Africa', both from Claire Robertson and Martin Klein (eds.), *Women and Slavery in Africa*.
38. Claire Robertson, 'Post-Proclamations Slavery in Accra', in Robertson and Klein, *Women and Slavery*, pp.220–242. See also her *Sharing the Same Bowl: A Socioeconomic History of Women and Class in Accra, Ghana* (Bloomington, Indiana, 1984).
39. Barbara Cooper, *Marriage in Maradi: Gender and Culture in a Hausa Society in Niger, 1900–1989* (Oxford, Portsmouth, New Hampshire, 1997).

Slavery and the Slave Trade as International Issues 1890–1939

SUZANNE MIERS

This chapter discusses the international anti-slavery campaign between 1890 and 1939. The slavery issue was used by the colonial powers during the partition of Africa to further their own ends, but, once their rule was established, they took only minimal action to end the institution and sometimes even supported it. The three slavery committees of the League of Nations were established not because of any increased anti-slavery zeal on the part of the colonial rulers, but in order to deflect persistent humanitarian calls for action. They nevertheless set standards for the treatment of labour and projected a number of social questions into the international arena.

Humanitarianism and Diplomacy 1890–1919

Slavery became a major international concern from the day in 1807 when the British outlawed their own slave trade. Once this step was taken it was clearly in Britain's interest to get rival colonial and maritime powers to follow suit in order to prevent this lucrative trade from passing into foreign hands and providing foreign colonies with needed manpower. In 1815 the British tried to get other powers to outlaw it and even to establish a permanent committee to monitor progress. However, their rivals saw this as an attack on their commerce and on their colonies. They would only agree to append a declaration to the Treaty of Vienna proclaiming that the slave trade was 'repugnant to the principles of humanity and universal morality'. This was an important step in the direction of the present human rights movement, but it had no practical value. There followed a long and bitter campaign, during which, by bribery and cajolery, the British secured a network of treaties giving the Royal Navy unique powers to search and seize suspected slavers flying the flags of other nations.[1] As the result of this campaign, the British came to view themselves as the leaders of an international 'crusade' against slavery, the burden of which they had borne almost alone. British statesmen recognized that the cause was popular with the electorate and that Parliament would sanction expenditure and high handed action against foreign countries if these were presented as anti-

SLAVERY AND THE SLAVE TRADE AS INTERNATIONAL ISSUES   17

MAP 5
NORTH EAST AFRICA, c.1930

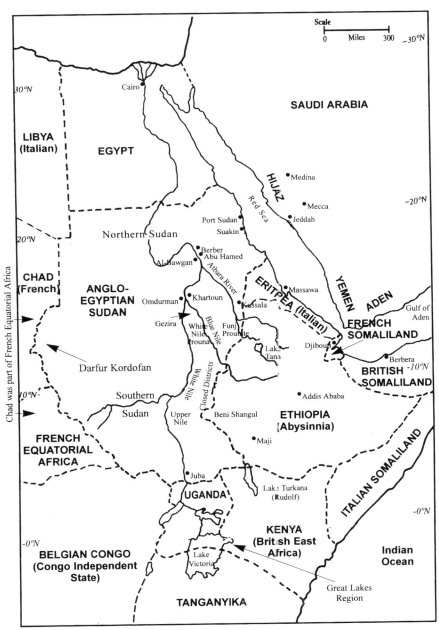

MAP 6
NORTH EAST AFRICA AND ARABIA

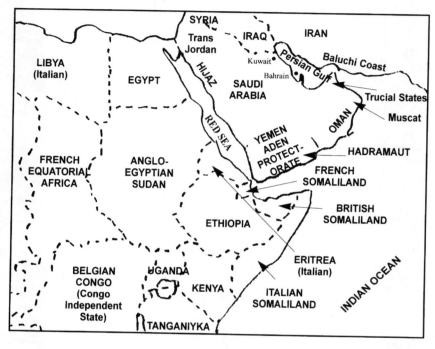

slavery measures. Thus, the 'crusade' could often be used to further other interests – a fact not lost on rival powers.

The spearhead of the anti-slavery movement was the British and Foreign Anti-Slavery Society.[2] A middle-class and largely Quaker organization, it wielded an influence out of proportion to its tiny membership and minuscule budget because of its close links with members of both Houses of Parliament, with government officials and missionary societies, and its ability to mount impressive propaganda campaigns.

By the 1870s the Atlantic slave traffic was a thing of the past. The trade, however, still flourished in Africa and there was an active export traffic to the Muslim world. Attention was forcefully drawn to this by European traders and missionaries penetrating ever further into the interior as the European colonial powers began to partition the coast in the 1880s. Africans took up arms against the intruders and by 1888 the French Cardinal Lavigerie found his missions on the Great Lakes under attack. In response, he launched an anti-slavery 'crusade' of his own, with papal blessing, calling for volunteers to combat this scourge in the heart of Africa.[3]

SLAVERY AND THE SLAVE TRADE AS INTERNATIONAL ISSUES   19

The British, anxious to retain their leadership of the anti-slavery movement and worried at the prospect of unofficial crusaders rampaging around Africa, persuaded Leopold II of Belgium, ruler of the Congo Independent State, to invite the leading maritime and colonial powers, together with the Ottoman Empire, Persia and Zanzibar, to Brussels to discuss concerted action against the export of slaves from Africa. The colonial powers, led by the wily king, proceeded to negotiate a treaty against the African slave trade on land, as well as at sea, and carefully designed it to serve their territorial and commercial ambitions.

The Brussels Act of 1890 was a humanitarian instrument in so far as it reaffirmed that 'native welfare' was an international responsibility; and bound signatories to prevent slave raiding and trading, to repatriate or resettle freed and fugitive slaves, and to cut off the free flow of arms to the slaving areas.[4] But it had important practical advantages for the colonial rulers. By binding them to end the trade in slaves and arms, it not only dealt a blow to African resistance, but was an attempt to prevent unscrupulous colonial administrations from attracting trade to their territories by allowing commerce in these lucrative products. By stating that the best means of attacking the traffic was to establish colonial administrations in the interior of Africa, to protect missionaries and trading companies, and even to initiate Africans into agricultural and industrial labour, it put an anti-slavery guise on the colonial occupation and exploitation of Africa.

For the British it had the added advantage that the maritime clauses of the Act committed the other colonial powers to allow mutual rights to search their shipping and prevent their flags from being used to cover slaving operations. Finally the Act broke new ground by establishing the first international supervisory machinery – bureaux in Brussels and Zanzibar – for the exchange of information on the slave traffic and on the antislavery legislation of signatory powers.

It was the first comprehensive international treaty against the slave trade, but it dealt only with the African traffic. The maritime clauses applied only to the Red Sea, Persian Gulf and part of the Indian Ocean and then only to small 'native' vessels. Moreover, the French parliament rejected even this reduced right to search their shipping, although the French did agree to better policing of their own flag. The major loophole, however, was that the treaty contained no provisions for its enforcement. The bureaux in Brussels and Zanzibar were little more than information offices, and the only weapons against signatories who failed to carry out their obligations were publicity and protest.

Humanitarianism and African Realities

Most notably, the Brussels Act did not bind signatories to suppress slavery. None of the colonial powers was prepared to commit itself to this, although they all believed that it should be ended, and they all knew that as long as there was a market for slaves the traffic would continue. British experience with abolition had not been happy. In plantation colonies, freed slaves, instead of becoming more productive wage labourers, had where possible, opted to work for themselves as artisans or in other occupations, or to become subsistence farmers. Production had declined. In the tiny British footholds on the West Coast of Africa fear of losing their slaves threatened to drive away the native merchants upon whom the colonies depended, while in South Africa abolition had been a factor in promoting the Boer exodus known as the Great Trek.

In their Indian empire, however, the British devised a form of emancipation which minimized these dangers and provided a model to be used in Africa as new territories were acquired.[5] They merely declared that slavery no longer had any legal status. This meant that no claims could be countenanced in court on the basis of slavery, hence slaves who wished to leave might do so. But slave holding was still legal, and slaves were not actually freed. This model of abolition was ideal for the government. It was cheap – no compensation needed to be paid to owners. The impact could be delayed by not informing the slaves of their rights. There was thus no large scale sudden departure and very little disruption of the economy or alienation of masters. The humanitarians, also disappointed with the results of outright abolition in the colonies, were willing to accept this solution because slavery in India was considered 'benign' – that is less cruel than its counterpart in the Americas – and slaves would not be suddenly freed without means of support. This, therefore, became the model of abolition used in most of British Africa.[6] As the empire expanded colonies, in which slavery had to be outlawed, were kept to a minimum and new annexations became 'protectorates' in which full colonial administrations did not have to be introduced, and 'native' customs including slavery could continue even if it had lost its legal status. Other powers found similar legal subterfuges to avoid freeing slaves, or they outlawed slavery but then did not enforce their laws.[7]

As the scramble for Africa gained momentum none of the colonial rulers had the resources to risk alienating slave-owning elites, upon whose cooperation they often depended, or disrupting the economies of their nascent dependencies. They justified their failure to attack slavery by claiming that African slavery was also benign, and that once robbed of its cruellest features – slave raiding, kidnapping, and trading – it would die out

SLAVERY AND THE SLAVE TRADE AS INTERNATIONAL ISSUES   21

gradually to the benefit of the slaves themselves. It was certainly expected to end as the result of colonial rule. For the British abolition was an integral part of a package which included the imposition of the *pax Britannica*, the rule of law, the spread of Christianity, and the establishment of a free market economy – a package which provided the moral justification for the conquest of Africa. The Brussels Act reinforced this expectation in the mind of the European public. It was reinforced still further as wars of conquest were justified as wars against slavers – an excuse made easier because in many cases the fiercest resistance came from rulers whose raids regularly reaped thousands of slaves, or from peoples heavily involved in the slave traffic.[8]

Between 1892 and 1914 all the colonial powers took steps to end large scale slave raiding and trading, as well as the export of slaves from Africa – measures clearly in the interests of orderly government. They enforced these laws, however, in highly variable fashion, depending on their political and economic interests.[9] In Angola, for instance, in the first decade of the twentieth century, even Portuguese officials participated in the slave trade in order to supply workers to the cocoa producing islands of Principe and São Tomé.[10] The French in Dar al-Kuti did not stop slave raiding but diverted it away from their own trading posts.[11] The Germans allowed raiding and trading to continue in northern Cameroon throughout their rule, and neither the French nor the British, who succeeded them, had ended it by 1920.[12] Slave raiding in the Sahara continued to the end of colonial rule.[13] Slave trading on a large scale soon disappeared everywhere, but an underground traffic continued even in areas under close control.

None of the colonial rulers was in any hurry to tackle slavery itself. In fact, as other chapters in this volume make clear, in many areas they discouraged slaves from asserting their freedom and used various methods to uphold the institution. They returned fugitive slaves to their owners, denied them access to land or wage labour, forced them to ransom themselves, arrested them as vagrants, or put them to work for the administration. They often referred slave cases, which could not be heard in colonial courts, to Native or Muslim courts, usually to the detriment of the slaves. Chiefs and other owners found ways to prevent slaves from reaching European administrators, who were in any case few on the ground. They failed to inform slaves of their rights, while often assuring owners that they would be allowed to keep their slaves. The ability of slaves to strike out on their own depended not so much on anti-slavery legislation, or the goodwill of the colonial administration, but on such variables as their gender and age, whether they had access to land, water, livestock, tools and seeds, or whether they could find wage labour. Conversely the fate of masters depended upon their being able to keep control of such resources and maintain administrative and judicial powers.

By 1914 in a few areas, notably in French West Africa, slaves had departed *en masse*, forcing a change in colonial policy,[14] but in most of Africa the majority had stayed where they were. Many, however, had renegotiated the terms of their dependency. Although no longer as pervasive or exploitative, slavery was still widespread, and most colonial administrations had no desire to interfere with it, although their long-term aim was to develop a wage labour force or to promote peasant production. Meanwhile slavery served their purposes. Colonial rule produced a huge new demand for labour for the construction of roads, railways, dockyards and buildings, for work on European plantations, mines and other projects, as well as for increased food production. Colonial officials found it convenient to leave agricultural production to slave owners or to call on them for the labour required for public, and even private, purposes. Moreover, desperate to make their territories economically viable, they resorted to various devices for mobilizing unfree labour themselves. These included forced labour, conscription into the army or police forces, and the recruitment of contract labour by dubious means. The Congo Independent State and the French bought slaves to serve in their armed forces. The Portuguese demanded workers from chiefs who could only get them by buying or capturing slaves. All the colonial powers drove Africans into the labour force by regressive taxation and land alienation. The French, Belgians and Portuguese forced them to produce cash or food crops.

The League of Nations and Slavery

By 1919 the occupation of the African coast by European powers had reduced the export of slaves to a small smuggling traffic to Arabia and the Persian Gulf. Slave raiding had been eradicated in all but the remotest areas of Africa. Slave dealing had been outlawed and in most colonial possessions slavery no longer had a legal status. The Brussels Act had lapsed during the First World War and in 1919 the colonial powers had no desire to renew it. They wished to be free of its commercial clauses[15] and believed that the slave traffic was now so small that it was no longer needed. To the regret of the humanitarians, they abrogated it. Instead a single clause was inserted into one of the treaties signed at St. Germain-en-Laye in 1919 binding signatories to try to secure 'the complete suppression of *slavery in all its forms*' as well as to end the slave trade. Moreover, article 23 of the Covenant of the newly established League of Nations bound members to 'secure and maintain fair and humane conditions of labour and the just treatment of the native inhabitants under their control'. This enlarged the scope of the international obligation to include the suppression of slavery and other abuses of 'native labour' and extended it beyond Africa.

SLAVERY AND THE SLAVE TRADE AS INTERNATIONAL ISSUES   23

Significantly, however, no time limit for action was laid down and no definition of 'fair and humane conditions of labour' was attempted. The major African colonial powers wanted no international supervision of their colonial policies. They could not avoid it in the case of the former German colonies, which were now divided between Britain, France and Belgium to be administered as League Mandates, supervised by the Permanent Mandates Commission. But they were determined not to accept any scrutiny of their policies in other territories. They doubtless hoped that the slavery clauses in the treaty of St. Germain and the League Covenant were a sufficient sop to allay whatever remained of European and American interest in slavery.

They reckoned without the Anti-Slavery Society, now called the Anti-Slavery and Aborigines Protection Society.[16] The moving spirit of the Society, from 1910 until his death in 1940 was John (later Sir John) Harris.[17] He was particularly adept at mobilizing members of parliament by feeding them questions, engineering debates and standing by to provide information. He was an indefatigable organizer of press campaigns, and travelled the country incessantly, speaking to all and sundry, from humble church gatherings to prestigious civic groups. He was not a radical reformer, but was sceptical about the benefits of colonial rule for indigenous people. Government officials thought him unsympathetic to what they considered vital imperial interests and none too scrupulous with the truth, but they had a healthy respect for his ability to embarrass them in press and Parliament. It was Harris who brought the League of Nations into the anti-slavery campaign. He went to Geneva in 1920 to lobby delegates. After five of the 'most strenuous weeks' of his life, he realized that the League 'opened up an entirely new method' of dealing with colonial issues. Whereas governments could brush aside the appeals of small humanitarian societies, he believed they would not be able to ignore questions raised by the League, and he had found sympathetic ears. While planning his strategy, he heard news about slaving in Ethiopia which spurred him into action.

In 1919 an Anglo-Ethiopian commission had been sent to the southwest borders of Ethiopia to investigate persistent incursions into British East Africa and the Sudan and to finalize the delimitation of the frontier. The British members reported evidence of widespread slave raiding by Ethiopian officials and their followers, who were unpaid and forced to live off the land. Slaving and looting were endemic and slave trading rampant.[18] British Foreign Office officials knew that if Harris heard of this he would demand action. This would irritate the Ethiopian government and prejudice important British interests, including the expansion of commerce, and the building of a dam on Lake Tana to control the waters of the Blue Nile in order to regulate irrigation agriculture in Egypt and Sudan, and expand cotton production in the Gezira. Protection of these interests was complicated by rivalry between Britain, France and Italy, parties to the tripartite agreement of 1906, which guaranteed the independence of Ethiopia but allotted each of them a sphere of operations in case the government should collapse. As the Italian sphere straddled the Blue Nile, Britain was reluctant to take any action which might weaken the Ethiopian government – an unstable triumvirate dependent upon the very provincial authorities who were slave raiding and trading. The British believed that only combined pressure by the three powers would force them to introduce reforms. French and Italian participation was highly unlikely, and anyway might topple the Ethiopian government. They were afraid to publish the commission's reports for fear of precipitating a call for action in Britain. So they sent a consul to southwest Ethiopia and exhorted the governments of Kenya and Sudan, neither of which wanted to incur the expense, to police their borders. They had no illusions that anything would change.

Early in 1922 the storm they dreaded broke in the British press with a series of articles on slavery in Ethiopia, and editorials suggesting the question be referred to the League of Nations. To make matters worse reports from across the Red Sea showed that newly imported slaves from Ethiopia were being openly sold in the Hijaz, where the new Hashemite king, Hussein, had come to the throne with British help. Not only was he allowing the traffic, he was taxing it. Pilgrims, who came to the Holy Cities from all over the Muslim world, were also being enslaved.[19] The Turks, who had been expelled from the Hijaz during the war, had been parties to the Brussels Act and had allowed the British to patrol their territorial waters, police their flag, and manumit slaves who took refuge in the British consulate in Jeddah. King Hussein, however, refused to stop the slave trade or slavery and objected to British ships patrolling his waters, and to consular manumission. The Foreign Office, anxious for his recognition of British and French mandates over Iraq, Transjordan and Syria, was unwilling to press him too far. In June 1922, however, fuel was added to the agitation Harris was now orchestrating, when the Royal Navy captured a dhow carrying thirty young Ethiopian slaves. The ensuing trial revealed that the victims had been embarked in French Somaliland and highlighted loopholes in Britain's powers of jurisdiction which enabled some of the slavers to go free.

Finding the British government unwilling to take action, Harris persuaded the New Zealand delegate to the League, Sir Arthur Steel-Maitland – a British member of parliament – to raise the question of slavery at the League Assembly in September 1922.[20] As a result, in an entirely new departure, the League launched an investigation into slavery everywhere and asked all members for reports on their own territories. This widening of

SLAVERY AND THE SLAVE TRADE AS INTERNATIONAL ISSUES 25

its scope was a vain attempt to disarm Portuguese suspicions that the inquiry was really directed against their oppressive labour policy, which Harris had long attacked. To Harris' consternation Britain, the only power with eye-witness accounts from southwest Ethiopia as well as the Hijaz, ducked the whole issue by simply reporting that there was no slavery in the British Empire. When pressed in Parliament, the government published a White Book to show that the slave trade in Ethiopia was declining.[21] Harris marshalled his cohorts for a debate in the House of Lords, and, in July 1923, the Foreign Secretary was forced to promise to send for up-to-date information for the League. Both the peers and the press reminded him of Britain's traditional role as leader of the anti-slavery movement.[22] The message was clear – the cause was still popular.

At this point the Ethiopians applied for admission to the League, hoping this would protect them from British or Italian aggression. The move was instigated by the French, who believed the agitation in Britain was the prelude to an attack on Ethiopian independence. The British opposed Ethiopian admission but, finding they could not prevent it, insisted that the Ethiopians agree to restrict the arms trade, to send the League full information on slavery, and to consider any recommendations it might make.[23] The British soon found that Ethiopia's admission was a cloud with a silver lining. They could now tell Harris and his supporters that only the Ethiopians could report to the League on slavery in their own country. Britain, absolved from the responsibility of denouncing a fellow member, could simply say that it would support any action the League undertook. This effectively internationalized the question and, as will be shown, guaranteed that nothing would be done.

The Ethiopians, however, took fright and passed important legislation providing stiff penalties for raiding and trading and issuing regulations which would end slavery as existing slaves died. The result merely drove the trade underground. Raiding and trading continued and slaves were still exported to Sudan and across the Red Sea.[24]

The Temporary Slavery Commission (TSC) 1924–25

Meanwhile, the League, set in motion by the resolution of 1922 and finding little response to its appeal for information, appointed the Temporary Slavery Commission in 1924 to inquire into slavery world wide. This body, carefully designed by the colonial powers to have no bite and very little bark, set the pattern for those that followed.[25] To keep down costs, it was limited to eight experts on slavery – private individuals appointed by the League, not by their governments, hence theoretically 'independent'. But six were nationals of the leading colonial powers – Britain, France,

Portugal, Italy, Belgium and Holland. To ensure that they understood the problems that faced colonial administrations and were not irresponsible 'faddists', all of these but the Italian were either serving or retired colonial officials.

The British member was Sir Frederick (later Lord) Lugard. His qualifications were impeccable.[26] He had fought Swahili/Arab slavers on the shore of Lake Nyasa as a young man and had tackled slavery in various capacities on the Kenya coast and in Uganda. As the first Governor of Northern Nigeria, he had found ways to prevent wholesale slave desertions in order to avoid ruining the economy and alienating powerful slave owners. As Governor-General of all Nigeria he had presided over the final abolition of the legal status of slavery. He was convinced that in the interests of both slaves and masters slavery should end gradually but he was also convinced that it must be ended. Unlike many of his contemporaries, he believed Africans would respond to market incentives and should not be driven into the work force by devices such as forced labour, regressive taxation and land alienation.

The French expert was Maurice Delafosse, whose qualifications matched Lugard's.[27] As a young man, he had joined the 'Armed Brothers of the Sahara' to fight slave traders, and subsequently he had been a colonial administrator. He agreed with Lugard that Africans were not lazy by nature and he too opposed forced labour and other forms of colonial exploitation. The most notable of the other members was Harold Grimshaw, who represented the newly formed International Labour Organization (ILO), which wanted to take over all labour questions. It had been founded on the premise that if labour was to be protected anywhere it had to be protected everywhere; otherwise those powers which allowed slavery and other abuses would have an advantage over rivals who insisted on the payment of fair wages and good working conditions. The only non-European was a Haitian, L.D. Bellegarde. Appointed as window dressing, he proved a valuable antidote to the former governor of Angola, A. Freire D' Andrade, who was bent on protecting Portuguese interests and believed that Africans had a duty to enter the colonial workforce.

The colonial governments, fearful of damaging revelations, and determined not to allow any supervision of their colonial administrations, insisted that the TSC be both temporary and purely advisory. It had no power to launch investigations and could only take evidence from non-governmental organizations (NGOs) approved by their own governments. States had to be able to reply to accusations against them before these could be considered. Finally, to limit its only real weapon – publicity – it met in private and the League decided whether or not to publish its reports, which, of course, were carefully vetted by the imperial governments.

SLAVERY AND THE SLAVE TRADE AS INTERNATIONAL ISSUES   27

Circumscribed as it was, the TSC went much further than the colonial powers, including the British, wanted. Led by Lugard and Grimshaw, under the rubric 'slavery in all its forms', it condemned serfdom, the sale of children for domestic service, concubinage, and slave dealing under guise of adoption or marriage. In the case of pawning (the pledging of a person for credit) and peonage or debt-slavery, it recommended restricting the amount of labour that could be demanded for the debt, and that the debt be extinguished on the death of the debtor. It discussed child betrothal, inheritance of widows, dowry payments and even polygyny, but shied off condemning them outright. As for slavery, it merely recommended abolition of its legal status so that those slaves who wished to remain with their owners could do so, but it urged that slaves be told that they could leave.

To the surprise of the Foreign Office it also dealt with forced labour. Claiming that this often deteriorated into slavery, it recommended that it be limited to essential public works and be adequately paid, that administrators should not be allowed to recruit labour for private enterprises, and chiefs should not be allowed to use it for themselves. Finally it suggested that the protection of indigenous labour should be taken on by the ILO. Grimshaw and Lugard had hoped to draw up a 'charter' of rights for native labour but objections from the colonial governments killed the idea.

All members of the TSC played the anti-slavery card to further national interests. For instance, the French and Italians insisted that its report endorse their campaigns against the Tuareg and Sanusi in the Sahara desert on the grounds that they were attacking slave raiders. Lugard got the TSC to recognize the British 'right' to manumit and repatriate fugitive slaves who took refuge with their officials in Arabia and the Persian Gulf – a question on which Britain wanted support from other powers.[28] The French reinforced their position as the defenders of Ethiopia by ensuring that the TSC's report praised the Ethiopian reforms of 1924, and by persuading Lugard to withdraw his proposal for a League commission of inquiry.[29] So it went on.

Its most fruitful recommendation was that the League negotiate a convention against the slave trade, slavery and forced labour. This unwelcome proposal might have died had Lugard not forced the hand of the British government by sending them a draft treaty. He opened up a veritable Pandora's box. The Foreign Office was sympathetic – only a few weeks before the House of Lords had again complained that Britain was not playing its traditional role – but his proposals sent alarm signals through other departments. The Admiralty objected to the proposed stricter policing of the Red Sea, for fear of encouraging France and Italy to increase their naval forces in this strategic region. The India Office feared that the proposals ran counter to land tenure practices in the sub-continent, some of which bound tenants to the soil and in effect condemned them to forced labour. Moreover, they did not want to be pushed into taking action in the still unadministered regions of Assam and Burma, or in the Indian Princely States with whose internal administration they were forbidden by treaties to interfere. The Dominions Office was worried that chiefs in the High Commission Territories of southern Africa would have to be paid more if they lost their rights to call out 'tribal labour'.[30] The Colonial Office had no desire for any treaty that might force them to eradicate slavery or change their labour policies. It was decided, however, that some action was needed to placate the humanitarians and to ensure that no other power stole Britain's thunder as leader of the anti-slavery movement. An interdepartmental committee, therefore, hammered out a watered down version of the treaty, which was presented to the League. The anti-slavery lobby led by Harris demanded more, and other colonial powers demanded less than the British asked for, but finally the Slavery Convention of 1926 was signed.[31]

The Slavery Convention of 1926

This treaty, which is still in force, was the first international instrument specifically directed against slavery. The colonial powers saw to it that it was a paper tiger. Neither France nor Italy would agree to declaring the maritime traffic piracy, which would have deprived slavers of the protection of their national flags. France would not even concede the right to search. The convention therefore merely stated that a further treaty on the seaborne trade would be negotiated. This was never done.

Slavery, vaguely defined as 'the status of a person over whom all or any of the rights attaching to ownership are exercised', was to be suppressed 'in all its forms'. But the forms were not spelt out and suppression was to be undertaken only 'progressively and as soon as possible'. Thus even Ethiopia, where slavery was still legal, could sign the Convention. New ground, however, was broken by a clause which declared that forced labour was only to be used for public purposes and had to be adequately remunerated and performed from home. Again much of the force was lost because its use for private enterprises was to be phased out 'progressively and as soon as possible'. Significantly, the Convention contained no machinery for enforcement. France and Italy would not even accept a commitment to send reports to the League. All that could be agreed was that each member should keep the League informed of its anti-slavery regulations.

Nevertheless, the Convention had important repercussions. The League invited the ILO to take action against forced labour resulting in the Forced

SLAVERY AND THE SLAVE TRADE AS INTERNATIONAL ISSUES   29

Labour Convention of 1930 – the first in a series of agreements for the protection of indigenous labour. As for slavery, publicity surrounding the meetings of the TSC and the discussion of the Convention kept the question before the public for several years. In the British empire this had an impact at the grassroots level. Colonial administrations were ordered to review their laws to ensure that slavery no longer had any legal status. Hence the spate of new ordinances issued at this time in Sierra Leone, where slaves were now told of their rights, and in the Gold Coast and a number of other territories.[32] In Sudan more vigorous action was taken to end slavery and to resettle fugitive slaves from Ethiopia.[33] In many cases these new laws simply reaffirmed existing ones, while in others results were meagre. In Bechuanaland, for instance, administrators had refused to admit that there was any servitude. Now they had to agree that by the League definition the domination of hunters and gatherers by pastoral groups was indeed a form of slavery. But only minimal action was taken until the Acting Chief of the Bangwato fell out with the Resident Commissioner in the 1930s.[34] In most of Britain's African possessions, however, more uniform and stronger laws were now on the statute books, even if they were not always enforced.

The Committee of Experts on Slavery of 1932 (CES)

The Convention of 1926 did not rid the British of their dilemma over Ethiopia, or do much to eradicate slavery in Africa. The Ethiopian reforms of 1924 defused criticism at the TSC, thanks to the French, but raiding and trading continued and Britain was still faced with having information she did not wish to use.[35] Half-hearted attempts to get France and Italy to join her in pressing the League to take action failed.[36] Moreover, there was still a small slave trade across the Red Sea, and the traffic continued in Arabia, in the British Aden Protectorate and the small British satellites on the Persian Gulf. In China and among the Chinese in the British territories of Hong Kong, the Straits Settlements and what is now Malaysia, little girls continued to be sold into domestic service as *mui tsai*.[37] In Liberia indigenous peoples were impressed as contract labour for the Spanish island of Fernando Po.[38] Forced labour was still used by the colonial powers.

The Anti-Slavery Society kept up its pressure on the British government to establish a permanent League committee, pointing out that they could send it information on other powers that they were reluctant to bring to the League Assembly. The advent of a more sympathetic Labour government in 1929 gave the Society unusual influence, particularly after one of its vice-presidents, Sir John Simon, became Foreign Secretary in 1931. Foreign Office officials had already decided that instead of refraining from pressing the slavery issue for fear of damaging other interests, they could use the

League to bring pressure on recalcitrant powers and gain 'kudos' with the public in the process.[39] They therefore proposed revival of the TSC, in spite of objections from the Colonial and India Offices. As expected this was opposed by the other colonial powers, and Ethiopia, Liberia and Thailand, who delayed consideration of the proposal for a year. In 1930 the British, growing bolder, demanded a permanent League slavery commission with powers to conduct its own investigations. It took another year and much wrangling, and the promise of supplementary funds from the British and Italian anti-slavery societies, before the other powers agreed to the appointment of the Committee of Experts on Slavery (CES). Always fearful of any threat to their sovereignty, led by Portugal and France, they saw to it that this committee was even more emasculated than its predecessor.[40] It was appointed for only one year to investigate the workings of the 1926 Convention, identify the main obstacles to the eradication of slavery, and suggest any modifications needed in the League machinery. It was not to discuss forced labour. Its meetings were to be private and it could only consider evidence supplied by or through governments. Accusations could only be considered after the accused government had responded. If they were denied, the information was to be treated as non-proven.

The CES was composed of nationals of all seven European colonial powers – Britain, France, Portugal, Italy, Belgium, Spain and the Netherlands. The ILO merely sent an 'observer'. To satisfy women's organizations, the Portuguese member was a woman. Inevitably Lugard was appointed. He was past his prime and, because he was an 'independent member', he was not specifically briefed – a fact the Foreign Office was to regret. The French member, Gabriel Angoulvant, in contrast, was accompanied by a high official of the Ministry of the Colonies. Angoulvant was the very antithesis of Lugard. An authoritarian technocrat, he had made good use of forced labour as Governor of the Ivory Coast and then Governor-General of French West Africa. He had introduced compulsory crop production and concessionary companies on the model of the Belgian Congo.[41]

The thorniest question at the CES was Ethiopia.[42] Here the mere threat of the League committee had already had an impact. In 1931 Haile Selassie, newly installed as Emperor, fearing that he might be forced to accept a League investigation and possible loss of independence, invited the Anti-Slavery Society to send a delegation to offer him advice.[43] This mission, headed by Lord Noel-Buxton, spent a month in Ethiopia in 1932 and proposed that the emperor ask for a League adviser and a loan to help end slavery.[44] Haile Selassie promised to end slavery within twenty years but rejected Buxton's proposals as infringing his sovereignty and certain to arouse public feeling against him. Noel-Buxton and Harris both gave

SLAVERY AND THE SLAVE TRADE AS INTERNATIONAL ISSUES   31

evidence at the CES over the objections of the French, who defended the Emperor, although well aware of the extent of slaving in his territories. Haile Selassie, however, succeeded in deflecting criticism by establishing a new Slavery Department with an Englishman, Frank de Halpert, as Adviser.

Apart from this indirect result, the CES achieved little. It was hampered by lack of information, and contention between Britain and France. Angoulvant played a trump card by attacking Britain for failing to suppress slavery in the Indian Princely States, Bahrain, the Trucial Sheikhdoms and the Hadhramaut. Lugard knew nothing about the subject and Foreign Office officials, chagrined at his lack of spirited defence, found to their dismay that although the British had reduced the maritime trade to these regions to a mere trickle, they had virtually no control over the interior of the Trucial States or the Hadramaut.

Much time was spent in acrimonious discussion about whether slaves were still slaves once the legal status of slavery had been ended. Lugard insisted that by the League's definition they were slaves until they actually left their owners. Angoulvant called them serfs (or predial or domestic[45] slaves) and insisted that the CES report stated that this 'serfdom' maintained political, social and economic equilibrium and should be left to die a natural death. This was in keeping with the policy of all the colonial administrations, as the various chapters in this volume make clear. Angoulvant reported to his government that the advantage of his definition was that France could claim that there were no slaves in her African empire.[46] The whole discussion was confused and bedevilled by lack of consensus on terminology.

Moreover, it begged the question of what had actually been done to enable slaves to leave their owners, as well as how far it was possible to free a slave by simply announcing that slavery was no longer a legal institution. This raises the problem of what former slaves understood by freedom. To some it meant complete integration into the kin groups of the free or forming kin groups of their own on terms of social, economic and even spiritual equality. In societies in which intermarriage with the free was possible, or where manumission was recognized, such equality might be achieved, at least by the descendants of slaves, but in many societies it was impossible. In Muslim societies freed slaves and their descendants became clients of descendants of their former owners ad infinitum.[47] Ex-slaves thus often settled for various degrees of 'freedom'. The variations were infinite, as the chapters in this volume make clear.[48]

The only concrete result of this committee was that it unanimously recommended the appointment of a permanent League commission to inquire into slavery. This was what the British had wanted from the outset,[49] and endorsement by the TSC made it difficult for other powers to object.

32 SLAVERY AND COLONIAL RULE IN AFRICA

Nevertheless they succeeded in delaying its first meeting until 1934. They also curtailed its powers so that, like its predecessors, it was purely advisory, met in private, and could not conduct investigations or take evidence from private sources. Governments were to see any communications which concerned them. To prevent it from supervising colonial policies, it was only to meet every two years 'if necessary' and was merely to study the documents sent to it concerning slavery, and submit reports. Again it was not to discuss forced labour.

The Advisory Committee of Experts on Slavery (ACE)

This committee, known as the Advisory Committee of Experts on Slavery, consisted of nationals of the seven European colonial powers only. Lugard was passed over in favour of Sir George Maxwell, a retired civil servant who had served in Malaya – a choice the British were soon to regret. Maxwell was peppery, outspoken, conscientious, tireless and dedicated. He was new to Geneva and initially suffered from the delusion that members of the League really wanted the ACE to achieve results. Where his colleagues were mainly content to defend national interests, he was determined to make the committee effective.[50] He immediately tried to change the rules of procedure. After initial setbacks, he worked out a successful strategy which enabled the committee to hold annual meetings. He got around the prohibition on evidence from unofficial sources by getting it agreed that members of the ACE could supply any information that came their way by virtue of their 'special knowledge', thus enabling him to conduct his own investigations.

He successfully extracted information from reluctant British government departments by flooding them with memoranda based on published information and, when they protested that he had not done them justice, demanding full reports. He drew attention to a wide range of questions including debt-bondage in India, child labour in Ceylon, bridewealth in Africa, the plight of the Basarwa in Bechuanaland, slavery in Islam, and the sale of Chinese girls as *mui tsai*. He insisted on voluminous and truthful reports, pointing out contradictions, hypocrisy and shortcomings. He sent questionnaires for indignant governors and if the replies were not satisfactory, he incorporated criticisms in ACE reports which were published by the League.[51]

He raised questions British colonial administrations had no desire to face, such as why so many slaves had not left their owners when the legal status of slavery ended. He refused to believe that they were contented with their lot and wanted a complete 'census' of these 'voluntary slaves' and an inquiry into why they had stayed. This not only ran counter to the policy of

SLAVERY AND THE SLAVE TRADE AS INTERNATIONAL ISSUES   33

gradual suppression, but it infuriated the Colonial Office because it entailed extra work for already understaffed colonial administrations. They also baulked at the cost when Maxwell suggested land and credit be made available to ex-slaves to speed up their real emancipation. He tried to force the India Office to take responsibility for the policies of the Indian Princely States and for the continued legal existence of slavery in the Trucial States. He spurred a reluctant administration into negotiating treaties against the slave trade with rulers in the Aden Protectorate.

Although the Colonial Office thought Maxwell had a grudge against them, it seems more likely that he was trying to get the government to work with him to raise the prestige and value of the ACE. He hoped to defuse the opposition of other powers, by having it deal only with chattel slavery, slave raiding and trading, and pawning. He thus sought to narrow the definition of slavery which the TSC had broadened with its interpretation of 'slavery in all its forms'. He tried to pass trafficking in children to the Social Questions Committee of the League, and to have the ILO deal with all forced labour and other abuses, including peonage. Both claimed they were too busy. African marriage practices he wanted left to colonial governments. Predial slavery or serfdom, which had so divided the CES, he considered could be left to die out. The immediate aim of the ACE should be to free those slaves who had themselves been bought or captured.

The result of Maxwell's prodigious efforts and fertile mind was that he supplied the ACE with the bulk of its material. His colleagues worked cordially enough with him, and doubtless watched with satisfaction as he piled up voluminous reports on the British empire. Of the 97 pages of the 1935 report, for instance, only 20 did not deal with British possessions, giving the impression, Foreign Office officials complained bitterly, 'that slavery was peculiarly a British problem'. The 1936 report highlighted the 'vestiges of slavery in the British empire while passing lightly over the other colonial territories' and actually stating that there was no slavery in Portuguese or Italian colonies. Thus ironically, far from proving Britain's anti-slavery zeal to an admiring world, Maxwell provided the material for attacks on British policy from, as the Foreign Office put it, 'quarters whose real record in the matter of slavery will not bear comparison with ours'. They considered redrafting some reports to conceal the facts and avoid a possible 'small but embarrassing humanitarian storm' but decided against it.[52] Not surprisingly, by 1937 the Foreign Office thought the committee had outlived its usefulness.

By this time significant changes had taken place both in the international situation and in Africa which reinforced this view. In 1936 Italy conquered Ethiopia using the slavery issue as propaganda and declaring the institution illegal in all occupied areas. In 1938 Italy withdrew from the League of

34 SLAVERY AND COLONIAL RULE IN AFRICA

Nations, and hence from the ACE. On the opposite shores of the Red Sea, the British, faced with the growing threat from an ever more ambitious Italy, and anxious to improve relations with Saudi Arabia, renounced their 'right' to manumit slaves who took refuge in their consulate in Jeddah. In return the Saudis undertook to forbid the import of slaves, and to regulate the sale and manumission of those already in the country.[53] At the time slaves were still being imported into Arabia from Ethiopia, India, the Baluchi coast, and under guise of pilgrims, from as far away as China and West Africa. The British had no illusions that this would end but, faced with rising tensions in Europe, they wanted to play down the slavery issue. Moreover, the Red Sea slave trade, so active a decade earlier, was now believed to be very small and no slaver had been caught by the Royal Navy since 1922.

By 1938 the committee was dying of attrition. The Italians had withdrawn. As the civil war engulfed Spain, the Spanish member no longer came to Geneva. The Portuguese delegate ceased to attend. Maxwell agreed with the Foreign Office that little more could be done now that information would not be forthcoming from the previous main areas of chattel slavery, Ethiopia and Saudi Arabia. Moreover, the legal status of slavery had been abolished in all colonial territories. Slavery had been eroded in most of Africa by the economic, social and political changes which accompanied colonial rule – including the imposition of peace, the monetization of the economy, the development of a wage labour force, the levelling influence of colonial labour and taxation policies, and the development of modern communications. There was also less incentive to acquire or keep slaves as prestige no longer depended on the number of a man's followers but on the accumulation of money and possessions. Slavery was still legal in Arabia. In Africa small-scale slaving continued, mainly in children, and many former slaves retained ties with their ex-owners, but even Maxwell felt that the committee could now be disbanded. He had called attention to and written reports on every conceivable form of slavery and he hoped to hold a final meeting in 1939 to wind up its affairs 'honourably' – its job largely done – and to pass its responsibilities to other bodies. However, he found no support, and the outbreak of the Second World War in September sealed its fate. Although not formally dissolved, it never met again.

The Impact of the League Committees

In the realm of human rights the League of Nations committees have an important place. They gave notice that slavery was under attack and helped to get the question of forced labour and the protection of native labour taken up by the ILO. In practical terms the TSC resulted in the negotiation of the Slavery Convention of 1926 – the first international instrument specifically

SLAVERY AND THE SLAVE TRADE AS INTERNATIONAL ISSUES   35

directed against slavery. Because of the insistence of the committee, this convention also condemned practices 'analagous to slavery'. Although these were not spelt out in the treaty, the TSC report described them. These now, therefore, became international questions. In 1956 the United Nations negotiated a Supplementary Convention on slavery and related institutions which identified them. As chattel slavery gradually died out – outlawed everywhere by 1970,[54] although not completely ended[55] – so these became the main focus of international attention. Today they are discussed annually at the United Nations Working Group on Contemporary Forms of Slavery which has met every year since 1975.

This committee has some advantages over its predecessors. It meets in public, and takes evidence directly from non-governmental organizations. However, like the League committees it is advisory only, and although the United Nations has negotiated a series of treaties against practices 'analogous to slavery', it has no powers of enforcement. Its only weapon against recalcitrant governments remains, as in the past, the publicizing of their shortcomings. During the Cold War it was as politicized as any of the League committees had been. Although there has been a marked improvement in the last few years, it is only effective if governments are willing to carry out its recommendations.

ACKNOWLEDGEMENTS

The initial research for this chapter was made possible by a grant from the Rockefeller Foundation in 1980–81. I am at present working on a book on Britain and the suppression of slavery 1890–1990.

NOTES

1. See *inter alia* Suzanne Miers, *Britain and the Ending of the Slave Trade* (henceforth *Slave Trade*) (London, 1975).
2. For the early history of this society see Howard Temperley, *British AntiSlavery 1833–70* (London, 1972).
3. F. Renault, *Lavigerie, l'esclavage Africain, et l'Europe*. 2 vols. (Paris, 1971).
4. For the Brussels Conference and the Brussels Act, see Miers *Slave Trade*, pp.206 ff.; for an earlier reaffirmation see *inter alia* Suzanne Miers, 'Humanitarianism at Berlin: Myth or Reality', in S. Forster, W.J. Mommsen and R. Robinson (eds.), *Bismarck, Europe and Africa: The Berlin Africa Conference 1884–1885 and the Onset of Partition* (Oxford University Press, London, 1988), pp.333–45.
5. For the end of slavery in India see Temperley 1972; D.R. Banaji, *Slavery in British India* (Bombay, 1933); L. Caplan, 'Power and Status in South Asian Slavery' in J.L. Watson (ed.), *Asian and African Systems of Slavery* (Oxford, 1980), pp.169–94; B. Hjejle, 'Slavery and Agricultural Bondage in South India in the Nineteenth Century' in *The Scandinavian Economic History Review*, XIV, 2 (1966) pp.71–126; D. Kumar, 'Colonialism, Bondage and Caste in British India' in Martin A. Klein (ed.), *Breaking the Chains: Slavery, Bondage and Emancipation in Africa and Asia* (Madison, Wisconsin, 1993) pp.112–30
6. See chapters by Falola, Hargey, Opare-Akurang, Rashid and Stilwell in this collection. For

further examples see chapters in Miers and Roberts, and *inter alia* Paul Lovejoy and Jan Hogendorn, *Slow Death for Slavery: the Course of Abolition in Northern Nigeria 1897–1936* (henceforth *Slow Death*) (Cambridge, 1993).

7. See chapters by Clark, Cordell, Deutsch, Eckert and Klein. For other examples see Miers and Roberts, *End of Slavery.*
8. See chapters by Falola, Ohadike and Stilwell in this collection.
9. For examples see Miers and Roberts, *End of Slavery.*
10. J. Duffy, *A Question of Slavery* (Harvard, 1967); Linda M. Heywood, 'Slavery and Forced Labour in the Changing Political Economy of Central Angola, 1850–1949', in Miers and Roberts, *End of Slavery*, pp.415–36.
11. Dennis Cordell, 'The Delicate Balance of Force and Flight: The End of Slavery in Eastern Ubangi-Shari', in Miers and Roberts, *End of Slavery*, pp.159–61.
12. See chapter by Eckert; James H. Vaughan and A. Kirk-Greene (eds.), *The Diary of Hamman Yaji: Chronicle of a West African Muslim Ruler* (Bloomington, Indiana, 1995).
13. See chapter by Klein, and E.Ann McDougall, 'A Topsy-Turvey World: Slaves and Freed Slaves in the Mauritanian Adrar, 1910–1950', in Miers and Roberts, *End of Slavery*, pp.362–88.
14. Richard Roberts and Martin A. Klein, 'The Banamba Slave Exodus and the Decline of Slavery in the Western Sudan', *Journal of African History*, 21, 3 (1980) pp.375–94; Richard Roberts, 'The End of Slavery in the French Soudan, 1905–1914', in Miers and Roberts, *End of Slavery*, pp.282–307; Martin A. Klein, 'Slave Resistance and Slave Emancipation in Coastal Guinea', in Miers and Roberts, *End of Slavery*, pp.203–19; Martin A. Klein, *Slavery and Colonial Rule in French West Africa* (Cambridge, 1998).
15. Miers, *Slave Trade* pp.286 ff.
16. The British and Foreign Anti-Slavery Society amalgamated in 1909 with the Aborigines Protection Society. (henceforth ASAPS)
17. The discussion of Harris' activities which follows is based on his voluminous correspondence in the archives of the ASAPS in Rhodes House, Oxford.
18. Suzanne Miers, 'Britain and the Suppression of Slavery in Ethiopia', *Slavery and Abolition*, 18 no.3 (December 1997), pp.257–88 (henceforth 'Ethiopia').
19. Suzanne Miers, 'Diplomacy versus Humanitarianism: Britain and Consular Manumission in Hijaz 1921–36' (henceforth 'Hijaz'), *Slavery and Abolition*, 10 (1989), pp.102–28.
20. Minutes on Steel-Maitland to MacNeil, 5 December 1922, FO 371/7148; Harris to Steel-Maitland, 12 October 1926, ASAPS mss. Brit.Emp.s.19 G444 file 5.
21. *Abyssinia*, no.1, 1923, Cmd. 1858.
22. Minutes by Curzon on memoranda in FO 371/8404, and on article by Darley in *Outward Bound*, 2 September 1923, FO 371/8406. *Hansard*, 31 July 1923; *The Times*, 1 August 1923.
23. Miers, 'Ethiopia'.
24. Ibid.
25. For correspondence on composition and powers of TSC see FO 371/9531, and League of Nations archives in Geneva (henceforth LA) S1670/9, and the League publication A.24.VI, A.42 (a) 1924 VI. For proceedings of TSC see its minutes A.18.1924 and C.426.M.157. 1925 VI. For reports of the two sessions see A.17.1924.VI and A.19.1925.VI. Memoranda of members were not published but are in the League archives.
26. M. Perham, *Lugard: The Years of Adventure 1858–1898* (London 1956), *Lugard: The Years of Authority 1898–1945* (London 1960). For his work in Nigeria see Lovejoy and Hogendorn, *Slow Death.*
27. For Delafosse see C. Harrison, *France and Islam in West Africa, 1860–1960* (Cambridge, 1988) pp.102–5, 144–9; E.Van Hoven, 'Representing Social Hierarchy: Administrators and the Family in the French Soudan: Delafosse, Monteil, Labouret', *Cahiers d'Études Africaines*, 30 (1990), pp.179–98; S.Wooten, 'Colonial Administrators and the Ethnography of the Family in the French Soudan', *Cahiers d'Études Africaines*, 33 (1993), pp.419–46.
28. See Suzanne Miers, 'Hijaz', *Slavery and Abolition*, 10 (1989), pp.102–28.
29. Lugard memorandum LA CTE 36; Note by Clauzel, 1 Aug. 1925, Ministère des Affaires Étrangères (henceforth FMAE) SDN 940 and Clauzel to Delafosse, 8 July 1924, SDN 939 (references are to temporary enumerations in use when I saw the documents in 1980).

SLAVERY AND THE SLAVE TRADE AS INTERNATIONAL ISSUES 37

30. These territories were Bechuanaland (now Botswana), Swaziland, and Basutoland (now Lesotho).
31. Correspondence with Lugard and other government departments, minutes of interdepartmental meetings, and reports of negotiations at Geneva are in FO 371/10617. 11133, 11134, 11135.
32. See chapters by Opare-Akurang and Rashid.
33. See chapter by Hargey.
34. See Suzanne Miers and Michael Crowder, 'The Politics of Slavery in Bechuanaland: Power Struggles and the Plight of the Basarwa in the Bamangwato Reserve, 1926–1940', in Miers and Roberts, *End of Slavery*, pp.172–200.
35. Miers, 'Ethiopia'.
36. Foreign Office Confidential Prints (FOCP) 12911, 13082, 13134 and FO 371/11570 and 11571.
37. See *inter-alia* Suzanne Miers and Maria Jaschok, *Women and Chinese Patriarchy: Submission, Servitude and Escape* (London, 1994).
38. I.K. Sundiata, *Black Scandal: The United States and the Liberian Labour Crises, 1929–1936* (Philadelphia, 1980), and *From Slaving to Neo-Slaving: The Bight of Biafra and Fernando Po in the Era of Abolition, 1927–1930* (Madison, Wisconsin, 1996). The League investigated conditions in Liberia at the request of the Liberian government but not the deplorable conditions on Fernando Po.
39. Minute by Cadogan, 26 July 1929 on ASAPS to FO 18 July 1929, FO 371/13480.
40. Correspondence leading up to the appointment of this committee is in FO 371/15036.
41. François Manchuelle, 'Forced Labour in French West Africa 1881–1946: A Reappraisal Paper presented at the African Studies Association annual meeting November 1987.
42. The CES minutes are in LA C.E.E./1st session, P.V. and P.V. 2nd session, confidential. The Report is League Paper A 34. 1932 VI. 1 Sept.1935. The various drafts are filed in LA Carton 2358 6B/37985/1490. Lugard's report is in FO 371/16504. Angoulvant's reports are in FMAE SDN 943. For Lugard's behind the scenes machinations with regard to Ethiopia see Miers, 'Ethiopia'.
43. Miers, 'Ethiopia'.
44. For report of this mission see Report on Abyssinia by Lord Noel-Buxton and Lord Polwarth, enc. in FO to Secretary-General, 26 April 1932, Foreign Office Confidential Print 14116 no.61.
45. With reference to Africa the term 'domestic' slave was normally used to describe a person born into slavery.
46. See Angoulvant's report on second session of CES, FMAE SDN 943. His carefully worded final statement is in the CES report.
47. See chapter by Sikainga.
48. For a recent discussion see Igor Kopytoff, 'The Cultural Context of African Abolition', in Miers and Roberts, *End of Slavery*, pp.485–503. See also *inter alia* Carolyn Browne, 'Testing the Boundaries of Marginality: Twentieth-Century Slavery and Emancipation Struggles in Nkanu, Northern Igboland, 1920–29', *Journal of African History*, 37 (1996) pp.51–80.
49. Lugard to FO confidential 15 April 1932, and FO minutes, FO 371/16503.
50. Maxwell's correspondence and memoranda from 1934 to 1939 are too voluminous to detail here. They are to be found in the Foreign Office series 371, in archives of the Colonial, Dominions and India Offices and in the League of Nations archives Geneva.
51. CCEE 138.C159 M.113, 1935, VI; C 189 (1) m.145, 1936; C.188 M.173.1937, VI; C.112 M.98, 1938.VI.
52. Minutes FO 371/20517, W1949/154/52, pp.27ff.
53. Miers, 'Hijaz'.
54. Saudi Arabia outlawed it in 1962, the Trucial States during the 1960s and Muscat and Oman in 1970.
55. See chapters by Klein and Hargey.

No Liberty, Not Much Equality, and Very Little Fraternity: The Mirage of Manumission in the Algerian Sahara in the Second Half of the Nineteenth Century

DENNIS D. CORDELL

France does not have only free men among its Muslim subjects; Algeria includes, in addition, a very small number of black slaves. Should we allow slavery to continue on soil that we control? One of our neighbouring Muslim princes, the Bey of Tunis, has declared that servitude is abolished in his empire. Can we do any less?

It is therefore to be desired that one can soon make it disappear, and the Commission has expressed the most formal wishes about it. Without doubt, it is necessary to proceed towards the abolition of slavery with the utmost precaution and deliberation. We have reason to believe that [if] dealt with in this manner, it will not provoke any serious resistance and will not put us in peril.

Alexis de Tocqueville
Rapport sur l'Algérie (1847)[1]

On 27 April 1848, a year after Tocqueville's report to the Assemblée Nationale, the France of the great revolution of 1789, the cradle of 'liberty, equality, and fraternity', indeed proclaimed the legal abolition of slavery throughout the empire. This paper is about what that decree meant in the Algerian Sahara in the last half of the nineteenth century.[2]

In Algeria, the reaction of the military government to the prospect of abolition was anything but enthusiastic. In 1847, when the Minister of War asked Maréchal Bugeaud his opinion of the draft proclamation, the conqueror of Algeria responded with both anger and contempt, raising the objections that would reappear in military and civilian reports from the colony for the rest of the century:[3]

You request, Monsieur le Ministre, my proposals and my observations. Proposals! I have only one, which is to postpone indefinitely this measure which is politically unwise and somewhat barbarous, despite the cloak of philanthropy. As for my observations, I will not be brief. I present them without reserve, so much so that the *négrophiles* will say to the 'first chief' that I am barbarous or retrograde.

Bugeaud goes on to list his objections in substantial detail. In response to claims that abolition was a great success in Tunis, Constantinople and Egypt, he suggests that the measure had no impact at all beyond the walls of the city of Tunis itself and that the situation was probably the same in Turkey and Egypt: 'In the capitals and in the large cities, blacks were liberated, but in the countryside their habitual status has not changed.' Bugeaud also believed that such a measure could bring armed resistance among France's Algerian subjects:

You have conquered them, they have bowed their heads under the yoke of force, but if they are resigned [to French control] it is because they believe that you will keep your promises to respect their religion, their customs, and their property. Although vanquished, they remain armed. They could take to the battlefield again without great delay, and it would take three or four hundred thousand disciplined troops to defeat them.

The Maréchal developed this argument further, noting that French imposition of forced labour, forced cultivation of certain crops, and forced military service on the people of Algeria was absolutely necessary, and that abolition would add unnecessary insult to injury. He advocated beginning with the French Caribbean, where the French slave-owning class was small and weak, thus avoiding the discontent of three or four million Arabs in Algeria.

Bugeaud then shifted the discussion to the nature of slavery in North Africa, voicing an argument that became commonplace in the following decades; namely that slaves in Algeria, unlike their counterparts in the Caribbean, were part of the family, and that their culture was indistinguishable from that of their owners: 'They enjoy the same lifestyle; they are only rarely mistreated, the Arabs often marry black women, and children born of concubines are treated exactly as the others.' Bugeaud goes on to cite the fragile French presence in Algeria and France's dependence on local elites to control the population – the very people most likely to own slaves. He further raises the spectre feared by all bureaucrats, a runaway budget resulting from the importation of an 'army of agents' to enforce the decree. He conjectures that while urban dwellers would accept emancipation with resentment and resignation, the 'tribes' of the rural areas,

40 SLAVERY AND COLONIAL RULE IN AFRICA

whose 'chiefs, even the least important, owned black men and women slaves', would become restless. Bugeaud concludes his analysis with the observation that outlawing slavery would threaten trans-Saharan commerce. And then, despite his refusal to do so at the outset, he presents two alternative propositions – either to put off the proclamation indefinitely, or to delay such a declaration until 1 January 1850, and even then to limit abolition of slavery and the slave trade to areas occupied by French troops or under French civilian administration.

Despite Bugeaud's vocal opposition, the French government indeed abolished slavery throughout the empire the next year. In Algeria, Governor General Charon named a commission to study implementation of the decree. That body concluded that efforts at manumission should be the responsibility of the central government in Algiers. In reality, however, jurisdiction came to reside with regional and local military and civilian authorities. In the mid-nineteenth century, Algeria consisted of 'the Tell' or lands along the Mediterranean coast, and 'the Sahara', a band of French influence extending a hundred kilometres into the desert to the south – as far as Biskra in the east, Laghaouat in the centre, and Sidi-Yahya in the southwest. In both areas the *Bureaux arabes,* an administration created by ministerial decree on 1 February 1844 and staffed by military and civilian officials deemed to be specialists in Muslim and Arab affairs, governed local populations.[4] Whether they acknowledged it or not, the administrators of the Bureaux arabes shared Bugeaud's concerns about the impact of freeing the slaves in Algeria. And more often than not, they responded to Tocqueville's appeal for a 'measured' policy regarding emancipation. Further south, French authority was negligible in 1848, but in the second half of the century the army founded posts ever deeper in the desert.[5] Dependent on local elites for support, French commanders in the Great Sahara displayed, if anything, even less enthusiasm for freeing the slaves than their compatriots farther north. Such a lack of enthusiasm also stemmed from the central role played by slave labour in the Algerian Sahara.

Slavery and Societies in the Algerian Sahara

Slavery was a crucial component of the social reproduction of Algerian societies in the last half of the nineteenth century. Estimates of the proportion of the Algerian population that lived in servitude in the mid-nineteenth century are lacking. In neighbouring Morocco, Ennaji suggests that slaves may have constituted as much as a tenth of the population.[6] Ennaji also cites qualitative evidence to demonstrate that black African slaves were ubiquitous in Morocco – among wealthy urban households as

THE MIRAGE OF MANUMISSION IN THE ALGERIAN SAHARA   41

well as among their neighbours of more modest means, among rural agricultural populations, and among desert nomads.[7] In the Sahara, slaves lived in the desert camps of the Arab Chaamba and the Tuareg, and among the oasis populations subject to their authority. Bataillon suggests that captives made up a larger part of the population in the southern desert which lay closer to the sources of the slave trade.[8]

In North Africa as elsewhere, the conditions of servitude varied according to context. In 1849, just after emancipation, Durrieu penned a benign view of slavery just south of Algiers in the Médéa subdivision of the Tell:

> The state of black slaves is far from being in the Médéah [*sic*] subdivision as abject and as rough as it is in our American colonies. No where does one find a group of black slaves exploited by an owner and subjected to heavy labour. In the Titery, the black slave is purchased by rich families and is only used for domestic labour. He becomes a member of the family and only rarely complains about his fate.[9]

The social roles and work organization of slaves differed according to whether they were attached to farming communities in the Tell, or whether they were dependents of nomadic peoples, and the relationship between oasis and nomadic societies in the part of the desert where they lived. Among nomadic peoples such as the Tuareg, for example, slaves remained almost a caste apart.[10] In a recent comparative study of genetic markers among the social classes in Idelès, an oasis community tributary to the Tuareg in the Hoggar Mountains of the central Sahara, Lefèvre-Witier notes that clearly discernible genetic divisions remain today between the Tuareg, the Haratin or descendants of freed slaves and former slaves or *iklan*.[11] Such distinctions were reflected in the differing economic roles of each of these social groups a century earlier.[12] Gender distinctions were also important. Some female slaves became concubines of their masters and enhanced their social position by giving birth to their children. But despite apparent advantages associated with being a concubine or wife, the case studies included in the last section of this essay clearly demonstrate that the ambiguous status of female slaves in the Algerian social context frequently made it more difficult for women to free themselves from oppressive masters.

The labour of slaves in the Algerian Sahara resembled the work of captives elsewhere in the desert. Slaves and haratin, men and women who were technically free but who remained dependent on patrons – European observers often likened them to serfs[13] – were the mainstays of agriculture and crafts production. In 1857, French reconnaissance columns visited the oases of Ouargla and Negouea, located about 700 kilometres south of Algiers, and sent a description of their inhabitants to Dr. Cosson, Secretary of the Société Botanique de France:

> The inhabitants of the city are of the colour and [possess] some of the traits of the Negro race. On the outskirts of the town in the sand, they cultivate fruit trees, vegetables, tobacco, cotton and a lucerne which is not our *Medieago satira*.[14]

In most parts of the desert, date production also occupied many slaves. Lelong, for example, noted that Haratin, who were legally free when he wrote in the early 1940s but who in many respects remained as dependent as slaves in earlier times, did all the work in the 'avenue of the palms', the stretch of oases commanded by *ksour* or fortified settlements between Figuig and Tidikelt in northwestern Algeria.[15] His description of the nobles, who did little work, was indeed quite acerbic:

> About forty *ksour* were spaced along [the] course [of the 'avenue of the palms'], inhabited by harratine [*sic*] cultivators and the Cheurfas, nobles claiming descent from the Prophet, who, due to this status, lived from the work of others.[16]

In the nineteenth century slaves also provided a large part of the labour necessary to build, tend and maintain the irrigation systems necessary for agricultural production in the Sahara. Needs and technology varied from one part of the desert to another. The French military expedition to Ouargla and Negouea cited above also reported that 'gardens are watered from shallow, non-artesian wells whose water is first dumped into a basin located above the ground from which it flows into small square parcels of land.'[17] Farther south, however, the water table is much deeper. In the eastern Algerian desert, oases are watered by deep artesian wells. Settlements in the west and south depended upon extensive networks of underground irrigation tunnels or *foggara*. In the oasis of Tamentit, for example, the foggara extended for forty kilometres at a depth of sixty metres![18] In 1908, an administrative report from the Territoires du Sud – the Saharan administrative districts – testified to the immense reserves of labour required to maintain such systems:

> Everywhere numerous crews are working to repair old wells or dig new ones. In Touat and the Gourara, under the direction of officers and men of the *Compagnie saharienne*, the inhabitants are making greater and greater efforts to expand water resources, either by drilling to increase the volume of existing foggara or by putting back into service others long ago abandoned.[19]

THE MIRAGE OF MANUMISSION IN THE ALGERIAN SAHARA 43

Writing in the 1940s, Gautier noted that 'each [oasis dweller] recalled the memory of a grandfather or other elder who came as a slave from the Soudan' or the desert-edge.[20] Lelong concludes that Haratin were essential for life in the desert; the same might be said of slaves who were not yet freed.[21]

Patterns of settlement in the Algerian Sahara resembled those farther south and west.[22] (See Klein and Sikainga chapters.) Some slaves in the nineteenth century, like their successors in the twentieth, lived in separate, settled communities where they enjoyed some autonomy, while others were attached to the households of their owners. Still others, both women and men, accompanied their nomad masters into the desert where they helped tend their herds.[23] Viewed from the Sahara, then, where slaves and their labour were crucial to social reproduction, the French emancipation proclamation of 1848 must have seemed quite irrelevant even to those who were supposed to make it reality.

The Ambiguity of Abolition in Algeria and the Neighbouring Desert

The parliamentary decree of 1848 outlawed slavery from one day to the next. But despite the prompt nomination of a commission to implement the decree in Algeria, and ensuing administrative circulars which at least formally aimed at abolishing slavery and the slave trade, the colonial archives record nary a soul who advocated so rapid and unambiguous an end to slavery in any part of the colony. While most colonial administrators and military leaders expressed their philosophical agreement with the decree, almost to a man (there were no women) they echoed Tocqueville's appeal for restraint, and shared Bugeaud's scepticism about the entire enterprise. Writing in 1848, Defoug, who was attached to the colonial military administration in Médéa, argued that the only way to prevent the slave trade was to stop the importation of slaves from the south. As for the abolition of slavery itself, Defoug noted that the slave population of the subdivision was between 1,600 and 1,700 people, who represented a capital investment of a half million francs. He suggested that only the colonial state could afford to reimburse such a sum to Arab slave owners, and that a failure to do so would lead to general discontent, if not revolt. He went on to recommend a ten-year plan for abolition, during which time the colonial state would free one-tenth of the slaves annually and reimburse their owners.[24] Describing the situation in Médéa the following year, Durrieu is even more ambiguous. After his almost positive description of slavery in Médéa cited earlier, he takes the philosophical high road, assuring us of his conviction that 'one can only contemplate with pain the shameful traffic which has the slave as its object and the insult to the dignity of man that slavery represents.'[25] However, in the same breath he preaches caution and counsels recruiting the newly 'freed' slaves for the colonial labour force:

> Seeing that the emancipation of the black slave race in Algeria represents a threat to Arab property, it should be undertaken only gradually. Begin with the coastal cities, and extend it to those of the interior, and from there to the Arab tribes, by which time we will be able to indemnify slave owners for the capital that they spent in acquiring them. The great public works of Algeria, to which black slaves could be called, could perhaps be the means whereby the government could provide them the benefits of liberty.[26]

A decade later the situation had not apparently improved. In both 1857 and 1858, the Maréchal Gouverneur Général, the highest ranking military officer in Algeria, felt compelled to issue circulars to French administrators admonishing them to obey the law. On 12 November 1857 he wrote to his General in Algiers that,

> [...] slaves have been recently sold in certain markets of Algeria. I do not need to remind you that this commerce is against the law, but I must recommend that you take great care to assure that the letter of this law is respected. Black men and women brought into Algeria to be sold must be immediately liberated without allowing the traders to claim any indemnity whatsoever. Indeed to assure the repression of this commerce, such traders will be detained for whatever length of time you determine.[27]

The following year he had to write again to the same General; this time he sent copies to all the *Commandants supérieurs*, the officials who administered subdivisons, the territorial unit just below the level of the province:

> Infractions of the law of 27 April 1848 have recently occurred in large numbers. In several parts of the province we have had to apply the dispositions of the Governor General's circular of 22 November 1857. I do not have to insist on the reasons which, in these circumstances more than any other, make it desirable to prevent infractions [of the law] rather than to have to suppress them. I request that you bring to the attention of the Commandants supérieurs and the heads of the Bureaux arabes in the *cercles* [local administrative districts] the necessity to leave no stone unturned in attaining this objective. The investigations which precede the granting of permits to whose who request permission to travel afford the natural occasion for ascertaining the intentions of those who might be susceptible to engaging in the slave trade and for warning them of the consequences that could result from [such activity].[28]

THE MIRAGE OF MANUMISSION IN THE ALGERIAN SAHARA   45

Ambiguity about the abolition of slavery (and even the slave trade) continued into the latter decades of the nineteenth century. In an 1877 report on trade and exploration in the Sahara, Flatters suggested that the slave trade was the most important component of trans-Saharan commerce, and cites conversations with informants throughout Algeria who advocated tolerance of the trade. His choice of words is ironic to say the least:

> Local people most familiar with the Tidikelt, Touat, Gourara, Hogger, Ghadames, etc., are unanimous on this point: [... T]he only way to create lasting ties with Saharan regions outside European control is to render free the commerce in slaves. To suppose that without this tolerance we can establish commercial ties of another nature with any real importance is a chimera.[29]

Two years later, the president of the Algiers Chamber of Commerce echoed this analysis, citing a report by Féraud, the French Consul General in Tripoli, that attributed the loss of commerce to the abolition of slavery and the slave trade in Algeria. Féraud, in fact, went so far as to suggest that abolition was responsible for the depopulation of settlements in the Algerian Sahara such as the El Goléa group of seventy oases, many of which had been abandoned by 1879. To remedy the situation, Féraud proposed, and the Chamber passed on to the Préfet of Algiers, a policy similar to that advocated by Durrieu earlier in the century – namely that the colonial administration recruit black slaves in the central Sahara, in places such as El Goléa, Ouargla, Gardeïa, and Insaleh, and bring them into the colony as 'free men', where, in exchange for their freedom, they would either serve in the army for five years, work for French or Arab landowners, or agree to resettle the abandoned oases. The proposal even included a clause whereby inhabitants of Algeria would be authorized to purchase female slaves whom they wished to marry, 'thus emancipating them'![30] The Governor General's response was brief, but the fact that he did not dismiss the plan out of hand suggests that such proposals were not viewed as being extreme: 'The means that you indicate to bring the return of the slave trade to Algeria seems to me to be fraught with difficulty. Nonetheless, the question merits study.'[31] Indeed, the situation appears to have changed so little by the latter decades of the century that in 1887 the Governor General once again issued the 1857 circular abolishing the slave trade.[32]

The law and the circulars abolishing slavery and the slave trade were clear, but the ambiguity in attitudes persisted until the end of the century and beyond. As late as 1906, a Lieutenant-Colonel of an oasis in the heart of the Algerian Sahara noted that the populations of southern Algeria viewed the slave trade as a licit trade, and insisted that if local authorities tried to eliminate the commerce, they would have take on the entire local

46 SLAVERY AND COLONIAL RULE IN AFRICA

population.[33] Such attitudes compelled no less an authority than the President of the French Republic to issue a decree in July 1906 reiterating the illegal character of the slave trade in Algeria.[34] But despite French prevarication, the provisions of the law seemed clear enough to many fugitive slaves who presented themselves at French posts throughout Algeria in the last half of the nineteenth century.

Slaves Who Sought Freedom (even if they did not seek '*Liberté*')

While the French debated the merits of abolishing slavery and the slave trade in Algeria and the Sahara, individual slaves continually confronted the authorities with demands for freedom. In Algeria itself, black African men and women fled their owners and appealed to French authorities for asylum. Others fled to Algerian soil from Morocco in the west and Libya in the east, lands where slavery and the commerce which supported it remained legal. The tales of black African slaves who sought relief from slavery between 1848 and World War I in the territories that comprise today's Algeria are incomplete narratives reported in letters and reports generated by the colonial administration in the course of deliberations about their fate. While these African men and women probably did not understand *liberté* in the way intended by the French authors of the abolition decree of 1848, they clearly knew that they could appeal to European authority for asylum from masters who were abusive and who neglected their welfare.

In the decade or so after 1848, the cases of flight recorded in the archives illustrate quite clearly that slaves preferred to appeal to French civilian officials for their freedom than to the military authorities who ruled indigenous Arab and Berber populations. If Maréchal Bugeaud's negative reaction to the abolition decree is any indication of thinking about manumission that prevailed in military circles, it is not surprising that slaves from zones under military control chose to claim asylum in areas under civilian authority; or that others seized the occasion of a visit with their owners to towns under French civilian control to ask for refuge. Such appears, for example, to have been the strategy of Mohamed ben Zerouali, a black slave who presented himself on 11 January 1854 to the *préfet* in Oran, the chief civilian authority in the *département*, 'to invoke the benefits of the decree of 27 April 1848 on the abolition of slavery.'[35] He identified one Si Ali ben Hammadan as his owner, whom he charged with total neglect, and appealed to French civilian authorities to allow him to settle and make his own living in the 'black quarter' (*quartier nègre*) of Oran. Although civilian authorities wrote to the director of Arab affairs for the subdivision or military district of Oran requesting instructions on how to handle the case, it is clear they were inclined to grant Mohamed's wish.

THE MIRAGE OF MANUMISSION IN THE ALGERIAN SAHARA 47

Civilian authorities were more circumspect in the case of Fatima, a black woman who appeared around the same time at the préfecture in Oran. Fatima and her owner were from Mascara subdivision, located about 100 kilometres southeast of Oran in the Atlas Mountains. She took advantage of a sojourn in Oran to seek refuge in the black quarter. Later unidentified circumstances led her to appear at the préfecture, where she charged her owner with beating her and planning to sell her. In this instance, a civilian official simply recounted the incident to military authorities, and requested instructions without expressing any opinion. Penned across the document is a terse note – presumably from a military official – noting that because the woman had left her *duar* (or camp) without permission she should present herself to the Bureau arabe in Mascara within 13 days.[36] The archives are unfortunately silent on Fatima's fate.

At the end of the decade, slaves continued to flee to zones of civilian authority in search of freedom. In 1859, the case of a male escapee named Barka left two letters in its wake which illustrate quite explicitly the conflict between civilian and military officials over manumission.[37] On 7 June the Préfet of the Oran préfecture replied to a letter dated 4 June from the general commanding the Oran subdivision. The general had requested the return of Barka, whom he charged with theft and flight from military authority. The Préfet observed that the slave showed signs of a recent beating, and repeated Barka's declaration that he had fled his owner Rabah ben Moussa because of ill treatment. The Préfet emphasized that Barka had fled to escape servitude, not because he sought to elude military authority. He went on to say that 'not being able to refuse to apply to him the benefits of the decree of 27 April 1848', he had on 23 May inscribed Barka as number 332 on the *corporation des nègres*, the black civilian register.

To bolster his position further, the Préfet noted that Rabah ben Moussa himself had admitted to purchasing Barka three years earlier for 130 *durus* (or 650 old francs), thus violating the law by participating in the slave trade. Moreover, he intimated that Rabah had invented the charge of theft since he waited a month after Barka's escape to raise the issue. The Préfet explained that the charge of theft was under investigation by the Conseil de Guerre, but expressed the opinion that if Barka were cleared, he should be allowed to remain in Oran. Finally, in a sentence clearly meant to smooth over the disagreement, the Préfet apologized for not getting 'the facts' to the general earlier, 'vowing to take care to let you know the names of blacks, who, with the motive or under the pretext of slavery, seek refuge from military territory in civilian territory.' But the general was apparently not to be assuaged and said so in a letter on 9 June. The Préfet addressed a strongly worded reply to him the following day:

48   SLAVERY AND COLONIAL RULE IN AFRICA

> It is impossible for me, Monsieur le Général, to share your sentiment
> about the situation of this inhabitant in light of the by-law of 4
> November 1858 executing the decree of 27 April 1848. I am therefore
> obliged to refer [the matter] to His Excellency the Minister of Algeria
> and the Colonies and to suspend until his ruling the return [of the
> individual] whom you request.

Following the abolition decree and for the rest of the century, slaves from
the neighbouring territories of Morocco and Tunisia also fled to French
authorities in Algeria in quest of freedom. The military seemed to be more
receptive to granting refuge to slaves from lands beyond French control. In
some cases, however, civilian authorities felt compelled to continue to
pressure them to adhere to the law. As late as 1880, for example, no less an
official than Governor General Albert Grévy wrote to the commanding
general in Algeria reminding him he was obliged to protect black women
from Morocco who had sought refuge in Algeria 'to obtain their liberty
under the protection of our laws', despite rulings by local qadis who wanted
to return the women to their owners.[38] A series of eight letters written
between 7 July and 20 August 1893, for example, recounts the tale of
Abdallah El-Guelman, Abdallah and Othman, three slaves from the Gourara
located on the southern edge of the Great Western Erg deep in the Sahara.
They had somehow made their way from Gourara 450 kilometers northeast
to the French post at El-Goléa, where they appealed for asylum to the
commanding officer, Captain Godron. He not only granted their request, but
when their two (former) owners appeared shortly thereafter, he told them
that according to French law slavery had been abolished, and said that he
would only return the slaves if the former captives agreed to it.[39] They did
not, and in letter written two weeks later, Godron reported that two of the
three men were employed by the local administration and a third was a paid
employee of the *caïd*, or chief, of the Mouadhi, the people of the oasis.[40]

The same year, another series of documents treated the case of
Mohamed, a young black slave about 18 years of age, who presented
himself to the civil inspector at the oasis of Tozeur in Tunisia, and made the
following declaration:

> Two years ago slave traders kidnapped me from Afjou [in central
> Algeria] with about twenty other black men and seven black women,
> and took us to the market in Ghadames. There I was purchased, along
> with six other young blacks like myself, by El-Hajj Ammar of the
> Troud of Wadi Souf. Three other Algerians belonging to the Troud
> acquired four black men and were part of the same caravan. I watched
> the herds of my master until this year, when he forced me to leave. I
> followed three black men and two black women who fled to Nefta. I

THE MIRAGE OF MANUMISSION IN THE ALGERIAN SAHARA 49

first sought shelter, a month ago, with Mbarek ben el-Khazem, and then, the day before yesterday, with the Khalifa of Nefta where I want to stay.[41]

The 'Affaire Mohammed' sufficiently preoccupied the French to provoke the exchange of letters among J. Cambon who was the Governor General of Algeria, the commanding general in Constantine in eastern Algeria, and the French Resident General in Tunis. Apart from attempting to determine if Mohamed's story was true or not, the Governor General was particularly concerned to learn if the young man had been held as a slave on Algerian soil, which would have been illegal. The conclusion of the inquiry was ambiguous. But in a final letter written to the French Resident General in Tunis on 4 December 1893, Governor General Cambon nonetheless determined that the decree prohibiting slavery had not been violated – at least on Algerian soil:

> ... the young black Mohammed was purchased at the market in Ghadames [in Libya] several years ago from El Hadj Belkaum el Bellili by Aoun ben Zengui ben el Hadj of the Rebaïa of El-Oued [in Algeria], who was acting on behalf of Mohammed ben Massaoud of the same tribe who is mentioned in your letter of 28 September. Brought to El Oued, the young Mohammed stayed for two years at the home of Mohammed ben Messaoud. Without leaving the annexe of El Oued, he then served *in a state of liberty* [my italics] for four months with Ali ben Ahmed ben Amin of the Azazla and the caïdat of the Messaba, and [after that] for two months with El Hadj Amara bou Ibïa of the Oulad Djama of Achech. [...] Although this information does not completely agree with that supplied by the black [Mohammed], it is clear that he was not held as a slave by the various individuals with whom he has worked since his arrival in Algerian territory.[42]

The correspondence is not as clear as the Governor General's conclusion. To be sure, Ghadames, where Mohamad was sold, was an oasis in Libya, which was at that time part of the Ottoman empire. On the other hand, El Oued, an oasis located in the northern Sahara about 300 kilometres south of the French settlement of Constantine, lay within the zone of French influence, if not in the colony of Algeria as defined at that time. The Governor General calculated that Mohamed spent two years in El Oued. The French official noted that Mohamed had 'served' for six months 'in a state of liberty' *chez* Ali ben Ahmed ben Amin and *chez* El Hadj Amara bou Ibïa, an oxymoronic description that reflects the ambiguous and contradictory status of 'freed' slaves. He failed to comment, however, on Mohammed's status during the first 18 months of his sojourn in El Oued –

50 SLAVERY AND COLONIAL RULE IN AFRICA

a period of residence that followed the abolition decree of 1848. The Governor General, like most French administrators most of the time, followed the letter, and not the spirit, of the law.

If slaves played French military and civilian authorities against each in their efforts to gain their freedom, owners (or former owners) sought to blur the difference between slave status and other forms of dependency in a ploy to keep or regain their captives. Muslim legal authorities – to whom French authorities frequently turned for interpretations of family law – often supported slave owners in these endeavours. In much of the correspondence, investigations of the status of escaped black slave women are obfuscated by the claims of owners that these women were their wives. And these men frequently produced papers written by local *qadis* (judges) or other religious leaders to prove their claims. In a variation on this strategy, they also sometimes sent male slaves (who were, of course, not identified as such) to the authorities to request the return of black women whom they identified as their spouses.

Such was the scheme to force the return of Rahma, described in a letter ironically written on Bastille Day 1860 by the Préfet of Oran to the general commanding the subdivision.[43] Like the slaves described above, Rahma had fled military territory. She ultimately found her way to the civilian Bureau arabe in Oran, where, she told the associate director that 'she was fleeing slavery in the wake of poor treatment by her owner Si El Habib ben Zouaoui.' The official heard her case and then urged her to return to her home in Melita. Somehow Rahma found the wherewithall to 'refuse to return to her master', whereupon he 'returned with a black man named Salem who said he was married to Rahma'. The Préfet's narrative is telling at this point: 'It was no longer the master claiming his slave, but a husband requesting that his wife return to the conjugal residence'. The Bureau official asked for proof of marriage. Since Rahma had formally declared that she was not Salem's wife, and charged him, moreover, with inflicting a serious head injury, the associate director allowed her to stay in Oran pending presentation of the necessary documentation. Indeed, Salem did return with marriage papers, and the préfet of Oran concluded his letter to the commanding general by writing that 'I have given orders that this black woman be placed at your disposition so that you may force her to return to her husband's tent'.

The Préfet's letter is the only record left of Rahma's ordeal. Without other evidence it is impossible to determine with absolute confidence who was telling the truth, Rahma or Salem. However, it is fair to suspect that the marriage was concocted after the failure of Rahma's owner to retrieve her himself. The letter intimates that her owner had first tried to retrieve her (the Préfet does not mention this first attempt, but he notes that her former owner

THE MIRAGE OF MANUMISSION IN THE ALGERIAN SAHARA   51

'returned' with Salem), and only when he returned a second time did he bring Salem who claimed Rahma as his wife.

Similar episodes are described in other narratives about women who attempted to escape slavery. For example, the month after Rahma fled, the captain who administered the Annexe of Aïn Temouchent wrote to the captain in charge of the Bureau arabe in Oran to ask what to do about qadis who issued suspicious marriage contracts.[44] The captain wanted to know how to respond to demands of a black man named Faradji Ouled el Miloud for the return of his wife Zineb, who had sought refuge at the French post and who refused to rejoin him. The translation of the marriage contract accompanying the captain's letter revealed quite clearly that Bouchentouf Ouled el Monkour, the black man's patron (and perhaps his former owner), had sponsored the marriage, supplying the funds to pay the *sadaqha* or brideprice, as well as promising to support the couple and provide them with clothing. In exchange, the contract stipulated that Faradji would remain with Bouchentouf Ouled el Monkour as his *khammès* (or tenant farmer),[45] and that 'the fruits of his labour' would accrue to the tent. The captain closes by asking what to do with qadis who presided over such questionable marriage contracts, if a document written in such circumstances was valid, what rights were retained by the black man, and what to do with the black woman.

The letter says very little about Zineb, other than to note that the *sadaqha* would be paid in two instalments, half at the time of marriage and half ten years later – a common clause in marriage contracts in the region.[46] The question here is not whether Zineb was a slave; she both was and was not. In the eyes of the French administration she was not a slave because slavery had been abolished in 1848. However, Muslim law continued to sanction servitude. But Zineb's case illustrates the way that slave owners played on gender relations to retain control over women. In a gender alliance between male owners and slaves, Bouchentouf Ouled el Monkour first provided Faradji with a slave woman as his wife. When Zineb escaped, both men used that relationship of dependency to legitimize claims for her return. In this case, Muslim legal authorities supported the strategy, probably not only because they regarded it as a way around a French decree that they regarded as illegitimate – the abolition decree of 1848 – but also because the custom of an owner sponsoring the marriage of his slave was perfectly legitimate in their eyes. On occasion, however, the *fuqaha* or Muslim legal authorites – particularly those in the urban areas – supported women's appeals for freedom. Christelow writes that,

> [o]n this score, I have come across one interesting incident. The fuqaha of Mostaganem – which meant above all Ben Barnu of the

Conseil de Jurisprudence – cooperated with the Sub-Prefect in annulling the marriage of a black woman who had fled to civil authority, to her former master. Thus not only did they in effect support a slave's demand for freedom, but they recognized a crude disguise for slavery – marriage – for what it was, and acted accordingly.[47]

In many cases these claims were dubious, but they probably do reflect the fact that many women slaves had sexual relations with their owners. They also suggest that slave women were valued for their reproductive capacities. As for the marriage claims, it seems highly likely that when confronted by the authorities, the owners of female slaves would have married them in an effort to avoid punishment. While it is true that female slaves and wives both occupied social and legal positions inferior to those of their male owners and husbands, the strategies outlined in the cases of Rahma and Zineb did not issue from the failure of slave owners to distinguish between the legal statuses of female slaves and wives. Islamic law generally, and the Maliki *madhdhab* or legal school predominant in the Maghrib in particular, make clear distinctions between them.[48]

Other cases deal with the fate of African women later in the century, such as Messaouda, who in 1893 reported to authorities that she was purchased by one Mohammed ben Mahoud of Ouargla, taken to his house, and then resold by him to another man.[49] Authorities investigated the case, finding that Messaouda had been given to Mohammed ben Mahmoud by two men from Ouargla as repayment for a loan.

The slaves who attempted to escape their servitude undoubtedly did not have the same understanding of *liberté* as the French authorities who proclaimed it for them. But it is likely that they were familiar with the restraints and responsibilities that the *Shari'a* imposed on slave owners. As Sikainga notes in this collection, 'slaves were severely punished for disobedience', and 'responded to their harsh treatment by fleeing, seeking sanctuary in the shrines of holymen, or demanding that their owners sell them.'[50] And so, just as abused slaves appealed to Muslim authorities, secular and religious, so escaped slaves appealed to the French officials in Algeria for sanctuary after 1848. If the French remained undecided for a half century and more about whether or how they should implement the emancipation decree, slaves in the colony of Algeria and the neighbouring Sahara, acting in accordance with their own understanding of the *Shari'a* and social practice, were prepared to force them to live up to the letter of the law and make the mirage of manumission a concrete reality.

THE MIRAGE OF MANUMISSION IN THE ALGERIAN SAHARA

GLOSSARY

Bureaux arabes (French)	An administration created in colonial Algeria by ministerial decree on 1 February 1844 to govern local Muslim populations
Caïd (Arabic)	Chief of an Arab camp or settlement in the Maghrib
Cercle (French)	Administrative district below the level of the Division or Département and the Subdivision in French Algeria
Duar (Arabic)	Arab camp or settlement in Algeria
Duru (Arabic)	Unit of currency in French Algeria equal to 150 old francs (anciens francs)
Faqih (s.)/ Fuquha (pl.) (Arabic)	Muslim legal authority or authorities
Foggara (Arabic)	Underground irrigation canals common in the oases of the southern Algerian Sahara
Haratin (Arabic)	Freed slaves or free descendants of slaves
Iklan (Tamashek)	Slaves
Ksour (Arabic)	Fortified settlements in Saharan oases
Préfet (French)	Chief civilian official of a Division or Département in French Algeria
Qadi (Arabic)	Judge in the Islamic legal system
Shari'a (Arabic)	Islamic law
Subdivision (French)	Administrative district below the level of the Division or Département in French Algeria

NOTES

1. Alexis de Tocqueville, 'Rapport sur l'Algérie (1847) – Extraits', in Alexis de Tocqueville, *De la colonie en Algérie* (Paris, 1988), pp.179–80.
2. This case study is drawn from ongoing research in the archives of the Gouvernement-Général of Algeria and its subdivisions found at the Centre d'Archives d'Outre-Mer (CAOM), a depository of the Archives Nationales (AN) in Aix-en-Provence, and from the Centre d'Accueil et de Recherche des Archives Nationales (CARAN), a depository of the Archives Nationales (AN) in Paris. This is the first published work from a research project on 'How much of the TransSaharan Slave Trade was Really TransSaharan? A Social and Demographic History of Saharan Societies.' I wish to thank the ex-Joint Committee on African Studies of the Social Science Research Council and the American Philosophical Society for grants in support of this project. At Southern Methodist University, the Stanton Sharp Endowment Trust for History in the William P. Clements Department of History, the University Research Council, and the Fund for Faculty Excellence provided additional assistance. Finally, I wish to thank my partner Gary W. Irvin for his affection and constant encouragement. He shared my concern to demonstrate that a dean can still do primary research.
3. Archives de l'Armée (Vincennes), 18Mi14 (formerly Carton 2EE7), Registre de la correspondance du Maréchal Bugeaud avec le Ministre de la Guerre, du mois de février au 27 mai 1847 (5 fragments), 'Observations sur le projet d'abolition de l'esclavage en Algérie, 1 mai 1847.' I am grateful to Yacine Daddi Addoun of the Department of History, York University, Ontario, who generously provided me with his transcription of Bugeaud's observations. The direct quotations from Bugeaud and paraphrased references attributed to him are all taken from this document.
4. Jacques Frémeaux, *Les bureaux arabes dans l'Algérie de la conquête* (Paris, 1993), pp.18–21.
5. French expeditions reached Touggourt, an oasis in the northern desert south of Constantine, in December 1853 for the first time, and Ouargla the following month. The army returned to Ouargla in January 1857. See Jean Lethielleux, *Ouargla, cité saharienne des origines au début du XXè siècle* (Paris, 1983), pp.249–50.

54 SLAVERY AND COLONIAL RULE IN AFRICA

6. Mohammed Ennaji, *Soldats, domestiques et concubines: L'esclavage au Maroc au XIXè siècle* (Paris, 1994), 18. Ennaji cites estimates ranging from 50,000 to 500,000, concluding that 'slaves were found in quite high numbers'.
7. Ibid., pp.19–22.
8. C. Bataillon, 'La tribu', 31, and 'Modernisation du nomadisme pastoral', 171–72, both in UNESCO (ed.), *Nomades et nomadisme au Sahara* (Paris, 1963).
9. CAOM-AN (Aix), Algérie, Gouvernement-Général, 50II265, No.6, 1849.05, Durrieu, 'Renseignements sur l'introduction et le commerce des nègres esclaves dans la subdivision de Médéah', 1849.05.
10. André Bourgeot, *Les sociétés touarègues: Nomadisme, identité, resistances* (Paris, 1995), pp.53–68.
11. Philippe Lefèvre-Witier. *Idelès du Hoggar. Biologie et écologie d'une communauté saharienne* (Paris, 1996).
12. CAOM-AN (Aix), Fonds Algérie, Gouvernement-Général, Ricaud, 'Renseignements sur la région d'Idelès', 1893.04.29.
13. CAOM-AN (Aix), Alger, Oasis, Dossier 31, Duclos, 'Rapport sur la situation des tribus Ajjer à l'automne 1916', Chapitre 1, 1916.
14. CAOM-AN (Aix), Algeria, Gouvernement-Général d'Alger, 22H26, Expédition d'Ouargla, Colonne de Laghouat, 'Itinéraire de la colonne de Laghouat accompagné de l'énumération des vegétaux ligneux observés dans le Sahara algérien pendant l'expédition d'Ouargla', to Monsieur le Docteur Cosson, Secrétaire de la Société botanique de France, 1857.
15. M.-H. Lelong, *Le Sahara aux cent visages* (Paris, 1945), pp.189–245.
16. Lelong, *Le Sahara*, p.191.
17. CAOM-AN (Aix), Algeria, Gouvernement-Général d'Alger, 22H26, Expédition d'Ouargla, Colonne de Laghouat, 'Itinéraire de la colonne de Laghouat accompagné de l'énumération des vegétaux ligneux observés dans le Sahara algérien pendant l'expédition d'Ouargla', to Monsieur le Docteur Cosson, Secrétaire de la Société botanique de France, 1857.
18. E.F. Gautier, *Le Sahara* (Paris, 1946), pp.194–5, 199.
19. CARAN-AN (Paris), 200Mi874, AOF, 12G22, Gouvernement Général de l'Algérie, 'Situation politique des Territoires du Sud, Mois de Juillet 1908'. The Gourara is a région in the western Algerian desert with its capital at Timimoun (see Gautier, *Le Sahara*, 86). It appears that older foggara and wells fell into disuse in the Algerian Sahara following the decline of slavery and consequent loss of labour in the late nineteenth century. Such certainly seems to have been the case further east in southern Libya. See Gustav Nachtigal, *Sahara and Sudan I:Tripoli, the Fezzan and Tibesti*, Allan G. B. Fisher and Humphrey J. Fisher, trans. (London, 1974) and *Sahara and Sudan II: Kawar, Bornu, Kanem, Borku, Ennedi*, Allan G. B. Fisher and Humphrey J. Fisher, trans. (London, 1980). In the 1990s, Lefèvre-Witier reported that the maintenance of the foggara in Idelès in the Hoggar Mountains required endless labour (see *Idelès du Hoggar*, 76–77).
20. Gautier, *Le Sahara*, pp.203–04.
21. Lelong, *Le Sahara*, p.223.
22. For a description of slavery in the southwestern Sahara, see the essay by Martin Klein in this collection.
23. CAOM-AN (Aix), Fonds Algérie, Gouvernement-Général, 12H50, Division d'Alger, Subdivision de Laghouat, Affaires Indigènes No. 32 , 'Objet: Territoires du Sud, Cercle de Laghouat', Vigy to M. le Gouverneur Général de l'Algérie.
24. CAOM-AN (Aix), Fonds Algérie, Gouvernement-Général, 50II265, No.21, Defoug, 'Rapport sur l'extinction de l'esclavage dans la subdivion de Médéah établie conformément à la dépêche No [unreadable] du 31 août 1848', 1848.
25. CAOM-AN (Aix), Algérie, Gouvernement-Général, 50II265, No 6, 'Renseignements sur l'introduction et le commerce des nègres esclaves dans la subdivision de Médéah', 1849.05.
26. Ibid.
27. CAOM-AN (Aix), Fonds Algérie, Gouvernement Général, 20J42, Gouvernement Général de l'Algérie/Cabinet/Bureau politique des Affaires arabes/ No 131, Objet: Au sujet des ventes d'esclaves, Circulaire No 256, Le Maréchal Gouverneur Général de l'Algérie à Monsieur le Général Commandt la Subdivision de Mascara, Alger, 1857.11.12.

THE MIRAGE OF MANUMISSION IN THE ALGERIAN SAHARA 55

28. CAOM-AN (Aix), Fonds Algérie, Gouvernement-Général de l'Algérie, 20J42, Province d'Oran, Direction des Affaires Arabes No. 23, 'Objet: Circulaire au sujet de la vente des esclaves, Oran', 1858.08.15.
29. CAOM-AN (Aix), Fonds Algérie, Gouvernement-Général de l'Algérie, 22H46, Subdivision de Médéah, Cercle de Laghouat, No.102, Objet: Rapport complémentaire sur le commerce et l'exploration du Sahara central et du Soudan. Suite aux rapports du 2 Juillet 1876, No. 342 et du 18 octobre 1876, No.502.
30. CAOM-AN (Aix), Fonds Algérie, Gouvernement Général d'Algérie, 22H26, Chambre de Commerce d'Alger, No.21782, 'Objet: Sahara et Soudan, Caravanes. Au sujet des propositions de M. Le Consul Général de France à Tripoli pour faire refluer, vers l'Algérie, le commerce du Soudan', letter to M. le Préfet d'Alger, Algiers, 1879.10.28.
31. Ibid.
32. See note 27.
33. CAOM-AN (Aix), Fonds Algérie, Gouvernement-Général, 12H50, Affaires indigènes, No. 182, Le Lieutenant-Colonel Laperrine, Objet: Suppression de la traite, 1906.03.24.
34. Le Mobacher: Journal officiel paraissant deux fois par semaine 58, No.4851, 1906.07.25, 3. A copy of the decree may be found in CAOM-AN (Aix), Fonds Algérie, Gouvernement-Général de l'Algérie, 12H50.
35. CAOM-AN (Aix), Fonds Algérie, 66Miom251, Number 4, Département d'Oran, Préfecture, No.147, Le Conseiller Secrétaire Général délégué pour le Préfet to M. Le Directeur des Affaires Arabes de la Province d'Oran, Au sujet de nègre Mohamed ben Zerouali qui a quitté son maître. 1854.01.02.
36. CAOM-AN (Aix), Fonds Algérie, 66Miom251, Number 4, Département d'Oran, Préfecture d'Oran, No. 89, Oliivier to Monsieur Capitaine, 185?.01.12 (date not completed).
37. CAOM-AN (Aix), Fonds Algérie, 66Miom251, microfilm roll 4, No. 629, Préfecture d'Oran, Bureau arabe départemental to Monsieur le Général de Brigade, Commandant la Subdivision d'Oran, Dossier: Exécution du décret du 27 Avril 1848, A/s d'un nègre nommé Barka, Oran, 7 June 1859; No. 273, Préfecture d'Oran, Bureau arabe départemental, A/s du nègre Barka réclamé par le Né Rabah ben Moussa comme son esclave, 10 June 1859. The préfet underscored that slavery was the issue at hand by his decision to identify the *dossier* as treating the execution of the decree of 27 April 1848.
38. CAOM-AN (Aix), Fonds Algérie, Gouvernement Général d'Algérie, 20J42, File 11, No. 128, Au sujet d'esclaves réfugiés sur le territoire algérien, 1880.08.30.
39. CAOM-AN (Aix), Fonds Algérie, Gouvernement-Général d'Algérie, 22H38, File: 'Esclaves nègres venus de Gourara et réfugiés à El-Goléa', Division d'Alger, Etat-Major de la Division, Section des Affaires Indigènes, No. 576, Au sujet de trois nègres arrivés du Gourara, Le Général Swiney to Monsieur le Gouverneur Général, 7 July 1893. Various military authorities wrote eight letters about this incident between 7 July and 20 August, which illustrate, among other things, the important role played by Muslim legal authorities in efforts by Muslim owners to reclaim their slaves. See earlier sections of this essay.
40. Ibid., Division d'Alger, Annexe d'El Goléa, Affaires indigènes, No. 392, Au sujet d'une lettre adressée par deux caïdas du Gourara au caïd des Mouadhi, El Goléa, 1983.07.16.
41. CAOM-AN (Aix), Fonds Algérie, Gouvernement-Général, 12H50, Gouverneur-Général au Général Commandant la Division de Constantine, Alger, 1893.01.30.
42. CAOM-AN (Aix), Fonds Algérie, Gouvernement-Général, 12H50, J. Cambon, Gouverneur-Général to Monsieur le Résident Général in Tunis, No. 2843, 'Au sujet du jeune nègre Mohammed', Algiers, 1893.12.04.
43. CAOM-AN (Aix), Fonds Algérie, Préfecture d'Oran, 66Miom251, roll 4, Préfet to the Général commandant la Subdivision d'Oran, Letter No.28, Au sujet de la négresse Rahma réclamée par le nègre Salem son mari', 1860.07.14. The subsequent quotations in this paragraph all come from the Préfet's letter. The Préfet's remarks in the penultimate paragraph cast doubt about the seriousness of the official investigation of Rahma's charges: 'As for the reply presented by the caïd [or chief of the black quarter] to the *chaouich* or Arab official at the military Bureau arabe, there was an error in the report… The caïd never saw the chaouich.' However, the Préfet concluded that this inaccuracy was of no consequence since the documents 'attested that Rahma was married to Salem'.

44. CAOM-AN (Aix), Fonds Algérie, Préfecture d'Oran, 66Mion251, roll 4, Division d'Oran, Annexe d'Aïn Temouchent, Letter No. 433, 1860.08.26., Le Capitaine, Chef de l'Annexe to M. le Capitaine, Chef du bureau arabe à Oran.
45. The term means one-fifth, referring to the portion of the harvest that such farmers owed to their patrons (see Lefèvre-Witier, *Idelès du Hoggar*, p.250). Ennaji uses this term to describe rural field slaves in his study of slavery in Morocco in the nineteenth century. See Ennaji, *Soldats, domestiques et concubines*, p.57.
46. Allan Christelow, *Muslim Law Courts and the French Colonial State in Algeria* (Princeton, 1984), p.68.
47. Christelow, *Muslim Law Courts*, 121. Christelow includes the relevant archival citation: Fonds Algérie, Division d'Oran, 1JJ12, Letter to Gouvernement Général, 8 February 1859. Mostaganem is located on the coast about 75 kilometres east of Oran. Christelow also records 'a similar care where a rural qadi reached an opposite decision' in the eastern part of the colony (Division de Constantine, Subdivision de Sétif, 40KK19, Letter to Division de Constantine, 20 June 1866).
48. Ennaji, *Soldats, domestiques*, pp.64–67. See Sikainga chapter in this collection.
49. CAOM-AN (Aix), Fonds Algérie, Gouvernement-Général, 12H50, Division d'Alger, Subdivision Laghouat, Cercle de Ghardaïa, Affaires indigènes, No.49, Chef de Bataillon Marignac à M. Le Cmdt Militaire du Territoire de Ghardaïa, Objet: A.S. du trafic de nègres dans le M'Zab à Ouargla, Ghardaéa, 1906.01.24.
50. Ibid.

Slavery and Muslim Jurisprudence in Morocco

AHMAD ALAWAD SIKAINGA

The aim of this article is to examine the link between the Muslim legal system and slavery in Morocco and to shed light on the conditions of Moroccan slaves as reflected in the records of the Muslim courts. Its primary interest is in the vein of social rather than legal history. Beyond the intricacies of Muslim jurisprudence as it pertains to slavery, the article focuses on the way in which Islamic law was used by the slaveholders to justify and maintain their control over the slaves, how the slaves themselves used the tenets of Islam to resist domination and assert their equality, and the response of both groups to colonial anti-slavery policies in the twentieth century.[1] The article will also address the question of what abolition meant in the Moroccan context and to what extent it affected the status of slaves and their descendants.

This study is based on Muslim court records as well as the writings of the Moroccan *'ulama* (Muslim scholars and theologians) who wrote legal decrees and opinions known as *fatawi* (sing. *fatwa*) and *nawazil* (sing. *nazila*).[2] Muslim court records consisted of rulings in disputes over such matters as the purchase of slaves, marriage, inheritance, concubinage, manumission, and so forth.[3] The *fatawi* and *nawazil* were written by learned scholars and jurists in response to questions from judges, administrators, and commoners. Before analysing some of these writings and court cases, it is appropriate to provide a brief account of the nature of Moroccan slavery and the role of slaves in Moroccan society.

The Evolution of Slavery in Morocco

Slavery was an ancient institution in Morocco.[4] Located at the northern terminus of the trans-Saharan trade routes, for many centuries Morocco received a continuous influx of slaves from West Africa, the Sahara, and the Mediterranean regions. However, the majority of slaves in Morocco came from the Western Sudan through the trans-Saharan trade. A large number of captives were taken from the Western Sudan during the Sa'adiyyin invasion of the kingdom of Songhay at the end of the sixteenth century. The import of West African slaves into Morocco continued until the late nineteenth

58   SLAVERY AND COLONIAL RULE IN AFRICA

century when the French occupied the region. Slaves were brought to Tafilalt in southern Morocco via Tuwat, from which they were distributed to the rest of the country.[5] Although the French succeeded in curtailing the slave trade from West Africa, clandestine slave trafficking continued throughout the first two decades of the twentieth century. Slave markets existed in major Moroccan cities such as Fez, Rabat, and Marrakesh.[6] In Rabat, for instance, at the beginning of this century the slaves were sold and auctioned in hotels.[7] In Fez, in the late nineteenth century, the slave sale was conducted daily at a textile market called al-Barka.[8] The mechanics and the complex process of the slave sale will be examined later. What will be stressed here is the role and the status of slaves in Moroccan society.

As elsewhere in Africa and the Middle East, Moroccan slaves performed various tasks particularly in the domestic and the agrarian sectors. However, one of the most notable aspects of Moroccan slavery that drew a great deal of scholarly attention was the conscription of slaves into the army. In the late seventeenth century, Moulay Isma'il, the 'Alawite sultan, created an army of black slaves to avoid having to rely on tribal forces whose loyalty was suspect. The creation of a slave army was part of the sultan's effort to consolidate his power, to expand the kingdom, to suppress internal dissent, and to repulse the European and Ottoman threat.

Although the use of slave soldiers had several precedents in Islamic history, Moulay Isma'il's experiment generated a great deal of opposition from some of the leading Muslim scholars in Fez because it involved the forcible recruitment of the Haratin who were Muslims.[9] The Haratin are people of ambiguous social and racial status. Their origin is a subject of debate. According to some accounts the Haratin were manumitted slaves. Yet it is generally believed that they were perhaps the aboriginal inhabitants of North Africa and the Sahara region who were displaced by Berber and Arab immigrants.[10] The Haratin were dark-skinned, landless farmers and craftsmen. Although they were legally free, the Haratin resembled the slaves in that they were kinless and were regarded as socially inferior by the Arab and Berber among whom they lived. The Haratin did not form a single ethnic group; rather they were scattered among the Berber and Arab groups with whom they maintained dependent relationships.[11] Some *'ulama* from Fez opposed the recruitment of the Haratin into Moulay Isma'il's army because, in their view, they were Muslims who could not be legally enslaved. Although the sultan succeeded in coercing some of the *'ulama* to endorse his endeavour, the protest continued and led to the imprisonment and execution of a jurist who refused to bend to the Sultan's will.[12]

The army that Moulay Isma'il had created was called the *'Abid al-Bukhari*.[13] While earlier studies have suggested that the 'Abid al-Bukhari were captives and refugees from the Western Sudan, the recent studies of

SLAVERY AND MUSLIM JURISPRUDENCE IN MOROCCO

Allen Meyers have stressed that nearly all of these slave and Haratin soldiers were Moroccan-born.[14] Many of the slave soldiers were either confiscated from their masters or given as tribute to Moulay Isma'il.[15] By 1727, the slave army numbered 50,000 soldiers who were stationed in garrisons in various parts of the country and became responsible for maintaining internal security as well as the conquest and administration of tribal territories.[16] The 'Abid al-Bukhari helped Moulay Isma'il resolve his immediate political crises and strengthen his power.

In addition to military functions, the slaves and the Haratin played an important role in agricultural production, particularly in the oases of southern Morocco. These tasks included tending crops, drawing water, pasturing cattle, and so forth. In Tuwat, for instance, in the late nineteenth century, the Haratin formed approximately 40 per cent of the population and the slaves about 9 per cent.[17] As mentioned earlier, the Haratin were landless and hence they became a source of cheap labour for the Berber and Arab landlords with whom they forged patron-client relations hips. The Haratin made share-cropping arrangements with their patrons, according to which they received a small share of the crop. For instance, the Haratin would receive only one-tenth of the date harvest.[18] The social and economic distinction between the Haratin and the rest of the population was recognized in the customary law in southern Morocco.[19]

In administrative and urban centres such as Fez, Marrakesh, Rabat, and Meknes the great majority of the slaves were used for domestic purposes in the households of government officials, military commanders, merchants, religious leaders, and commoners. According to Mohammed Ennaji, slave ownership in Morocco was associated with prestige and high status.[20] Although slaves from both sexes were involved in domestic work, the overwhelming majority were females. In addition to being concubines, female slaves were responsible for household chores and child rearing and provided entertainment for the urban elite.[21]

The conditions and status of slaves in Moroccan society have been a subject of debate. While some scholars have held the view that Moroccan slaves were treated well and were integrated into the owners' households,[22] Mohammed Ennaji has argued that the condition of slaves in Morocco was a complex web of paternalism and oppression.[23] He drew attention to the hard work and miserable conditions of farm slaves.[24] The slaves were considered the absolute property of the master who could sell them at will. Upon the master's death, the slaves were listed with livestock and other forms of property and were distributed among the heirs of the deceased owner.[25] As elsewhere in the Middle East, Moroccan slaves were given peculiar names to distinguish them from the free-born persons.[26] It was reported that the newly-purchased slave would be asked about his name. If

60 SLAVERY AND COLONIAL RULE IN AFRICA

his name resembled the names of free-born persons, it would be changed to one of the typical slave names.[27] Slaves were severely punished for disobedience. Such punishments often involved whipping, expulsion from the owner's home, or sale.[28] The slaves responded to their harsh treatment by fleeing, seeking sanctuary in the shrines of holy men,[29] or demanding that their owners sell them.[30] Some slave owners manumitted their slaves as an act of religious piety. Female slaves who bore children to their owner were automatically freed. As elsewhere in Africa and the Middle East, liberated slaves had no alternatives for survival and often continued to be attached to and work for their former owners.[31]

West African slaves brought many cultural influences to Moroccan society. They retained a great deal of their cultural heritage and introduced new traits that continue to have significant impact on Moroccan popular culture and religious practices. Although this subject is beyond the scope of this study, suffice it to say that West African cultural traits in Morocco are evident in such customs as ecstatic dancing, spirit possession, and blood sacrifices.[32]

Slavery in the Muslim Legal System

The status of slaves in Muslim societies has generated a great deal of scholarly debate during the past three decades.[33] A major part of this debate revolves around the questions of whether or not slavery in Muslim societies was benevolent and on the existence or the absence of colour prejudices among Muslims.[34] This approach was criticized by Frederick Cooper who pointed out that the main problem of both apologists and critics of Muslim slavery was their conception of religion as a determinant of social structure and their attempt to find a universal essence of Islamic slavery.[35] The status of slaves in Muslim societies cannot be determined merely by looking at the Quranic injunctions and the legal texts. Rather, it is important to stress the way which Muslim law was used by different groups in the society and the dialectical relationship between social relations and their conception in religious terms.[36] Although the message of Islam is essentially singular, 'it assumes different forms and manifestations for different groups and societies and at different times and circumstances.'[37] There were differences between theologians who were more concerned with the essence of the Islamic faith, jurists who were concerned with the formulation and the application of the *Shari'a*, and philosophers who sought to reconcile reason with religious revelation.[38]

The *Shari'a* laws were formulated by jurists in the early centuries of Islam. Eventually four schools of jurisprudence, or *madhahib* (sing. *madhab*) emerged: Maliki, Hanafi, Shafi'i, and Hanbali. Jurists eventually

SLAVERY AND MUSLIM JURISPRUDENCE IN MOROCCO

declared that the work of interpreting the Quran and the *sunna* as positive law was complete. The *'ulama* were supposed to be the guardians of the sacred law who ensured its proper application by the rulers. However, in reality, many *'ulama* in Muslim societies became closely linked with the ruling elite and the dominant groups. Athough the role of the *'ulama* may be compared with that of Gramsci's intellectuals, who play a major role in shaping the cultural norms that ratify the structure of the society, yet the *'ulama* were not a monolithic group. As will be shown later, some *'ulama* broke rank with the rulers and defied them when they felt that the latter did not follow the *Shari'a*.

The Quranic concepts regarding slavery consisted mainly of broad and general propositions of an ethical nature rather than specific legal formulations. In theory, Islam obliges the slave owner to bring his slaves into the Muslim community and to teach them Islam. The owner is the guardian, responsible for the slave's action. The Quran admonishes the owner to treat the slaves well, and to look after their needs. If the owner fails to meet these obligations, the *qadi* (Muslim judge) can compel him/her to fulfil them or else either sell or emancipate the slave. The owner is forbidden to overwork the slave, and if he does so to the point of cruelty, he is liable to incur a penalty that is, however, discretionary and not prescribed by law.[39]

As in other matters, the *Shari'a* rules on slavery varied from one school to another. In general, the *Shari'a* ruled that the only legal criterion for enslaving a person was that he or she was an unbeliever, with whose people the Muslims had a no non-aggression pact and whose territory had been forcibly overrun in accordance with the rules governing *jihad* (Muslim holy war).[40] In theory, a free-born Muslim could not be enslaved. Slaves had both legal rights and limitations. Technically, the master owned both the slave and what the slave possessed; but if a contract of manumission had been entered into, the slave was allowed to earn money to purchase his freedom and similarly to pay a marriage dowry. The slave could marry, but only with the consent of his master. While the Hanafi and the Shafi' schools of jurisprudence allowed a male slave to marry two wives, the Maliki permitted him four, thereby making no distinction between slave or free-born male. Theoretically, a male slave could marry a freeborn woman, but this was discouraged in practice, a reflection of racial consciousness and social status among Arabs. If a male slave married a slave woman, the children belonged to the woman's owner. A slave woman could marry a free man, including her master, but she should be freed before the marriage was contracted.[41] A slave's testimony was not admitted in courts. A penalty for an offence by slave was half that of a free person. The owner was responsible for paying fines incurred by a slave. In civil matters, a slave had

62 SLAVERY AND COLONIAL RULE IN AFRICA

no rights or legal powers and could not enter into a contract, or hold or inherit property.

Islam encouraged *'itq* (manumission) and provided several procedures to facilitate it. The first method is *mukataba*, or a contract of manumission between the owner and the slave, whereby the latter would pay the former a fixed sum of money. The second is *tadbir*, by which the owner would declare that a slave would be freed after the owner's death. A third method is a verbal proclamation by the owner that a slave is free. Fourth, a slave could be freed as a *kafara* or penance for accidental homicide, breaking an oath, or other offences.[41]

Perhaps no area was treated in more detail than the status of female slaves who were regarded as concubines by the *Shari'a*. A slave concubine who bore children to her master would be elevated to the status of *um walad* (mother of his child), and their offspring were considered co-equal to the masters' free-born children. Such a woman could not be sold and was to be freed upon her master's death. If a man claimed a female slave as a concubine before a *Shari'a* court, she could establish a claim at his death, which would entitle her to a share in his estate. If a concubine was manumitted, she could not have a legal status as a wife; she would be living with her master as his mistress and her children would be regarded as bastards. If a slave woman decided to desert her master, she would lose the custody of her children. If the slave woman had children from a man who did not belong to her owner's family, the children would be considered as the property of the owner. The same applied if she had children from another slave.[43] But there is no reason to assume that such strictures were any more effective among Muslims than others. The status of slaves in many parts of Africa and the Middle East and their day-to-day existence was determined by social reality and by other considerations such as their economic roles and the cultural norms of the society.

Slavery and Muslim Jurisprudence in Morocco

For several centuries, the judicial system in Morocco was based on the *Shari'a* and followed the Maliki school of jurisprudence. However, customary law prevailed among many Berber groups and other segments of the population. Successive Moroccan rulers assumed the Muslim title, the *khalifa*, and tried to legitimize their authority by seeking the support of the *'ulama*, particularly those of the Qarawiyyin Mosque in Fez. In addition to advising the rulers, Moroccan *'ulama* have written extensively on various aspects of the *Shari'a* and tried to ensure its application in all aspects of life. They also advised judges and administrators on various legal problems. Their writings were contained in voluminous *fatawi* and *nawazil*.[44] Slavery

SLAVERY AND MUSLIM JURISPRUDENCE IN MOROCCO

was one of the subjects that has figured prominently in the *fatawi* and *nawazil* books.

One of the earliest recorded theological and legal debates on the subject of slavery occurred in the late seventeenth century, when a group of people from Tuwat in southern Morocco sought the advice of Ahmad Baba, the Western Sudanic scholar in Fez, on the question of which West African groups could be enslaved. In response, Ahmad Baba wrote a lengthy treatise in which he delineated the regions and the ethnic groups whose people were the legitimate target of enslavement. According to this treatise, captives from Bornu, Kano, Katsina or Songhay should not be taken as slaves since the inhabitants of these regions were long-standing Muslims. However, Ahmad Baba identified several non-Muslim groups in the same region, such as the Mossi, Gurma, Busa, Borgu, etc. These groups were in fact a major source of slaves for the kingdom of Songhay.[45]

It is clear that the people of Tuwat were trying to legitmize the acquistion of slaves and to practice slavery within an Islamic ideological and legal framework. In essence, the *fatwa* of Ahmad Baba's treatise had laid the ground rules for enslavement and made black and non-Muslim West African communities a legitimate target for enslavement. Indeed, the association of blackness and unbelief with servitude was deeply rooted among North Africans.[46]

Perhaps the most notable scholarly debate on the subject of slavery in Morocco, took place in the late seventeenth century in response to the efforts of Moulay Isma'il to recruit the Haratin into his slave army.[47] As mentioned previously, the 'Alawite sultan tried to persuade the *'ulama* of Fez, particularly those of the Qarawiyyin mosque, to endorse his policies. He asked them to scrutinize and approve the conscription of the slaves whose names were placed in a register. The slaves whose owners were known were purchased at a fixed price, while those whose owners were unknown were recruited 'free of charge'.[48] One of the leading *'ulama* who supported the sultan was Muhammad 'Alilish who became the chief recruiting officer. However, the majority of the *'ulama* of Fez opposed the conscription and declared it illegal, particularly when it became indiscriminate and involved free-born persons such as the Haratin. Their disapproval was articulated in letter by Sidi Muhammad ibn 'Abdel Qadir al-Fasi who argued that' the basic condition of man is freedom', and that if the slave-status of a person cannot be proven, then such a person is 'the master of his soul.'[49] Moulay Isma'il was enraged and tried to discredit the *'ulama* of Fez. He humiliated Burdula, the Qadi of Fez, dismissing and reinstating him several times. But it was Sidi Al-Hajj 'Abdel Salam Jasus who offered the most daring challenge to Moulay Isma'il: it was reported that Jasus had held a debate with 'Alilish in which he criticized the *fatawi*

64 SLAVERY AND COLONIAL RULE IN AFRICA

that sanctioned the forced conscription of the Haratin, arguing that they were free Muslims. Jasus was immediately seized and imprisoned in Meknes for three months in 1708. He was then released on condition that he pay a fine and stop agitating against the recruitment of the Haratin as slaves. He was not prepared to do either. Upon the orders of the governor of Fez, Jasus was reimprisoned and tortured, his books and property were confiscated, and he was finally executed on 4 July 1709.[50] Jasus's controversy illuminates several important points: First, it underscores the fragility of the power of the religious establishment and the fact that the slave army was much more important for the sultan than the allegiance of the *'ulama*. At the same time, from the perspective of the slaves, the episode can be regarded as a struggle among the ruling establishment. The *'ulama's* opposition was not against the idea of a slave army, rather it was against the manner in which it was conducted; they tried to ensure that it adhered to the *Shari'a* rules.

Conflicting Legal Systems

The French occupation of Algiers in 1830 increased the pace of European intervention in Morocco. In addition to France, Britain and Spain had strong economic and strategic interests in the country. The weakness of the Moroccan government in the late nineteenth century provided an opportunity for these European powers to expand their holdings on Moroccan soil. For instance, in the 1950s Spain occupied Tetuan and Mellila. However, it was France that had the strongest interest in Morocco. After a series of military interventions in the late nineteenth and early twentieth centuries, France finally proclaimed Morocco as a French protectorate in 1912.

The disintegration of the Moroccan government and the beginning of European intervention in the nineteenth century led to the erosion of the Muslim judicial system, as new European courts were established in different parts of Morocco. These included a new government independent judicial apparatus that was administered by tribal leaders and provincial governors who began to strengthen their authority at the expense of *Shari'a* judges.[51] Moreover, with the establishment of the European protectorates in different parts of the country, European law was applied not only to European nationals but also to Moroccan citizens who were living in the protectorates.

Following the establishment of the French protectorate in 1912, the judicial system was reorganized and several court systems were established. In addition to French, British, and American Courts, there were *al-Mahakim al-Makhazania* (Government Courts), *al-Mahakim al-Shar'iyya* (Shari'a

SLAVERY AND MUSLIM JURISPRUDENCE IN MOROCCO 65

Courts), *al-Mahakim al-'Urfiyya* (Courts of Customary Law), *al-Mahakim al-Isra'iliyya* (Jewish Courts), and *al-Mahakim al-Ist'nafiyya* (Courts of Appeal).[52]

The *Shari'a* courts dealt with personal matters such as marriage, divorce, inheritance, slavery, and so forth. As mentioned earlier, these courts followed the Maliki *fiqh* (jurisprudence) which was laid down and explained by the *'ulama* in different works. These books were divided into three categories. The first consisted of *kutub al-Isoul* (original works) such as *Mukhtasar al-Shaykh Khalil* and *Tuhfat ibn 'Asim*. The second category consisted of the *fatawi* and *nawazil* such as *Mi'yar al-Wanshrisi* and *al-Mi'yar al-Jadid* of al-Wazzani. The third category included interpretative works such as *al-'Amal al-Fasi* by 'Abdel Rahman 'Abdel Qadir. These texts became the legal references upon which Moroccan *'ulama* and judges relied.

Like other European colonial powers in Africa, the French adopted a gradual approach in the abolition of slavery. A series of laws was enacted over a period of time. The French law of February 1848 prohibited slavery in all territories under French control. In June 1880 the supreme court in Algeria issued a decree to the effect that the relationship between the slave and his owner would not be recognized by law. A similar law was introduced in Tunisia after the establishment of French rule there.[53] However, in Morocco anti-slavery legislation was introduced in piecemeal fashion. Moroccan judges assumed that since Morocco was a French protectorate and slavery was prohibited in French possessions, then slavery was illegal in their country.

In July 1916 the Supreme Council of Justice in Rabat issued a decree to the effect that the son of a concubine would no longer be regarded as the son of her owner unless the owner acknowledged his relationship with the slave woman and recognized the paternity of the child.[54] However, it was only in 1925 that a law explicitly prohibiting slavery in Morocco was introduced and all clauses recognizing servitude were removed from the personal matters code.[55]

As elsewhere in Africa, the official abolition neither led to the sudden death of slavery nor brought a substantial change in the relationship between freed slaves and their former owners. In Muslim countries, the problem was compounded by the fact that servitude was sanctioned by the *Shari'a*. This provided them with both an ideological and a legal framework to maintain their control over their slaves and resist colonial anti-slavery laws. It is not surprising, therefore, that disputes involving slaves and slaveowners continued to arise and the *Shari'a* courts became a major arena of the struggle between the two groups. The following examples involve disputes emanating from the selling of slaves and the 'defects' of the slaves,

66   SLAVERY AND COLONIAL RULE IN AFRICA

inheritance, and child custody. Although these are limited examples that do not give a complete picture, they do provide important insights into the conditions of the Moroccan slaves and the problems they endured during slavery and after emancipation.

Purchase of Slaves

As mentioned previously, the *Shari'a* ruled that the only legal criterion for enslaving a person was that he or she was an unbeliever, with whose people the Muslim community had no non-aggression pact and whose territory had been forcibly overrun in accordance with the rules governing the *jihad*. However, once the slave was acquired and became a property, then s/he could be sold. The *Shari'a* contains elaborate rules governing the buying and selling of the slaves. Slaves were classified with livestock; their sale was regulated by the same rules applying to camels, sheep, and goats.[56]

The *Shari'a* placed great emphasis on the physical and mental conditions of the slaves and stressed that the slave should be free of any 'defects' at the time of his sale. According to *Tuhaft Ibn 'Asim*, a major reference for Moroccan judges, the slave defects were defined and divided into three groups: The first are the permanent defects such as stroke, blindness, loss of body parts, leprosy, vitiligo, and any permanent facial or body defects. The second group includes mental illnesses, urinating in bed, and any other recurring defects. The third group include behavioural defects such as stealing, lying, adultery, etc.[57] Buyers were usually given several days to discover any defects in a newly purchased slave, after which the sale was considered complete. The slave defects and the sale procedure were discussed in great details in many legal texts. The seller was required to disclose these defects at the time of sale and to describe them in the contract. If the buyer discovered a defect that was not disclosed, he had legal a claim on the seller. The emphasis on the health of the slaves underscores the importance of their productive and reproductive functions. The slaves were usually assigned to heavier household duties, including cooking, washing, cleaning, lifting and so forth.

In nineteenth-century Morocco, slaves were bought either privately through dealers or from the slave markets. As mentioned earlier, these markets existed in all major cities such as Fez, Marrakesh, Rabat, and Meknes. In Fez, slaves were sold in open markets and the sale was done through written contracts. These contracts included full description of the slaves and any known defects. In Rabat, slave markets were held in hotels. Newly purchased slaves were kept in the buyer's house for a three-day testing period, after which they would be returned if the buyer discovered any defects. If an owner decided to sell one of his female slaves, he would

SLAVERY AND MUSLIM JURISPRUDENCE IN MOROCCO

take her to the house of an old woman called the *amina*, who would look after the slave woman until she was sold. After the slave was sold, the seller would reimburse the *amina* for all her expenses.[58]

The prices of slaves varied depending on their gender and physical conditions. In general, female slaves commanded higher prices. For instance, in Fez markets in the late nineteenth century, a 16-year-old female slave was sold for 500 francs.[59] However, after the prohibition of the slave trade in the late nineteenth century, slaves were sold privately and their prices increased, particularly female slaves.[60]

The selling and buying of the slaves was a source of numerous legal disputes. These disputes illuminate important matters such as the health condition and the exploitation of individual slaves. There were many disputes involving pregnant female slaves, who were often sexually exploited by their owners. For instance, in 1898, Ahmad ibn al-Mamoun al-Balgithi al-Fasi, who was a retired judge, wrote a *nazila* in response to a dispute involving a pregnant female slave from Rabat: the buyer decided to return her after a brief period, arguing that he was defrauded by the seller because the slave woman had a miscarriage. A group of *'ulama* from Fez replied that he had a legal claim against the seller. But when al-Fasi was asked by a judge, he replied that the buyer had no claim since the seller was not aware of the pregnancy. He further argued that the miscarriage of the foetus ended the pregnancy and the defects no longer existed. However, he pointed out that the buyer would have had a legal claim against the seller if the miscarriage had caused any permanent physical damage to the slave woman.[61] This case illustrates the degradation of female slaves as a result of the sexual exploitation of their owners and other members of the owners' households. The slave woman in this case was considered a 'used property' by the buyer who was not willing to take her. In another case dated in 1914, a prominent merchant in Azrou brought a legal claim to Muhammad ibn Rashid al-'Iraqi, a judge at Azrou, against a man who after marrying one of the merchant's manumitted female slaves, divorced her and decided to sell her. However, the judge ruled in favour of the merchant and upheld the free status of the woman.[62]

These cases raise important questions that have much wider implications. First, they demonstrate the fact that according to the *Shari'a*, the slaves were just a commodity that could be bought, sold, used and exchanged. Second, the 'legal defects' of the slaves cannot be defined without reference to time and place. The Muslim world encompasses a vast geographical area, with different climatic conditions and diseases. Apparently, early Muslim jurists did not take these variations into account. Third, perhaps most of the so-called slave defects were associated with the harsh conditions of enslavement; the long journey involved in the

68 SLAVERY AND COLONIAL RULE IN AFRICA

transportation of the slaves and their encounter with different climatic conditions as well as the physical and sexual abuse of the slaves by their owners.

Concubinage and Child Bearing

As mentioned previously, the slave concubine who bore a child to her master would be elevated to the status of *um-walad* and would be freed upon her master's death; and her children would be regarded as co-equals to their free-born brothers. In a case dated November 1967, a freed slave woman took her stepson to court, alleging that he was the father of her two children and demanded that she should be paid child support.[63] Her stepson denied the allegation and brought witnesses who testified that the slave woman was the concubine of his father and that after his father's death she came under the custody of his mother. The court accepted the woman's claim and ordered him to pay child support. The stepson then appealed against the ruling and the case was brought to the Supreme Council of Justice which overturned the verdict. In its deliberation, the Supreme Council of Justice provided three reasons for its decision. First, the junior court ruling was contrary to the law of the land which prohibited slavery. The council referred to the 1925 law which had removed all clauses recognizing slavery from the penal code. The council also cited the Moroccan constitution which stipulated that all Moroccan citizens are equal before the law enjoying the same rights and liberty. Second, the council criticized the verdict on technical grounds arguing that all the parties involved in the case were not present during the court proceedings. The council was referring to the concubine's sons who neither made a claim nor appeared in court. Finally, the council stated that the junior court should not have awarded the woman an unspecified amount of child support. The council then referred the case to the provincial court in Casablanca. It is not clear how the case was finally decided by the provincial court.[64]

Inheritance

According to the *Shari'a*, the estate of a deceased freed male slave who had no children would be divided between his widow and his former owner, with the former receiving one-fourth and the latter receiving three-fourths. If the former owner was dead, his share would be inherited by his nearest relatives. The estate of a deceased freed female slave with no offspring would be divided equally between her husband and her former master. If the former master was deceased and had no surviving heirs, his share of the estate would be claimed by the *bayt al-Mal* (Muslim public treasury).[65]

SLAVERY AND MUSLIM JURISPRUDENCE IN MOROCCO

In 1931 in Fez, a case was brought by the bayt al-Mal to Judge Muhammad ibn Ahmad Al-'Alawi of Fez, against two prominent religious figures, Ahmad ibn Hamad ibn 'Ali and his cousin Muhammad ibn Moulay Al-'Arabi. The latter was the nephew of a prominent Fasi woman named Umm Kalthoum Ghatsa who was owner of a slave woman called 'Anbar. As an act of piety in her old age, Ghatsa wrote a will in which she declared that after her death 'Anbar should be freed and should be married to a free-born man. After Ghatsa's death, 'Anbar was married to a free-born man but he died without children. 'Anbar herself died at Fez in May 1931, leaving behind a significant estate. The inheritance of her estate became the subject of dispute between the public treasury and the aforementioned Fasi men. The representative of the *bayt al-Mal* argued that since the deceased woman was manumitted and had no children, her estate belonged to the *bayt al-Mal*. The two men, on the other hand, claimed that since 'Anbar was owned by their aunt and had no heirs, they were legally entitled to her estate. They invoked a well-established Muslim tradition known as *wala'*, which was a perpetual bond between the manumitted slave and his former owner. The judge ruled in favour of the two men, and even though the *bayt al-Mal* appealed the rulings, the Supreme Council of Justice upheld the judge's ruling.[66] This particular ruling and the concept of *wala'* deserves further attention. According to Muslim jurists, manumission does not nullify the eternal bond between the slave owner and his *mawla* (freed slave). In pre-Islamic Arabia, the word *mawla* (plural *mawali*) referred to a category of people who lacked kinship ties within Arabian society. They included vagabonds, slaves, freed slaves, and non-Arabians.[67] Mawla is also a concept based on the premise that once the slave was freed, he needed an affiliation with society. Through the *wala'*, the freed slaves were formally established as full members of society. Although this practice was common in pre-Islamic Arabia, it was also strongly encouraged by Islam and was sanctioned by Muslim jurists.[68] The *wala'* was one of the ways in which Arabian Muslim society tried to avoid the social consequences of manumission. Without *wala'*, it was assumed the freed slave would be let loose and would pose a danger to the society. If the *mawla* died without heirs, his estate would be inherited by his former owner. In short, the *wala'* meant that, despite manumission, the slave owner would still maintain control over his ex-slaves who would continue to be dependent upon him.

Conclusion

From the preceding narrative it is evident that there was a strong link between slavery and Muslim jurisprudence in Morocco. Moroccan *'ulama* and jurists made conscious efforts to ensure that the practice of slavery

70   SLAVERY AND COLONIAL RULE IN AFRICA

conformed to the *Shari'a* rules and the Islamic concepts. As a group that was closely linked with the ruling elites and the slave-holders, the *'ulama* and the jurists tried to explain and legitimize the existing social order and to provide an ideological framework for the slave-holders to maintain their domination of the slaves. But, as we have seen, the *'ulama*'s conception of the social order often conflicted with that of the ruling establishment and the slave-holders. The latter needed slaves for building their political and economic power as well as prestige, and were prepared to use 'illegal' methods to obtain slaves. However, Islamic norms could be a double-edged sword that would also be used by the slave in their struggle against the owners. As the above cases show, the slaves themselves used the tenets of Islam to assert their moral equality and independence.

The establishment of French colonial rule created a complex and paradoxical situation. It eroded the power of the ruling elites, the slave-holders, and the *'ulama*. At the same time, it imposed a European model of abolition that did not necessarily conform with Muslim concepts of slavery and freedom. This situation posed a major challenge to the *'ulama* and the jurists. Despite the efforts of the slave-holders to use Islamic law to maintain their control over the slaves, the *'ulama* tried to provide interpretations that would conform to the new reality and to establish an ideological framework that would ratify the new social order.

ACKNOWLEDGEMENT

I am indebted to the J. William Fulbright Program and the Moroccan-American Commission for Educational and Cultural Exchange for awarding me a Fulbright fellowship in 1996–97 academic year, which enabled me to conduct research for this essay.

NOTES

1. On this perspective, see Frederick Cooper, 'Islam and Cultural Hegemony: The Ideology of Slaveowners on the East African Coast', in Paul E. Lovejoy (ed.), *The Ideology of Slavery in Africa* (Beverly Hills and London, 1981), pp.271–307.
2. The *fatawi* and *nawazil* are replies and opinions written by the *'ulama* in response to legal questions posed by judges, administrators, and sometimes common people.
3. For the utilization of court records for the study of slavery see, Terence Walz, 'Black Slavery in Egypt During the Nineteenth Century as Reflected in the Mahkama Archives of Cairo', in John Ralph Willis (ed.), *Slaves and Slavery in Muslim Africa, vol. II, The Servile Estate* (London, 1985), pp.137–60.
4. Although there are numerous references to slavery in Morocco, the most recent single book on the subject is Mohammed Ennaji's, *Soldats, Domestiques et Concubines. L'esclavage au Maroc au XIXe Siècle* (Casablanca, 1994).
5. 'Abdel 'Aziz al-Khimlishi, 'Tijarat al-Raqiq fil Maghrib fil Qarn al-Tasi'ashar', *Majalat Dar al-Niyaba*, 7, Summer of 1985, pp.37–44; Muhammad Zarruq, 'Qadiyat al-Riq fi Tarikh al-Maghrib', *Pirasat fi Tarikh al-Maghrib* (Casablanca, 1991), pp.7–23.
6. Roger Letourneau, *Fes qabl al-Himaya*, vol.1, translated by Mohamed Lakhdar and

SLAVERY AND MUSLIM JURISPRUDENCE IN MOROCCO

Mohamed Hajji (Beirut, 1986), p.296; Pierre Loti, *Morocco* (Philadelphia, n.d.), pp.182–3; Nura al-Tabba' and Bahiyya al-'Azraq, 'Jawanib min al-Hayat al-Iqtisadiyya bi madinat al-Rabat fil Qarn al-Tasi'ashar, 1850–1912', MR Thesis, Mohammed V University, 1985, pp.94.

7. Ibid., p.94. See also, Louis Brunot, *Textes Arabes de Rabat* (Paris, 1931), p.193.
8. Letourneau, pp.296–7.
9. On this subject see, Allen Meyers, 'Slave Soldiers and State Politics in Early Alawi Morocco, 1668–1727', *International Journal of African Historical Studies*, 16, 1 (1983), pp.39–48 and Aziz Abdalla Batran, 'The Ulama of Fas, M. Ismail, and the Issue of the Haratin of Fas', in J.R. Willis (ed.), *Slaves and Slavery in Muslim Africa*, pp.1–15.
10. For a discussion of the term Haratin see, Ahmad b. Khalid al-Nasiri, *al-Istiqsa' li-Akhbar Duwal al-Maghrib al-Aqsa'*, vol.7 (Casablanca, 1966), p.58; Georges Colin, 'Hartani', *Encyclopedia of Islam* (new series), 3 vols. (Leiden, 1960–74), III, p.230; Ann McDougall, 'A Topsy-Turvy World: Slaves and Freed Slaves in the Mauritanian Adrar, 1910–1950', in Suzanne Miers and Richard Roberts (eds.), *The End of Slavery in Africa* (Madison, 1988), pp.362–88.
11. Mohamed A'fif, 'Musahama fi dirasat al-Hayat al-Ijtima'iyya wal Siyasiya li Mujtama' al-Wahat fil Janub al-Maghribi: Tuwat fil Qarn al-Tasi'ashar', Diploma Thesis, Mohamed V University, 1982, pp.160–75.
12. Batran, 'The *'ulama* of Fas', pp.1–15.
13. The army was called so because soldiers were asked to swear the oath of allegiance on Imam al-Bukhari's book which is regarded as the most authentic text which contains the Prophet Muhammad's sayings.
14. Allen R. Meyers, 'Class, Ethnicity, and Slavery: The Origins Of The Moroccan 'Abid', *The International Journal of African Historical Studies*, X, 3 (1977), pp.427–42.
15. Allan R. Meyers, 'Slave Soldiers And State Politics In Early 'Alwi Morocco, 1668–1727', *International Journal of African Historical Studies*, 16, 1 (1983), p.43.
16. Ibid..
17. 'Afif, p.160
18. Ibid., p.175.
19. Ibid.
20. Ennaji, p.198.
21. See Mustafa al-Shabbi, *al-Nukhba al-Makhzaniyya fi Maghrib al-Qarn al-Tasi'ashar* (Rabat, 1995), p.139; Letourneau, p.298; al-Tabba' and al-Azraq, pp.95–6.
22. Letorneau, p.298, Zarruq, p.7.
23. Ennaji, p.157.
24. Ibid., pp.102–4.
25. For instance, in their study of the economic life in Rabat, Nura al-Taba' and Bahiyya al-Azraq reported that al-Yamani b. Said al-Nasiri used his female slaves to pay off the debts of his wife. Moreover, the slaves were commonly included in the estate of deceased persons for distribution among their heirs, see al-Tabba' and al-Azraq, pp.95–6.
26. Examples of slave names were Sa'ida (happy) for females and Mubarak (blessed) and Rabih (winner) for male slaves, see al-Tabba and al-Azraq, p.96; Brunot, p.86.
27. Ibid.
28. Brunot, p.95
29. In Fez, for example, slaves took refuge in the shrines of famous holymen such as Sidi Abdel Qadir al-Fasi and Ahmad al-Tijani, founder of the Tijaniyya brotherhood, see Letourneau, p.298.
30. Ennaji, pp.77–90.
31. Ibid., p.96.
32. Meyers, 'Class, Ethnicity, and Slavery', p.439.
33. Examples of this literature include, Bernard Lewis, *Race and Slavery in the Middle East* (Oxford, 1990); John R. Willis, *Slaves and Slavery in Muslim Africa*; Allan Fisher and Humphrey J. Fisher, *Slavery and Muslim Society in Africa* (London, 1970).
34. Examples of studies that emphasized the benevolent nature of slavery in Muslim societies include Muhammad Abdel-Wahab Fayid, *al-Riq fil-Islam* (Cairo, n.d.); Muhammad Shwkat

72   SLAVERY AND COLONIAL RULE IN AFRICA

al-Tunisi, *Muhammad Muharir al-Abeid* (Cairo, 1975); and Hammouda Ghoraba, 'Islam and Slavery', *The Islamic Quarterly*, II, 3 (October 1955), pp.152–9.

35. Frederick Cooper, 'Islam and Cultural Hegemony', pp.271–307.
36. Ibid.
37. Abdel Salam Sidahmed, *Politics and Islam in Contemporary Sudan* (New York, 1996), p.3.
38. Ibid., p.2.
39. For a discussion of slavery in Islam see Walid Arafat, 'The attitude of Islam to Slavery', *Islamic Quarterly*, 10 (1966), pp.12–18; Hammouda Ghoraba, 'Islam and Slavery', *The Islamic Quarterly*, II, 3 (October 1955), pp.152–9; Muhammad Abdel Wahab Fayid, *al-Riq fil-Islam*, Cairo, n.d.; Bernard Lewis, *Race and Slavery in the Middle East* (New York, 1990); and John Hunwick, 'Black Africans in the Islamic World: An Under-studied Dimension of the Black Diaspora', *Tarikh*, 5, 4 (1978), pp.20–40.
40. Hunwick, 'Black Africans', p.21.
41. Walid Arafat, pp.12–18.
42. Fayid, *al-Riq fil-Islam*, pp.82–90.
43. Ibid.
44. The most distinguished group of Moroccan scholars were those based at al-Qarawyyin mosque in Fez.
45. J.O. Hunwick, 'Notes on Slavery in the Songhay Empire', in John Ralph Willis (ed.), *Slaves and Slavery in Muslim Africa, vol.II*, p.21.
46. John Hunwick, 'Islamic Law and Polemics Over Race and Slavery in North and West Africa (16th–19th Century)', Paper presented to the SSHRC/UNESCO Summer Institute, York University, Canada, 14 July–1 August 1997, pp.1–10.
47. Batran, pp.2–4.
48. Ibid.
49. Ibid.
50. Ibid.
51. Muhammad Khayr Faris, *Tanzim al-Himayya al-Firinsiyya fil Maghrib, 1912–1939* (1972), pp.251–3.
52. *Al-Majala al-Maghribiyya lil Qawanin wal-Madhahib wal-Ahkam al-Ahliyya*, no.1 (1935), pp.2–3.
53. Ibid.
54. Ibid.
55. *Majalat Dar al-Niyyaba* (1983), p.396.
56. Abi al-Hasan ibn 'Abdel Salam al-Tusuli, *al-Bahja fi Sharh al-Tuhfa*, vol.2 (Beirut, 1991), p.67.
57. Ibid., pp.68–9.
58. Brunot, p.86.
59. Loti, p.183.
60. Al-Tabba' and Al-Azraq, p.95.
61. *Nwazil wa fatawi wa Ahkam Ahmad ibn al-Ma'moun al-Balgithi al-Fasi, vol.1*, 1347, Ref. No. 370 Sabihiyya Library, Salé, p.199.
62. *al-Majala al-Maghribiyya lil Qawanin wal Madhahib wal-Ahkam al-Ahliyya*, No.6–7 (1937–38), p.21.
63. *Majalat Dar al-Niyaba*, 1983, pp.396–8.
64. Ibid.
65. Walz, pp.152–3.
66. *al-Majala al-Maghribyyiya lil Qawanin wal Madhabih wal-Ahkam al-Ahliyya*, No.6–7 (1937–8), pp.22–4.
67. Daniel Pipes, 'Mawlas: Freed Slaves and Coverts in Early Islam', *Slavery and Abolition*, 1, 2 (September 1980), p.134.
68. Ibid., p.136.

Slavery and French Rule in the Sahara

MARTIN A. KLEIN

French law to date has had no effect at all in the real desert for two reasons. The French do not know what is going on, and the slaves do not know that they can get their freedom – though sometimes a slave does escape and claim his freedom in Timbuktu. But there is another reason why slaves do not escape. If their master is a marabout, they believe he can reach them with his gris-gris ... Then again, a slave may be too far in the desert for him to be able to escape.

Former slave, Timbuktu, in 1959[1]

Official proclamation of the abolition of slavery in 1980 gives Mauritania a kind of notoriety by making it seem one of the last, if not the last country in the world where slavery was officially tolerated. In fact, it has a record for abolition, having in 80 years, known three de facto abolitions, one with the colonisation of Mauritania by the French from 1903, one which followed from ratification by Mauritania of the Universal Declaration of Human Rights, and finally that of July 1980.

Abdel Wedoud Ould Cheikh[2]

In January 1894 French troops under Étienne Bonnier sailed down the Niger and landed at Timbuktu. Lacking defences, the city submitted immediately. Bonnier left a garrison in the city and then set off along the river to meet forces moving overland under Commandant (=Major?) J.J.C. Joffre. Camped near Goundam, Bonnier's force was massacred by the Tuareg in a night attack. Thus began the effort of France's African army to bring the Sahara under control. The lesson of their humiliating defeat was one the French learned slowly, for three years later a squadron of Spahis was massacred.[3] It was not the last French defeat in the desert. The conquest the Sahara was one of the more irrational episodes in the history of colonialism. An area with no known resources, the Sahara could be conquered only by a commitment of resources no metropolitan government was willing to give for a vast expanse of desiccated land inhabited mostly by nomads. Its attraction was both a romantic fascination with the proud lords of the desert

74 SLAVERY AND COLONIAL RULE IN AFRICA

and a desire to show other peoples of the region they had the power to control the desert raiders. The French effort to establish a loose suzerainty in the desert was a slow struggle, which often victimized the servile villages that provided grain and labour for the nomads. To conquer and hold the Sahara, the French had to both defeat and compromise with the men who ruled it.

The conquest took place just as French policy towards slavery was changing and massive numbers of slaves were heading home in the agricultural areas just south of the desert. This paper looks at why policies carried out in the savanna were not introduced to the Sahara and how slavery was altered under French rule.[4] It is concerned with two areas, the Mauritanian desert ruled by Arabic-speaking nomads called Beydan and the Tuareg areas of what is now Mali and Niger. The Sahara was administered by the French military into the 1930s, and in some areas until the end of colonial rule.[5] The argument is that French policy was determined by their dependance on allies and the difficulties they had operating in the desert. They had limited forces, long supply lines, and as to slavery, had to accept Tuareg and Moor institutions France had long condemned. Hence they oscillated between freeing servile dependants to weaken their masters and recognizing the masters' control over them. The French presence brought real change, but to the end of colonial rule and in some areas up to the present, the Sahara was one of the rare areas where traditional forms of servitude persisted.

There were different patterns of nomadism in the desert. In the deeper desert, nomads depended primarily on camels, were based around oases, and ranged over long distances in the quest for pasture. Closer to the savanna, they also herded goats, sheep and cattle and were confined by their need for water to fixed transhumant cycles. Seasonal migrations generally took them south during the dry season to settlements of clients and servile peoples, and then back into the desert in the rainy season. Many Beydan tribes were linked to European commerce as producers of gum in the area north of the Senegal river and as slavers.[6] The Tuareg had no involvement with Europeans, but they controlled Timbuktu and other important desert-side entrepots and dominated the trans-Saharan trade. Both areas produced salt and minerals. The search for pasture for different animals meant that peoples dispersed frequently into camps as small as 20 to 30 persons. Commercial and political interests, however, brought them together in larger tribal federations capable of demanding tribute from weaker desert-dwellers, from merchants, and from desert-side cities. Servile peoples did much of the herding in nomadic camps and all of the agricultural work in oases and desert-side areas. Nomads depended on servile peoples for the grain which provided much of their sustenance and for cloth.

SLAVERY AND FRENCH RULE IN THE SAHARA 75

Desert society was very hierarchical. At the top were the politically dominant warrior tribes. Below them were client and marabout tribes. In Mauritania, the marabout tribes were originally Berber-speakers, who were brought under controlled and 'disarmed' by Arabic speaking invaders in the seventeenth century. The marabout tribes came to specialize in both learning and commerce and eventually became richer. Beneath warrior and marabout were artisans and the servile groups, who were a majority of the desert population. Among the Tuareg, for example, servile dependants were anywhere from 10 per cent to 20 per cent of the population deep in the desert and from 70 per cent to 90 per cent in desert-side areas.[7] In Mauritania, they were at least half.[8] As in the savanna, servile peoples can be divided into two groups. The true slaves are called *abd* in Arabic, *iklan* in Tamacheq. The second category is often defined as freed slaves. They are called *Haratin* among the Beydan and *Bella* among the Tuareg.[9] Haratin and Bella could own property, enter into contracts, negotiate their own marriages, and bequeath to their children. They were still tied to families that had owned them, sometimes shared their camps, owed them hospitality, paid tribute, and could be asked to do work. The relationship between noble and servile varied considerably from place to place, depending on their mutual dependence, the balance of forces and the ecological situation. Most Haratin and Bella lived in separate settlements. The transition from Abd to Hartani or Bella was not automatic. Europeans have often seen the differences as racial. Beydan means white, though miscegenation often blurred visible differences.[10] The most important distinction was probably between Haratin and Bella who lived in their own settlements and those who lived in the camps with Beydan and Tuareg.

The condition of slaves was probably harsher among the Moors and particularly among marabout tribes because they exploited slave labour more systematically. The demand for labour was high. Slaves were used to produce gum, to mine salt and copper, to grow dates, to transport these products to market, and to feed those otherwise employed. Herding also demanded a lot of labour because different animals had different needs. At the same time, life was harsh in the Sahara, and mortality rates were high. Slaves, Haratin and Bella were subject to raids, drought and epidemics. Cordell has suggested that high mortality rates led to constant import of slaves and is now trying to verify this hypothesis.[11] McDougall has supported this with evidence of a large flow of slave labour into the Sahara during the nineteenth century.[12] Though slaves were acquired by different methods everywhere, the Moors relied more on purchase and the Tuareg on raiding. Those settled in desert-side villages were probably better off than those in the camps. Left alone most of the year, they owed an annual tribute. Most paid about 80 to 100 kg. a year, which was about a third that paid in

76

slave villages among the Soninke and Fulbe.[13] Near Timbuktu, Bella paid 150 kg. of millet per male and 75 kg. per female.[14] Bella and Haratin also received loans of animals. Some moved from servicing the dry season needs of the Tuareg to becoming merchants.[15] During uncertain times, servile status may have provided Bella and Haratin of desert-side villages some security.

Conquest and Slave Policy

Once the Anglo-French agreement of 1898 completed the partition of West Africa, the French military turned to the Tuareg who dominated the area north of Timbuktu and east almost to Lake Chad. Some Tuareg were also settled in the Bend of the Niger as far south as northern Burkina Faso.[16] They were dangerous, mobile and highly effective opponents, who knew how to live and move in the desert. The French attempt to establish a loose suzerainty in the desert was a slow struggle to deny the tribes access to water, to pasture and to the savanna trade. There was no single moment when the Sahara was theirs. Submission for Tuareg tribes was often a tactical move to enable them to withdraw and lick their wounds until their herds had been replenished and were safe. With limited forces, the French needed allies, pasture for their mounts, and knowledge of where water could be found. It also involved a struggle for control of the Bella. In order to weaken the Tuareg, the French encouraged the autonomy of the desert-side dependants.[17] Many Bella took advantage of the French presence, but the French did not understand either Bella reluctance to accept new masters or the interest they had in remaining on good terms with the Tuareg. The French were thus not always happy with Bella behaviour. Thus, in 1902, the Commandant at Dori spoke of the 'turbulent and independent mood' of Bella who were reluctant to give up one set of obligations for another and did not want to work for the French as porters.[18] The French were more cautious about freeing slaves in the Tuareg camps. Inspection reports often mention the failure to apply laws against slave-trading. One report cites a comment by a Regional Commandant that the Ulliminden Tuareg sold men like cattle, but notes that they were not charged with slave-trading.[19] Another inspection report suggests that only five prosecutions for slave-trading at Djerma in a three-year period implied a lack of zeal.[20]

It was clear, however, from administration responses that the French lacked the personnel to survey the nomads and to travel with them in the desert. This also meant that they could not protect servile peoples or totally end the slave trade. Deprived of revenue from both predation and their desert-side slaves, the Tuareg were bound to resist, and that resistance simply intensified the French approach to the Bella. The Ulliminden north

SLAVERY AND FRENCH RULE IN THE SAHARA

of Gao submitted in 1903, but revolted in 1908. A year later, administrators were told:

> We must make the nobles understand that the Imrad and Bella are men like themselves ... we must recognize them immediately as owners of herds they guard ... we must make Imrad and Bella understand that they should raise their heads, that they should submit claims directly to us without fear of the nobles, and finally should expect to become owners of the herds confided to their care.[21]

The Bella were concerned about protection, land, possession of stock they received as loans and control of their children. The Tuareg claimed the right to take slave children to work in the camps, girls at domestic chores and boys as herders or to be given as servants to newlyweds. In Voltaic regions, Bella often submitted to the French before their Tuareg masters did, but when discretion dictated, they continued, renegotiated or resumed tribute relations.[22]

In Mauritania, there was a longer period of penetration. The commercial houses of St. Louis had close links with the gum-producing states of the Senegal River, Brakna and Trarza, and had no desire to place them under colonial rule. Xavier Coppolani, an administrator and student of Islam, was able to sell a programme of peaceful penetration, but only over the objections of authorities in Senegal. In 1903, Coppolani signed treaties with Brakna and Trarza and Mauritania became a civil territory, the last colony in French West Africa. Following the assassination of Coppolani while on a mission to the Adrar in 1905, the military completed the conquest by arms.[23] The French were more solicitous of the Beydan than they were of the Tuareg. The Moors were better armed and more tied into the colonial economy. Their raids also posed a threat to the peoples of the Senegal river. Coppolani and his heirs offered to insulate the Moors from laws applied south of the river if they stopped raiding Senegal. The Moors submitted on condition that their 'customs, values property and religion' be respected. 'It was well understood,' one administrator later wrote, 'that their slaves would [be permitted] to stay with them.'[24] In 1906, Lt. Col. Montané insisted that France had committed itself 'to change nothing in the social situation of the country and its customs, such as that of slaves, who are considered by the Moors as their property and their things'.[25] In the rest of French West Africa, slavery policy had already changed. In 1903, administrators had been told that they were no longer to return slaves to their masters, and in 1905, Governor-General Ernest Roume proclaimed a comprehensive anti-slavery law, which forbade any transactions in persons. This led to hundreds of thousands of slaves leaving their masters.[26]

Governor General William Ponty (1908–15), a prime mover in the attack

78 SLAVERY AND COLONIAL RULE IN AFRICA

on slavery, insisted that the French had 'no reason to make Mauritania an exception where slavery will be maintained contrary to our traditions and to the principle that the Government General has made prevail across the territory'.[27] Ponty could do nothing about it. Mauritania remained a military fief, where many soldier-administrators refused to enforce prohibitions of the slave trade. Only slaves showing evidence of serious mistreatment were freed.[28] For slaves living near the Senegal River, flight was possible, but further into the Sahara, the Moors were more secure in their control of their slaves. The French depended on Mauritanian allies to move in the desert. They were limited in their ability to coerce by their need for mounts, pastures and provisions.

Revolt and Reaction

In northern Mauritania, resistance to French conquest went on until 1934, especially in the north, where it was led first by a cleric named Ma el Ainin, and then by the camel-herding Reguibat. The French also faced two strong revolts from the Tuareg, who took advantage of the reduction in the French military and administrative force during World War I. In the first the Ulliminden, who once controlled Timbuktu and the area around it, rose under Fihroun, the *Amenokal* or traditional leader. In the second, Kaosen, a leader outside the traditional structure, reported to be the son of a slave woman, rallied the Air in Niger and put Agades under siege. Kaosen used arms left behind when the Italians withdrew from southern Libya and was supported by the Sanusi, a Muslim brotherhod that was fighting the Italians in the Libyan Sahara. Fihroun was speedily defeated, but Kaosen was killed only in 1919 and the last dissidents were defeated only in 1920.[29] The Tuareg suffered heavy losses. Their warriors and herds were decimated. Their leaders were hunted down.

The French were determined that they would not rise again. They broke up the confederations, creating smaller units and releasing tributaries from their allegiance to traditional chiefs.[30] They continued to encourage Bella to free themselves, but as so often in French slave policy, they eventually retreated from this, not because they decided it was wrong, but because it conflicted with two other priorities, preventing the depopulation of the desert and maintaining good relations with the traditional elite, on whom the administration depended. Thus, Bernus writes that 'Colonial policy oscillated between two extremes according to events and the personality of the administrator in place'.[31] The decease of a powerful chief could provoke a conflict over herds he had loaned to Bella. There were constant negotiations and constant shifting positions. Once the tribal confederations had been broken, the French tended to let the Tuareg regulate relations with

SLAVERY AND FRENCH RULE IN THE SAHARA

their servile dependants and, if necessary, confirm their arrangements. Thus, in 1942, an administrator worked out an agreement between Tuareg and Bella that affirmed Bella dependence. Another administrator suggested a few years later that 'it would be wise to support the Tuareg who apply customs we cannot impose because of our egalitarian principles. As they have Bella, we should be afraid of an evolution which is too rapid and would provoke social disorder.'[32]

The American anthropologist, Horace Miner, who spent seven months in Timbuktu in 1940, described the situation there. Timbuktu was a city of some 5,000 or 6,000 people, a majority of them slaves or freed slaves. Though small, it was very diverse ethnically with many Bella and slaves of Arabs living in compounds on the edge of the city. 'The French', Miner reported,

> have eliminated some aspects of slavery. They have forbidden the use of the French word 'slave' and substituted 'captive.' The capture of new slaves and the sale of slaves, except for concubines, has been stopped ... A mistreated slave may appeal to the French for freedom and simply run away, for now, the danger of being re-enslaved is gone. The determining fact in the eyes of the French as to whether a person is freeman or slave is who pays the head tax – the individual or the master.[33]

Large numbers of slaves had freed themselves, though others lived in huts within or adjacent to their masters' compounds. Slaves were much inhibited by economic insecurity. Timbuktu was a poor city in a hostile environment. A woman could earn a living as a prostitute and many did. Female slaves and women of slave descent also engaged in petty commerce, and when free-born Arabs hired a servant, they spoke of hiring a slave. Slaves and former slaves also farmed on river floodlands.[34] Miner comments on 'the ruthlessness with which families were broken up' under the pre-colonial system, but elsewhere, he describes a rather benign form of servitude.

We have a fuller picture of change in Mauritania. In spite of French reluctance to threaten slave owners, there were two important changes in slave-master relations.[35] First, over the half-century after the conquest, Abid were gradually converted to Haratin.[36] Children of Abid did not automatically become Haratin. The master could free a Hartani if he wished. The persistence of kidnapping along the desert's edge also meant that new Abid were always flowing into the system. The second change was the loosening of control over both Abid and Haratin. This took place in spite of French policy, which local administrators often ignored. They heard court cases, in which slave status was openly recognized and the slave's wishes were often ignored.[37] In 1929, a French court recognized that slaves could

80   SLAVERY AND COLONIAL RULE IN AFRICA

be inherited, though this clearly violated the 1905 anti-slavery law. Nevertheless, while the French reinforced the masters' control over slaves, they also created a labour market and a money economy. The demand for cooks, servants, guards, interpreters and shepherds was met primarily by Haratin. Haratin also supplied French military posts with milk and meat and, from that, extended their commercial activities down into Senegal, where the growth of the groundnut economy created a demand for camels to carry the harvest to market. Recruits to the army were usually slaves 'given' to the French, who became Haratin. Many Haratin came to own slaves and some sought a French education. Slave and Haratin women also married soldiers. Some administrators facilitated these relationships, though others tried to block the departure of the wives, seeing it as an exchange of one form of slavery for another. This, of course, reflected their assumption that marriage in Africa was a form of servitude.

Depression and drought stepped up these processes. The Mauritanian economy was tightly linked to Senegal. Mauritanians sold meat, provided transport services, and were petty traders in Senegal. With the collapse of the Senegal market in the 1930s, many merchants sold off slaves. At the same time, drought forced nomads to range more widely in search of pasture. Slaves left behind flocked into towns, where most joined the unemployed. The early 1930s saw a sharp increase in prostitution. Impoverishment of many masters left some former slaves in a new kind of poverty, but the increased possibility of earning money provided an opportunity for others. There was a shortage of skilled labour in the date plantations, hitherto slave work. As a result, those who worked the date groves were able to negotiate better terms and even acquire land. Others sought agricultural land along the Senegal River.[38] Many Abid and Haratin successfully competed in the job market, in both Mauritania and Senegal. Perhaps the best measure of change was that slave owners increasingly complained of women refusing to work, showing disrespect and exercising more control over their children.[39] Some slaves bought their freedom. Others disappeared, mostly to Senegal. Most remained in some form of dependance.

Renewed Resistance

Thus, slowly, many Bella and Haratin drifted away from their masters. Their numbers were much reduced by the end of colonial rule, but up to independence, Bella would sometimes return to renegotiate their relationship to the Tuareg. Colonial administrators were often unhappy with Bella, who frequently ignored their wishes and preferred to deal with the Tuareg.[40] When negotiation took place between Tuareg and Bella, it was

SLAVERY AND FRENCH RULE IN THE SAHARA 81

shaped by a series of factors: the policies of the administration, the personality of the administrator, the existence of options for the Bella, and the development of a money economy.[41] Even in the Sahel, Tuareg often maintained control over servile dependents. Loiseau tells of the heads of Tuareg families coming to the administrator in the 1950s to complain when a Bella fled to the freed slave quarter of an administrative centre. The lake region southwest of Timbuktu was an area of conflict. Here the annual flood of the Niger filled a series of lakes, and a rich harvest was possible as the flood plain gradually dried out. In this area Tuareg, Fulbe and Songhay intersected, each with its servile communities. The Kel Antessar had 4,650 Bella and the Tinguereguif had 1,685. These Bella were still slaves, Guemas wrote, but because they had to feed themselves, their 'masters generally left them half of their harvest to meet their needs'.[42] Dupeyron's 1957 study of budgets in a village on Lac Faguibine confirms this. Both the slaves of the Songhay and the Bella had become sharecroppers dependant on free families who controlled the land. They owed half their harvest and provided fish and sometimes cloth to their masters. The slave family Dupeyron studied worked hard, but barely managed to feed themselves, and that thanks largely to fishing. Their only luxuries were kola nuts, a good garment for festive occasions, and the sacrifice of a sheep for the Muslim Tabaski festival. The wife had a single piece of jewellery, a bracelet inherited from her mother.[43] Control of land here permitted Tuareg and Songhay masters to maintain a control over servile dependants almost as tight as in earlier periods. In fact, Bella gave a higher share of their crop than elsewhere, perhaps because the floodplain gave a good yield, perhaps because isolation made it difficult for them to break away from Tuareg control.

This does not mean that slaves accepted their status. They not only fled but also staged a series of revolts after World War II around Kayes and Nioro and in the bend of the Niger.[44] Despite earlier movements of liberation, about 50,000 Bella remained under control of Tuareg masters in the *cercles* of Niafunke, Goundam, Timbuktu and Gao.[45] Then, in 1946, at Menaka, among the Imajoren Tuareg, 'there was an explosion. The word liberation spread like wild fire. Bella arrived at the post to seek the "peace paper".' Many took stock. Others left fields unharvested. Overnight, the authority of chiefs and masters disappeared as Tuareg struggled to save their herds and keep a few Bella in their camps.[46] The commandant tried to mediate, divide stock and form Bella into two nomadic fractions of Black Tuareg.[47] That was not the desire of the Bella, who knew that they would never be seen as equals by the Tuareg. By 1949, many Bella near Gao were also heading south to seek better lands. The local commandant was told to try to control vagabondage and aimless wandering, but also belatedly 'to remedy the real causes of the departures by better regulating conflict

82   SLAVERY AND COLONIAL RULE IN AFRICA

between masters and slaves and improving the condition of the Bella population'.[48]

Further west, there were similar problems at Yelimané and Nioro. In the area between Kayes and Nioro, there were about 30,000 Haratin, who lived in agricultural villages, paid annual dues to and were taxed through their Beydan masters. In addition, many travelled with their masters when caravans moved into the Soudan during the dry season. Administrative reports show that desert-side Haratin were increasingly limiting the demands of their masters. In 1944, a border rectification transferred crucial districts to Mauritania in an effort to establish a more rational border between Sudanese agriculturalists and Mauritanian nomads. The problem was that Moors of the Hodh came to their Haratin villages in the Sudan every dry season. Whereas in Mauritania property rights of the masters were protected, in the Sudan, Haratin were exposed to 'propagandists of new ideas'. Yelimané, furthermore, was populated largely by former slaves of both Moors and Bambara who had freed themselves over the years. As increasing numbers of Haratin took refuge at Nioro and Yelimané, many Beydan refused to come south for fear of losing their Haratin. Others took hostages. The commandant at Nioro expected the smooth liberation of agricultural villages, but feared that liberation of Haratin herders would lead Beydan to quit the desert. He undertook negotiations to avoid that.[49] The French were still worried about keeping population in the desert. Both Moor and Tuareg were increasingly unable to maintain control over desert-side populations. In general, the years since 1945 have seen a continued southward movement of Bella and Haratin seeking better watered land and freedom from former masters.[50] Since 1968, these migrations have also been pushed by drought and have often influenced Bella to move far from their desert masters. The administrator's fear that the Beydan would leave the desert reflected the similar concern of earlier administrators that if the slaves were freed, masters would not work. In fact, those who survive in the desert do so because of dogged desire to survive. Most of the Beydan know no other life.

Persistence of Slavery

In spite of this, a 1951 report suggested that it would be 'premature, even maladroit' to think of emancipating the slaves.[51] This was not, of course, what the larger world was told. In a report to the United Nations Economic and Social Council, the French wrote:

> It is undeniable that in the borderlands of southern Morocco, numerous families keep in their service a category of individual who, without being properly speaking slaves, are part of the family

SLAVERY AND FRENCH RULE IN THE SAHARA

83

patrimony. They are often born of slave parents or from concubines of members of the family with slaves and they remained attached to the family within which they are not mistreated.

In Timbuktu, it was still possible to buy a slave. In 1958, several months after the referendum that gave France's African colonies self-government, Robin Maugham visited Timbuktu under the auspices of the Anti-Slavery Society and Aborigines Protection Society. He interviewed slaves and masters and bought a slave.[52] In Timbuktu, slaves had the right to freedom and many had taken it. Some fled to the city, where they could find work in the quarries, could become prostitutes or could farm, but many Bella still lived in Tuareg camps outside the city. Men in the camps worked for their masters and some Tuareg males considered Bella women theirs to take. Maugham was told that young men would often send a Bella girl out to collect firewood, then follow and rape her.[53] Slaves at Timbuktu were sometimes sent into the city when there was not enough work for them in the camps. They could be sold, Maugham was told, but only if they agreed to the sale. One chief paid for his trip to Mecca by selling several slaves there. Slaves were often harshly treated. Those who fled were beaten if caught or followed into the city. Those safely established in the city were often visited and reminded that the French were leaving. Maugham was convinced that Bella stayed with masters sometimes because of coercion and sometimes because they accepted their station in life. 'Of course a slave can go to the Commandant,' one informant told him,

> and the Commandant will tell him that by law he is not a slave, and by law, his master is not his master. But the slave probably knows that already. In his head, he knows that he is a free man. But in his heart, he does not believe it. He knows that he is a Bela [sic] – and a Bela is a slave. If he buys his freedom from his master, that is different. But otherwise, he believes that he belongs to his master, and so do his children.[54]

The slave Maugham bought was freed before witnesses under Quranic law. Maugham's account is compatible with that of Orsini, who mentions kidnappings of children in the 1940s and the beating to death of a woman who tried to escape. He cited a price of 60 camels for a female slave. Orsini's description suggests that slaves in Saharan society had no rights at all, not even the right to testify in court cases.[55]

Slave-raiding and slave-trading also persisted in Mauritania. Le Boulleux knew of the kidnapping of a 14-year-old girl in 1948 and a 13-year-old shepherd boy in 1950. An 18-year-old male could be bought for 20 camels or about $1,600, a female for 30 camels. Le Boulleux claimed that

84 SLAVERY AND COLONIAL RULE IN AFRICA

slaves were well-treated though he knew of one who died from a beating after trying to escape. Like many of his predecessors, he feared that a brusque change would only create unemployed vagabonds. Similar feelings must have been held by a minister in the de Gaulle government who attended a camel fair in Reguibat territory in northern Mauritania in 1959, a year after the grant of self-government. The Reguibat are camel herders who wander across desert regions of Mauritania, Morocco and Algeria and have maintained through the colonial period both the possession of their slaves and a high degree of autonomy. The most important question the Reguibat asked the Minister was whether they would be allowed to maintain control over their slaves. His response was that they would if they treated their slaves well.

A year later, both countries were independent. The heritage of French rule is different in Mali and Mauritania. In Mali, independence was won by the Union Soudanaise, a party based in the socialist intelligentsia, which was opposed to traditional forms of exploitation and more willing than the French to recognize the rights of various servile peoples. Hostile to the new rulers, the Tuareg revolted from 1962 to 1964. Two other factors were important in weakening Tuareg control. First, increased opportunities to earn wages made it possible for Bella to leave or to purchase land and livestock. Second, a generation of drought decimated Tuareg herds. Tuareg had no animals to loan, and neither the capacity to coerce or sustain.[56] In some cases, Tuareg became dependent on Bella. Others followed Bella into the quest for wages. Some Bella remain in dependent relationships, but others have developed their mixed agriculture, often moving elsewhere. Another large group lives in poverty on the outskirts of various Sahelian towns. In 1989, the hostility of the Tuareg to the hegemony of the savanna peoples erupted again in a war. Among the militias that rallied around the Malian state was a group of Bella organized as the Ganda Koy.

Mauritania had to deal with the same economic and climatic variables, but the political situation is different. There, power since independence has been in the hands of a Beydan minority, though many posts in state and army were held by members of non-Arab ethnic groups and a few by educated Haratin. The Beydan have been faced with radical changes. First, Mauritania experienced real economic change. The 1950s saw the opening of iron mines, independence and the construction of a new capital. Colonial Mauritania had been ruled from St. Louis, the capital of Senegal. Slaves and Haratin were numerous among those seeking, work, and with an income, accumulating property. Second, as in Mali, drought destroyed most of the herds. In 1965, the country was 83 per cent nomad. In 1987, the percentage was down to 23 per cent. A whole generation has grown up that has never lived in the desert and knows only life in Nouakchott, now a city of over

SLAVERY AND FRENCH RULE IN THE SAHARA

700,000 people, or one of the smaller towns. Third, Beydan hegemony was increasingly challenged both by Haratin and by non-Arab ethnic groups. In 1974, El Hor was founded by the members of the Haratin elite.[57] In 1980 Mauritania abolished slavery.[58] The law specified that masters should be compensated for the loss of their property, which the government has not done. Masters, supported by many of the religious authorities, ignore the law. Many slaves, however, have slipped away from the control of their masters, either because impoverished masters cannot support them or by successfully fleeing to Nouakchott, where they can receive help, particularly from a local organization called SOS-Esclave founded in 1995.[59] Ferment in the cities has fed back into rural areas, where there is increasing conflict about land, about dams and about inheritance. Recent writers on Mauritania have described efforts of Haratin to use new revenues to accumulate livestock and land. This has involved both struggles to establish their right to property and struggles over inheritance. Masters in Mauritania still claim the property of their deceased slaves.[60]

The government of Lt. Col. Taya, which seized power in 1980, found a scapegoat, the Black Africans, who are largely related to the peoples of Senegal. After a minor border confrontation in 1989, the Taya regime purged the government and army, expelled tens of thousands of people reputed to be of Senegalese origin, and expropriated lands worked by people, mostly Fulfulde-speakers, whose families had lived north of the Senegal river for generations. Pursued with great brutality, these actions opened up promotions within the military, provided jobs in the civil service and land, which is now largely owned by Beydan and worked by Haratin and Abid. In response, Senegal expelled people of Mauritanian descent, many of them Haratin who no longer spoke Arabic. One effect of the conflict was to prevent an alliance between Haratin and the non-Arab ethnic groups. Many of those expelled from Senegal ended up in a Mauritania they never knew, working lands seized from those expelled for being 'Senegalese'. The Taya regime has harassed SOS-Esclave and human rights activists within Mauritania. Slaves are still forced to work for masters and are brutally punished, exchanged, separated from spouses and children.[61]

Conclusion

In the savanna lands of French West Africa, slaves who remembered an earlier home often returned to it during the early twentieth century. For others, there was a slow process of change in which operation of the law was often inhibited by the identification of administrators with and dependance on chiefs. Nevertheless, throughout much of the savanna, the exploitation of slave labour either disappeared or became inconsequential.

In many parts of the savanna, former slaves are as well off today as their former masters, and in some cases, better off. The desert was different for two reasons. First, both slaves and freed slaves had fewer options. There were no cities to flee to, and if the slave remembered an earlier home, it was far away. A slave walking across the desert risked being re-enslaved or dying of thirst, but most did not remember an earlier home.

Second, the Bella and Haratin were born in the desert. They speak Arabic or Tamacheq. Even those kidnapped during the colonial period were taken young and probably assimilated to their master's culture. Harsh as their slavery seems, Bella and Haratin were part of desert society and often identified as such. It is difficult to say how much their subjection is influenced by a discourse on slavery that shapes that desert society, but it is echoed by different interviews. 'God created me to be a slave,' a slave woman told an American journalist, 'just as he created a camel to be a camel'.[62] As Maugham's informant suggests, subjection is ordained by religion and reinforced by an ideology that divides society between the honourable and dishonourable. Slaves do work the freeborn scorn. Freeborn women must cover themselves and maintain their modesty. Slave women have no such obligations and can be used sexually. The hegemonic ideology which ordains subjection in the slave also ties the Haratin in to the world-view of their masters. Meskerem Brhane has described how educated Haratin claim equality by seeing their relationship to the master's culture in kinship terms. It is this very desire to be accepted in the world of their masters that has made it possible for the state to separate Haratin from Black Africans of the Senegal valley. The Haratin are raised in Arabic culture, see it very much as their own, seek respectability within it, and identify more with the Beydan who subjected them than with fellow Blacks. When anti-Senegalese riots broke out in Nouakchott in 1989, most of the violence was committed by Haratin.

There is not much evidence that the French wanted to do much for servile peoples. The Sahara has often attracted men who romanticize the desert. 'We were attracted,' Philippe Loiseau wrote, 'by the prestige of the desert, by a society whose somewhat feudal character attracted our intelligence and our sensibility. We were seduced and attracted by a living society that we helped to destroy.'[63] I am not sure that all of his predecessors were so torn. Furthermore, had they wished to really transform desert society, it would not have been easy to do so. Distances were great and the environment was hostile. The French learned to live in the desert, but they suffered the same restraints as the nomads. They had to maintain herds of camels and forces that could ride those camels.

SLAVERY AND FRENCH RULE IN THE SAHARA

GLOSSARY

Abd (pl. abid)	Slave (Arabic)
Bella	Servile dependants of Tuareg, between slave and free in status
Beydan	Noble Moors; comes from Arabic word for white
Hartani	Arabic term for servile dependants, between slave and free in status
Ighwellen	Tamacheq term for Bella
Iklan	Tamacheq term for slave

Abbreviations:

ANM	Archives Nationales du Mali
ANSOM	Archives Nationales, Section Outre-Mer (France)
ARS	Archives de la République du Sénégal
AWF	Archives of the White Fathers, Rome
CHEAM	Centre de Hautes Études d'Administration Musulmane

NOTES

I would like to thank Dennis Cordell, Meskerem Brhane, Annemarie Bouman, Andrew Clark and Suzanne Miers for their comments on this paper. I am particularly grateful to Ann McDougall, who taught me much of what I know about the Sahara.

1. Robin Maugham, *The Slaves of Timbuktu* (New York, 1961), p.170.
2. 'L'évolution de l'esclavage dans la société maure', in Edmond Bernus, Pierre Boilley, Jean Clauzel, Jean-Louis Triaud (eds.), *Nomades et commandants: Administration et sociétés nomades dans l'ancienne A.O.F.* (Paris, 1993), p.181.
3. Father Mahiet, 15 Oct. 1897, *Chroniques*, #77, Jan. 1898, AWF.
4. This paper is a by-product of the research for Martin Klein, *Slavery and Colonial Rule in French West Africa* (Cambridge, 1998). My original concern with the Sahara was understanding why its history was different from the savanna. I eventually realized changes in the desert echoed those in the savanna, but played themselves out in different ways.
5. Edmond Bernus, *Touaregs Nigériens. Unité culturelle et diversité régionale d'un peuple pasteur* (Paris, 1981), pp.95–104; E. Bernus, P. Boilley, J.Clauzel and J.-L. Triaud, *Nomades et commandants: Administration et sociétés nomades dans l'ancienne A.O.F* (Paris, 1993); Finn Fuglestad, *A History of Niger 1850–1960* (Cambridge, 1983), pp.54–78; André Salifou, *Histoire du Niger* (Paris, 1989), pp.166–88.
6. James Webb, 'The Trade in Gum Arabic: Prelude to French Conquest in Senegal,' *Journal of African History*, 26 (1985), pp.149–68; *Desert Frontier: Ecological and Economic Change along the Western Sahel 1600–1850* (Madison. Wisconsin, 1995), ch. 5.
7. See Jean-Pierre Olivier de Sardan, *Quand nos pères étaient captifs* (Paris, 1976), ch. 2, for the traditions of a Songhay servile community. See also Fuglestad, *Niger*, pp.28–9; Bernus and Bernus 1975; Bernus 1981, pp.91–4; Edmond and Suzanne Bernus, 'L'évolution de la condition servile chez les Touregs sahéliens', in Claude Meillassoux (ed.), *L'esclavage en Afrique précoloniale* (Paris, 1975), pp.27–48; Pierre Bonte, 'Esclavage et relations de dépendance chez les Touaregs Kel Gress', in Meillassoux, *Esclavage*, pp.49–76; André Bourgeot, 'Rapports esclavagistes et conditions d'affranchissement chez les Imuhag', in Meillassoux, *Esclavage*, pp.77–98; Priscilla Starrett, 'Tuareg Slavery and Slave Trade', *Slavery and Abolition*, 2 (1981), pp.83–113; Lloyd Cabot Briggs, *Tribes of the Sahara* (Cambridge, 1960), ch. 5.
8. Abdel Wedoud Ould Cheikh, 'L'évolution de l'esclavage dans la société maure', in E. Bernus *et al.*, *Nomades et commandants*, p.182.
9. *Haratin* is an Arabic word (*s. hartani*), also used sometimes in Tuareg areas. The Tamacheq word is *ighwellen*, but I am using the more common term Bella to limit confusion. Colin defines them as 'a kind of caste, formed of men of inferior status,' G.S. Colin, 'Hartani', in

88 SLAVERY AND COLONIAL RULE IN AFRICA

Encyclopedia of Islam, III (1971), 231. On the meanings of Haratin in Morocco, see article by Sikainga in this volume.

10. Timothy Cleaveland describes the development in Walata of a Beydan elite which is racially not very different from the slaves who work for them. 'Nineteenth Century Walata and the Power of Women', Paper presented to the Annual Meeting of the African Studies Association, Orlando, Florida, November 1995.

11. Dennis Cordell, 'Black Africa and the Sahara: The Demographic Implications of the Muslim Slave Trade in the Late Nineteenth Century', Paper presented to American Historical Association, San Francisco, 1983.

12. Ann McDougall, Unpublished manuscript, chapter 7. I am grateful to McDougall for showing me this work.

13. Bernus and Bernus, 'Evolution', p.33.

14. Report on Timbuktu in 1894, ARS, K 14; reports on Sumpi, Ras-al-Ma and Douzou in 1904, ARS, K 19.

15. See Stephen Baier, *An Economic History of Central Niger* (London, 1980), pp.48–9; Stephen Baier and Paul Lovejoy, 'The Tuareg of the Central Sudan: Gradations in Servility at the Desert Edge (Niger and Nigeria)', in Suzanne Miers and Igor Kopytoff (eds.), *Slavery in Africa* (Madison, 1977), pp.391–414; Starrett, 'Tuareg Slavery', p.93; Briggs, 'Tribes', pp.93–4.

16. J.-M. Kambou-Ferrand, *Peuples Voltaiques et Conquête Coloniale 1851–1914* (Paris, 1993), pp.351–56.

17. Jean-Pierre Olivier de Sardan, *Les Sociétés Songhay-Zarma (Niger-Mali)* (Paris: Karthala, 1984), ch. 9. See 'Directives Générales pour les Officiers Commandant les Circonscriptions Administratives du Territoire Militaire', enclosure with Meray report, ARS, 4 G 11; Political Report, Oct. 1901, First Military Territory, ARS, 2 G 1/15; Kambou-Ferrand, *Peuples Voltaiques*, pp.356–61.

18. Political Report, Dori, June 1902, ARS, 2 G 2/8 and 6 Feb. 1901, ARS, 2 G 1/15. See also Kambou-Ferrand, *Peuples Voltaiques*, pp.356–61.

19. Report on Gao, 24 Jan. 1910, ARS, 4 G 11. See also Report on Timbuctou, ibid. On Bella in Dori, see ANM, 1 E 32.

20. Inspector Maurice Meray, Report on Cercle of Djerma, 21 Dec. 1909, ARS, 4 G 11.

21. Bernus, *Touaregs*, p.108. There was often conflict between higher and lower authority as a court case at Timbuktu demonstrated. Two slaves of Abdullah Ould Mohammed fled. A nephew was sent after them with a camel. He caught them and was taking them to Arawan. During a halt, the slaves fled with the camel. The nephew died of thirst. The sentence of one year apiece was reversed by a higher authority, who suggested that Abdullah should have been before the court, guilt of 'having concluded with his nephew an agreement for the alienation of the liberty of a third person'. Report on Justice Indigène, Military Territory, 4th quarter 1910 and decision of 10 June 1911, ARS, M 122.

22. Maurice Meray, Report on Timbuktu, 8 Dec. 1909, ARS, 4 G 11. Political reports for 1907 and 1908 show a struggle for autonomy and a concern of Tuareg and Fulbe about their slaves. See for Timbuktu, ANM, 1 E 79; for Dori, ANM, 1 E 32; for Gao, ANM, 1 E 36. On the Tuareg efforts to keep control of Songhay villages, see Chroniques, #132, Nov. 1907, AWF, Rome.

23. Pierre Bonte, 'L'émir et les colonels, pouvoir colonial and pouvoir émiral en Adrar mauritanie', in Bernus *et al.*, *Nomades*, pp.69–80; Francis de Chassey, *Mauritanie 1900–1975: De l'ordre colonial à l'ordre néo-colonial entre Maghreb et Afrique Noire* (Paris, 1978), pp.15–47.

24. E. Ann McDougall, 'A Topsy-Turvy World: Slaves and Freed Slaves in the Mauritanian Adrar, 1910–1950', in Miers and Roberts, *End of Slavery*, p.366; G. Désiré-Vuillemin, *Contribution à la Mauritanie* (Dakar, 1962).

25. Cited by Inspector Demaret of Guyho mission on Kaédi, 6 Jan. 1908, ANSOM, Contrôle 909.

26. Klein, *Slavery and Colonial Rule*.

27. Ponty to Commissaire du Gouvernement-Général en Mauritanie, 29 May 1908, ARS, 4 G 6. On colonial rule in Mauritania, see Chassey, *Mauritanie*, pp.35–165.

SLAVERY AND FRENCH RULE IN THE SAHARA

28. McDougall, 'Topsy-Turvy', pp.366–9.
29. Bernus, *Touaregs*, pp.99–104; Salifou, *Niger*, 1973.
30. Bernus, *Touaregs*, pp.105–8; Kélétigui Mariko, 'L'attitude de l'administration face au servage', in Bernus *et al.*, *Nomades*.
31. Bernus, *Touaregs*, p.109.
32. Ibid., pp.109–11
33. Horace Miner, *The Primitive City of Timbuktu* (Princeton, 1953), p.39.
34. Miner, *Timbuktu*, pp.36–44 and 50.
35. McDougall, 'Topsy-Turvy'; Chassey (1978), pp.92–6.
36. Abdel Wedoud Ould Cheikh, 'L'évolution de l'esclavage dans la société maure,' in Bernus *et al.*, *Nomades*, 1993, p.182 argues that today about half of the Arab population of Mauritania is of servile origin. He cites in support of this a 1964–65 census that indicated that 13 per cent of Arabic-speakers were Abid and 29 per cent were Haratin. The Abid were certainly a higher percentage of the population in 1900.
37. See case cited in McDougall, 'Topsy-Turvy', p.369.
38. Chassey 1978, p.94.
39. McDougall, 'Topsy-Turvy', pp.378–79.
40. Kambou-Ferrand, *Peuples Voltaiques*, pp.359–61.
41. In three Tuareg communities surveyed in Meillassoux, *Esclavage*, differences are striking. Bella were 10 per cent in the community most involved in a cash economy. Bonte, 'Touaregs Kel Gress', p.54. They were 15 per cent in a second desert-side community. Bernus and Bernus, 'L'évolution', p.44. Among the Ahaggar of Algeria, they were over 40 per cent while at Gurma in northern Burkina Faso, Bella were 70 per centof the Tamacheq-speaking population.
42. Marc Guemas, 'Bellahs et Harratines', Mémoire, École National de la France d'Outre-Mer, Paris, 1957.
43. G. Dupeyron, 'Bintagoungou, Village de Faguibine: budgets et niveau de vie', *Cahiers d'Outre-mer*, 12 (1959), pp.26–55.
44. Gov. Soudan to Gov.Gen., 9 Feb. 1950, ARS, 2 K 15 (174).
45. Gov. Soudan to Gov.Gen., #16, January 1950, ARS, 2 K 15 (174).
46. Gov. Soudan to Gov.Gen., 7 July 1950, ARS, 2 K 15 (174). Bella were about 43 per cent of a population of over 25,000. The nobles were less than 5 per cent.
47. Capt. Forgeot, Report on Bellah, n.d., ARS, 2 K 15 (174).
48. Dir. Affaires Politiques to Gov. Soudan, 9. Sept. 1949, ARS, 2 K 15 (174).
49. Cmdt. Nioro to Gov. Soudan, 6 April 1948; Gov. Soudan to Gov. Gen., ARS, 2 K 15(174).
50. On Haratin seeking 'to escape the close attentions of their former masters', see Camilla Toulmin, *Cattle, Women and Wells. Managing Household Survival in the Sahel* (Oxford, 1992), p.22. On earlier moves to better watered lands, see Richard Roberts, 'The End of Slavery in the French Soudan', in Miers and Roberts, *End of Slavery*, 1988.
51. Cited in Le Bouleux, 'L'esclavage', 1963.
52. Maugham, *Slaves*, pp.201–4.
53. Ibid., p.168.
54. Ibid., p.164.
55. Orsini, 'Survivances'.
56. 'Slavery in the Sahel: a report of Ducan Fulton on West African Sahelian States', Anti-Slavery Society.
57. '*Hor*' means noble or pure and is usually used to describe Beydan. In contrast, Haratin has a connotation of 'mixed' or 'impure', See Meskerem Brhane, 'My Master is My Cousin' and other ambiguities of subservience among the Haratines of Mauritania,' paper presented to 1997 meeting of African Studies Association, Columbus, Ohio. Slavery in Mauritania has been regularly reported on by Anti-Slavery International, Human Rights Watch and Amnesty International. See for example Human Rights Watch, *Mauritania's Reign of Terror: State-Sponsored Repression of Black Africans* (New York, 1994).
58. John Mercer, *Slavery in Mauritania Today* (Edinburgh, 1982). A United Nations mission to Mauritania was convinced that 'slavery as an institution protected by law has been genuinely abolished in Mauritani', though it recognized that *de facto* slavery still existed. United

90 SLAVERY AND COLONIAL RULE IN AFRICA

Nations, Economic and Social Commission. E/CN.4/Sub.2/1984/23; E/CN.4/Sub.2/1985/26.

59. Elinor Burkett, 'God Created Me to be a Slave', *New York Times Magazine*, 12 Oct. 1997, pp.56–60.

60. Urs Peter Ruf, 'Dams and ramparts, cattle and goats: recent configurations of territoriality, social hierarchy and dependence in the Tagant and Aftout Regions of Mauritania', Paper presented to 1997 meeting of Brhane and African Studies Association, Columbus, Ohio, 'My Master is My Cousin'.

61. Burkett, 'God Created Me to be a Slave', See the submission of Anti-Slavery International (formerly the Anti-Slavery Society) to the Working Group on Contemporary Forms of Slavery, Commission on Human Rights, United Nations Economic and Social Council, June 1997 for an example of exploitation as harsh as those Burkett describes.

62. Burkett, 'God Created me to be a Slave', p.56. Burkett does not tell us what the actual word was, but it was probably *abd*.

63. Philippe Loiseau, 'L'administration et les rapports nomades/sédentaires', in Bernus *et al.*, *Nomades*, p.164.

'The Ties that Bind': Servility and Dependency among the Fulbe of Bundu (Senegambia), c.1930s to 1980s

ANDREW F. CLARK

The ending of slavery in Africa during the colonial period has recently generated considerable interest among scholars [1] Many ex-slaves, whether migrating or remaining with their former masters, transformed slave relations of production into other ties of dependence and interdependence. Historians have tended to focus on the early colonial period, especially prior to the First World War, when rapid changes occurred. Many scholars have also concentrated on the serviles who left, rather than on the majority of ex-slaves who, after abolition, remained in the vicinity of their former owner but fashioned new relations of servility. This negotiation process continued through the late colonial and into the independence periods. Ex-slaves who migrated obviously influenced the practice of slavery for those who remained, but those who stayed were equally instrumental in transforming the bonds of servility into other forms of dependency and their activities and experiences deserve to be given the same attention. Some serviles did seek to escape from slave status and create new lives away from former masters. While their actions certainly influenced the practice of slavery for those who remained, slavery as a set of ties linking people in different social categories was not eliminated and most ex-slaves sought to benefit from its transformation into new types of dependency. Many were women with only limited choices, or men with no access to land or wage employment. They were willing to accept certain restrictions if it also meant maintaining certain rights.

Slavery in West Africa was always a dynamic rather than a static institution. Servile ties were continually being transformed over the years. Thus, prior to legal abolition, slaves of the Fulbe of Bundu, a Muslim society in eastern Senegambia, normally progressed from newly acquired captives, or trade slaves (*diawambe*), to domestic slaves (*maccube*) who possessed fictive kinship ties with the freeborn. French anti-slavery measures caused slavery's demise as a labour system but did not end dependency and discrimination based on slave descent. The social structure, including the inherited division between free-born and persons of slave descent, was maintained. After legal abolition, former slaves and former masters worked out a complex series of rights, responsibilities and obligations that transformed slavery into a new type of dependency between two social categories without seriously disrupting Fulbe economy and society. This transformation of ties of servility and dependency has continued into the contemporary period.[2]

This essay considers the transformation of the ties between the *maccube*, or persons of servile descent, and the freeborn Fulbe of Bundu in eastern Senegambia, from approximately the 1930s to the 1980s. While most of the major legal and economic changes in slavery and servile relations of dependency had occurred by the end of the First World War, *maccube* continued to struggle to transform ties of servility and dependency throughout the late colonial years and have continued to do so since independence in 1960. Slave status has been retained but its meaning has been transformed. From the 1930s to the 1980s, ties between former serviles and free-born among the Bundunke Fulbe were solidified and codified, setting the stage for contemporary interactions between the two groups. Given the reliance on oral sources and the unfolding and gradual nature of the process of negotiation, exact dates for specific changes in relations cannot be determined with precision. Emphasis in this article is thus given to the situation in the 1980s to demonstrate the changes that have occurred in the twentieth century. Because of the sensitivity of some of the issues, the article is written in the past tense and ends with the 1980s. Yet the still unfolding transformation of ties between freeborn and persons of servile heritage constitutes a significant force in contemporary West African economy and society.[3]

Sources for this study include a variety of written and oral materials. Despite their insistence, after 1905 when slavery was legally abolished in the region, that serviles were not slaves but domestic servants who voluntarily remained with their former masters, French colonial officials periodically addressed questions of servility and dependency in archival correspondence and reports until the eve of independence. Documents from the League of Nations shed some light on the issue in the 1920s and 1930s. Oral testimonies from the 1980s and 1990s collected throughout Bundu in Pulaar, the local dialect of the Fulbe language, provided the most substantial evidence for both the distant and more recent past. Descendants of both free-born and servile persons were interviewed and their behaviour was observed over the course of several extended research trips in Bundu.[4]

The Local Context of Slavery and Abolition

Slavery characterized the pre-colonial and early colonial political economy of the Bundunke Fulbe, a strongly Muslim society.[5] Islam played a critical

SERVILITY AND DEPENDENCY AMONG THE FULBE OF BUNDU   93

role in all aspects of Bundunke Fulbe life, including slavery. People were often enslaved in the name of Islam and the practice of slavery followed similar patterns to other parts of Islamic West Africa.[6] In the late nineteenth century, approximately two-thirds of the population was listed as of servile descent.[7] The Fulbe considered captives (*diawambe*), or trade slaves, acquired through raids, kidnapping, purchase, debt payment, or punishment for crimes, as kinless outsiders without a social identity. Trade slaves of the Fulbe primarily originated from non-Fulbe, non-Muslim groups in neighbouring areas, especially to the east and south of Bundu. Besides providing their labour in the most arduous tasks, trade slaves functioned as investment and currency. Second or later generation slaves (*maccube*), having achieved a degree of ethnic, linguistic and cultural affinity with their Fulbe owners, customarily were sold only in times of great hardship. Masters treated slaves as 'perpetual minors', who usually took their masters' family names, and often carried out tasks similar to those of junior or female members of the kin group. *Maccube* never achieved complete assimilation into Fulbe society, remaining *maccube* even after formal manumission.

Depending on the season and their masters' primary occupation, servile persons worked in agriculture, pastoralism, craft production, commerce, and domestic service. During the rainy season, lasting from late May to early October, the majority of agricultural slaves reportedly laboured in their owners' fields five days a week, from sunrise until two in the afternoon but, at harvest time, slaves generally spent from dawn to sunset in their owners' fields. Slaves used their free time to cultivate their own small plots, given them by their masters. Servile workers often cared for livestock. Dry season activities centered on craft manufacture, including textile production, which contributed substantially to household income. While a few large exclusively slave villages existed in eastern Bundu, most slaves lived in their masters' compounds or in a particular part of the village reserved exclusively for *maccube*.

The French tolerated slavery and the slave trade in the upper Senegal valley, including Bundu, even after the consolidation of colonial rule in the 1890s. Colonial officials repeatedly insisted that domestic slavery could not be abolished without causing massive upheaval and completely destroying agricultural, craft and commercial production among the Bundunke Fulbe, their staunchest supporters in the region. French concerns centred on collecting taxes and tariffs, encouraging economic productivity, maintaining order, and ensuring the cooperation and loyalty of local Fulbe leaders, most of whom owned very large numbers of slaves.[8]

Official French policy toward slavery and abolition in West Africa, never uniform and varying from place to place, underwent a transformation

94 SLAVERY AND COLONIAL RULE IN AFRICA

in the period between approximately 1900 and 1905.[9] Governors of French West Africa moved slowly against slavery, hoping to prevent massive population movements and the disruption of production. As a first step, in 1900, all slave caravans in colonial territory were ordered stopped and freed slaves put into *villages de liberté*, or freedom villages.[10] A year later it became illegal for slaves in areas under direct civilian administration, including Bundu, to be returned to their masters, a decree extended to all of French West Africa in 1903. Masters were also forbidden to reclaim slaves in French courts. The new laws did not end slavery, and not all local administrators enforced the policies uniformly. However, the decrees did reflect a shift in official policy and eventually opened some avenues for slaves seeking freedom. In the early twentieth century, local colonial administrators stopped using the term *esclaves* (slaves) and referred to all persons of servile descent as *captifs* or *domestiques* (domestic slaves).

Slave initiative was the primary motivating force behind the transformations in domestic slavery in the early years of the twentieth century. Between 1905 and 1908, the major slave exodus of the colonial period occurred in French West Africa, with an estimated 200,000 to 500,000 slaves and ex-slaves leaving their masters. Some sources suggest even higher numbers. Whatever the total, among the Fulbe of Bundu, only a few slaves participated in this exodus,[11] but many migrated from the region during the famine of 1913–14 which affected the entire Sahelio–Sudanic belt of West Africa. During this famine, masters excused slaves from normal labour obligations and some persons of servile descent, although not officially liberated, received permission from their masters to leave the area, migrating to the groundnut basin of Senegal or coastal regions.[12] Sources on the famine in Bundu do not contain figures on the numbers involved in migrations and liberations, either formal or informal, but the 1913–14 famine altered and undermined slavery as an economic institution in much of West Africa.[13] The transformation of slavery was further hastened by the recruitment and mobilization during the First World War from 1914 to 1918. Many slaves and ex-slaves volunteered or were drafted to serve in the war effort.[14] After the war, many ex-slave veterans from Bundu refused to return to their former villages and set up communities near Bakel and Kayes on the Senegal River. Even today informants refer to these communities as *maccube* settlements.[15]

Despite further migrations and liberations throughout the 1920s and 1930s, most persons of servile descent among the Fulbe of Bundu either remained with their ex-masters or maintained strong ties of dependency even after having moved away. Serviles who migrated often left daughters married in local villages, necessitating the maintenance of some ties. The majority of people of slave descent became tenant farmers, working for

SERVILITY AND DEPENDENCY AMONG THE FULBE OF BUNDU   95

free-born families. Individual heads of households decided what labour obligations they had to fulfil. According to informants, these labour obligations usually lasted only one generation before serviles became independent farmers. Other serviles immediately set up independent households but they relied on their former owners for land, seeds, tools, loans, and other types of material assistance. Former masters, determined to keep control over labour but also aware of anti-slavery legislation, granted serviles concessions but still regarded them as *maccube*.[16]

Throughout the late colonial years and even after independence, local and Muslim courts in Bundu, which generally operated on local matters independently of the central government, recognized *maccube*, and continued to settle disputes between freeborn and servile persons. According to informants, these local courts and councils codified many of the rights and responsibilities of *maccube*. In some villages, the *chierno*, or *marabout*, or local religious leader decided disputes between freeborn and serviles, setting precedents for later cases.[17] Bundunke Fulbe considered slave status hereditary and immutable. No one could be newly enslaved, but all descendants of ex-slaves retained their servile status in society. Persons of servile descent could leave, renegotiate ties of dependency, and engage in some economic activities previously limited to free-born persons, but their social status of *maccube* did not change.

Pawning – the pledging of a person for a loan – which had largely disappeared in French West Africa by the 1920s, experienced a resurgence with the Great Depression of the 1930s.[18] In Bundu, pawns were almost exclusively women and young girls, but, according to an informant, by the 1930s a freeborn could no longer pawn a *maccudo* as had been the most common practice in the past.[19] A person could only pawn his kin. The same informant also insisted that pawning was not slavery because it was a temporary condition, not an inherited status. Although pawning was illegal, the French initially adopted the position that pawns were not slaves and were therefore subject to different laws.[20] No incidents of pawning in French West Africa were reported in the archives after the outbreak of World War II. An informant in Bundu insisted that the practice had been abandoned by then.[21] It is unclear precisely what impact the resurgence of pawning had on servile relations among the Bundunke Fulbe but in the 1930s, while the freeborn maintained some control over the *maccube*, they could no longer use them as pawns; nor did pawns become *maccube* or pass on servile status.

French conscription policies, both for forced labour and military recruitment projects, involved issuing local or regional quotas for manpower, based on census figures, to be met by local chiefs and colonial officials. The French practised forced labour in French West Africa from the

96 SLAVERY AND COLONIAL RULE IN AFRICA

beginnings of the colonial era until 1946.[22] Bundunke Fulbe and *maccube* both participated in forced labour projects. No distinctions were made either by the colonial administration or by local people between free-born and servile persons in labour quotas. A freeborn could not send a *maccudo* to fill his labour requirements. Related freeborn and servile families did assist one another if a household was short of labour at harvest time and requested assistance.[23]

Both freeborn and *maccube* from Bundu served in a variety of capacities during World War Two. A freeborn could not require a servile to fill a wartime obligation but related families did assist one another when necessary. When *maccube* returned after military or other service, they did not change their status. Some servile veterans served in France and a number remained to work in Europe. Yet they retained their ties with free-born Fulbe families in Bundu, sending remittances and periodic gifts. In the post-war years, serviles who migrated overseas from Bundu generally kept their ties with freeborn families as many planned to earn enough for marriage and then return. While the serviles were away, the free-born families protected their interests in Bundu by taking care of any problems that arose. After independence in 1960, increased numbers of young, male free-born Fulbe from Bundu joined with related servile families already established in Europe, especially France. The servile host families were responsible for supporting the new arrivals and helping them secure employment, usually in factory or menial labour jobs. Some migrants engaged in petty trading. This responsibility continued with increased emigration in the 1970s and 1980s.[24]

Independence in 1960 had no discernible impact on servile status in eastern Senegal. The Senegalese government took it for granted that the French had abolished slavery in the early twentieth century and thus had no reason to pass any legislation or take any action. The Bundunke Fulbe continued to maintain the status of *maccube* and the ties of dependency between serviles and freeborn. Like the French, the Senegalese government did not want to disrupt the economy and had very little enforcement power in remote eastern Senegambia. It was easier to ignore the existence of servile ties or servile status. The Bundunke Fulbe were content to accept the new government as it did not interfere with their social hierarchy and traditional way of life.[25]

Bundunke Fulbe Social Divisions

It is unclear in fact what the new government of independent Senegal could or should have done after 1960 in view of the great changes which had taken place in the position of the *maccube* since 1900. The following discussion

SERVILITY AND DEPENDENCY AMONG THE FULBE OF BUNDU 97

focuses on the situation in the 1980s by which time most of the changes had occurred. In the early to mid-twentieth century, the precise meaning of the term *maccudo* in Pulaar changed among the Bundunke Fulbe from denoting 'slave' to signifying 'servile', 'former slave' or 'person of servile descent', which was the case in the 1980s. The term *maccube* continued to demarcate people descended from slaves or former slaves who had certain restrictions, rights, responsibilities and obligations. *Maccube*, whether loosely translated as clients, retainers, servants, 'quasi-relatives', or persons of servile descent, continued to exist as a clearly separate group in Fulbe society. This distinction certainly existed in the 1980s. The word *maccudo* was still used in daily conversation in the 1980s, connoting a person descended from slaves or former slaves of the Fulbe. *Maccube* were distinct from free-born or 'pure' Fulbe, primarily in matters of marriage, religion, ritual and social obligations. Abolition among the upper Senegal Fulbe eliminated extreme economic dependency but not the distinct inherited and immutable social category of *maccube*.

Bundunke Fulbe divided their social structure into freeborn, artisan, and servile levels, with further distinctions operating within each status.[26] The freeborn consisted of nobles, or *toorodbe* (sing. *toorodo*), and the vast majority of non-noble Fulbe (*Fulbe*; sing. *pullo*). Freeborn nobles and non-nobles intermarried, performed similar political, religious and social activities, and interacted freely. The distinction of noble descent was primarily honorary.

Artisans (*waabe*; sing. *bailo*) belonged to specialized, hereditary, endogamous, occupational groups, including ironworkers, silver and gold smiths, wood workers, leather workers, and entertainers, or *griots* (praise singers and musicians). Oral traditions stress the 'foreign', non-Muslim and non-Fulbe origins of artisans. Most local Fulbe, both freeborn and servile, attributed Mande or Soninke origins to artisan castes. Artisans inherited their position and maintained artisanal status even if they did not practice a craft. Only artisans engaged in smithing, both jewellery and agricultural tools, and woodworking. Ironsmiths made hoes, repaired carts, fashioned brands, and did other metal work, generally on a commission basis. Silversmiths fashioned arm and leg bracelets, and rings. Goldsmiths made earrings, pendants, and other jewelry on commission. Wood workers created mortars and pestles for pounding millet. and also made furniture and tools. *Waabe* worked their fields during the rainy season and did most smithing during the dry season. The demise of artisanal activities during the colonial and post-colonial period did not result in the ending of smith status or the weakening of artisans' rights, responsibilities and restrictions.

Slaves belonging to the Bundunke Fulbe originally consisted of non-Fulbe, and usually non-Muslims, acquired through capture or purchase,

98 SLAVERY AND COLONIAL RULE IN AFRICA

primarily from the east or south. The first generation were *diawambe* (sing. *diamdo*) and their descendants, or those 'born in the house', were *maccube* (sing. *maccudo*). According to traditions, the large numbers of slaves that came into the area in the later nineteenth century were victims of the wars of *al-Hajj* Umar Tal and his successors to the east and of Samori Toure in the Guinean region to the south.[27] In the 1980s, the term *maccube* applied to all people of servile descent. 'Once a *maccudo*, always a *maccudo*' was a common local Fulbe expression, usually invoked when a person of slave heritage did or said something a *pullo* did not like or condone.[28]

Freeborn Fulbe in Bundu possessed all political and legal power in their villages. Villagers elected male chiefs for life, generally from certain prominent free-born families. The chief ran local affairs, assisted by a council of elders who were heads of households. Villagers elected the heads of other local organizations. The Senegalese government had set up a system of village offices for each settlement. The local elected chief was always freeborn, as were heads of the women's association, young men's association, and any other village-wide organizations. Any supervisory position involving money or labour, either at the village or local government level, required free-born status. A village council of freeborn elders advised the chief on important matters, and also settled all legal disputes that households could not solve within or among themselves. In legal matters, the word of a freeborn counted for twice as much as that of a *maccudo*. Two *maccube* had to witness a crime and to testify in order to charge a freeborn. Fines for crimes committed by people of slave descent against the freeborn were usually double those for crimes committed by freeborn against *maccube*. Often the fines levied by the village council against *maccube* included labour obligations for the victim, whatever his or her social status. For example, if convicted of theft, the *maccudo* had to return or pay for the stolen item, and work for the victim for several days. Freeborn convicted of crimes usually only had to pay a fine, either in coin, crops, or livestock, but never had to work for the *maccudo* victim.

Frequently, usually at public meetings to settle disputes, informants stressed that all men were *neena goto, baaba goto* (meaning 'same mother, same father'), regardless of their descent, and all men and women were *maccube Allah* ('slaves of *Allah*'). Both free-born and servile descent people thus agreed publicly that all people were equal in the sight of *Allah*. In private, often after a disagreement with someone of a different social category, freeborn attributed to the *maccube* qualities opposite to those considered desirable among the Fulbe. According to this stereotype, people of servile descent were irresponsible, shameless, uncivilized, uncouth, noisy, disrespectful, and troublesome. They tended to lie, cheat, and steal. Freeborn described *maccube* as black, coarse, fat and unclean, all negative

SERVILITY AND DEPENDENCY AMONG THE FULBE OF BUNDU 99

physical attributes to a free-born *pullo* who prized cleanliness, modesty, a sense of reserve, honesty and intelligence. Fulbe often dismissed the words and actions of a *maccudo* as not to be taken seriously. Arguments between a free-born and a *maccudo* often ended with someone privately informing the *pullo* to remember that the other was only a *maccudo*.[29]

Informants of both free-born and servile descent insisted that, formerly, *maccube* always used a respectful language when talking to or addressing pure Fulbe. A form of this speech has persisted among the *maccube*, most notably in public places and at village meetings. All villagers likewise used this type of formal, respectful speech when speaking to *marabouts* and chiefs. The language was formalized and stylized, and included the use of certain forms of address, avoiding certain words or expressions, and using key words repeatedly. Facility in speech ranked very highly among the Bundunke Fulbe. They considered understanding the Pulaar language, and using it correctly and well, particularly important. Demonstrating linguistic skills was equated with intelligence; knowledge of the Pulaar language meant an understanding of the Fulbe way of life (*pulaaku*). Speaking Pulaar meant becoming Fulbe. Parents frequently and consistently corrected their children's speech. People often joked about non-Fulbe trying to learn Pulaar. Sometimes freeborn told stories and jokes about artisans and *maccube* who had made grammatical errors. Informants noted that newly-acquired slaves who did not speak Pulaar remained marginal until they had learned the language well.

Beginning especially after World War Two, some young men of all social groups migrated, temporarily and permanently, to other areas and overseas, especially to France, seeking work and a cash income. These migrations increased with the Sahelian drought of the 1970s and the lack of economic opportunities in the region in the 1980s. *Maccube* who migrated generally maintained ties to their related freeborn family. Migrants of servile descent sent remittances and gifts to their free-born counterparts while away. The freeborn in turn assisted *maccube* migrants whenever possible, usually interceding with local *marabouts* for special prayers to ensure health and success. Migrants of servile descent on return visits to the village generally brought substantial gifts for their related free-born family, often in the form of cash. In migrant communities in France, social divisions were strictly maintained, with *maccube* migrants doing certain chores for freeborn migrants.[30]

Even after death, *maccube* remained a distinct group, being buried in a separate section of the cemetery. Freeborn and artisans, however, were buried in the same section. Burial rituals differed slightly between freeborn and *maccube*. The latter were buried more quickly, with fewer participants, and fewer prayers said at the gravesite.[31]

Bundunke Fulbe Labour Divisions

Throughout the colonial period and after independence, Fulbe villagers in Bundu did similar agricultural work, consisting of the hand-hoe farming of millet, corn, groundnuts and cotton. Some villagers also tended small gardens adjacent to their compounds. Villages generally were situated near the centre of the fields. The freeborn tended to have fields closer to villages, whereas *maccube* and artisans often had fields several kilometres from the dwellings. Villagers planted similar crops, used similar tools and techniques, and generally produced similar harvests.

The Fulbe considered themselves superior herders whereas freeborn sometimes cited *maccube* as better and more productive farmers. Pastoralism was the only 'pure' work for a *Pullo*. According to oral traditions, the Fulbe had taken up farming out of necessity, not personal preference.[32] Ecological and environmental changes in the twentieth century affected the Bundunke Fulbe economy and society. With increasing droughts and desertification in Bundu in the twentieth century, agriculture became increasing central.[33] Fewer and fewer Fulbe could rely exclusively or even primarily on pastoralism. After the Sahelian drought of the 1970s, agriculture definitively dominated the regional economy. In addition, both the colonial administration and independent government of Senegal encouraged farming by the Fulbe by providing them with seeds and pesticides, and buying their crops through cooperatives. The establishment in the 1960s and 1970s of Niokola Koba National Park in an area where many cattle had been previously herded further encouraged the pursuit of full-time agriculture. Despite the shift from pastoralism to agriculture in recent decades, Fulbe in Bundu still identify the 'Fulbe way' (*pulaaku*) with pastoralism.

Cattle-raising distinctively marked the *pullo*, not only in Fulbe society but among neighbouring ethnic groups as well. Cattle were the distinguishing asset of a *pullo*, and only freeborn Fulbe inherited the 'secrets' of cattle-raising. *Maccube* families usually hired a freeborn to herd their cattle, or joined their herds with that of a freeborn family to ensure proper care and growth. Most often, *maccube* and freeborn with joint herds consisted of families with prior master-slave relations.

Maccube could work alongside artisans, as they worked alongside freeborn, but a servile could never become more than an apprentice or student of artisan work. Some *maccube* acquired considerable artisanal skills, yet they never worked independently and never achieved the status of artisan. No matter how skilled, a *maccudo* remained a *maccudo*.

Cotton grew very well in Bundu, and farmers of all social groups cultivated it extensively. Each compound grew its own cotton for household

SERVILITY AND DEPENDENCY AMONG THE FULBE OF BUNDU 101

use and for sale to the government which encouraged cotton cultivation by providing seeds and insecticides. Cotton money was usually the only large cash income villagers received each year. People used the money to buy millet and groundnuts to tide the households over the dry season, and to pay taxes, which required cash.

Only male *maccube* wove cotton cloth. Elderly women of all social groups carded and spun cotton. Informants insisted that previously carding and spinning were done only by slave women who spent most of their dry season time in spinning to produce an adequate supply of cotton thread for the male slave weavers.[34] Elderly women unable to perform sustained agricultural labour spun thread as one of their contributions to the household. Weavers worked only with already spun cotton thread.

Weavers charged a small fee to weave the cotton which they placed on narrow strip looms. Weavers generally set up the locally made looms during the dry season under a shade tree in their compounds. They sometimes worked all day, weaving narrow strips of cotton from the spun cotton thread. The thread's owner then sewed together the strips. Dyeing, particularly indigo-dyeing, was done in Soninke villages by Soninke women dyers, also of slave descent. Both Fulbe and *maccube* men and women wore garments made on the looms. While most clothing consisted of purchased, factory-made textiles produced either in Senegal or abroad, locally woven traditional cotton textiles had a definite niche among residents. Traditional ceremonies, such as baptisms, initiations, weddings, and funerals, required very specific types of traditionally woven cloth.

In addition to weaving, certain other occupations remained the exclusive preserve of *maccube*, including such dangerous or menial jobs as the digging, deepening and repair of wells; latrine and grave digging; butchering; disposing of animal carcasses; and carrying heavy loads over long distances. *Maccube* were credited with possessing considerable healing powers. They alone reportedly could cure certain diseases, including particular types of fevers, mental disorders, and skin rashes. They were believed to have an acute knowledge of plants and herbs, and to be able to cast spells and to ward off evil spirits and bad spells. *Maccube* 'medicine', whether for good or ill, was renowned among the Fulbe of Bundu. Many midwives were *maccube*, although some artisan females also assisted in childbirth.

Maccube Rights and Obligations

A complex series of rights and responsibilities operated between freeborn and serviles. Every free-born compound had its related *maccudo* compound, and vice versa. Within the related compounds, individuals further

102

established special ties. Individual partnerships often included: the heads of the freeborn and *maccube* compounds; the senior wives of each compound head; junior wives of household heads; senior wives of the head's brother; elderly widows in both compounds; and junior male and female members of each compound with someone of the same gender.

The special partnership between compounds and between individuals in the compounds came into operation at times of need and celebration. Theoretically, neither freeborn nor *maccube* could refuse any reasonable request for assistance, either monetary or labour, by the other. Although the definition of the term 'reasonable' may have varied, a free-born compound generally honoured the requests of a *maccudo* family. Usually, these requests involved a loan of money, or assistance in harvest, ceremonial or compound activities.

Related compounds of free-born and servile descent visited one another on every major public holiday and participated together in most important social occasions, including births, baptisms, weddings and funerals. At religious ceremonies, mainly baptisms and weddings as well as Islamic feasts, including *Tabaski* or the end of Ramadan, the fasting month, an artisan killed the sheep or goat at the home of a free-born Fulbe. Each free-born family then gave a large, select portion of meat to an associated *maccudo* compound. Members of the related compounds visited one another throughout the day with free-born members giving visitors of servile descent gifts of money and/or cloth. The *maccube* then recited the praises of the freeborn, eliciting further gifts. Free-born women often gave their *maccube* counterparts head scarves or pieces of cloth on special days. Slave heritage women brought gifts of food, usually millet or groundnuts, to their freeborn counterparts. No money passed from *maccube* to freeborn on holidays whereas fairly large amounts passed from freeborn to persons of servile descent.

Islam and the Maccube

Divisions between persons of free-born and slave heritage were particularly entrenched in religious matters. The Fulbe in Bundu of all social categories were Muslim. All men attended mosque prayers as equals. The Bundunke Fulbe belonged to the Tijaniyya brotherhood, introduced by Fulbe clerics from Futa Toro in northern Senegal, most notably *al-Hajj* Umar Tal in the 1850s.[35] The Tijaniyya maintained a tradition of loyalty to particular *marabouts*, or religious leaders, all freeborn although not all nobility (*toorodbe*). The descendants of major *marabouts* exercised considerable authority and influences. Fulbe *marabouts* in Bundu wielded enormous prestige and power, not only among local Fulbe but other ethnic groups as

SERVILITY AND DEPENDENCY AMONG THE FULBE OF BUNDU   103

well. Every large village had a local religious leader. There were also several Fulbe *marabouts* in Bundu whose reputation passed far beyond the region. Many had studied for years in Futa Toro in northern Senegal and a few had made the pilgrimage to Mecca. These *marabouts* were all free-born Fulbe. Other social groups could not advance in this hierarchy. Control of religious offices contributed substantially to continued free-born social domination and the persistence of social divisions.

Religious men of servile descent could gain enormous respect but they did not become *marabouts*. One striking example involved a *maccudo* in a large Fulbe village in western Bundu. Al-Hajj Mahamadou N'Diaye reportedly travelled overland, mostly by walking, to Mecca in 1936, returning to his village several years later. Because he was a *maccudo*, he had to secure his master's, as well as the local *marabout*'s, permission to make the pilgrimage. According to N'Diaye, the journey took approximately two years. He spent about a year in Mecca and then took two years to complete the return walk. Even after returning from the pilgrimage, al-Hajj N'Diaye retained his *maccudo* status, with its accompanying restrictions. Villagers accepted his claims about the pilgrimage, and always referred to him as al-Hajj N'Diaye. Every indication confirmed his story. He could name cities and towns he had passed through, discuss certain details about Mecca, and had objects he had carried back from the pilgrimage. Since then, he had rarely left his village. He died in 1985, revered but still a *maccudo*.

Al-Hajj N'Diaye enjoyed enormous prestige in Bundu for his pilgrimage, his piety and also his healing powers. People, both Fulbe and non-Fulbe, spoke highly of his successful healing of numerous mental disorders. Several people who had suffered temporary mental disorders recounted their first-hand experiences with N'Diaye's healing powers. Many people knew someone who had been cured of mental illness or had 'evil spirits' driven away by al-Hajj N'Diaye. He had four wives, numerous children, and one of the largest compounds in the village. Every member of his compound was of slave descent. He constantly received visitors from all over Bundu and Senegal in general. His cattle herd, augmented by gifts from people who sought him out, was one of the largest in the area. Weddings in his compound were lavish and well-attended, reflecting his wealth and prestige.

Despite his credentials, prestige, wealth, and powers, al-Hajj N'Diaye never led mosque prayers. He was never referred to as a *marabout*, a teacher or a religious leader. He had no *talibés* or students. He exercised no political power in the village. When questioned as to why a man who walked to Mecca, cured mental disorders, and received visitors from all over the country never led mosque prayers and was never involved in important village decisions, villagers responded that al-Hajj N'Diaye was a *maccudo*. The pilgrimage to Mecca, his religious devotion, the healing powers he apparently possessed, and material wealth could not erase his social level. 'Once a *maccudo*, always a *maccudo*.' Villagers confided that, because he was both an al-Hajj and a *maccudo*, he possessed extraordinary healing powers, far exceeding those of many religious Fulbe *marabouts*. Informants agreed that *marabouts* had religious learning and political power but al-Hajj N'Diaye had healing powers. One informant confided that al-Hajj N'Diaye was 'not a typical *maccudo*, but he was still a *maccudo*.[36]

Initiation and Marriage among the Bundunke Fulbe

The Fulbe of Bundu had an age-set system based on initiation. Men of all social groups born within a year or two of each other belonged to the same initiation set. The strongest ties across social group lines existed among men who had been initiated together as young boys, usually between the ages of eight and eleven. Initiations occurred every two or three years, depending on the number of boys ready for the ceremony. Ceremonies included circumcision, done by the head blacksmith; extended isolation in the bush; group marches throughout the area; learning songs and Fulbe rituals from older men; and general preparation for the responsibilities of adulthood. Freeborn, artisan, and *maccube* boys were all initiated together and all shared the same age-set.

Upon completion of the initiation, the boy's family prepared a celebratory feast. Associated freeborn and *maccube* compounds, if both had an initiate, sometimes celebrated together, combining resources for the celebration meal and activities. A sheep or goat was killed, and the meat divided up between free-born and slave descent families. If a freeborn compound had an initiate, the associated *maccube* compound was invited, and the freeborn received an invitation if a boy of servile descent had been initiated.

Among Bundunke Fulbe, young girls of all social categories underwent limited excision at an early age in a private ceremony. Wives of blacksmiths performed the operations in their compounds and then the girls were sent home to recover in seclusion. There were no group activities involved. Young girls of all social groups were excised under similar circumstances.

Marriage occurred strictly within social levels. Free-born, artisan and servile persons married within their own social group. Some informants insisted that Islamic law dictated that men and women only marry within their own social status. Whether under traditional Fulbe practice or Islamic law, villagers invariably married someone from the same social level. Children inherited their parents' status.

SERVILITY AND DEPENDENCY AMONG THE FULBE OF BUNDU   105

The ideal marriage was stable, peaceful and familiar. Villagers claimed that marriage with an approved relative was best, and certainly marriage with someone from the same village was preferable to marriage with someone from another village or area. Marriages between people of different ethnic groups periodically occurred, yet even in inter-ethnic marriages, the partners belonged to the same social status. The recurring theme was that marriage was best between two people who shared relatives, neighbours, religious beliefs, and social group affiliation. A woman from another village might become lonely and homesick and spend too much time away from her husband, travelling back and forth to her parents' compound. It was better to marry a woman from the village to avoid a wife's absences. Marriage outside of the social group, however, was incomprehensible and apparently forbidden by Fulbe custom. Each group had certain rights and responsibilities that would conflict if there were intermarriage between different social groups. As one informant asked, if a woman of slave descent married a free-born man, would she be his wife or his slave, and would their children be free or slave descent?[37]

Checking social origins in Bundu was relatively easy and straightforward. People's genealogies were widely known and easily verified. Both first and last names often distinguished freeborn, artisans, and *maccube*. Artisans had unique family names. Because women retained their family names after marriage, checking social origins was further facilitated as both father's and mother's family names were known. Acquaintances also knew the prospective mate's social status. The names and status of one's relatives likewise served as indicators of a person's social status. Because of the importance of social status among the Bundunke Fulbe, learning anyone's origins was not difficult or complicated. While it was usually done indirectly, checking social status directly was also acceptable and considered appropriate when discussing marriage.

No matter how wealthy, religious or respected, an artisan or *maccudo* could not marry out of his or her social group. The largest herd of cattle did not make a person of servile descent the equivalent of a freeborn individual when it came to marriage. If a free-born man or woman were ever unknowingly to marry a *maccudo* and then to discover it, the marriage would be dissolved. If a free-born man unknowingly married a woman of slave heritage, the marriage payment would be returned, and the woman's family would be additionally fined by a local or Muslim court. The *maccudo*, whether male or female, was held responsible for any breach of marriage between social groups. Concealing and lying about one's social status were grounds for divorce and ostracism.

Informants noted that formerly a man could take a *maccudo* woman as a concubine, but this was no longer the case. Freeborn women could never have become concubines or marry outside their social group. Villagers could not say precisely when the practice of free-born men taking *maccube* concubines stopped, although some informants said that 'the French' had stopped it by taxing a man for every wife and concubine he had living in his compound. Other informants said it had been made illegal during colonial rule and men had to give up their servile concubines. Polygamy has continued among all social categories and within the categories. Owing to financial considerations, only a minority of men had more than one wife, and all wives had to belong to the same social group as the husband. A few sexual liaisons apparently existed between young free-born men and young servile women prior to marriage, but these never led to marriage. The liaisons ended as soon as one or the other became engaged to someone from their own social category. If the young servile woman became pregnant by a freeborn, the young man's family paid a fine but had no further obligations.[38]

Conclusion

The importance of slavery among the Bundunke Fulbe is reflected in its vestiges in contemporary society. While slavery was abolished as a legal and economic system in the early twentieth century, its function as a social category has persisted. Persons of slave descent still have certain restrictions, rights and responsibilities in Bundunke Fulbe society. These specifications have evolved over time through a series of subtle negotiations between persons of free-born and slave descent in response to changing conditions. *Maccube* have retained their social status and their place in the social structure while altering their interactions with freeborn Fulbe. These interactions continue to reflect the dependency nature of the relationship between freeborn and serviles in Bundunke Fulbe society.

The process of refashioning ties of dependency has continued among the Fulbe of Bundu in eastern Senegambia. There does not appear to be a move towards abolishing those ties, or changing the social structure, although this could have been done a long time ago. Freeborn, artisans and *maccube* have worked out a complex series of social and economic interactions. An understanding of those ties, and the dynamic process involved in refashioning them, is essential to an understanding of Bundunke Fulbe society both past and present.

SERVILITY AND DEPENDENCY AMONG THE FULBE OF BUNDU

NOTES

1. See, e.g., S. Miers and R. Roberts (eds.), *The End of Slavery in Africa* (Madison, Wisconsin, 1988); M. Klein (ed.), *Breaking the Chains* (Madison, 1993); P. Lovejoy and J. Hogendorn, *Slow Death for Slavery* (Cambridge, 1993). On Senegal specifically, see M. Mbodj, 'The Abolition of Slavery in Senegal, 1820–1890: Crisis or the Rise of a New Entrepreneurial Class?', in Klein (ed.), *Breaking the Chains*; B. Moitt, 'Slavery and Emancipation in Senegal's Peanut Basin: the Nineteenth and Twentieth Centuries', *International Journal of African Historical Studies* (hereafter *IJAHS*), 22 (1989); idem, 'Slavery, Flight and Redemption in Senegal, 1819–1905', *Slavery and Abolition*, 14 (1993), pp.27–50; and A. Clark, 'Slavery and its Demise in the Upper Senegal Valley, 1890–1920', *Slavery and Abolition*, 15 (1994) pp.51–71.
2. On precolonial and colonial Bundu, see P. Curtin, *Economic Change in Precolonial Africa* (Madison, 1975); and M. Gomez, *Pragmatism in the Age of Jihad: The Precolonial State of Bundu* (Cambridge, 1992). Colonial accounts include A. Rancon, *Le Boundou* (Bordeaux, 1894); and E. Roux, *Notice historique sur le Boundou* (Saint-Louis du Sénégal, 1893). On the Fulbe of Bundu from the precolonial era to the 1980s, see A. Clark, 'The Fulbe of Bundu: From Theocracy to Secularization', *IJAHS*, 29 (1996).
3. This article is part of a full-length manuscript on slavery and its ending in eastern Senegal, entitled 'The Ties that Bind: Servility and Dependency in the Upper Senegal Valley, 1890–1990' (in progress).
4. The archival sources include *Archives Nationales du Sénégal* (hereafter ANS) K. Series ('Esclavage et Travail') as well as documents in ANS 2K series. Other reports can be found in ANS 2G, 'Rapports politiques et economiques'. League of Nations documents are contained in League of Nations files Geneva (hereafter LN). Oral interviews are in the author's collection and are being prepared for deposit at the Archives of Traditional Music at Indiana University. On collecting oral sources on slavery in the region, see A. Clark, 'The Challenges of Cross-Cultural Oral History: Collecting and Presenting Pulaar Traditions on Slavery from Bundu, Senegambia (West Africa)', *Oral History Review*, 20 (1992).
5. See Gomez, *Pragmatism in the Age of Jihad*; Curtin, *Economic Change*; and Clark, 'The Fulbe of Bundu'.
6. See P. Lovejoy, *Transformations in Slavery* (Cambridge, 1983) and P. Manning, *Slavery and African Life* (Cambridge, 1990).
7. See the census for Bundu in ANS K. 17.
8. Relevant archives are in ANS K., esp. K. 18 and K. 25. and ANS 13G and 15G. See also Clark, 'Slavery and its Demise'.
9. See previous note as well as F. Renault, *L'abolition de l'esclavage au Sénégal* (Paris, 1972); and Klein, 'Slavery and Emancipation in French West Africa', in *Breaking the Chains* (1993), pp.171–196.
10. D. Bouche, *Les villages de liberté en Afrique noire française* (Paris, 1968); and A. Clark, 'Freedom Villages in the Upper Senegal Valley, 1890–1920', *Slavery and Abolition*, 15 (1994), pp.311–30. Archival references can be found in these two works also.
11. On the slave exodus, see R. Roberts and M. Klein, 'The Banamba Slave Exodus and the Decline of Slavery in the Western Sudan', *Journal of African History* (hereafter *JAH*), 21 (1980), pp.375–94. On Bundu in particular, see Clark, 'Slavery and its Demise'.
12. A. Clark, 'Internal Migrations and Population Movements in the Upper Senegal Valley (West Africa), 1890–1920', *Canadian Journal of African Studies*, 28 (1994).
13. See archival references and the description in A. Clark, 'Environmental Decline and Ecological Response in the Upper Senegal Valley, West Africa, from the late Nineteenth Century to World War I', *JAH*, 36 (1995).
14. On World War One in general, see M. Echenberg, *Colonial Conscripts* (Portsmouth, New Hampshire, 1991), esp. Ch.3. For Bundu, see Clark, 'Slavery and its Demise', and idem, 'Environmental Decline and Ecological Response'.
15. See, e.g., interview with S. Bathily at Bakel, 15 Aug. 1996.
16. Interview with B.I. Kante at Kanioube Mayo, 20 Sept. 1987 and 5 Aug. 1996.
17. Interview with Chierno M. Sow at Goudeseyni, 27 Sept. 1987 and 20 Aug. 1996.

18. See especially the documents from French West Africa from the 1930s in LN, 'Committee of Experts on Slavery (CES)', and 'Advisory Committee of Experts (ACE)'. Further references can be found in A. Clark, 'France, the League of Nations, and the Suppression of Slavery in French West Africa', unpubl. paper presented to ASA Conference (1995). See also, M. Klein and R. Roberts, 'The Resurgence of Pawning in French West Africa during the Depression of the 1930s', *African Economic History*, 16 (1987), pp.23–37.
19. Interview with M. B. Sow at Bidiancoto, 28 July 1996.
20. LN, ACE, Annex 11, Report from the French Government (Feb., 1937), p. 53. See also Clark, 'France. The League of Nations and the Suppression of Slavery'.
21. See previous notes.
22. On forced labour in French West Africa, see B. Fall, *Le travail forcé en Afrique occidentale française, 1900–1945* (Paris, 1993). Fall's book contains extensive archival references from the ANS. On Senegal, see M. Mbodj and B. Fall, 'Forced Labour and Migration in Senegal', in A. Zegeye and S. Ishemo (eds.), *Forced Labour and Migration: Patterns of Movement within Africa* (London, 1989).
23. Interview with O. Ba at Tambacounda, 13 Aug. 1996.
24. Interviews with A. Keita at Reims, France, 19 June 1988; I. B. Sow at Pantin, France, 10 June 1988.
25. See A. Clark, 'The Fulbe of Bundu'.
26. On the Fulbe in general, see M. Dupire, *Organisation sociale des Peul* (Paris, 1970).
27. On Umar Tal, see D. Robinson, *The Holy War of Umar Tal* (Oxford, 1985). On Samori Toure, see Y. Person, *Samori: une évolution dyula* (Dakar, 1968–1975).
28. See, e.g., interview with M. B. Sow at Bidiancoto, 3 Aug. 1996.
29. See, e.g., previous note.
30. I observed the distinctions between freeborn and *maccube* among Bundunke emigrants in France during research trips in 1988, 1991 and 1993.
31. Informants were reluctant to discuss death and burial matters but I was able to observe some of these practices during my research stays. For comparison, see the discussion of the burial of griots among the Wolof of Senegal in D. Conrad and B. Frank (eds.), *Status and Identity in West Africa* (Bloomington, Indiana, 1995), pp.4–7.
32. See, e.g., interview with S. Ba at Bidiancoto, 4 Aug. 1996.
33. See Clark, 'Environmental Decline and Ecological Change', and *idem*, 'The Fulbe of Bundu'. .
34. See, e.g., interview in n. 28.
35. On the Tijaniyya brotherhood in general, see J. Abun-Nasr, *The Tijaniyya* (London, 1962). On Umar Tal, see Robinson, *Holy War*.
36. Interview with M. B. Sow at Bidiancoto, 10 May 1981.
37. Interview with M. Sow at Bidiancoto, 8 Sept. 1987.
38. Among the numerous interviews on the subject of marriage, concubinage and current practices, see especially L. Camara at Bidiancoto, 30 Aug. 1987 and S. Ba at Bidiancoto, 15 Aug. 1987.

The 'Freeing' of Slaves in German East Africa: The Statistical Record, 1890–1914

JAN-GEORG DEUTSCH

Between 1890 and 1914 about 60,000 people, roughly 10 to 15 per cent of the total slave population of about half a million, received 'Letters of Freedom' or *Freibriefe* from the colonial authorities in German East Africa.[1] This article will examine the reasons why, where, and to whom these certificates were issued.[2]

The data which the German colonial administration collected for statistical purposes contain valuable information about slavery and the slave trade in East Africa. Between 1893 and 1896 copies of very detailed district slave records were sent to the Colonial Department of the Foreign Office in Berlin, and they are now available in the Colonial Records Section of the Federal Archives in Berlin. They include, among other information, the names, age, gender, origin, and sometimes even the profession of the 3,700 slaves who obtained the *Freibrief* in this period [3]

After a short introduction these documents will be analysed in the second part of this article. The article will conclude with a brief discussion of German anti-slavery policy in the wider context of the dismantling of slavery in early colonial East Africa.

Colonial Legislation and Administrative Practice

After the German conquest in 1890 the long-distance and export-oriented commercial slave trade was firmly suppressed in German East Africa, but slavery itself was never formally outlawed in the German colonial period, nor were slave owners legally prevented from selling their slaves in small numbers to local African buyers. Rather than abolishing slavery, the German colonial authorities enacted three distinct pieces of legislation designed to regulate the relationship between African slaves, their owners and European employers.

The first legal regulation in this respect was an ordinance issued by Governor von Soden in September 1891 which specified the conditions under which slaves could receive a *Freibrief*. The second ordinance, issued by Chancellor von Bülow in November 1901, aimed at transforming the relationship between slaves and their owners into some kind of serfdom,

110   SLAVERY AND COLONIAL RULE IN AFRICA

MAP 7
ISSUE OF 'LETTERS OF FREEDOM' IN GERMAN EAST AFRICA ACCORDING TO
DISTRICT (1891–1912)

Source: Bundesarchiv Berlin, R.1001, Files No. 7410–7415.

(Adapted fromf J. Koponen, Development for Exploitation, Helsinki 1995, p.110)

THE 'FREEING' OF THE SLAVES IN GERMAN EAST AFRICA 111

while the third ordinance, again issued by von Bülow in December 1904, stipulated that all children born to slaves after 31 December 1905 would be 'free'.[4] In addition, a number of internal decrees were sent to local district officers which in very general terms stipulated how they should proceed. Sometimes these decrees contradicted official statements made at the same time by colonial officials in Berlin to the German press. In any case, both the ordinances and the decrees were only broad guidelines. In practice, local district officers were able within certain limits to design their own anti-slavery policy, which meant that there was no common approach, for instance, to the very important question of whether fugitive slaves should always be returned to their owners. Local district officers were allowed to decide such issues according to their moral preferences and to local political circumstances. In fact, there was great confusion about government policy. Thus, in 1901 the district officer A. Leue lamented that:

> Nobody knows what the score is. Neither the slave owners nor the district officers have a clear idea of what they have to do or what is forbidden to them. Likewise, the slaves are ignorant about their rights and duties.[5]

Still, this legislation provided a rudimentary framework, especially for the issue of 'Letters of Freedom'. The most important was the *Freibrief* ordinance of September 1891 which outlawed the outright purchase of slaves by 'non-natives' (*Nicht-Eingeborene*), including not only Zanzibaris and people of Indian origin, but also Europeans, especially German nationals. Yet at the same time the ordinance specifically allowed the 'temporary acquisition' of slaves. In order to satisfy the ever increasing European demand for African labour, plantation owners were granted the right to conclude redemption agreements with slaves and their owners. These contracts had to state the sum of money which the redeemer agreed to pay to the former owner for the slave and the period of time the slave had to work for his new employer in order to pay off the ransom. The money was then deducted monthly from a previously agreed wage. Usually after two to three years the slaves were free and would receive their official redemption certificate. Both the contract and the certificates were registered by the local district officer.[6]

However, the ordinance also mentions in passing that *Freibrief* certificates could be issued for other reasons. The ordinance itself is rather vague as to what these were, but an accompanying decree specifically names 'manumission by the owner', 'death of the owner', 'freed on a military campaign', 'birth of children' (to the owner) and 'unknown'.[7] Moreover, in their local law making and enforcing capacity, district officials were free, for instance, to issue emancipation certificates to any slave whose

SLAVERY AND COLONIAL RULE IN AFRICA

owner they believed was morally or politically unfit to own slaves. Certificates were also issued in accordance with the Brussels Act of 1890 which required signatory powers to issue 'Letters of Freedom' to fugitive slaves who came from abroad.[8] These certificates had also to be registered. Thus, there were basically three broad patters of slave 'liberation': (third party) *redemption, manumission* by the owner, and official *emancipation.*

It is important to note that paragraph three of the ordinance of November 1901 stipulated that slaves had the right to redeem themselves.[9] Until then only some district officers had informally allowed slaves to buy their own 'freedom' even against the will of their owners, while other district officers had handled this issue with the utmost restraint.[10] Thus, from the very beginning of certification, the category of 'redemption' covered both self-redemption of slaves as well as redemption by others, such as European plantation owners, African employers and even family relations of the slaves. Unfortunately, the overall record for the period 1891–1912 does not distinguish between the two and there is thus room for conflicting interpretations.[11] Similarly, 'official emancipation' took place for a variety of reasons, ranging from mistreatment of the slave to non-residence of the owner within the boundaries of the colony. Frequently, no specific reason was given as to why the district officer emancipated a particular slave.

The Statistical Record

If one looks at the overall number of slaves who received *Freibriefe*, there was a steady increase between 1891 and 1912 (see Table 1). Until the mid-1890s, only a few hundred were issued but then their numbers increased to 2,000–3,000 in the second half of the 1890s and early 1900s. In 1909 the 4,000 mark was reached. Thus, although there are no data available for the years 1913 and 1914, one can safely assume that in the period 1890 to 1914 about 60,000 *Freibriefe* were issued by the local administration, since according to the records exactly 51,632 slaves had received such certificates by the end of 1912. Detailed records for the years 1891 and 1892 are missing, but for the period 1893 to 1912, the available figures show that of the total of 50,818 slaves liberated in this period, 19,311 were redeemed, 17,374 were manumitted by their owners, and 12,263 were officially emancipated. All other reasons, such as 'death of the owner' and 'freed on a military campaign', accounted for only 1,870 *Freibriefe*.

Tables 2a and 2b show the development of the various *Freibrief* categories over time. In the period 1893–1912 the number of slaves who were manumitted by their owners, redeemed themselves or were redeemed by others steadily increased, reflecting both the diminishing social importance of slavery and the growth of the colonial economy. The number

TABLE 1
ISSUE OF 'LETTERS OF FREEDOM' ACCORDING TO DISTRICT, 1891–1912

	1891	1892	1893	1894	1895	1896	1897	1898	1899	1900	1901	1902	1903	1904	1905	1906	1907	1908	1909	1910	1911	1912	Total
Kilwa	5	103	64	121	185	654	445	471	1122	447	538	489	535	611	327	379	565	505	506	473	700	590	9835
Lindi	7	66	95	100	113	61	451	88	104	109	167	100	219	347	380	608	362	623	818	973	499	1118	7408
Pangani	3	22	24	56		43	130	97	49	162	144	262	264	178	574	436	372	348	177	186	522	92	4141
Tanga	7	270	97	168	78	186	268	122	91	63	190	171	172	118	157	157	215	224	200	208	216	156	3550
Bagamoyo	16	174	72	172	90	110	97	68	60	74	221	186	217	108	243	158	339	156	289	202	290	204	3546
Tabora					96	64	46	80	30	23	84	42	114		150	242	223	274	371	265	581	591	3276
Dar-es-Salam		131	72	113	150	264	184	152	58	116	85	175	114	127	126	108	184	118	162	203	152	206	3000
Mohorro-Rufiji									59	121	112	155	207	248	105	199	196	183	137	197	245	190	2354
Udjidji						14		134	74	36	117	69	124	65	53	101	187	196	293	236	197	250	2146
Iringa							162	262	114	67	80	171	196	113	65	190	182	123	73	65	94	48	2005
Morogoro													170	274	260	99	129	147	336	300	139	55	1909
Mikindani		2	24		124	177	106	59	122	75	121	77	57	123	119	159	129	186				244	1904
Saadani		8	15		25	17	82	31	11	8	48	13	34	19	53	58	136	152	168	72	42	26	1018
Handeni																			57	240	159	185	641
Muanza							1	49	44	3	18	19	5	12	11		24	44	87	206	39	14	576
Bukoba								21	28	10	149	56	69	38	26	52	12	17	26	15	18	19	556
Kilimatinde							72	58	20	26	39	7	13	26	44	16	29	33	47	58	38		526
Kilossa							69	115	13	38	102	89										66	492
Mpapua							24	54	30	10	23	15	11	13	12	11	35	108	29	43	41	15	463
Usumbura									3	52	38	224	32	23	31	16	32	32	23	36	28	21	446
Wilhelmsthal								40	11	10	29	18	12	23	30	18	22	18	11	25	25	15	351
Bismarckburg									45	4	35	25	34	2	1	3	32	13	7	16	13	13	290
Songea								57	49	8	5	7	9	10	15		31	13	19	13	13	17	256
Irangi								4			12	2	8	11	9	12	16	30					172
Kisaki				5	10		7	37	21	17	16	22											135
Mahenge										11		4		17	11	6	5	7	4	11	17	11	106
Langenburg							16	18	10	5		11	4	5	2	3	6		6	5	6	5	102
Urundi																	19	12	21	23	13	12	100
Moschi				41			32	13	12	6	3	3	8		2	2			2	12		1	137
Schirati											28	8											36
Dodoma																						47	47
Rubschugi															12	29							41
Ussuwi																	19						19
Singidda													1	3	2	2		5	1			11	11
Aruscha																							9
Mkalama																	3						8
Mkondva								4		3													7
Kifumbiro																						6	6
Ruanda																					1	4	6
Ubena																						2	2
Total	38	776	468	781	861	1590	2192	2034	2180	1504	2404	2420	2631	2514	2820	3080	3504	3554	3870	4083	4094	4234	51432

Source: Bundesarchiv Berlin, R.1001, Files No. 7410–7415.

Note: The archival spelling of place and district names has been retained in the tables.

TABLE 2a
ISSUE OF 'LETTERS OF FREEDOM' 1893–1912
Reasons for Issue
Total Numbers

	Redemption	Manumission	Emancipation	Others	Total
1893	74	93	210	91	468
1894	150	142	391	98	781
1895	209	274	281	97	861
1896	229	207	1043	111	1590
1897	283	624	818	467	2192
1898	369	603	906	156	2034
1899	389	617	1088	86	2180
1900	365	665	440	34	1504
1901	691	783	830	100	2404
1902	723	673	965	59	2420
1903	738	922	901	70	2631
1904	781	983	690	60	2514
1905	1052	1093	633	42	2820
1906	1525	940	353	262	3080
1907	1642	1332	474	56	3504
1908	1782	1358	362	52	3554
1909	1922	1464	476	8	3870
1910	1980	1338	754	11	4083
1911	2186	1534	368	6	4094
1912	2221	1729	280	4	4234
1893–1912	19311	17374	12263	1870	50818

Source: Bundesarchiv Berlin, R.1001, Files No. 7410–7415.

of slaves who were officially emancipated, however, slowly declined from about the turn of the century. This was largely due to the fact that the period of colonial conquest had come to an end by that time. Up to about 1900, coastal aristocrats or chiefs further inland who had resisted or were suspected of having opposed the establishment of colonial rule in their area were often relieved of their slaves. This policy was also a subtle but highly effective strategy to exert a strong measure of control over local elites. They often owned large numbers of slaves and their loss often meant their immediate financial, social, and thus political ruin. In any case, after the turn of the century the number of slaves who received a *Freibrief* for that particular reason declined.[12] This was probably also the main reason why in the year 1900 the overall number of *Freibriefe* dropped so sharply. It was almost entirely due to a decrease in the numbers of official emancipation *Freibriefe* issued in that year.[13]

The geographical distribution of certification varied greatly (see map). Between 1893 and 1912 about half of the slaves who received *Freibriefe* lived in or near the four coastal districts of Kilwa, Lindi, Pangani, and

TABLE 2b
ISSUE OF 'LETTERS OF FREEDOM' 1893–1912
Reasons for Issue. Total Numbers

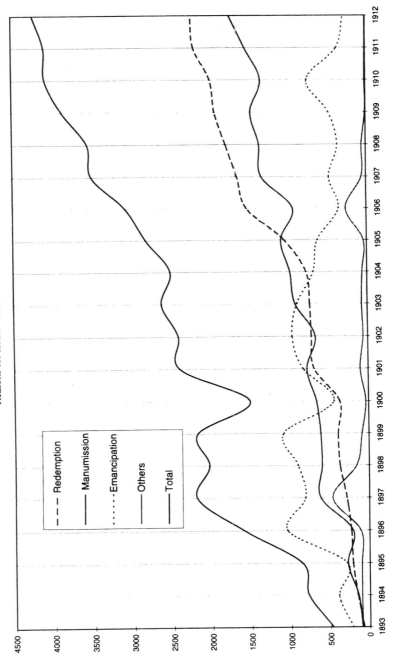

Source: Bundesarchiv Berlin, R.1001, Files No. 7410–7415.

116   SLAVERY AND COLONIAL RULE IN AFRICA

Tanga. This is hardly surprising since these districts harboured large numbers of slaves and were effectively controlled by the German colonial government much earlier than the inland districts.[14] Yet there are certain important local variations in this pattern. In the inland districts, in which, according to administrative reports, very large numbers of slaves could be also found, especially in Tabora, Ujiji, Songea and Iringa District, few slaves obtained their 'freedom' by certification. In these districts the unmaking of slavery followed a different local historical trajectory.[15] Moreover, it should be noted that while most of the European owned plantations were located in or near the four coastal districts mentioned above, the largest number of African labourers (about half of the 50,000 African employees in 1910) worked in or near Tanga and Pangani Districts, while in Lindi and Kilwa Districts this number amounted to less than 5,000.[16] Yet it was in these districts that most slaves were redeemed. It therefore appears that there was no direct geographic-numerical connection between the location of redemption and the activities of European plantation owners.

The reasons for the issue of *Freibriefe* also varied geographically (see Tables 3 and 4). For instance, manumission by the owner played a major role only on the coast, particularly in Kilwa, Bagamoyo and Dar es Salaam Districts, where many Muslim slave owners lived. According to the teachings of Islam manumission was considered to be a pious act and it conveyed considerable social prestige to the slave owners. In the inland districts, the number of slave owners who were devout Muslims was much smaller. Yet it would be wrong entirely to attribute the increase in the number of manumissions after 1900 to an increase in religious piety on the coast, since manumission was probably also a means of purchasing some social benefits from a situation which had become politically and socially untenable. Arguably, after the turn of the century the development of the colonial economy slowly eroded the hold which owners had over their slaves and the increase in the number of manumissions was a sign of that.

In Tabora District, which was said to have harboured more than 200,000 slaves in the 1890s, the number of redemption *Freibriefe* only started to increase steadily in the second half of the 1900s and early 1910s. By that time, however, the local slave population had already declined to probably less than 100,000.[17] Finally, it should be noted that the number of fugitive slaves who received their *Freibriefe* in accordance with stipulations of the Brussels Act was rather small, 36 to be precise. But this figure is misleading. There were certainly several hundred, probably even thousands, of both male and female slaves who received *Freibriefe* on account that their owners resided abroad and that they had run away from them. Since, however, these slaves had already lived in German East Africa for some

TABLE 3
ISSUE OF 'LETTERS OF FREEDOM', 1891–1912 (SELECTED DISTRICTS AND MAIN REASONS ONLY)

	1891	1892	1893	1894	1895	1896	1897	1898	1899	1900	1901	1902	1903	1904	1905	1906	1907	1908	1909	1910	1911	1912	Total
Kilwa	5	103	64	121	185	654	445	471	1122	447	538	489	535	611	327	379	565	505	506	473	700	590	9835
Redm.	n.a	n.a	3	8	29	25	46	41	n.a	61	86	192	56	88	64	103	79	106	101	122	320	232	1762
Manu.	n.a	n.a	6	26	102	59	284	286	n.a	270	296	206	304	307	221	256	449	349	267	317	350	325	4680
Eman.	n.a	n.a	41	74	52	554	114	144	n.a	116	156	91	175	216	42	20	37	50	138	34	30	33	2117
Lindi	7	66	95	100	113	61	451	88	104	109	167	100	219	347	380	608	362	623	818	973	499	1118	7408
Redm.	n.a	n.a	30	76	69	13	21	17	n.a	10	41	21	38	132	99	412	183	350	409	402	254	535	3112
Manu.	n.a	n.a	13	19	11	8	41	54	n.a	54	52	35	67	116	145	112	145	220	302	255	138	452	2239
Eman.	n.a	n.a	12	5	25	29	107	16	n.a	42	61	30	101	99	128	56	22	53	100	316	107	131	1440
Pangani	3	22	24	56		43	130	97	49	162	144	262	264	178	574	436	372	348	177	186	522	92	4141
Redm.	n.a	n.a	4	24		16	19	35	n.a	91	84	48	139	92	314	124	270	226	105	114	243	49	1997
Manu.	n.a	n.a		6		5	11	15	n.a	43	48	33	86	73	206	95	102	113	72	66	279	39	1292
Eman.	n.a	n.a	20	26		22	99	44	n.a	24	12	181	39	13	54	17		5		6		4	566
Tanga	7	270	97	168	78	186	268	122	91	63	190	171	172	118	157	173	215	224	200	208	216	156	3550
Redm.	n.a	n.a	17	11	14	42	90	48	n.a	31	83	63	52	52	65	97	117	100	86	114	92	62	1236
Manu.	n.a	n.a	29	16	21	50	54	45	n.a	27	73	73	86	42	87	76	98	123	114	90	124	94	1322
Eman.	n.a	n.a	47	99	43	87	119	17	n.a	5	32	33	34	16	4		1		4				541
Bagamoyo	16	174	72	172	90	110	97	68	60	74	221	186	217	108	243	158	339	156	289	202	290	204	3546
Redm.	n.a	n.a	5	9	2	21	21	10	n.a	15	104	51	54	55	79	69	177	90	131	74	98	99	1164
Manu.	n.a	n.a	28	50	29	33	34	20	n.a	25	62	101	94	41	134	85	155	58	144	110	186	97	1486
Eman.	n.a	n.a	27	89	55	41	13	24	n.a	11	50	34	69	12	30	4	7	8	14	14	6	8	516
Tabora						96	64	46	80	30	23	84	42	114	150	242	223	274	371	265	581	591	3276
Redm.						43	5	13	10	n.a	11	18	4	45	92	188	159	201	229	197	363	340	1918
Manu.						3					1	5	3		42	38	19	50	62	48	125	231	627
Eman.						50	59	21	60	n.a	8	52	35	69	16	16	38	23	80	20	93	20	660
Dar-es-Salam		131	72	113	150	264	184	152	58	116	85	175	114	127	126	108	184	118	162	203	152	206	3000
Redm.			4	20	25	26	21	42	n.a	46	25	58	17	51	53	60	95	64	62	66	81	106	922
Manu.			7	25	72	29	113	52	n.a	60	28	59	64	48	43	42	78	28	86	128	80	89	1111
Eman.			49	49	17	178	39	33	n.a	3	23	40	14	10	20	3	11	15	14	9	11	11	549
Mohorro-Rufiji									59	121	112	155	207	248	105	199	196	183	137	197	245	190	2354
Redm.									n.a	8	13	5	20	35	24	66	66	67	76	133	140	102	755
Manu.									n.a	76	78	73	105	172	55	24	82	107	59	61	103	88	1083
Eman.									n.a	37	21	77	82	41	26	109	48	8	2	3	2		456
Udjidji							14	134	74	36	117	69	124	85	53	101	187	196	293	236	197	250	2146
Redm.								6	22	16	85	38	47	36	24	57	157	126	128	142	142	166	1192
Manu.							1				5	4	8	12	8	29	14	24	148	61	44	65	423
Eman.							8		108	20	27	27	66	8	21	15	16	46	17	33	11	18	441
Iringa							162	262	114	67	80	171	196	113	85	190	182	123	73	65	94	48	2006
Redm.								9	32	35	33	122	161	89	46	167	8	102	51	59	64	25	1003
Manu.											1	7	10	1	8	3	4	12	2	20	22		90
Eman.								152	178	27	47	49	13	11	13	5	170	6	10	2	10	1	694
Others	0	10	44	51	149	194	409	560	419	286	666	600	469	599	640	486	679	804	844	1075	598	789	10371
Total	38	776	468	781	861	1590	2192	2034	2180	1504	2404	2420	2631	2514	2820	3080	3504	3554	3870	4083	4094	4234	51632

Redm.: Redemption   Manu.: Manumission   Eman/: Emancipation   n.a.: not available

Source: Bundesarchiv Berlin, R.1001, Files No. 7410–7415.

118
SLAVERY AND COLONIAL RULE IN AFRICA

TABLE 4
REASONS FOR ISSUE ACCORDING TO DISTRICT, 1893–1912
(1899: Data not avalaible)

	Redm.	Manu.	Eman.	DeO.	BoC.	BrA.	MiC.	Others	Total
Kilwa	1762	460	2117	45	0	0	1	0	8605
Lindi	3112	2239	1440	81	5	1	245	108	7231
Pangani	1997	1292	566	1	0	0	1	210	4067
Tabora	1875	627	660	66	0	4	0	14	3246
Bagamoyo	1164	1506	516	88	0	3	8	11	3296
Tanga	1236	1322	541	56	2	14	0	11	3182
Mohorro-Rufiji	755	1083	456	0	0	0	0	1	2295
Dar-es-Salam	922	1111	549	58	8	12	85	66	2811
Iringa	1003	90	694	18	3	0	27	56	1891
Udjidji	1192	423	441	1	0	0	1	14	2072
Mikindani	567	820	258	53	19	0	0	63	1780
Morogoro	843	304	739	0	0	0	0	23	1909
Saadani	370	361	257	6	0	0	3	2	999
Handeni	591	49	1	0	0	0	0	0	641
Bukoba	91	43	389	0	0	0	0	5	528
Kilossa	94	124	168	1	2	0	54	36	479
Muanza	142	36	320	2	0	0	0	32	532
Kilimatinde	207	91	127	1	2	0	70	8	506
Usumbura	66	24	318	0	0	0	0	35	443
Mpapua	107	117	199	7	1	0	0	2	433
Wilhelmsthal	190	81	69	0	0	0	0	0	340
Bismarckburg	132	40	70	1	0	0	0	2	245
Songea	127	57	17	1	0	0	0	5	207
Irangi	77	66	29	0	0	0	0	0	172
Kisaki	46	15	49	1	1	0	0	2	114
Mahenge	43	33	29	0	0	0	1	0	106
Langenburg	44	14	31	0	0	2	0	1	92
Moschi	47	12	63	1	1	0	0	1	125
Schirati	0	36	0	0	0	0	0	0	36
Rutschugi	14	4	18	0	0	0	0	5	41
Urundi	35	18	10	0	0	0	0	6	69
Dodoma	24	18	5	0	0	0	0	0	47
Ruanda	24	10	2	0	0	0	0	0	36
Ussuwi	0	0	19	0	0	0	0	0	19
Singidda	9	2	0	0	0	0	0	0	11
Aruscha	3	3	3	0	0	0	0	0	9
Mkalama	7	1	0	0	0	0	0	0	8
Mkondva	2	0	5	0	0	0	0	0	7
Kifumbiro	2	3	0	0	0	0	0	1	6
Ubena	0	2	0	0	0	0	0	0	2
Total	18922	16757	11175	488	44	36	496	720	48638
in %	38.8	34.5	23.0	1.0	0.1	0.1	1.0	1.5	100

Redm.: Redemption Eman.: Emancipation BoC.: Birth of Children BrA.:
Manu.: Manumission DeO.: Death of Owner MiC.: Military Campaign Brussels A.

Source: Bundesarchiv Berlin, R.1001, Files No. 7410–7415.

THE 'FREEING' OF THE SLAVES IN GERMAN EAST AFRICA 119

time, many district officers did not regard such slaves as fugitives in the narrow sense of the Brussels Act and therefore abstained from issuing *Freibriefe* under this category. Instead, such slaves received emancipation *Freibriefe*. For instance, of the 171 *Freibriefe* issued in Tanga in the year 1894, 89 carried the heading 'official emancipation'. A closer inspection of these *Freibriefe* reveals that 86 were issued because the owner of the slave resided on the island of Pemba which at that time belonged to the British Protectorate of Zanzibar.[18]

District Records, 1893–96

While the aggregate numbers of *Freibriefe* issued in the period 1891–1912 provide a broad outline of major trends, district records for the years 1893–96 allow a more subtle interpretation of the statistics. But it would be wrong to suppose that slaves who received *Freibriefe* in the 1893–96 period were representative of the whole slave population of German East Africa at the time, nor can it be assumed that the interpretation of the data for this period is equally valid for the whole 1890–1914 period. However, despite these restrictions it is possible to make a few cautious observations on the slave trade as well as ownership, employment, gender, age, and ethnicity of slaves in East Africa around the turn of the century.[19]

Most owners whose slaves were 'freed' were men, though there were also a few women. These men and women usually owned one or two slaves, though there were others, like certain chiefs in the interior or local aristocrats on the coast who apparently owned hundreds. These men were often part of the local social and political elite, and it was among them that the German administration chose their local representatives (called *Sultans*, *Akidas* and *Jumbes*). This was one of the main reasons why the German administration was so reluctant to abolish slavery outright in the colony, since it would have greatly diminished the social and political power of those through whom the administration wished to rule the country.[20]

Most 'freed' slaves, both male and female, were previously employed as agricultural labourers. But not all slave owners, at least on the coast and in the 'coastal' towns in the interior like Tabora and Ujiji, were landowners. A few slave owners seemed to have acquired slaves solely for entrepreneurial purposes, for instance long-distance trade, in which slaves, usually male, were employed as caravan porters. Moreover, it appears that some owners deliberately diversified the employment of their slaves. For instance, when in 1894 Abdallah bin Sef, resident on the island of Mafia, was for political reasons relieved of his 55 slaves, his workforce included not only 41 agricultural labourers but also seven seamen, three blacksmiths, two agricultural overseers, one carpenter and one personal servant.[21]

120 SLAVERY AND COLONIAL RULE IN AFRICA

According to the *Freibrief* records, only a few Europeans or German nationals owned slaves. One notable case is the Hauptmann of the *Schutztruppe,* Hermann Stigl, after whom Stigl Gorge in Tanzania is named. In 1895 he manumitted his female slave Sassonsi, a 25-year-old woman from Tabora.[22] But such cases were a rare exception, since after all 'non-natives', especially members of the German civil administration and the *Schutztruppe*, were strictly forbidden to own slaves. More common were the cases in which owners of Indian origin manumitted slaves, although as British subjects they also were not allowed to own slaves. Thus, according to the classification system employed in the records the vast majority of slaves were owned by either 'Arab', 'Swahili' or 'African' owners, although it is not entirely clear how the administration, for instance in towns like Tabora or Lindi, defined these three groups. As far as the profession of the owners is concerned, it is noticeable that many African owners carried Germanized Swahili honourary titles, such as *Jumbe*, *Sultan*, and *Akida*. Finally, it appears that a certain number of female slaves who were manumitted or redeemed had been previously owned by African *Askaris* of the *Schutztruppe*, especially non-commissioned officers, although slave ownership was forbidden to them as well.[23]

As already mentioned, the majority of slaves who received *Freibriefe* in the period 1893–96 were previously employed in agriculture. Most of them worked on the farms or plantations of their owners. Some district officers made a distinction between those slaves who were only employed as agricultural labourers and those who farmed on their own. It appears that especially on the coast some large land-owning aristocrats had settled slaves on their land not so much because they were interested in the labour power of these slaves, but rather in order to obtain a portion of the vegetables and the grain they produced. The social prestige of such '*shamba*' slaves was considered to be much higher than that of agricultural labourers, since their status was similar to sharecroppers and other clients and dependants of the local Swahili aristocracy.[24]

A minority of 'freed' slaves had occupations other than agricultural work. These varied with the structure of the local economy and included such professions as seaman, fisherman, net-maker, trader, blacksmith, carpenter, butcher, bricklayer, porter, hunter, herdsman, mat-maker, basket-maker, dressmaker, shoemaker, tailer, potter, stone carrier, domestic servant and 'native doctor'. The majority of these 'professional' slaves were men. Women apparently only dominated the mat-making business.

There was, however, one 'profession', called *Suria*, in the documents which was exclusively the domain of women. These were female slaves who were bought by prosperous men as concubines or second-class wives, usually without bridewealth payments or an Islamic or other kind of

THE 'FREEING' OF THE SLAVES IN GERMAN EAST AFRICA

marriage ceremony. Most of these women were in the 15–25-year age group and their redemption prices often exceeded those of female agricultural labourers in the same age group by a factor of two to three. They were often ransomed by *Askaris*, though there were also a few instances in which German nationals redeemed such women. However, the fact that European men redeemed African *Surias* is in itself no proof for the existence of more than casual sexual relationships between African slave women and European men in this period. Still, one might speculate why these men paid such extraordinarily high redemption prices for these women.[25]

Only a small number of the slaves, perhaps less than ten per cent of all 'freed' slaves, worked in the households of their owners. This surprisingly low figure seems to contradict much of the contemporary writing about slavery in East Africa. According to this literature most of the slaves in German East Africa were employed as domestic servants.[26] However, there is probably a bias here in the records, since for instance older slaves, especially the ones who were born in the household of their owner, were less likely to be redeemed than other slaves because of their firmer attachment to the families of their owners. Conversely, slaves who remembered where they had been enslaved or had recollections of their birthplace were more likely to seek redemption than second or third generation household slaves. In this context it should also be noted that the great majority of slaves who received *Freibriefe* were not born in the location of certification or in the place of their owners' residence. But, in any case, it appears that the incidence of household slavery had been to some extent exaggerated in the official portrayal of slavery in East Africa at the time, probably because it allowed slavery to be painted as a 'mild' and 'patriarchal' institution whose abolition was not required for humanitarian reasons.[27]

The overall majority of 'freed' slaves, including even those who were previously employed in agriculture, were female slaves. There is thus reason to suggest that the majority of slaves in East Africa were indeed women. Tables 5 and 6 show that almost two-thirds of all manumitted slaves and over half of all redeemed slaves were female slaves, most of whom were less than 25 years old. But like the uneven regional distribution of certification and the variable professional status of the slaves, the place of certification is significant in this respect. While in some districts the gender balance of the 'freed' slave population was almost even, in other districts the number of 'freed' female slaves greatly exceeded the number of 'freed' male slaves. There is moreover some evidence to suggest that women played a far greater role in agriculture than colonial reports published at the time acknowledged. As mentioned above, a number of coastal aristocrats were relieved of their slaves because they opposed the German

122 SLAVERY AND COLONIAL RULE IN AFRICA

administration. In the case of Abdallah bin Omari of Kilwa Kivindji whose slaves were officially emancipated in 1896, it appears that of the 226 slaves concerned, 120 were women, most of whom were less than 30 years old and employed as agricultural labourers.[28]

The *Freibrief* records also reveal that on the whole female slaves were more highly valued than male slaves of the same age group. For instance, for younger women in the 15–25 year age group the redeemer had usually to pay about 60 to 80 Rupees, while male slaves in the same age group fetched only 40 to 60 Rupees. The redemption price was usually the local 'market rate' for slaves, fixed by the district officer after consulting local opinion, since all such transactions were supposed to be tightly supervised by him. The amount which slave owners received for their slaves varied greatly between different locations. In general, slaves were more highly valued on the coast than in the interior, although for highly priced slaves, such as *Surias*, redemption costs tended to be similar everywhere.

In this context it should be noted that the difference between the redemption prices for male and female slaves of the same age group and profession was greatest in the 15–25 year age group and that redeemed female slaves were generally younger than their male counterparts. This suggests that female slaves were valued for other reasons than their productive capacity. It is impossible to ascertain on the basis of the *Freibrief* records the reason for these differences, but younger female slaves were probably in greater demand, because after redemption they could be more easily controlled than young men. Younger women were probably also more highly valued for their putative reproductive capacities, since after redemption they usually stayed with their redeemers. Thus it appears that under the disguise of redeeming young women some sort of small-scale clandestine female slave trade was conducted in which African men, the *Askaris* of the *Schutztruppe* and even German plantation owners, military officers, and members of the civilian administration seem to have had their share. Finally, there is some circumstantial evidence which suggests that younger female slaves conferred higher social prestige on their redeemer than young men.[29]

As to the question who redeemed slaves, five distinct groups can be identified. About half of the 662 'freed' slaves in this category were redeemed by Europeans, mostly German nationals (see Table 6). The other half were either redeemed by Africans, by the so called Arabs, and a few by people of Indian origin. Only a small number of slaves redeemed themselves. Such cases constituted less than ten per cent of all the redemptions in the *Freibrief* records in the 1893–96 period, though their numbers may have been higher as occasionally the name of the African redeemer was not included in the registers. European redeemers comprised

THE 'FREEING' OF THE SLAVES IN GERMAN EAST AFRICA   123

two plantations, two priests acting on behalf of the Catholic Missions in Bagamoyo and Lindi, and a number of individuals, mostly members of the civil administration.

The largest single group of slaves was redeemed by the manager of a coffee plantation called Nguelo in the vicinity of the Usambara mountains in 1895. Sixty-one slaves of all age groups (30 women and 31 men) were redeemed from an almost equal number of different slave owners. The plantation paid 55 Rupees for each female slave and 50 Rupees for male slaves. This was not a very large sum of money considering that domestic servants usually received wages of 8 to 12 Rupees per month from their European employers at that time. The 'freed' slaves were supposed to work for 18 months on the plantation, after which they would receive their *Freibriefe*. In this period food and shelter would be provided by the plantation. Interestingly, in this case, at the time of their redemption all the 'freed' slaves already lived on the plantation. This suggests that the plantation owner had previously rented slaves from slave owners and now redeemed them in order to turn these slaves into his permanent wage labour force. A year later, the plantation redeemed another 60 slaves, 26 men and 34 women, most of whom belonged to the 15–25-year age group and none of whom had previously lived on the plantation. In both 1895 and 1896 the great majority of the 'African' and 'Arab' owners had only sold one or at most two slaves to the plantation.[30]

A further 40 slaves (14 women and 26 men) were redeemed by G. Rowehl who owned rubber plantations near Lindi and Mikindani. The 'freed' slaves comprised all age groups and apparently already lived on the plantation. Unfortunately little more is known about this transaction. Thus, all in all 161 slaves were explicitly redeemed by plantation owners in the period from 1893 to 1896. There may have been a few unrecorded or unidentified cases, but the overall picture shows that about half of the slaves redeemed by Europeans and about a quarter of all redeemed slaves were ransomed in order to employ them on European owned plantations (see Table 6). Even assuming that there might have been a handful of cases in which European plantation owners had not been recorded as redeemers in the *Freibrief* registers, it seems implausible to argue that redemption was a means by which the European plantation owners solved their perennial labour shortage problems.[31] First, the number of slaves redeemed by the European plantations was too small in comparison with the total workforce employed by them, even at that early stage of the development of the European-owned plantation sector. Secondly, large scale redemption by plantations seems to have been limited to the coastal area and a few individual plantation owners. It was thus a local phenomenon and not a general pattern.

124 SLAVERY AND COLONIAL RULE IN AFRICA

On the whole, European redeemers preferred male slaves to female slaves in contrast to other redeemers, though the difference between them and other redeemers in this respect is less pronounced than might be expected. It is also noteworthy that Europeans usually paid higher prices, especially for female slaves, than other redeemers. Missionary redemption constituted a special case of European redemption. In 1895 the Catholic mission in Lindi redeemed 60 male and eight female slaves, most of whom were less than ten years old. To the great embarrassment of the mission, some of these boys had to be given back to their parents, since it turned out that they had been enslaved by some local entrepreneurs for the purpose of obtaining redemption money from the mission.[32]

One intriguing aspect of the *Freibrief* records concerns the origin of the slaves who received a *Freibrief* in the coastal districts. Although – as has been pointed out above – there might be a negative bias in the records concerning the number of slaves who were born in the location of their certification, the overall picture is probably correct. It appears that the coastal towns with large slave populations depended on different long distance trade routes for the supply of their slaves. These can be divided into a northern and a southern half, each representing different local and long-distance trade systems. In the northern part of the coast, place and ethnic names recorded in the registers (for instance, Masai, Bagamoyo, Pangani) suggest that many 'freed' slaves were born in the town where they received their *Freibrief* (Tanga, Bagamoyo, Pangani) or in nearby villages (such as Kaule) and neighbouring areas, but the majority of them came from areas adjacent to the great nineteenth century northern and central trade routes. According to the records, these 'imported' slaves were born in Tabora or Ujiji or were said to come from 'Manyema' country, a geographically imprecise name for a vast area in the eastern Congo (formerly Zaire), which borders on the western shores of Lake Tanganyika. Similarly, in southern towns, many slaves who were 'freed' in Lindi, Kilwa and Mikindani were locally born or born in the vicinity (for instance in the case of Lindi on the Makonde Plateau), but the majority were said to have come either from 'Nyassa', again an imprecise name for a vast area bordering Lake Malawi or from Yao country in what is today Mozambique.[33]

According to the *Freibrief* records there was thus little crossover between the northern and southern slave supply systems. In this respect it is noteworthy that most of the slaves who received *Freibriefe* in Tanga and Bagamoyo because their owners resided in Pemba or Zanzibar were said to have been born near Lake Nyasa (Lake Malawi). Further evidence for the existence of two different slave supply systems is to be found in the cases in which the local district administration stopped slave caravans and issued the slaves with emancipation *Freibriefe*. Of 61 slaves freed in Bagamoyo,

TABLE 5

ISSUE OF 'LETTERS OF FREEDOM', 1893–96
Age Group / Reason for Issue / District and Gender

	BAGAMOYO			DSM			KILWA			KISAKI			LINDI			MIKINDANI			MOSCHI			PANGANI			SAADANI			TANGA			UDJIDJI			TABORA			ALL DISTRICTS			in %
	M	F	T	M	F	T	M	F	T	M	F	T	M	F	T	M	F	T	M	F	T	M	F	T	M	F	T	M	F	T	M	F	T	M	F	T	T	M	F	
1 to 5	9	10	19	15	14	29	38	27	65	0	0	0	35	15	50	12	10	22	0	0	0	0	0	0	1	2	3	26	20	46	1	3	4	0	0	0	238	137	101	6.4
6 to 10	33	32	65	45	47	92	52	42	94	0	0	0	64	30	94	31	20	51	0	1	1	4	4	8	4	2	6	14	17	31	3	0	3	0	3	3	448	250	198	12.1
11 to 15	25	29	54	36	61	97	46	37	83	3	1	4	19	14	33	43	26	69	1	4	5	11	12	23	9	3	12	16	16	32	0	1	1	5	20	25	438	214	224	11.8
16 to 20	23	86	109	43	120	163	56	82	138	0	5	5	20	46	66	25	43	68	16	16	32	16	29	45	7	7	14	50	70	120	4	0	4	19	61	80	844	279	565	22.8
21 to 25	23	55	78	13	59	72	40	93	133	0	1	1	16	28	44	14	29	43	2	1	3	12	16	28	5	10	15	34	53	87	0	0	0	6	26	32	536	165	371	14.5
26 to 30	23	39	62	17	48	65	73	121	194	0	2	2	10	22	32	9	15	24	0	0	0	6	9	15	0	4	4	28	46	74	0	0	0	4	16	20	492	170	322	13.3
31 to 35	15	13	28	8	14	22	58	57	115	1	0	1	10	15	25	11	9	20	0	0	0	2	0	2	1	1	2	27	45	72	1	0	1	0	0	0	288	134	154	7.9
over 35	7	22	29	19	40	59	93	109	202	1	1	2	10	15	25	18	10	28	0	0	0	1	1	2	1	0	1	39	28	67	1	0	1	0	0	0	416	190	226	11.2
Manu	41	99	140	30	103	133	80	113	193	0	0	0	19	32	51	34	29	63	0	0	0	4	7	11	1	5	6	50	66	116	0	0	0	0	3	3	716	259	457	19.4
Eman	81	131	212	111	182	293	325	396	721	4	7	11	33	38	71	37	40	77	19	20	39	34	34	68	20	20	40	123	153	276	5	3	8	23	86	109	1925	815	1110	52.0
Redm	11	26	37	34	41	75	31	34	65	0	2	2	101	87	188	74	77	151	0	2	2	14	30	44	2	1	3	36	48	84	5	1	6	1	4	5	662	309	353	17.9
DeO	22	23	45	3	8	11	20	24	44	0	0	0	26	22	48	3	2	5	0	0	0	0	0	0	2	3	5	24	27	51	0	0	0	10	33	43	252	110	142	6.8
MiC	2	5	7	15	64	79	0	0	0	0	1	1	0	0	0	0	0	0	0	0	0	0	0	0	3	0	3	0	0	0	0	0	0	0	0	0	90	20	70	2.4
Unkn	1	2	3	3	5	8	0	1	1	1	0	1	5	6	11	15	14	29	0	0	0	0	0	0	0	0	0	1	1	2	0	0	0	0	0	0	55	26	29	1.5
Total	158	286	444	196	403	599	456	568	1024	5	10	15	184	185	369	163	162	325	19	22	41	52	71	123	28	29	57	234	295	529	10	4	14	34	126	160	3700	1539	2161	100

Manu.: Manumission DeO.: Death of Owner
Eman.: Emancipation MiC.: Military Campaign
Redm.: Redemption Unkn.: Unknown

Source: Bundesarchiv Berlin, R.1001, Files No. 7410–7412.

TABLE 6

ISSUE OF 'LETTERS OF FREEDOM', 1893–96

Age Group / Reason for Issue / District and Gender

Age Grp	Manumission						Redemption						...recorded Redemptions by Europeans						All Reasons 1893-1896					
	Male		Female		Total		Male		Female		Total		Male		Female		Total		Male		Female		Total	
		in %		in %		in %		in %		in %		in %		in %		in %		in %		in %		in %		in %
0 to 5	20	7,7	17	3,7	37	5,2	48	15,6	13	3,7	61	9,2	22	11,6	1	0,7	23	6,9	137	8,9	101	4,7	238	6,4
6 to 10	24	9,3	36	7,9	60	8,4	91	29,4	35	9,9	126	19,0	65	34,2	6	4,2	71	21,4	250	16,2	198	9,2	448	12,1
11 to 15	26	10,0	36	7,9	62	8,7	38	12,3	50	14,2	88	13,3	40	21,1	29	20,4	69	20,9	214	13,9	224	10,4	438	11,8
16 to 20	31	12,0	113	24,7	144	20,1	65	21,0	125	35,4	190	28,7	39	20,5	64	45,1	103	31,0	279	18,2	565	26,1	844	22,8
21 to 25	40	15,4	83	18,2	123	17,2	26	8,5	49	13,9	75	11,3	11	5,8	20	14,1	31	9,3	165	10,7	371	17,2	536	14,5
26 to 30	39	15,1	78	17,1	117	16,2	19	6,1	42	11,9	61	9,3	8	4,2	12	8,5	20	6,0	170	11,0	322	14,8	492	13,3
31 to 35	33	12,7	39	8,5	72	10,1	12	3,9	21	5,9	33	5,0	4	2,1	7	4,9	11	3,3	134	8,7	154	7,1	288	7,9
over 35	46	17,8	55	12,0	101	14,1	10	3,2	18	5,1	28	4,2	1	0,5	3	2,1	4	1,2	190	12,4	226	10,5	416	11,2
Total	259	100	457	100	716	100	309	100	353	100	662	100	190	100	142	100	332	100	1539	100	2161	100	3700	100
in %	36,2		63,8		100		46,7		53,3		100		57,2		42,8		100		41,6		58,4		100	

Source: Bundesarchiv Berlin, R.1001, Files No. 7410–7412.

THE 'FREEING' OF THE SLAVES IN GERMAN EAST AFRICA   127

Tabora and Kilwa between 1893 and 1895, the majority were women under the age of 20. All of the slaves who were officially emancipated in Bagamoyo and Tabora were said to have been captured in 'Manyema' country, while those emancipated in Kilwa all came, according to the records, from Nyassa and Yao country.[34]

Another intriguing aspect concerns the age and gender composition of the 'freed' slaves. If we compare vital statistics of the slaves who were manumitted by their owners with those who were redeemed or officially emancipated, the former were considerably older (see Table 6). Moreover, redeemed younger women were generally more highly valued in monetary terms than older women. This suggests that the 'intersection between extrafamilial and intrafamilial stratification', the social interplay between slavery and patriarchy, is slightly more complicated than part of the secondary literature has so far suggested.[35] In this literature one finds the argument that since both women and slaves were socially marginal to the societies in which they lived, female slaves occupied the very bottom of the local social order. Implicit in such accounts is the assumption that gender roles and slave status reinforced each other. Yet, at least in East Africa in the 1880s and 1890s and particularly on the East African coast, gender roles as well as slave status changed during the life cycle of female slaves. Thus, the relationship between gender and slavery should rather be seen as the intersection of different sets of life chances which varied according to the age of the female slave.

Finally, in the few emancipation cases in which district officers took care to note that the slaves were 'freed' because they had fled foreign owners, the proportion of female slaves was much higher than one might expect. For instance, out of the 96 slaves whom the district office in Tanga supplied with 'Letters of Freedom' in 1893, a group of 14 slaves was clearly identified as fugitives from the neighbouring island of Pemba. In this particular case, a majority of the fugitives were men. But there were also five, mostly younger, women. While some were probably fleeing with their spouses, others fled individually or with other women, as far as one can judge from the records. This belies the stereotype of the docile female household slave. Arguably, female slaves were as eager as male slaves to 'break their chains' if and when the occasion arose, though their ability to do so was severely restricted in comparison to male slaves, not least because they often had children.[36]

Certification and the Dismantling of Slavery

The anti-slavery policy of the German colonial authorities, especially the certification of ever increasing numbers of 'freed' slaves, was primarily a

128 SLAVERY AND COLONIAL RULE IN AFRICA

means of avoiding the outright abolition of slavery in German East Africa. The colonial authorities believed that abolition would harm their immediate economic and political interests by destroying the pillar on which both the old pre-colonial economy and the new lower level political system rested – large-scale slave-ownership. In addition, slave ownership was seen as a means of social control which would prevent the emergence of a 'floating proletariat'.[37] Only towards the end of the German colonial period had the colonial economy and the local political system matured to such an extent that it appeared to at least part of the administration that it could safely sacrifice its pre-colonial, slave-owning allies.[38]

While certification was the centrepiece of German anti-slavery policy, it is an open question whether the same can be said for the long-drawn-out process which eventually led to the dismantling of slavery in German East Africa. After all, certification concerned only a minority of the slave population. According to official estimates the number of slaves in German East Africa (excluding Ruanda and Burundi) decreased from around 500,000 in 1890 to perhaps less than 160,000 in 1914.[39] Only part of this decline can be attributed to the 60,000 'Letters of Freedom' issued by the administration.

Yet these numbers are probably to some extent misleading. First, in the period concerned large-scale enslavement was vigorously suppressed within the boundaries of German East Africa. Moreover, from 1905, children born to slave parents were regarded as 'free' at least as far as the administration was concerned. Moreover, a natural decline in the resident slave population by death has to be taken into account. Thus slave owners were less and less able to replenish their dwindling stocks of slaves. For these reasons, the numerical importance of certification in relation to the total slave population increased in greater magnitude than the numbers above seem to suggest.

Secondly, and what is more important, certification was just one option for slaves who wished to leave their owners. Arguably, third-party as well as self-redemption were alternatives to flight. From the point of view of the slave owner, redemption was thus often the only way of obtaining some economic benefit from an institution which was dissolving in front of his eyes. This explains why more and more slave owners, especially the great chiefs of slave holding societies in interior areas like Tabora, apparently had an interest in having their male slaves redeemed or accepted some token-self-redemption money from their slaves.[40] Thus it appears that growth of the colonial economy, especially of the wage labour sector, was instrumental in undermining the foundation of the pre-colonial economy by offering economic opportunities for both fugitive slaves and for those who wanted to earn the money for their self-redemption.

THE 'FREEING' OF THE SLAVES IN GERMAN EAST AFRICA 129

Finally, it seems that the increasing opportunity of both self-redemption and flight influenced the relationship between slaves and their owners. There is some evidence to suggest that as opportunities for both flight and self-redemption increased, slave owners felt more and more compelled to treat their remaining slaves as second-rate clients rather than chattels.[41]

Conclusion

In this essay the question was raised why, where, and to whom *Freibriefe* were issued. Moreover, the statistical evidence was examined for what it reveals about slavery and the slave trade in East Africa around the turn of the century. It was argued that German certification policy was primarily a political means of avoiding the abolition of slavery, that the majority of slaves were 'freed' on the coast and that there were, by and large, three different groups of slaves, who received 'Letters of Freedom': those who were manumitted by their owners, those who were redeemed or redeemed themselves, and those who were officially emancipated by the local district administrator. Examination of the 1893–96 district slave registers showed that in this period the majority of 'freed' slaves were young women, most of whom had previously worked as agricultural labourers. It was also argued that younger female slaves had different life chances than older female slaves in this period.

The slave registers also reveal that the link between growth of the European plantation sector and the incidence of redemption and self-redemption is less strong than the secondary literature has suggested. In particular, it was shown that there was no direct geographic numerical connection between the location of redemption and the locations of European owned plantations and that the number of slaves redeemed by Europeans was small in comparison with the number of labourers they employed on their farms. However, it was also pointed out that growth of the colonial economy slowly undermined the power base of African slave owning elites. Finally, it was argued that records of origin of 'freed' slaves suggest that coastal slave owners obtained their slaves through two different trade systems which apparently had little in common. Unfortunately, little is known about what happened to the slaves after they received their 'Letters of Freedom'. They were regarded as 'free' by the colonial administration and thus there are no archival records dealing with them. In local memory about the dismantling of slavery, certification plays little role, probably because it was just an outward sign of the much greater social upheaval which the end of slavery had brought about.[42]

I would like to conclude this paper with an exceptional, fairy-tale like biographical sketch of a 'freed' female slave named Faida, in order to draw

130 SLAVERY AND COLONIAL RULE IN AFRICA

attention to the fact that the statistical data presented in this article describe events which for the slaves concerned was one of the most important experiences in their lives. Faida received an emancipation certificate in October 1893. According to the *Freibrief* register she was then about 14 years old and had only shortly before arrived in Dar es Salaam. Faida was born in 'Manyema'. She had been bought by Murgan, an Egyptian mercenary who very likely had been hired in Cairo by *Reichskommissar* (later Governor) H. von Wissmann in 1889 to take part in the suppression of the coastal uprising of 1889/1890. For a time they both lived in Dar es Salaam. In the early 1890s, however, these so called 'Sudanese' mercenaries were slowly phased out of the *Schutztruppe* and apparently Murgan returned first to Cairo and then to his home town of Alexandria, taking Faida with him. Faida lived with him in Cairo for one and a half years until she ran away and returned to Dar es Salaam in mid-1893. It is not known how she managed to travel from Cairo to Dar es Salaam on her own, but she apparently presented her case to the *Bezirksamtmann* von Strantz, and since she came from abroad she duly received her emancipation certificate.[43]

NOTES

1. Bundesarchiv Berlin (in the following BAB), R.1001/7410-7415, Sammlung der zur Mitteilung an das Spezialbüro in Brüssel bestimmten Nachweisungen, 1 Oct. 1892–31 May 1915. In the collection and preparation of data presented in this article I was greatly assisted by Vincent Ovaert whom I would like to thank. Of course, all remaining statistical errors are my responsibility. For an estimate of total slave population in German East Africa at the turn of the century, see J.-G. Deutsch, 'What Happened to All the Slaves? Colonial Policy, Emancipation, and the Transformation of Slave Societies in German and British East Africa (Tanganyika), c.1890–1930', *Collected Papers of the 38th Annual Meeting of African Studies Association*, Orlando, Florida, 3–6 November 1995.
2. This paper has profited from T. Sunseri, 'Slave Ransoming in German East Africa, 1885–1922', *International Journal of African Historical Studies*, 26, 3 (1993), pp.481–511, and from F. Weidner's semi-official study, *Die Haussklaverei in Ostafrika*, Veröffentlichungen des Reichskolonialamts Nr. 7, Jena 1915. The term 'Letter of Freedom', is a literal translation of the German word *Freibrief.* The term was chosen despite its highly ideological bias, because the alternative term 'Letter of Redemption' gives the impression that most slaves obtained these certificates on the basis of a commercial transaction which, as will be shown further down, was not the case. The terms 'free' and 'freedom' are highly value loaded terms. In this article they are used merely to refer to 'non-slave' status.
3. BAB R.1001/7410-7415, Sammlung der zur Mitteilung an das Spezialbüro in Brüssel bestimmten Nachweisungen, 1 Oct. 1892–31 May 1915.
4. For text, see F. Weidner, *Haussklaverei*, pp.203–209.
5. A. Leue, 'Die Sklaverei in Ostafrika', *Beiträge zur Kolonialpolitik und Kolonialwirtschaft*, 1900/01, p.608 (translation by J.-G. Deutsch). Of all colonial administrators who voiced their opinion on the question of slavery in East Africa, only Leue favoured its outright abolition.
6. Gouverneurs-Verordnung, betreffend den Freikauf von Sklaven. Vom 1. September 1891; reprinted in Weidner, *Haussklaverei*, p.203.
7. BAB R.1001/1003/81. Decree (*Runderlaß*) by Governor von Soden, 4 Sept. 1891.

THE 'FREEING' OF THE SLAVES IN GERMAN EAST AFRICA 131

8. See Generalakte der Brüsseler Anti-Sklaverei-Konferenz, nebst Deklaration vom 2. Juli 1890, Art. LXIV, published in: Kaiserliches Gouvernement von Deutsch-Ostafrika, *Die Landes-Gesetzgebung des Ostafrikanischen Schutzgebiets*, Tanga/Dar es Salaam 1911², p.56.
9. Verordnung des Reichskanzlers, betreffend die Haussklaverei in Deutsch-Ostafrika. Vom 29. November 1901, published in: Kaiserliches Gouvernement von Deutsch-Ostafrika, *Die Landes-Gesetzgebung des Ostafrikanischen Schutzgebiets*, Tanga/Dar es Salaam 1911², pp.331–2.
10. BAB R.1001/7382/27/pp.42–93. Berichte der einzelnen Verwaltungsstellen in Deutsch-Ostafrika über die Sklaverei, 1897–1901.
11. This is my main disagreement with the interpretation offered by T. Sunseri. He argued that most slaves who received a redemption *Freibrief* were in ransomed by the European owned plantations or redeemed themselves by working on these plantations as wage labourers ('Slave Ransoming', p.491). However, as will be shown further down, there is some evidence which suggests that this was not the case. Thus, his contention that *all* ransomed slaves entered the wage work force certainly needs revision.
12. See for instance, R.1001/7412/53. Nachweisung der in Kilwa im Jahre 1896 erteilten Freibriefe, 31 Dec. 1896. In this year, 226 of Abdallah bin Omari's slaves were issued with emancipation *Freibriefe* by the district officer, Freiherr von Eberstein. Abdallah bin Omari had been accused of having participated in a local resistance movement. See also the figures in Table 3, Iringa District, for the years 1897 and 1898.
13. Another reason for the decline might be that district officers took notice of a decree issued by Governor Liebert on 5 March 1899. It informed them that a new slavery ordinance would soon be enacted by the colonial authorities in Berlin (the 1901 ordinance) and until then nothing should be done which would endanger or anticipate its implementation. See R.1001/1004/184. Decree by Governor Liebert, 5 March 1899. Finally, it should be noted that apparently the number of slaves who received emancipation *Freibriefe* because their owners lived abroad (Pemba or Zanzibar) declined throughout the 1890s.
14. See BAB R.1001/7382/27/pp.42–93. Berichte der einzelnen Verwaltungsstellen in Deutsch-Ostafrika über die Sklaverei, 1897–1901.
15. This theme will be more thoroughly explored in my forthcoming post-doctoral *Habilitation* thesis 'Slavery and Abolition in German East Africa' which is in preparation as a book.
16. BAB R.1001/6286/156. Reichskolonialamt to Kolonialwirtschaftliches Komitee, 12 March 1910. According to this estimate, in 1910 European plantation and the railways employed about 50,000 Africans, mostly male labourers.
17. These figures are official estimates and they may not be very reliable. However, the direction and magnitude of the trend appears to be correct.
18. See BAB R.1001/7411/95. Verzeichnis der im Jahre 1894 im Bezirk Tanga erteilten Freibriefe. The reason for this attitude is not entirely clear, but one likely explanation is that as far as the district officers were concerned, the issuing of Brussels Act *Freibriefe* served no direct administrative purpose, since the export of slaves was in any case explicitly forbidden by law. See also BAB R.1001/7410/365. Verzeichnis der im Jahr 1893 im Bezirk Tanga erteilten Freibriefe.
19. Apart from edited volumes by Robertson and Klein and Miers and Roberts, this section of the paper has greatly profited from the works of Frederick Cooper, Marcia Wright, and Jonathon Glassman without which interpretation of the *Freibrief* records would have been almost impossible. See C. C. Robertson and M. A. Klein (eds.), *Women and Slavery in Africa* (Madison, Wisconsin, 1983); S. Miers and R. Roberts (eds.), *The End of Slavery in Africa* (Madison, Wisconsin, 1988); F. L. Cooper, *From Slaves to Squatters: Plantation Labour and Agriculture in Zanzibar and Coastal Kenya, 1890–1925* (New Haven, CT 1980); M. Wright, *Strategies of Slaves & Women. Life-Stories from East/Central Africa* (London/New York, 1993); J. Glassman, *Feast and Riots. Revelry, Rebellion, and Popular Consciousness on the Swahili Coast, 1856–1888* (London, 1995).
20. J.-G. Deutsch, 'Weidner's Slaves: A Misunderstanding in German Colonial Thought', *Working Papers*, 5 (1996), Institute of Development Studies, Helsinki.
21. BAB R.1001/7411/27. Verzeichnis der im Jahre 1894 im Bezirk Kilwa erteilten Freibriefe.
22. BAP R.1001/7411/258. Verzeichnis der im Jahre 1895 im Bezirk Dar es Salaam erteilten Freibriefe, No. 448.

132 SLAVERY AND COLONIAL RULE IN AFRICA

23. BAB R.1001/7410/385. Governor von Schele to Foreign Office, 31 May 1894.
24. On the social prestige of the various slave sub-groups see J. Glassman, *Feast and Riots*, pp.29–54 and 79–114.
25. See, for instance, BAB R.1001/4711/124. Verzeichnis der im Jahre 1894 im Bezirk Lindi erteilten Freibriefe.
26. See, for instance, Weidner, *Haussklaverei*, p.16.
27. For such a view, see for example BAB R.1001/1006/196. Memorandum 'Denkschrift über die Haussklaverei in Deutsch Ostafrika' by Governor H. Schnee, 28 Oct. 1913.
28. BAB R.1001/7412/53. Verzeichnis der im Jahre 1896 im Bezirk Kilwa erteilten Freibriefe.
29. This has been argued in the context of slavery by E. A. Alpers, 'The Story of Swema: Female Vulnerability in Nineteenth Century East Africa', in Robertson and Klein (eds.), *Women and Slavery*, pp.185–99.
30. BAB R.1001/4712/10. Verzeichnis der im Jahre 1895 in Mikidani (Bezirksnebenstelle) erteilten Freibriefe, and BAB R.1001/4712/108. Verzeichnis der im Jahre 1896 in Mikidani (Bezirksnebenstelle) erteilten Freibriefe.
31. T. Sunseri, 'Slave Ransoming', p.482 stated that over time slave redemption created a 'symbiosis between slave institutions and the colonial economy'.
32. BAB R.1001/7411/294. Verzeichnis der im Jahre 1895 im Bezirk Lindi erteilten Freibriefe.
33. Geographical and 'ethnic' names are unreliable and often misleading in the colonial records of this period. Archival versions of spelling have been retained in this article.
34. BAB R.1001/7410/331. Verzeichnis der im Jahre 1893 im Bezirk Kilwa erteilten Freibriefe; BAB R.1001/7411/43. Verzeichnis der im Jahre 1894 im Bezirk Bagamoyo erteilten Freibriefe; BAB R.1001/7411/200. Verzeichnis der im Jahre 1895 im Bezirk Tabora erteilten Freibriefe. This underlines the importance of the gender division of labour and honour in the study of African slave systems.
35. For this phrase, see Robertson and Klein, *Women and Slavery*, p.22.
36. BAB R.1001/7410/365. Verzeichnis der im Jahre 1893 im Bezirk Tanga erteilten Freibriefe.
37. For this argument see J.-G. Deutsch, 'Weidner's Slaves'. For the opposite, see Sunseri, 'Slave Ransoming', p.488.
38. This theme will be more fully explored in my forthcoming book on this subject.
39. See Deutsch, 'What Happened to All the Slaves?'.
40. F. O. Karstedt, 'Zur Sklavenfrage in Deutsch Ostafrika', *Deutsch-Ostafrikanische Zeitung*, XVI (1914) 8, 24 Jan. 1914.
41. BAB R.1001/1006/196. Memorandum 'Denkschrift über die Haussklaverei in Deutsch Ostafrika' by Governor H. Schnee, 28 Oct. 1913. For this argument, see also Sunseri, 'Slave Ransoming', p.482.
42. J.-G. Deutsch, 'Social Memories of Slavery and the Slave Trade in Contemporary Tanzania', paper presented at the School of Oriental and African Studies African History Seminar, London, 14 May 1997.
43. BAB R.1001/7410/338. Verzeichnis der im Jahre 1893 in Dar es Salaam erteilten Freibriefe, No.68.

Slavery in Colonial Cameroon, 1880s to 1930s

ANDREAS ECKERT

Introduction: Colonialism and Slavery in Cameroon

The 'slow death for slavery',[1] the complex and regionally very different ways in which slaves were emancipated during the colonial period, has received much attention in recent scholarship. So far the historiographical debate has more or less omitted the former German colonies. Among these, the issue of slavery was by far most important in German East Africa. In this territory, there were slave plantations on a major scale as well as a considerable trade in slaves, both visible to European travellers and early colonial administrators. Anti-slavery rhetoric played an important part during the colonial conquest.[2] In Cameroon, as in the other German territories[3] in Africa, slavery was never the great issue that it was in German East Africa. During the conquest of Cameroon, anti-slavery arguments only played a minor role.[4] It was the general feeling in Germany as well as among most Germans in Cameroon that slavery was no great evil in this territory and would solve itself in time.[5] The first governor, Julius von Soden, for example believed that the introduction of a money economy would result in its abolition, for Africans would soon discover that it was simpler to hire workers for the transport of goods into the interior than to rely on recalcitrant slaves.[6] In numerous other reports on slavery in Cameroon various colonial governors recommended that it was sufficient to let time pass and slavery would disappear by itself.[7] Von Soden's successor, Governor Eugen von Zimmerer, stated in 1892 that in many societies slaves were already a powerful force that masters found impossible to control. The Germans half-heartedly launched a number of ordinances against slavery and the slave trade,[8] but only occasionally made sure that these legal measures were translated into action.

Though contemporaries played down or even neglected the problem of slavery in colonial Cameroon, slavery was not a negligible quantity, but an important element of the transformation of local societies and sometimes even a factor in colonial politics. In many regions of what later became Cameroon, various forms of slavery played a critical role during the pre-colonial period.[9] Slavery remained an important feature in the early colonial

134 SLAVERY AND COLONIAL RULE IN AFRICA

period and was never seriously attacked by the Germans or by the subsequent French and British colonizers. The present article attempts to link the scattered literature on slavery in colonial Cameroon with my own research findings in order to provide an outline of a still very much under-researched topic. As will be shown, until the 1930s legal measures only had limited effects on the ground, even in coastal areas where the European presence and influence were comparatively strong. This chapter will include a discussion of legal measures and practical steps against slavery as well as an analysis of changes at the grassroots level, which were often little related to anti-slavery legislation and operation but which had a profound impact on the ground. Two regions will serve as main examples: the Littoral and Adamawa in the North of Cameroon. During the nineteenth and the first decades of the twentieth centuries, slavery was central to political, social and economic life in these areas.

Slavery in the Nineteenth Century

Various forms of slavery played a critical role in the historical development of the Duala of the Cameroon Littoral. Duala functioned as a minor but steady supplier to the Atlantic slave trade until the 1830s.[10] The Duala view of their own way of life and its relationship to outside groups is intricately bound up with conceptions of servitude. Historical evidence also makes it clear that servile groups constituted important sectors of Duala social, economic, and political organization. Slavery was an important part of a very complex precolonial system in the Littoral which Ralph Austen has accurately described as 'hegemony without control'.[11] Within nineteenth-century Duala society, slaves were at once the key element in the construction of an effective commercial organization and the exploited victims of such enterprises – exploited either indirectly through limiting their avenues of advancement, or directly as victims of petty warfare, ritual sacrifice or plunder. The slaves functioned, as Austen has put it, as 'productive capital and negotiable chattel'.[12] There were severe limits to the impositions which could be placed upon Duala slaves. By most counts slaves constituted a majority of the population in Douala throughout the nineteenth century and the only groups among them to be under close surveillance were those in relatively privileged positions as household retainers and crews of trading expeditions. The majority worked in agriculture or as auxiliary fishermen in relative autonomy from their masters. 'Household' (as opposed to 'field') slaves acted as the major agents of inland trade and other affairs where kinsmen could not as easily be relied on. Slaves in this position usually came from distant areas – in particular the Cameroon Grassfields – as children and consequently

SLAVERY IN COLONIAL CAMEROON

135

maintained no ties with their home areas, but they were still identified within Douala as a somewhat foreign element wielding considerable power. Some individuals of slave origins could rise to high positions in Duala society. The most striking example is David Mandessi Bell, a Grassfields child who was brought into the household of King Ndumbe Lobe Bell during the 1870s and eventually became a very successful entrepreneur and one of the most powerful figures in this dominant clan. His slave origins, however, prevented him from aspiring to the actual Bell chieftaincy.[13]

In the case of nineteenth-century Adamawa with its centre Ngaoundere in the North of Cameroon we are dealing with slavery on a major scale.[14] The Adamawa *jihad*, an extension of Usman dan Fodio's conquest of the Hausa states of Nigeria, was undertaken in the early nineteenth century by small groups of Fulbe who established a Muslim emirate and a number of lamidates. The Fulbe, however, were substantially outnumbered by the local 'pagan' groups of the region. Ngaoundere was no exception in this regard, and the rapid integration of conquered Mbum and other peoples into the Fulbe state, which transformed large numbers of former enemies into effective elements of the state political and economic apparatus, is remarkable. In addition to locally conquered 'pagan' peoples, the size of the servile population at Ngaoundere was further enlarged by slaves captured at distances of 200 to 500 kilometres from Ngaoundere town itself. These captives were brought back for resettlement at Ngaoundere either as domestic slaves or as farm slaves in slave villages.[15] This long-distance raiding, which was a regular occurrence from the 1850s up until the first decade of the twentieth century, was a large-scale phenomenon. European observers at the end of the nineteenth century estimated that as many as 8,000 to 10,000 slaves were taken on these raids annually. Those captives who were not settled at Ngaoundere were sold to Hausa or Kanuri traders, and Adamawa soon gained a reputation as a 'slave traders' Eldorado'.[16] By the second half of the nineteenth century, Adamawa had become the main source of supply for the Sokoto Caliphate.[17] The demographic situation at Ngaoundere in the nineteenth century can be summed up as follows: At no time following the establishment of the Fulbe state did the proportion of slaves and vassals to freemen ever fall below a one-to-one ratio, and for most of the period the ratio was probably more like two-to-one.

Whatever the exact number and proportion of slaves in the pre-colonial period, they were not all of uniform social and legal status.[18] Even among the slave population at Ngaoundere itself, there were marked variations in status. Slaves could be owned by private owners or by the state. In the case of private ownership, slaves normally performed farming or herding work or could serve as domestic slaves in the master's household. The state-ruler owned substantial numbers of farm slaves, but there was also a category of court slaves linked to the office of the ruler. Many of the latter performed domestic tasks in the ruler's compound while others served as officers in the government or military. One problematic issue with regard to the Fulbe system of slavery at Ngaoundere is the question of increasing rights enjoyed by at least some of the slaves who had been born in captivity. Some form of progressive modification of slave status was only logical in a situation where slaves might hold important public office and where, in theory at least, masters were under the obligation to convert their slaves to Islam. Although the full details of the practice are not clear, it appears that in the case of household and court slaves who had been raised as Muslims in their masters' households, their owners were morally, although not legally, barred from selling them. On the other hand, farm slaves in Ngaoundere were subject to a more severe regime, and they and their children were sold at their masters' will.

The structure of slavery in Adamawa in the nineteenth century was determined primarily by military and commercial factors. The involvement of slaves in production in Adamawa, while undoubtedly the source of much of the food on which the Fulbe states subsisted, was of relatively minor structural importance. The slave-raiding activities of Ngaoundere had their own inbuilt and self-perpetuating rationale. The majority of the slaves taken in raids were traded to other Fulbe states, and it was more as a means of exchange than as means of production that slaves constituted the principal source of Ngaoundere's wealth.

Slavery in the Cameroon Littoral during the Colonial Period

The internal traffic in slaves and domestic slavery slowly diminished with the imposition of colonial rule, but it did not cease. The influence of the authorities was limited to the coasts and around the few military posts in the interior.[19] Until the turn of the century there was no real effort on the part of the Germans to abolish the internal slave trade and slavery. Even in areas like Douala and the Littoral where the German presence and influence were comparatively strong, slavery was far from being suppressed. The German rulers of Cameroon not only hesitated to interfere with Duala slavery but for a time unwittingly encouraged its expansion. German policy up to 1902 was officially aimed at undermining slavery by indirect measures. Many Germans did not believe that legislation could or should be used to promote profound changes in the Duala social order. Theodor Seitz, the District Commissioner in Douala during the 1890s, retrospectively stated that the 'transformation of the entire native economy ... must, by itself, bring about the disappearance of slavery'.[20] The officials of the new German administrative court at Douala were willing to disturb local customs only

SLAVERY IN COLONIAL CAMEROON

when they directly affected European interests (for instance in trade); they therefore rendered numerous judgments enforcing property in slaves.[21] It was only in 1895 that Seitz announced that the government court would no longer entertain appeals for the restoration of slaves. But no such restriction was placed upon the purely African courts of first and second degree, officially established by the Germans from 1892 onward among the Duala and neighbouring peoples.[22] Moreover, an 1895 decree outlawing the internal Cameroon slave trade seems to have received little enforcement or even publicity for some years. As late as 1901 Manga Bell, the leading Duala chief, successfully persuaded the government to pardon two convicted slave traders because no native really understood that such transactions were illegal.[23]

The economic situation created by the German presence on the Cameroon coast even appears to have stimulated an increased demand for slaves among the Duala. The little data available on early colonial slave sales suggest that the demand for slaves may have gone down during the first decade of German rule but rose again around 1900. From the interior to the coast the value of a slave rose. A slave cost 5,000 cowries in Foumban and 10,000 in Bangou in 1900.[24] A slave bought among the Babimbi in 1901 valued at 6 marks was worth 50 marks further along the Ndogobesol river towards the coast, and 100 in Edea.[25] In Douala, an adult male slave cost between 100 and 160 marks, or even 200, a women 200 to 300, and a young man or a young girl half the price charged for an adult of the same sex.[26]

The shift in the internal Cameroon slave market coincided with the beginning of Duala commercial cocoa farming at the turn of the century.[27] There is some evidence that at least the early stages of Duala commercial cocoa-planting depended upon the labour of slaves. Slave settlements established by the Duala at various inland points for producing and helping with the trade in palm products were converted into centres for growing cocoa. More slaves were again purchased from the interior. Only towards the end of the German period did slave labour diminish in favour of paid workers, although this was not the result of deliberate intervention by the colonial state. When on 21 February 1902 the German colonial authorities, embarrassed by a couple of damning missionary reports on slavery and slave-dealing,[28] finally promulgated an ordinance for the gradual abolition of internal slavery in Cameroon, they presented themselves 'as virtual spokesmen for Duala institutions'.[29] The first article stated that 'the customary law established among the Duala people, whereby the children of domestic slaves are regarded as half-free, is to be applied throughout the Protectorate'. The second said that 'children born to half-free individuals after the promulgation of this ordinance are free'.[30]

These measures did not interfere much with Duala social relations. The

138 SLAVERY AND COLONIAL RULE IN AFRICA

only direct effect the German government probably could have upon servile institutions at this point was to hinder further recruitment of slaves from the hinterland. The increasing effectiveness of colonial rule in general must have made procurement of slaves far more difficult. In general, imposition of colonial rule provided new resources to the local 'bargaining process' between slaves and their Duala owners. Previously, flight was an option open only to comparatively few slaves. Desertion was extremely hazardous because of the danger of re-enslavement and of the violence this often entailed. When, however, the German colonial administration gradually undermined the coercive power of Duala slave owners and reduced the risk of re-enslavement in areas under its control, flight probably became more common. This in turn forced Duala slave owners to improve increasingly the treatment of their slaves. This was especially true of working conditions, in order to strengthen the tenuous ties of reciprocity and retain at least some measure of control over the lives of their slaves. More and more slaves obtained a greater measure of personal autonomy. When he created his first plantation, Duala chief Manga Bell faced the refusal of his slaves to plant cocoa, as it was unknown to them and its profitability compared to trade was not guaranteed.[31] Governor Jesco von Puttkamer stated in 1901 that Duala slave masters had to provide gifts in order to get their slaves to do specific work.[32] In many cases, slaves became dependent farm workers for their former owners, but this was an improvement of their former marginal social position. Oral evidence suggests that during the first decades of colonial rule, relations between master and slave still had a strong paternalistic aspect. The Duala word *sango* means father or head of the family, and this was what a slave called his Duala owner. Each slave working on a Duala plantation had some autonomy as he had the use of a patch of land sufficient to produce what he needed. Everything he could produce on his land during his leisure time belonged to him. As he would do for his own children, the *sango* paid the dowry for each of his adult slave's wives. However, the slaves' families could be dismantled at any time, notably by giving one or more members away as compensation for a debt.[33]

From 1908 on, German accounts of the Duala plantation system became more open. This may be because it had by this time become possible for Duala farmers to attract free labour. Most Duala planters employed workers who were apparently not part of their household units. Pastor Modi Din employed eight Bali people on his 60 hectares plantation near the Mungo. David Mandessi Bell, Manga Ndumbe and Paramount Chief Duala Manga employed several hundred people on their large estates. A list of Mungo plantations and their labour force compiled in October 1913 indicates that most of the workers came from traditional *bakom* groups. Bamileke are

SLAVERY IN COLONIAL CAMEROON

139

even cited as 'Bakumkum' (little slaves). But only two workers are specifically mentioned as slaves.[34] The rest of the people are listed according to their villages of origin, but that does not give a clue to their social status. All in all there is very little evidence available to reconstruct in detail the slow death of Duala slavery and the shift from slave labour to other forms of labour in the Duala agrarian enterprise.

In theory there should have been competition for labour between big German plantations around Mount Cameroon and Duala farmers: the Germans drew most of their workforce from inland regions, particularly the 'Grassfields', which had previously supplied slaves for Duala agricultural and trading efforts.[35] But the Duala do not seem to have experienced any labour problems, because they could mobilize slaves they already owned and draw upon sources of indentured labour not accessible to Europeans. Also relevant was the fact that employment on their farms offered a more attractive means for free labourers to earn cash for taxes and other purposes than the notoriously harsh German plantations, which were often regarded by Africans as a new form of slavery and on which labourers were known to die like flies.[36] Despite this enlarged Duala commercial agriculture, labour relations, especially on older plantations, kept a paternalistic ethos that recalled the period of slavery. Duala planters continued to give a plot of land to their workers, where the latter could produce what they needed for subsistence. Methods of recruitment were still far from any model of a true labour market. When they needed men, Duala planters went to a village in the interior and talked to the chief, to whom they offered presents such as soap. In exchange, the chief authorised recruitment of labourers, providing that the planters paid their head tax. Men either came alone or with their families, if they already had one, and most of them did not return home, because life on these plantations was allegedly better than in their villages of origin. Some married locally and had children who became 'Duala children', being absorbed into Duala society.[37]

World War I ended German rule in Cameroon, which was then divided into British and French Mandates. Douala and most of the Dualas' plantation areas became part of the latter. During the first decade of the mandate period, the French government consciously promoted the type of rural capitalism already practised by the Duala. Their plantations were most important for France's aim of a *mise en valeur* of the Cameroon territory, as the huge former German plantations were in British Cameroon. In the 1920s, Duala planters almost exclusively used non-Duala labour on their expanding cocoa farms. These outside labourers were not slaves, as the Protestant Mission (Société des Missions Evangéliques) asserted, but freely recruited male labourers who were fed and – irregularly – paid. The living conditions of these labourers, who still came for the most part from the former slave-recruiting areas of the Duala – the Grassfields and Bamileke Highlands – are difficult to determine. According to some French administrative reports of 1925, labourers had a tolerable existence. Later reports, however, insisted that their situation was hardly better than that of slaves.[38] In any case, the Duala planters seem to have had no difficulty obtaining manpower, probably because, as in the German period, Bamileke migrants and others preferred work on Duala plantations to work for European plantations or other European enterprises. The French came to depend far more than the Germans on direct taxation of the Cameroon population to balance the colonial budget. Duala planters initially benefited from new pressures on interior groups to enter the labour market. In this context, some contemporaries complained that the French forced labour policies enforced or at least helped to maintain slavery.[39] The French administration in Cameroon considered it necessary to explain to the Colonial Ministry in Paris that forced labour in Cameroon had nothing to do with slavery.[40]

In the Depression of the 1930s, Duala agricultural enterprise experienced a crisis from which it has never really recovered. The key reason was that the Duala, faced with falling cocoa prices, could not successfully maintain a paid working force of the size needed for their commercial farming.[41] However, there is some evidence that slavery was still a feature in Duala society in the 1920s and later. For instance, David Mandessi Bell provided in his will (probably drafted in the early 1930s) for payment for 'the children of women bought'.[42] Paramount Chief Richard Manga Bell wrote in his will that his daughter 'shouldn't be sold'.[43] In the immediate post-World War I period, French administrative reports had already stated that the only slaves still coming into Douala were young children 'adopted' into urban households, where they performed domestic tasks.[44] Informants in Douala also told me that some of their neighbours came to Douala in the 1920s as children who had been snatched in the Grassfields and then worked in the households of wealthy Duala. In this context we also have occasional complaints during the 1920s and 30s (mainly from missionaries) about the practice (not only in Douala) of old men buying girl babies at a low price and selling them when they come to maturity at a large profit.[45] Moreover, in the 1940s and 1950s the accusation of slave origin was used by Duala individuals to prevent persons of servile origin from claiming 'customary' rights to urban land plots.[46] In Duala society, the stigma of slave origin could never be fully erased. Even to this day it is considered highly impolite, even dangerous, to speak openly about the servile origins of any Douala resident, although everyone knows that a large part of the 'indigenous', i.e. Duala-speaking, population is descended from imported slaves.

Slavery in Colonial Adamawa

As to the suppression of slavery, there was even less colonial engagement in northern Cameroon. A statement by Governor von Puttkamer in his memoirs is very characteristic of German policy towards slavery in the Adamawa region: 'The German resident in Adamawa should rule as little as possible, he should leave it to the local rulers. In this context I also gave an order that the extremely mild domestic slavery should continue to exist unhindered'.[47] The recollections of Kurt von Morgen, leader of the first German expedition into Cameroon's hinterland, also offer some insight into German thinking. Morgen pointed out that slavery in Adamawa was not as cruel as most Europeans believed and was merely 'a kind of serfdom'; that slaves were happy; that masters drew their confidants from among the slave population; that the only cruel aspect of slavery was the slave raid, which ought to be stamped out; and that if a slave were set free he would regret his manumission![48]

Germany got the biggest part of Adamawa (even though its capital, Yola, fell under British rule) and a small area of Bornu.[49] All in all, there was relatively little German economic interest in this area. The main aim of the Germans was to divert part of its trade (mainly in ivory) to southern Cameroon. Hence the political and military influence of the Germans in northern Cameroon remained fairly weak, even after some successful military expeditions around 1900.[50] Although von Puttkamer in general disapproved of slavery, he claimed that it would be better for the Germans not to interfere. In a letter to Chancellor Otto von Bismarck in 1889 he asked Bismark to consider that slave owners had made free trade possible for everybody 'by subjugating the fetish-negroes, cannibals and other savages who before were completely shut off from the outside world.'[51] What is striking in von Puttkamer's arguments is his barely concealed admiration of the perceived absolutism/despotism of the Adamawa state, which – according to von Puttkamer's interpretation – had established law and order instead of an impenetrable chaos. Consequently he saw slavery as an 'admittedly somewhat cruel process of development', the fight against which should be left to the Africans.

According to the existing German anti-slavery legislation, it was part of the duty of German district officers to stop slave raids and the slave trade. But that was it. The colonial government kept to Bismarck's advice '*Noli tangere*' and when they published reports dealing with the situation in Adamawa they carefully deleted those passages where the existence of slavery was mentioned.[52] In 1907 the German district commissioner in Adamawa wrote: 'To punish each person who buys or sells a slave would mean to punish the whole of Adamawa.'[53] Governor von Puttkamer himself

142 SLAVERY AND COLONIAL RULE IN AFRICA

was convinced that slavery formed the basis of the political and economic position of the Fulbe and therefore had to be tolerated, otherwise 'they would be ruined'. Von Puttkamer also stressed that in order to promote a 'successful development' it was sufficient to stop the slave raids; according to him it would not be wise to interfere either in religious or in social matters.[54]

In view of this German policy, it is no surprise that for British Northern Nigeria, 'German Kamerun was a notorious source of slaves in the first decade of colonial rule'.[55] Adamawa had been a major source of slaves in the nineteenth century, not only for the Sokoto Caliphate but also for Borno and adjacent areas to the south and southwest. This vast region continued its traditional role under colonialism.[56] However, the numerous cases of slave trading were only recorded when the British or French in the neighbouring colonies were affected in one way or another and therefore there was a risk that the colonial administration would be accused of allowing slave dealing. In 1907 a clerk of the Royal Niger Company uncovered a lively trade in slaves from Ngaoundere to Bamun in western Cameroon whereupon the German administration reacted by cautioning the Lamido. However, the Englishman who had brought this inconvenient affair to light was criticized by the responsible German district officer Strümpel: 'As many Englishmen he doesn't take into consideration that an ancient custom such as the trading in slaves cannot be brought to an end overnight.'[57] German officials tended to turn down and even tried to make British complaints about slave dealing in German territory seem stupid. For instance, in February 1903, the British Resident in Yola wrote to his German counterpart in Garoua: 'Sir, I have the honour to inform you that slave dealing and raiding appears to be going on unchecked at Gaundri in German Adamawa where there is a large slave market. Numbers of slaves are constantly being purchased in Gaundri and brought into Yola Province. I am given to understand that the Chief of Gaundri makes periodical raids upon Sakka and neighbouring tribes for the purpose of keeping the slave market stocked'.[58] The German Resident responded in a laconic way: '... a place named Gaundri doesn't exist in German Adamawa, consequently at a place called like this there can be no slave market.' To the Governor the Resident wrote: 'Gaundri means without any doubt Ngaoundere. I have warned the Sultan Mai that he should stop slave raids and the trade in slaves.'[59] In 1906 the German district commissioner in Garoua noted with regret that there was a divergence in the views of British administrators in Northern Nigeria and the German administration in Cameroon about slavery, something which would cause constant frictions between the two colonial powers. The Germans considered the very strict British policy 'of severely punishing every trade in slaves' as 'inappropriate'. They agreed that professional slave traders

SLAVERY IN COLONIAL CAMEROON

should be punished but saw no need to proceed against 'minor cases'.[60] In essence, it is very difficult to say how much influence the German colonial regime had on slavery in Adamawa. However, it may be that slave dealing was at least made more difficult. Slave traders learned not to draw the colonial power's attention to themselves, as this would have restricted their freedom of action.

However, German northern Cameroon (especially the border area) produced even more slaves during World War I. The 'disturbed state of the Cameroons', as one British official observed, made it 'the happy hunting ground of the Hausa trader who does not care where he goes and what he deals in, provided he gets a large profit.'[61] As a result of the war, Hausa traders flocked to the Cameroons in search of slave children. In the course of the post World War I division of Cameroon into French and British Mandates, large parts of Adamawa fell under French administration and some areas or districts (those adjacent to Nigeria) were transferred to the British. The Treaty of Versailles in 1919 provided for a League of Nations which would oversee the administration of Cameroon and other ex-German territories as the representative of the international community. The agreement between Britain and France and the League over Adamawa called for the development of good administration and a speedy end to slavery and related ills. However, both French and British administrations had little impact on the ongoing slave trade in Adamawa. Especially in the British zone, slave dealing continued apace, especially in children. Kidnappings along the Cameroon frontier were reported regularly. By the mid 1920s, Adamawa local officials were more cooperative in suppressing the trade, even though children were still smuggled through for another decade at least.[62] British reports to the League of Nations in the period up to 1927 contained the encouraging news that slave dealing and slavery in Northern Cameroon were becoming extinct.[63] However, doubts must be entertained about the veracity of these reports. At least until the late 1920s, the British effort, if there was any, to abolish slavery in the Adamawa area was a failure.[64] During this period, the British needed the Fulbe 'slavocrats' to help implement and operate the colonial system. A good example of the ongoing existence of 'slavocrats' is Hamman Yaji, the District Head of Madagali. He remained a steadfast practitioner of slave raiding and continued to extend not curtail the slave regime in his district before he was removed from office by the British in 1927.[65] However, slowly but surely the quest for a workable system of local administration in the Adamawa Districts led to a more serious anti-slavery campaign. It is difficult to determine the role of the League of Nations in this development. The agencies of the League exercised a watchdog role and made recommendations to and exerted moral pressure upon Britain, but in the

144 SLAVERY AND COLONIAL RULE IN AFRICA

end, the League was never able to directly promote change. The real impetus for administrative change, which encompassed an attack on slavery, came from Britain itself. The British were anxious to further the commerce of Adamawa but recognised that unless slavery and slave raids were eliminated neither production nor exchange could flourish.[66] Similar things could probably said about French Adamawa, even though the evidence is still far too thin to establish a comparative perspective.[67] However, in spite of colonial anti-slavery efforts, slavery remained a major issue in the Adamawa region until the post World War II period. According to Froelich in 1950 there were approximately 23,000 Fulbe living in the Ngaoundere state as compared with 35,000 non-Fulbe who were still identifiable as ex-slaves or servants of the Fulbe.[68]

Conclusion

In the areas which are now Cameroon, slavery was the most important institution of labour mobilization during the pre-colonial period and remained important in many places during the first decades of colonial rule. Although it issued numerous decrees, the German colonial government was very reluctant to emancipate the slaves. Many officials seemed convinced that slavery would disappear by itself. Moreover the Germans recognized that the emancipation of slaves – especially in Adamawa – would bring significant social upheaval. Moreover, the desire to make their government in Cameroon as inexpensive as possible and to utilize cheap African labour encouraged them as well as the colonial powers who succeeded them, France and Britain, to turn a blind eye to slavery. The slow death of slavery in Cameroon was mainly unrelated to their efforts, but was primarily – as shows especially the Duala case – the result of changing economic and political conditions. However, in northern Cameroon the institution of slavery survived on a considerable scale until the 1950s.

NOTES

1. Paul Lovejoy and Jan S. Hogendorn, *Slow Death for Slavery. The Course of Abolition in Northern Nigeria, 1897–1936* (Cambridge, 1993).
2. Both archival evidence and secondary literature on slavery in German East Africa are comparatively rich, as the chapter by Deutsch in this volume demonstrates. See also Thaddeus Sunseri, 'Slave Ransoming in German East Africa, 1885–1922', *International Journal of African Historical Studies*, 16 (1993), pp.481–511; Jonathan Glassman, *Feast and Riots. Revelry, Rebellion, and Popular Conciousness on the Swahili Coast, 1856–1888* (London, 1995); Klaus J. Bade, 'Antisklavereibewegung in Deutschland und Kolonialkrieg in Deutsch-Ostafrika 1888–1890', *Geschichte und Gesellschaft*, 3 (1977), pp.31–58. For a contemporary text, see F. Weidner's very interesting semi-official study, *Die Haussklaverei in Ostafrika* (Jena, 1915).

SLAVERY IN COLONIAL CAMEROON

3. For slavery in Togo, see Donna J.E. Maier, 'Slave Labour and Wage labour in German Togo, 1885–1914', in Arthur Knoll and Lewis Gann (eds.), *Germans in the Tropics. Essays in German Colonial History* (New York, 1987). The literature on German Southwest Africa (Namibia) occasionally mentions the problem of slavery in the colonial period. Helmut Bley, *Namibia under Colonial Rule* (Hamburg, 1996, German original 1968) briefly mentions the campaign of missionaries to free slaves (p.123).

4. One of the few anti-slavery statements made in connection to the conquest of Cameroon was made by Adolf Woermann, one of the Hamburg businessmen who pushed Bismarck to annex Cameroon. Woermann argued in 1888 a debate in the Reichstag that slavery should be abolished because free workers were better workers. See *Stenographische Berichte, 7. Legislaturperiode, 4.Session, 15.Sitzung, 14.12.1888, p.305.*

5. Again, in comparison to East Africa, archival evidence in colonial Cameroon is very weak.

6. Letter v.Soden to Bismarck, 29 August 1885, quoted in Harry Rudin, *Germans in the Cameroons 1884–1914. A Case Study in Modern Imperialism* (New York, 1968 (1938)), pp.389ff.

7. *Bundesarchiv Berlin* (formerly Potsdam, hereafter BB), R. Kol. Amt 7367: Material zur Beurteilung der Sklavenfrage in den deutschen Schutzgebieten: Kamerun, 1886–1898.

8. Legislative pieces can be found in *Die deutsche Kolonialgesetzgebung. Sammlung der auf die deutschen Schutzgebiete bezüglichen Gesetze, Verordnungen, Erlasse und internationalen Vereinbabrungen*, ed. Riebow *et al.* (Berlin, 1893ff). See also Arthur Wege, 'Die rechtliche Bestimmung über die Sklaverei in den deutschen afrikanischen Schutzgebieten', *Mitteilungen des Seminars für Orientalische Sprachen*, 18, 3 (1915). For a detailed discussion of ordinances see Leonhard Harding, 'Die deutsche Diskussion um die Abschaffung der Sklaverei in Kamerun', in Peter Heine and Ulrich van der Heyden (eds.), *Studien zur Geschichte des deutschen Kolonialismus in Afrika* (Pfaffenweiler, 1995).

9. A recent issue of *Paideuma* (Vol.41, 1995) contains a number of articles dealing with slavery and slave-dealing in different regions of Cameroon in the nineteenth and early twentieth centuries.

10. 'Duala' is used here to refer to the ethnic group, 'Douala' to the city. The best account of Duala slavery is Ralph A. Austen, 'Slavery among Coastal Middlemen: The Duala of Cameroon', in Suzanne Miers and Igor Kopytoff (eds.), *Slavery in Africa. Historical and Anthropological Perspectives* (Madison, Wisconsin, 1977), pp.305–33. A slightly revised version of this article is 'Slavery and Slave Trade on the Atlantic Coast: The Duala of the Littoral', *Paideuma*, 41 (1995), pp.127–50. The following paragraphs draw heavily on Austen's work.

11. Ralph Austen and Jonathan Derrick, *Middlemen of the Cameroon Rivers. The Duala and their Hinterland, c. 1600–c.1960* (Cambridge, forthcoming).

12. Austen, 'Slavery', p.313.

13. Ibid. The *David Mandessi Bell Papers*, Douala, provide some good general information about Mandessi Bell's life and career. I thank his granddaughter, Evelyne Mandessi Bell, for giving me access to these papers. For more on Bell, see Andreas Eckert, *Grundbesitz, Landkonflikte und kolonialer Wandel. Douala 1880–1960* (Stuttgart, 1998).

14. On Adamawa slavery, see Philip Burnham, *The Politics of Cultural Difference in Northern Cameroon* (Edinburgh, 1996). For background, see among others Wendy James, 'Perceptions from an African Slaving Frontier' in Leonie J. Archer (ed.), *Slavery and Other Forms of Unfree Labour* (London, 1988), pp.131–41; Ulrich Braukämper, *Der Einfluss des Islam auf die Geschichte und Kulturentwicklung Adamauas. Abriss eines afrikanischen Kulturwandels* (Wiesbaden, 1970); Barbara Blanckmeister, *'Din wa dawla!' Islam, Politik und Ethnizität im Hausaland und in Adamaua* (Emscetten, 1989); Philip Burnham and Murray Last, 'From Pastoralist to Politician: The Problem of a Fulbe Aristocracy', *Cahiers d'études africaines*, 34 (1994), pp.313–58; Thea Buttner, 'Die sozialökonomische Struktur Adamauas im 19. Jahrhundert, in *Wissenschaftliche Zeitschrift der Karl-Marx-Universität Leipzig, Gesellschafts- und Sprachwissenschaftliche Reihe*, 15, 4/5 (1966), pp.603–26; Anthony Kirk-Greene, *Adamawa Past and Present* (London, 1958).

15. On categories of slaves, see Paul Lovejoy, *Transformations in Slavery. A History of Slavery in Africa* (Cambridge, 1991).

146 SLAVERY AND COLONIAL RULE IN AFRICA

16. Siegfried Passarge, *Adamaua. Bericht über die Expedition des Deutschen Kamerun-Komitees in den Jahren 1893/94* (Berlin, 1895), p.480.
17. Paul Lovejoy, 'Slavery in the Sokoto Caliphate' in Paul Lovejoy (ed.), *The Ideology of Slavery in Africa* (Beverly Hills, 1981), pp.201–41.
18. Philip Burnham, 'Raiders and Traders in Adamawa: Slavery as a Regional System', *Paideuma*, 41 (1995).
19. On German rule in Cameroon, see Rudin, *Germans in the Cameroons;* Karin Hausen, *Deutsche Kolonialherrschaft in Afrika. Wirtschaftsinteressen und Kolonialverwaltung in Kamerun von 1914* (Zürich, 1970); Helmuth Stoecker (ed.), *Kamerun unter deutscher Kolonialherrschaft*, 2 vols. (Berlin 1960/68).
20. Theodor Seitz, *Vom Aufstieg und Niederbruch deutscher Kolonialmacht*, Vol.1 (Karlsruhe, 1927), p.64.
21. In the *Archives Nationales du Cameroun, Yaoundé* (henceforth ANY) for the first four years of the Douala District Court, there are records of 21 cases dealing with restoration of slaves.. In one (1895/15), a defendant was forced to sell a slave for whom he had already been paid. See also Austen, 'Slavery.'
22. Gotthilf Walz, *Die Entwicklung der Strafrechtspflege in Kamerun unter deutscher Herrschaft, 1894 bis 1914* (Freiburg im Breisgau, 1981).
23. ANY FA 4, 1901/352. See also Austen, 'Slavery.'
24. J.J. Chandjou-Nganso, 'Les Bamiléké de l'Ouest-Cameroun: Pouvoirs, Economie et Société: 1850–1916', Unpublished thesis (Paris-I, 1976), Table 4.1.
25. Lauffer, 'Sklaverei und Sklavenhandel in Kamerun', *Afrika. Monatszeitschrift für die sittliche und soziale Entwicklung der deutschen Schutzgebiete*, 8 (1901), p.133.
26. For slave prices in Douala, see H. Bohner, 'Sklaverei und Sklavenhandel in Kamerun', *Evangelisches Missions-Magazin*, 37 (1893), pp.16–29; idem, 'Die Sklaverei in Kamerun', *Afrika*, 7 (1892), pp.513–21; BB R.Kol.Amt 7367: *Material zur Beurteilung der Sklavenfrage in allen deutschen Schutzgebieten, 1886–1898.*
27. We have no direct account of when and how the Duala committed themselves to extensive cocoa cultivation. Some German reports suggest a date around 1900. See Yvette Monga, 'Les entrepreneurs Duala, c.1890–c.1930' (Unpublished thesis, Aix-en-Provence, 1996); Andreas Eckert, 'Cocoa farming in Cameroon, c. 1914–c.1960', in W.G. Clarence-Smith (ed.), *Cocoa Pioneer Fronts since 1800. The Role of Planters, Smallholders and Merchants* (Basingstoke, 1996), pp.137–53.
28. See for example *Basel Mission Archives* (hereafter BM), E-2.14,17: (Missionary) Dietrich, 'Sklavenhandel und Sklaverei in Kamerun', January 1901. When the German Parliament (Reichstag) debated the issues of slavery and slave-dealing at length in 1901, the Social Democrats, probably fuelled by reports from missionaries, attacked the 'salutary neglect' of the colonial administration in Cameroon. See *Stenographische Berichte, 10.Legislaturperiode, 2.Session 1900/01*, 65.Sitzung, 11.3.1901; 71.Sitzung, 19.3.1901.
29. Austen, 'Slavery'.
30. 'Verordnung, betreffend die Haussklaverei in Kamerun', *Deutsches Kolonialblatt*, 13, 5 (1902), pp.107–8.
31. See Seitz, vol.2 (Karlsruhe, 1929), p.60.
32. BB, R.Kol.Amt 7736: 'Report von Puttkamer', 27.8.1901.
33. See interviews in Douala with Prince Rene Douala Manga Bell (5.2.1993); Maurice Doumbe-Moulongo (10.11.1992); Gaston Kingue-Jong (12.5.1992); Léopold Moume Etia (19.9.1992).
34. ANY FA 4/926: 'Report by Gardens' Officer Frommhold', 26.10.1913.
35. There is a considerable literature on German plantations and their labour recruitment. See Adolf Rüger, 'Die Entstehung und Lage der Arbeiterklasse unter dem deutschen Kolonialregime in Kamerun (1895–1905)' in Helmuth Stoecker (ed.), *Kamerun unter deutscher Kolonialherrschaft*, vol.1 (Berlin, 1960), pp.149–242; W.G. Clarence-Smith, 'Cocoa Plantations and coerced Labour in the Gulf of Guinea, 1870–1914', in Martin Klein (ed.), *Breaking the Chains. Slavery, Bondage and Emancipation in Modern Africa and Asia* (Madison, Wisconsin, 1993), pp.150–70.
36. Ralph A. Austen, 'The Metamorphosis of Middlemen: The Duala, Europeans and the

SLAVERY IN COLONIAL CAMEROON

147

Cameroon Hinterland, c. 1800–c.1960', *International Journal of African Historical Studies*, 16 (1983), pp.16ff. On forced labour, working and living conditions in Mount Cameroon plantations see various reports in BB, for example R. Kol.Amt 7813: 'Report Bezirksamtmann v. Krosigk', 16.12.1908; R.Kol.Amt 3232: 'Report Dr. Pfister' Sept. 1913; see also numerous reports of Basel Mission, for example BM E-2.17: 'Kamerun 1904 I.' Mark W. DeLancey, 'Health and Disease on the Plantations of Cameroon, 1884–1939', in Gerald W. Hartwig and K. David Patterson (eds.), *Disease in African History. An Introductory Survey and Case Studies* (Durham, NC, 1978), pp.153–79; W.G. Clarence-Smith, 'Plantation versus Smallholder Production of Cocoa: The Legacy of the German Period in Cameroon', in Peter Geschiere and Piet Konings (eds.), *Itinéraires d'accumulation au Cameroun* (Paris, 1993), pp.187–216.

37. Interviews in Douala with René Douala Manga Bell (5.2.1993); Emilien Bell (21.9.1992); Maurice Doumbe-Moulongo (10.11.1992); Isaac Eyobé Essawe (12.11.1992); Henri Manga (1.12.1994); Léopold Moume-Etia (19.9.1992).
38. For further details, see Eckert, 'Cocoa-farming'.
39. Raymond Leslie Buell, *The Native Problem in Africa*, Vol. 2 (New York, 1928); Léon Kaptué, *Travail et Main d'Oeuvre au Cameroun sous Régime Français, 1916–1952* (Paris, 1986).
40. Archives Nationales, Section d'Outre-Mer, Aix-en-Provence (hereafter ANSOM), Affaires Politiques 2689/1: 'Commissaire Cameroun to Ministre des Colonies', 21.8.1926; 2689/5: idem to idem, 18.6.1928. It is difficult to clearly delineate the connections between slavery, forced labour, French policy and the pressures from the League of Nations. More work is needed on these complex issues.
41. See Eckert, 'Cocoa farming'; Austen, 'Metamorphosis'.
42. Archives David Mandessi Bell, Douala.
43. BB R.Kol. Amt 4431: Will Richard Manga Bell', 6.7.1932.
44. ANY APA 11282: 'Douala administration to Government Yaoundé', 25.12.1922.
45. ANSOM, Série géographique Togo-Cameroun, C.30, Dos.271: Ministre des Colonies to Directeur de la Congrégation des Pères du St. Esprit, n.d. (April 1934); Buell, *Native Policy*, vol.2, p.314.
46. See for example *Archives Service Provincial des Domaines du Littoral, Douala*. Dossier Litre Foncier 1109: 'Tribunal du Deuxième Degré de Douala. Jugement N.70, 26.7.1951'; Dossier Titre Foncier 1415: 'Tribunal du Deuxième Degré de Douala. Jugement N. 55/54, 20.5.1954. See also Eckert, *Grundbesitz*, ch.5.
47. Jesco von Puttkamer, *Gouverneursjahre in Kamerun* (Berlin, 1912), p.307.
48. Curt von Morgen, *Durch Kamerun von Süd nach Nord. Reisen und Forschungen im Hinterlande, 1889–1891* (Leipzig, 1893). For similar judgments of other German travellers, army officers and administrators, see Eldridge Mohammadou, 'Les sources de l'exploration et de la conquête de l'Adamawa et du Bornou allemand (1893–1903): Passarge, Dominik, Bauer' in A.S. Kanya-Forstner and Paul E. Lovejoy (eds.), *The Sokoto Caliphate and the European Powers, 1890–1907* (Stuttgart, 1994), pp.37–66 (*Paideuma*, vol.40).
49. For diplomatic details, see Albert Wirz, *Vom Sklavenhandel zum kolonialen Handel. Wirtschaftsräume und Wirtschaftsformen in Kamerun vor 1914* (Zürich, 1972); Monika Midel, *Fulbe und Deutsche in Adamaua (Nord-Kamerun) 1809–1916. Auswirkungen afrikanischer und kolonialer Eroberung* (Frankfurt am Main, 1990); Martin Z. Njeuma, *Fulani Hegemony in Yola (Old Adamawa) 1809–1902* (Yaoundé, 1978). On slavery in Yola, see excellent article by Catherine VerEcke, 'The Slave Experience in Adamawa: Past and Present Perspectives from Yola (Nigeria)', *Cahiers d'Études Africaines*, 34 (1994), pp.23–53.
50. Albert-Pascal Temgoua, 'L'Hégémonie allemande au Nord-Cameroun de 1890 à 1916' (unpublished thesis, Yaoundé, 1990).
51. BB, Nachlass von Puttkamer, 8: 'Report von Puttkamer to Bismarck', 15.5.1889.
52. ANY FA 1/67: 'Annual Report Adamawa-Bornu 1905/06; FA 1/68: 'Annual Report Adamawa-Bornu 1906–07'.
53. BB R.Kol.Amt 6580: 'Manuscript of Annual Report for Cameroon 1906–07', incl. 'Annual Report Adamawa'.

148 SLAVERY AND COLONIAL RULE IN AFRICA

54. BB R.Kol.Amt 3308: 'Report Von Puttkamer on his expedition to Lake Chad in 1903', 7.4.1904. His remarks on slavery were not included in the version of the report subsequently published in the *Deutsches Kolonialblatt*.
55. Lovejoy and Hogendorn, *Slow Death*, p.267.
56. Information about enslaved people during this period is given in Gudula Kosack, 'Aus der Zeit der Sklaverei (Nordkamerun). Alte Mafa erzählen', *Paideuma*, 38 (1992), pp.177–94; Brian L. Oswald, 'Vers la Libération. R.P. Jean Bocquene et les Kwanja', unpublished manuscript (Nyamboya, 1994); Emily A. Schultz, 'From Pagan to Pullo: ethnic identity change in Northern Cameroon', *Africa*, 54 (1984), pp.46–64.
57. BB R.Kol.Amt 4229: 'Monthly Report Adamawa-Bornu, July to mid-August 1907'.
58. ANY FA 1/74: 'Angebliche Duldung von Sklavenjagden des Lamidos Mai von Ngaoundere durch die deutschen Behörden. Britischer Protest und deutsche Antwort', 20.2.1903.
59. Ibid.
60. ANY FA 1/67: 'Annual Report Adamawa-Bornu', 1905–06.
61. Quoted by Lovejoy and Hogendorn, *Slow Death*, p.267.
62. Ibid.
63. See various *Annual Reports to the Council of the League of Nations on the Administration of the Cameroons under British Mandate.*
64. Richard A. Goodridge, 'The Issue of Slavery in the Establishment of British Rule in Northern Cameroon to 1927', *African Economic History*, 22 (1994), pp.19–36.
65. Anthony Kirk-Greene and James Vaughan (eds.), *The Diary of Hamman Yaji. Chronicle of a West African Ruler* (Bloomington, Indiana, 1995).
66. Richard Goodridge, 'Slavery, Abolition and Political Reform in Northern Cameroons to 1937', in *Identifying Enslaved Africans. The 'Nigerian' Hinterland and the African Diaspora*, Proceedings of the UNESCO/SSHRCC Summer Institute, York University, Toronto, 14.7.–1.8.1997, pp.649–63.
67. For an overview on French administration, which ignores the problem of slavery, see Daniel Abwa, 'The French administrative system in the lamidate of Ngaoundéré, 1915–1945', in Martin Z. Njeuma (ed.), *Introduction to the History of Cameroon in the Nineteenth and Twentieth Centuries* (London/Basingstoke, 1989), pp.137–69.
68. J.C. Froelich, 'Le Commandement et l'Organisation Sociale chez les Foulbé de l'Adamawa', *Études Camerounaises*, 45–6 (1954), p.25; Akam Motazé, 'Contribution à l'étude sociologique du milieu rural dans le Nord du Cameroun' (Unpublished thesis, Yaoundé, 1984), pp.60–61.

The Administration of the Abolition Laws, African Responses, and Post-Proclamation Slavery in the Gold Coast, 1874–1940

KWABENA OPARE-AKURANG

This is a study of the administration of abolition laws and the emancipation of slaves in the Gold Coast between 1874 and 1940. The question has been the subject of considerable discussion. Robertson's case study of post-proclamation female slavery in Accra shows that the courts failed to act as an engine of freedom and sheds light on the demographics of the slaves who used the courts.[1] McSheffrey has argued that there was significant slave flight after the proclamation of emancipation and suggests that the courts were instrumental in freeing slaves.[2] Dumett and Johnson disagreed, arguing that the impact of the abolition was inconsequential and that the courts remained marginal to the freeing of slaves.[3]

The administration of the abolition laws remains a lacuna. The literature concentrates on the number of slavery cases dealt with by the courts, rather than on an assessment of how the abolition laws were administered and their relevance to emancipation.[4] More attention has been paid to the Colony, the coastal enclave that had contact with the Europeans from the fifteenth century, than to the Protectorate, the interior regions first brought under European rule in the late nineteenth century. In the Colony, British law applied and slavery was illegal, whereas in the Protectorate it was not outlawed, but merely lost its legal status.[5] However, the boundaries between the Colony and Protectorate were not defined until 1901. In that year, the Protectorate was merged with the Colony and slavery should have become illegal, but as will be seen, practice and theory were very different in southern Ghana. Existing studies have concentrated on the last three decades of the nineteenth century, essentially, the period of conquest.[6] Very little is known about the early decades of the twentieth century, that is, the period of consolidation of colonial rule. In addition to filling these gaps, I discuss administration of the abolition ordinance and have reevaluated the total number of slaves, who utilized the courts as avenues of freedom. Lastly, I examine the responses of African slave-holders and dealers to the implementation of abolition laws.

150   SLAVERY AND COLONIAL RULE IN AFRICA

I argue that implementation of abolition laws was largely confined to the Colony and those areas of the Protectorate, where Christian missions operated. I agree with Dumett and Johnson that abolition laws were erratically administered,[7] but this was truer in the Protectorate than in the Colony. From 1874 to 1940, there were three periods of vigorous enforcement. The first was just after the abolition in 1874.[8] The second was in 1889–90 when reports submitted separately by Inspector R.E. Firminger and the London-based Aborigines Protection Society (APS) alleged that slavery was widespread in the Gold Coast.[9] The most productive period, however, was in response to the pressures from international anti-slavery groups and the Colonial Office between the late 1920s and 1940.[10]

Abolition laws were vigorously administered only when the Colonial Office and anti-slavery groups in Britain pressured the colonial government into action. Flaws in the administration of the abolition laws partly accounted for post-proclamation slavery. I reject the suggestion that the initial surge in the use of the courts occurred in the Protectorate.[11] In the Protectorate it was limited to centres of missionary activity. I take issue with the existing literature which argues that slaves usually used the courts in the Colony in their quest for freedom. Even in the Colony, the courts failed to assist freed slaves in adjusting to freedom. This explains their return to forms of bondage and dependency, and not, as others have maintained, the benignity of slavery or the generosity of holders.[12] Thus I agree with Suzanne Miers that 'the [abolition] ordinances remained very largely a dead letter in [indeed, I would add, from] the 1880s'.[13] I reject the assertions of Dumett and Johnson that the British vigorously pursued the elimination of servile institutions in 1911.[14] This happened only from the late 1920s.

The Abolition Act

On 21 August 1874 the Earl of Carnarvon, Secretary of State for Colonies, asked Governor Strahan to consult his 'Law Officer' – Sir David Chalmers – on the legalities entailed in the proposed emancipation.[15] Carnarvon further ordered that emancipation should follow the British-Indian model[16] and suggested that compensation, self-redemption and emancipation by degrees should be considered. He authorized Strahan 'to prepare at once for an early declaration that all children born after the end of this year [1874] shall be born free.'[17] In his reply of 19 September 1874 Strahan outlined several proposals that were not markedly different from those proposed by Carnarvon.[18] They included 'immediate prohibition of slave-dealing in every form' and the rule that 'no court, English or native shall give effect to any right or claim affecting personal liberty'. This meant that legally slaves would not have to go to court for their freedom and their holders could not

SLAVERY IN COLONIAL SOUTHERN GHANA   151

reclaim them.[19] The Ordinance was to apply to the Gold Coast Colony and the 'Protected Territories'. It also stated that henceforth slaves who entered the Protectorate and the Colony would be automatically free.[20] Thus Strahan's policy sought modification of servile institutions rather than their elimination.[21]

The colonial court system, dating back to the 1850s, was revamped in 1876,[22] but very little is known about which courts administered abolition laws. Indeed, special courts were assigned to deal with slave dealing, 'matters open for summary jurisdiction in minor offences being given to Magistrates and Commandants, major offences being triable in the Supreme Court of the Colony'. In the Protectorate slave cases could 'be tried before whatever Tribunal' might 'be from time to time for all reasons the most eligible'.[23] Initially, the maximum penalty for 'aggravated cases' or 'repeated offenses' was five years but it was later changed to seven years, and fines could be imposed 'either in addition to or in place of any term of imprisonment'. Most important, the abolition laws excluded the chief's court from adjudicating slavery cases since 'it may be expected that their [chiefs] sympathies would be more with the offenders than with the law, and that trials by them would frequently be illusory'.[24] Also although the abolition ordinance did not provide for witnesses and jurors[25] they actually took part in slavery cases.[26]

The operation of the abolition ordinance was stagnant and erratic until the late 1920s, when pressure from foreign anti-slavery societies led to revisions, making it more viable as an instrument of legal status abolition. First, there was the Slave-dealing Abolition Ordinance of 1928 that strengthened the previous Ordinance.[27] Second, the 'Reaffirmation of the Abolition of Slavery Ordinance, 1930' clearly stated that 'slavery in any form whatsoever was unlawful and that the legal status of slavery did not exist'.[28] The same year, Ashanti Ordinance No. 10 of 1930 and Northern Territories Ordinance No. 6 made the same declaration.[29] Similarly, in 1932, the northern section of British mandated Togoland, the Krepi region, which had been a major source of slave supply, came under the 'law for the time being in force in the Protectorate'.[30] Lastly, the Ordinance Extension Ordinance, 1935, unified the Ordinances for the Northern Territories and Asante with that of the Colony, thus streamlining abolition policy for whole of what is now Ghana.[31]

The Legal System: Operation and Obstacles

After the abolition of 1874–75, Strahan met with the Chiefs of the Central and Western Provinces at Cape Coast to announce the abolition laws. Later, he also toured the Eastern Districts. Further dissemination of the abolition

152 SLAVERY AND COLONIAL RULE IN AFRICA

laws had to wait until 1888, when Governor Brandford Griffith instructed District Commissioners (DCs) to put up notices in the Colony to bring abolition laws to the attention of the inhabitants. These instructions were published in the Government *Gazette* of 30 June, 1888 and again on 29 June 1889. Lastly, on 14 July 1890, a circular was issued ordering all DCs to vigorously enforce the abolition laws, paying particular attention to 'apprenticed' children.[32] In spite of these efforts, slaves seem to have been poorly informed about their rights. They would doubtless have benefited from a greater effort to publicize the ordinance. There were slaves who knew about the abolition ordinance, yet could not make sense of it.[33] The Basel Missionary, Zimmerman, predicted that the Proclamation would only become known by degrees in the more distant parts of the Colony.'[34] This was also true for remote parts of the Protectorate.[35] Dumett and Johnson have emphasized the lack of literacy of slaves as a roadblock to their utilizing the courts,[36] but the problem partly lay with the inept dissemination of the abolition ordinance.

Most scholars writing on the question attribute slow implementation to indifferent attitudes of colonial officials towards slavery.[37] Johnson's model of 'Attitudes' towards slavery and how they allowed the perpetuation of slavery is insightful.[38] While abolition policy was being formulated and throughout the period of its implementation, colonial officials wrote reports claiming that servile institutions were benign. Consequently, they favoured gradual abolition instead of systematic and rigorous enforcement of the abolition ordinance.[39] Lesser officials also made variations of this argument throughout the post-abolition period. Many examples can be gleaned from responses of the DCs to Firminger's report in 1889–90.[40] As late as 1930, when they came under pressure from anti-slavery societies, colonial officials held tenaciously to the view that slavery was benign.[41]

Another important explanation is the paucity of colonial officials.[42] In the Gold Coast, there was a shortage of colonial officials with professional legal training and experience throughout the colonial period.[43] As the political structures of the colonial state developed, the onus of implementing the abolition ordinance devolved on the DCs. The DC's court was solely responsible for adjudicating cases of slavery from the late 1870s.[44] It is not clear how many DCs were available at the moment of the abolition, but only four colonial officers, namely Governor Strahan, Dr V.S. Gouldsbury, Captain E. Lees, and Sir David Chalmers were administrators of the abolition ordinance from its inception to the late 1870s.[45]

The paucity of colonial officials was highlighted in 1875, when the Basel missionaries in Akyem Abuakwa wrote that 'there should be colonial officials posted to every interior tribe – this would make an end to the godless misconduct of the constables'.[46] Similarly, in 1876, Governor

SLAVERY IN COLONIAL SOUTHERN GHANA 153

Stanford Freeling admitted that administering law and order in the 'interior districts of the Protectorate' had been hampered by the lack of 'resident commissioners'.[47] Three years later, the Colonial Office endeavoured 'to find a barrister who will be willing to go to the Gold Coast Colony for months in aid [sic] and in cleaning off the arrears in the courts'.[48] No one came forward, and by 1882, 'the magisterial work of the Colony is as a rule done by the Constabulary Officers.' Consequently, Administrator A. Moloney set up a commission to report on the efficacy of their 'legal work'.[49] Again, in 1883, the APS, quoting from their 'correspondent' on the Gold Coast, complained to the Colonial Office, that

> The false economy of our Government is certainly detrimental to the interests of justice and to ... the administration of the law. Young and inexperienced Constabulary Officers without the slightest pretensions to any knowledge of the law or any attempt to study it, are appointed to act as magistrates.[50]

Also in 1891, Governor Griffith explained that the Colony and the Protectorate covered an area of not less than 38,685 square miles with a seaboard of 350 miles and a population of at least 1,500,000, composed of different ethnic groups, who 'speak different languages',[51] and concluded:

> [W]hile the staff of European District Commissioners now on the coast, owning to the vicissitudes of sickness, leave, and vacancies, consists of only six officers, and in no circumstances, with the strength which is as yet provided for could there be more than eight such Commissioners present at one time in the Colony ... in addition to their judicial and executive functions as magistrates, these officers are charged with the fiscal and political supervision of their districts.[52]

During the first decade of the twentieth century, the number of European and African administrators increased, and the work of the DCs became purely administrative, devoid of the legal work that had encumbered it in the past. By 1905, there were Detective Branches at Accra, Cape Coast, and Sekondi, all coastal towns. Accra had the highest number of detectives with the most superior ranks. This is perhaps reflected on the statistics for crime for 1905, which recorded four slave-dealing cases in Accra and one at Cape Coast.[53] Reinforced by additional personnel, provincial courts began to assume responsibility for administering the abolition ordinance. However, this did not bring any marked change in their administration. The First World War again decreased the available number of officers, as they were needed for wartime duties. In 1915, for example, Governor Hugh Clifford explained that out of 95 officers, 25 were on military duties, and that since 1 January 1914, about one-third of the 25 officers were on leave at any

154

given time.[54] In addition, the high death rate from the influenza pandemic in the post-war years reduced the number of colonial officials, both African and European.[55] Thus eradication of servile institutions was hampered by a staff woefully inadequate in numbers and experience.

Thus British resources were stretched to the limit in the Gold Coast. Shortage of colonial officials limited the geographical extent of British administration and led to a policy of conciliation towards the Protectorate states, thereby facilitating slavery there.[56] It was also the chief reason that enforcement of abolition laws was confined to the Colony until the early decades of the twentieth century.[57] Until the 1880s, the colonial government tacitly supported the Basel Mission in its struggle to emancipate slaves and pawns in Akyem Abuakwa.[58] Colonial policy was to 'maintain political peace in the country at any price'.[59] There was a similar British policy in the Praso and Voltaic regions.[60] This made it possible for slave-dealers to continue to bring slaves into the Gold Coast from the interior ports of trade well into the early twentieth century.[61] Allowing slavery to thrive in the Protectorate permitted it to survive in the Colony.

In the coastal region, where there were more colonial officials, the abolition ordinance was arbitrarily administered because of poor coordination between DCs and the legal department.[62] This led, according to the APS, to an influx of slave children into the Gold Coast, as

> owners, as they are now under no fear of being punished, and believe that all risks of having their slaves taken away from them by the Government and liberated have terminated.[63]

We have noted that the abolition ordinance excluded the indigenous rulers from adjudicating slavery cases. Whether, the indigenous rulers, who were slave-holders, would have been effective agents of abolition is debatable. As agents of colonial rule, they were forced to do many things against their will. Therefore, it is the ordinance that excluded them that has to be called into question, but not the proposition that as slave-holders, they would have undermined its application. In 1876, for example, a relative of a slave approached King Sakitey of Krobo to obtain his freedom; however, King Sakitey unequivocally advised him that he 'had better gone to see the Commandant'.[64] In fact, the need for the inclusion of chiefs was recognized as early as 1875 by Carnarvon. Commenting on the extent of British territoriality and the abolition ordinance, he advised that 'native courts should be regulated' to revamp the abolition ordinance.[65] Similarly in 1877 and 1882, Governors Freeling and Samuel Rowe respectively harped on this, and pointed out the importance of empowering the indigenous rulers to administer the abolition ordinance.[66] Again, in 1890, Acting Governor Hodgson recommended to the Colonial Office that 'a portion of the fines

SLAVERY IN COLONIAL SOUTHERN GHANA

inflicted in any cases of slave-dealing... may prove an inducement to them [chiefs] to be more active in the matter [abolition].'[67] Despite these useful insights, successive colonial governments did not come up with cogent policies to involve indigenous elites in the abolition process.

Yet another weakness in the administration of the abolition ordinance was the failure of the courts to establish any systematic and coherent policies to assist freed slaves in their transition from bondage to freedom. For years, courts often returned freed and deserting slaves to their holders.[68] Between March and April 1890, for example, three such cases resulted from incompetence and the complicity of colonial officials.[69] Governor Griffith's detailed rebuttal of the APS's criticism against him for releasing a court-freed slave-girl to her former holder is revealing. He explained that slave children, when freed, had no means of survival. The only remedy was to give such 'freed' slaves back to their 'former' holders as apprentices. 'Apprenticeship' or custodial care was the placing of freed slaves and pawns into the care of former holders, Christian missions, and families, both African and European.[70] In theory, 'apprenticeship' was premised on a long term basis to equip the apprenticed freed slave with skills to enable him/her to make a successful transition from slavery to freedom. But in practice, apprentices became a source of cheap labour in lieu of their upkeep. It must be emphasized that some of the 'apprenticeship' practices defy categorization. They included returning court-freed slaves to their blood relatives, releasing court-freed slaves to their former holders, keeping court-freed slaves as 'servants' with colonial officials, and marrying off freed slaves to colonial soldiers.[71] When Governor Griffith released the court-freed slave to her former holder, it unleashed 'other applications for the retention of children by the persons who had bought them and had been fined by the Commissioner.'[72] As the APS proclaimed, such laxity in the administration of the abolition ordinance only served to perpetuate slavery.[73] The number of freed slaves and pawns placed in 'apprenticeship' is difficult to gauge. The colonial prisons and major administrative centres were located along the coast; therefore, 'apprenticeship' tended to exist there.

Freed slaves who were not returned to their former owners, but became 'apprenticed' wards of the colonial government, did not fare better. Some court-freed slaves, mostly children, were placed in the custodial care of prison matrons and warders.[74] This practice does not appear in the records until 1889–90. It is difficult to determine how widespread this was in the earlier decades. However, the evidence shows that it took place in the Colony; even some slaves freed in the interior were sent to Accra to be placed in the care of the government.[75] The prisons lacked facilities to help slaves in their transition from bondage to freedom. As it happened, some prison officials clandestinely returned freed slaves in their custody to their

156 SLAVERY AND COLONIAL RULE IN AFRICA

former holders.[76] Indeed, the fate of the freed slaves depended on the disposition of the court and prison officials rather than pragmatic colonial policies, hence the failure of the 'apprenticeship' policy.

Slaves and the Use of the Courts

It is difficult to calculate the number of slaves who utilized the courts in their quest for freedom.[77] Not all sources indicate figures and some are scattered in different sources. Some archival documents are not legible. The figures presented here are not foolproof, but they are sufficient to enable us to revise the numbers, and more importantly, to help in deciphering how the abolition laws operated.

As soon as abolition was proclaimed, relatives of slaves used the courts to free them. Chalmers detailed report on the responses to and impact of abolition, written five months into abolition, revealed that:

> Very numerous instances have occurred, and are still occurring, of persons seeking the intervention of the Courts to aid them in removing their relations from distant parts of the country, where they may be domiciled, and conveying them to the locality where their tribe or family has it [sic] home.[78]

We cannot determine the size of the slave population at the time of abolition or the number freed by the courts, but the nature of the 'persons seeking the intervention of the Courts' was noted by Chalmers:

> Cases of this nature constituted at least nine-tenths of all that have occurred in connection with the emancipation scheme, and deserve a word or two special remark, throwing, as they do, a curious light on the internal history of the Gold Coast.[79]

The internal history is a reference to 'the various petty wars of the Protectorate' during which 'prisoners have been made and taken off to the country of the captors who has either retained them... or sold them off to a person of greater wealth.'[80]

As noted earlier, McSheffrey identified slaves' use of the courts during the early phase of abolition in the Protectorate.[81] This is based on Chalmer's report which referred to 'distant parts of the country', 'different parts of the country', and the 'Protectorate'.[82] In general, geographical images in the Chalmer's report point vaguely to the Protectorate as a whole. However, the Basel Mission report mentions only areas in the Protectorate, namely Akwapim, Krobo, and Akyem, where there was a strong colonial and missionary presence.[83] Indeed, for most of the Protectorate, there were neither colonial courts nor enough personnel to attempt to free slaves.

SLAVERY IN COLONIAL SOUTHERN GHANA

Apart from the initial, popular utilization of the courts as a vehicle of freedom, Robertson has calculated that between 1874 and 1918, there were 131 court cases in Accra which dealt with slave dealing. Her figures are low and she is right in stating that some cases were not recorded.[84] In 1891 Governor Griffith indicated in his report to the Colonial Office that not all cases were recorded in the court books.[85] Other data indicates that in the Colony there were 307 slave-dealing cases from 1885 to 1889.[86] In addition, during the first seven months of 1890, there were 106 cases with 76 convictions, representing nine district centres in the Colony and three in the Protectorate.[87] Of these, 23 cases with 18 convictions were for the Accra district. The high figure of 106 and the 72 per cent rate of conviction was a result of pressure by Governor Griffith on the DCs in 1888–89 to enforce the abolition ordinance. He also instructed DCs to put up notices in the Colony to bring the abolition laws to the attention of inhabitants.[88]

For the early twentieth century, the Annual and Departmental Reports are significant statistical sources. Dumett and Johnson report an annual average of 29 slave-dealing convictions for the Colony and Protectorate between 1903 and 1911.[89] However, my total figure of 187 for the period 1903–1908 has an annual average of 31 court cases.[90] Further, Dumett and Johnson, reveal that there were about 51 and 81 cases of slave-dealing for 1911 and 1912 respectively, when the government became vigilant.[91] In addition, there were six slavery court cases between 1916 and 1918.[92] All together, that is Robertson's figure of 131 for the period 1874–1918; Dumett and Johnson's figures for 1911 and 1912 respectively and mine, add up to 763. If Robertson's overlapping figure of 131 is subtracted from the total of 763, it suggests that there were 632 court cases mainly in the Colony. This shows that the abolition ordinance was more effective in the Colony, especially the administrative centres, than in the Protectorate.

By the end of the First World War, there were fewer slavery cases because slavery was tapering off.[93] Foreign anti-slavery groups increasingly focused on forced labour instead of slavery.[94] Nevertheless, cases pertaining to slave inheritance, assimilation, and the rights of former slaves and pawns increased in the 1920s.[95] Indeed, as the colonial economy expanded and access to land became important, questions of slave origins increasingly became an issue in land tenure cases in the courts.[96] By 1945 the Supreme Court was inundated with land litigation, ownership, and inheritance and succession disputes. Therefore, the colonial government created a divisional court to deal with such cases.[97]

Undoubtedly more research is needed, but two major conclusions can be drawn. First, the fact that the figures were mainly for the Colony suggests that the courts were instrumental in the emancipation of slaves in the Colony, but not in the Protectorate. Second, in addition to the 632 court

158 SLAVERY AND COLONIAL RULE IN AFRICA

cases, the fact that some cases were not recorded, and the fact that nine-tenths of all slaves who sought freedom immediately following the proclamation used the courts, strongly suggest that the figure is higher than appear in the records.

African Responses to the Ordinance: Innovation and Continuity

One major gap in the historiography is how Africans responded to the ordinance and its impact on the effectiveness of the abolition. Indeed, Africans responded ingeniously to the operation of the abolition ordinance. Slave-holders and dealers adopted innovative measures to counter the abolition ordinance, hence making it difficult for colonial officials to detect enslaved persons.[98] Most cases of enslavement were brought to the attention of colonial officials through African informers or by the slaves themselves. The DC of Tarkwa, H. Vroom, suggested in 1889 that 'With a handsome reward to informers, I think Slave Trade might be repressed to a certain extent in the Protectorate territory'.[99] This suggests that Africans were better able to identify the nuances and complexities of the servile institutions that had emerged in response to the abolition ordinance than the colonial officials.

There was a shift from the use of slaves with facial scarifications to those without. Before abolition, facial scarification indicated a slave from the Northern Territories.[100] Colonial officials often used facial scarifications to identify slaves.[101] H. Vroom, the DC of Tarkwa, for instance, wrote in 1889, that

> slaves introduced into the Protectorate after the abolition of the traffic in 1874 do in most cases bear no tribal marks of any kind on them, for it is by the absence of those marks that detection is easily evaded; and such slaves are found out by the foreignness of their accents.[102]

How widespread this was has to await future research. Vroom's statement suggests that some colonial officials were able to identify slaves by their foreign accents. To avoid detection and hence prosecution, slave-dealers and holders encouraged their slaves to lose such foreign accents. For example S. Cole, the DC of Ada, claimed in 1889 that to 'evade detection, the masters of the slaves make it a point to teach them [slaves] thoroughly the Awuna and Adangbe dialect'.[103]

In addition, slave-dealers and holders claimed that their slaves were 'family' members. This ploy was testified to by Cole, who noted that whenever slave-holders were queried about their 'slaves' or 'families', they would trace their relationship so well that, except you know to the contrary, you will place implicit confidence in what they state.'[104] Most slaves

SLAVERY IN COLONIAL SOUTHERN GHANA

imported in the colonial period were children who usually could not explain their servile status to colonial officials.

Also, intricate information networks were developed by slave-dealers and holders to inform one another of the arrival of colonial officials. This enabled them to hide their slaves by moving them. Firminger raised this issue,[105] and one of his avid detractors, Mr C. Riby Williams, the DC of the Volta River District, substantiated it:

> It is almost impossible to verify this information [existence of slavery], because as soon as an officer enters Krepi, the news is carried forward, and by the time Kpanto [Kpandu] is reached all the slaves, if there are any, have been removed to other places.[106]

Communal religious practices and sanctions also served the interests of slave dealers and holders.[107] Slaves were made to swear oaths and 'drink fetish', ritually binding them to stay and refrain from reporting their servile status to colonial officials. For example, in 1875 a holder took a freed slave to 'King Tackie for the purpose of administering fetish oath so as to declare that she will no longer go back to the government'.[108] This bound the slave to the holder, as slaves feared that a breach of the oath or the 'fetish' would be catastrophic. Again, how prevalent this was is difficult to gauge. However, the 'fetish' and oathing sanctions have been powerful agencies of social and political control throughout Ghanaian history.

Dumett and Johnson argue that the 'most formidable roadblock against wholesale emancipation of slaves was the reluctance of slaves themselves to come forward'. Further they note that 'People also hesitated to inform against their neighbours'.[109] Witnesses were often reluctant to provide information that would lead to prosecution of slave-dealers and holders. The DC of Accra, L.N. Peregrine, for example, plaintively wrote, 'The difficulty in these cases is to prove actual purchases, and reliable evidence in these charges is most difficult to obtain.'[110] This was best summed up by the DC of Saltpond, Mr. Hayes Redwar, who wrote: 'I am, however, aware that it [slavery] does exist, although it is impossible to obtain evidence sufficient to obtain conviction in any case brought before the Court.'[111]

Some notable Africans had connections and access to government officials and those involved in slavery court cases, such as prison wardens and matrons. This enabled them to influence decisions of the courts or circumvent court decisions.[112] The case of Fanny Hagan, an influential society lady of Accra, is illustrative. On 26 March 1890, she was tried by the DC of Accra, Mr Edward MacMunn, and fined £3 for having bought a slave girl called Nyamie Domah. Mr. MacMunn then placed Nyamie Domah under the custodial care of a prison matron to be 'apprenticed according to law.'[113] However, '[a]lmost immediately afterwards... the DC

160   SLAVERY AND COLONIAL RULE IN AFRICA

was peremptorily ordered by [Governor]…Griffith to restore the child to the convicted slave owner.'[114]

This was not the only such case. Ellen Quartey, 'the concubine of a white resident', had her slave-dealing charges quashed.[115] Also, Kwame Fori, a royal of Akropong-Akuapem, was summarily released from prison for slave-dealing to be enstooled as the Okuapehene.[116] These examples do not mean that every prominent African had his/her way with the courts. For instance, in the case of King Enimil Quow of Wassaw, the abolition law was applied to the point of a travesty of due process, leading to his exile in Lagos, a convoluted policy that enabled the colonial government to control the Wassa gold-fields.[117]

Conclusion

It is difficult to estimate the numbers of the servile population or those who sought freedom. Inhabitants in the Protectorate and the Colony responded differently to the abolition laws. There was a stronger colonial presence in the coastal and administrative towns than in the Protectorate. Therefore, slaves in the Colony tended to have greater access to the courts than their counterparts in the Protectorate. There were some exceptions in the Protectorate, such as Akyem, Aburi, and Tarkwa, where European colonial activity was markedly strong. In addition, the servile population tended to use the courts more during the periods of vigorous implementation of the abolition laws, such as the first eleven months of 1890.

In sum, the law was effective only when colonial officials were jolted into action by outside pressure. The operation of the law was beset with problems that were located not in the law itself, but in colonial policies. Three major interrelated setbacks were the paucity of colonial officials, the exclusion of the chiefs, and the lack of coherent and systematic policies to assist freed slaves in their adjustment. Further, slave holders and dealers exploited the defects in the abolition laws in their quest to preserve servile labour. In reality, what freedom meant to slaves, even those freed by the courts, remained ambiguous. This explains slaves' unassertive use of the courts even in the Colony, as well as freed slaves' reversion into forms of bondage and dependency. Thus, the failings of the abolition laws to a large extent accounted for the post-proclamation slavery.

NOTES

1. Claire C. Robertson, 'Post-Proclamation Slavery in Accra: A Female Affair?', in Martin A. Klein and Claire C. Robertson (eds.), *Women and Slavery in Africa* (Madison, Wisconsin, 1983), pp.220–45.

SLAVERY IN COLONIAL SOUTHERN GHANA

2. Gerald McSheffrey, 'Slavery, Indentured Servitude, Legitimate Trade and the Impact of Abolition in the Gold Coast, 1874–1901: A Reappraisal', *Journal of African History*, 24 (1983), pp.350–6.
3. Raymond Dumett and Marion Johnson, 'Britain and the Suppression of Slavery in the Gold Coast Colony, Ashanti, and the Northern Territories', in Suzanne Miers and Richard Roberts (eds.), *The End of Slavery in Africa* (Madison, 1988), pp.88–9.
4. McSheffrey, 'Slavery', pp.355–6; Robertson, 'Post-Proclamation Slavery', pp.222–3; Dumett and Johnson, 'Gold Coast', pp.83–5 and p.88.
5. Carnarvon to Strahan, August 20, 1874, No. 2 in Correspondence Relating to the Queen's Jurisdiction on the Gold Coast and the Abolition of Slavery within the Protectorate, *Parliamentary Papers, 1875, C. 1139* (hereafter C. 1139); David Kimble, *A Political History of Ghana* (Oxford, 1963), pp.302–15; Francis Agbodeka, *African Politics and British Policy in the Gold Coast 1868–1900* (London, 1971), pp.55–61; and Adu Boahen, *Ghana: Evolution and Change in the Nineteenth in the Twentieth Centuries* (London, 1975), pp.57–60.
6. Agbodeka, *African Politics*, pp.56–7.
7. Dumett and Johnson, 'Gold Coast', p.84.
8. See for example C. 1139; and 'Further Correspondence Relating to the Abolition of Slavery on the Gold Coast', *Parliamentary Papers, 1875, C. 1159* (hereafter C. 1159).
9. See 'Correspondence Respecting the Slave Trade', *Parliamentary Papers, 1889, C. 6010* (hereafter 6010); 'Correspondence Respecting the Slave Trade', *Parliamentary Papers, 1890, C. 6053* (hereafter 6053); 'Correspondence Respecting the Slave Trade', *Parliamentary Papers, 1890, C. 6199* (hereafter 6199); 'Correspondence Respecting the Administration of the Laws Against Slavery in the Gold Coast Colony', *Parliamentary Papers, 1891*, C. 6354 (hereafter 6354).
10. See for example, *Report of the Committee of Experts on Slavery Appointed by the Council of the League of Nations*, 4 April 1933, National Archives of Ghana, Accra, CSO 41/33 (hereafter RCES). This file contains information on anti-slavery groups in Britain such as St. Joan's Social and Political Alliance and the British Commonwealth League, and their pre-occupation with persistence of servile institutions in the Gold Coast. I thank Thelma Ewusie, Archivist, National Archives of Ghana, Accra (hereafter NAGA) for bringing this file to my attention. See also League of Nations, *Slavery: Report of the Advisory Committee of Experts*, Slavery 1936. VI.B. 1., p.20. For a comparative perspective, see for example, Paul E. Lovejoy and Jan Hogendorn, *Slow Death for Slavery* (Cambridge, 1993), pp.270–86. See also Miers chapter.
11. McSheffrey, 'Slavery', pp.355–6 is based largely on the report by Sir David Chalmers on the response to and the impact of abolition in Strahan to Carnarvon, 14 August 1875, No.70 in 'Papers Relating to Her Majesty's Possessions in West Africa', *Parliamentary Papers, 1875, C. 1343* (hereafter C. 1343).
12. Dumett and Johnson, 'Gold Coast', pp.88–9.
13. Suzanne Miers, *Britain and the Ending of the Slave Trade* (New York, 1975), pp.158–9.
14. Dumett and Johnson, 'Gold Coast', p.84. See also Richard Roberts and Suzanne Miers, 'The End of Slavery in Africa', in Miers and Roberts (eds.), *The End of Slavery in Africa* p.20.
15. C. 1139, Carnarvon to the Officer Administering the Government of the Gold Coast, 21 August 1874, No.3.
16. See for example, Dumett and Johnson, 'Gold Coast', pp.79–80. For an explication of the British 'Indian Model', see Roberts and Miers, 'The End of Slavery in Africa', pp.12–13.
17. C. 1139, Carnarvon to the Officer Administering the Government of the Gold Coast, 21 August 1874, No.3.
18. C. 1139, Strahan to Carnarvon, 19 September 1874, No.5.
19. Ibid; and C. 1139, Strahan to Carnarvon, 28 December 1874, Encl. 2 in No.21.
20. C. 1139, Strahan to Carnarvon, 19 September 1874, Encl. 4 in No.5; and C. 1139, Strahan to Carnarvon, 28 December 1874, Encl. 1 in No.21.
21. See enclosures in C. 1139, Strahan to Carnarvon, 28 December 1874: Encl. 1 in No.21; Encl. 2 in No.21; Encl. 3 in No.21; and Encl. 4. in No.21.

162 SLAVERY AND COLONIAL RULE IN AFRICA

22. H.W. Hayes Redwar, *Comments on Some Ordinances of the Gold Coast Colony with Notes on a few Decided Cases* (London, 1909), pp.1–10; and Heather Dalton, 'The Development of the Gold Coast Under British Administration 1874–1901', M.A thesis, University of London, 1957, pp.112–16.

23. C. 1139, Strahan to Carnarvon, 19 September 1874, Encl. 4 in No.5.

24. Ibid. See also NAGA, Case No. 101, 28 October 1875, SCT 17/4/2; Gold Coast Despatches from Governor to Secretary of State, 1879–80, 21 January 1880, No.22, NAGA, ADM 1/2/23. For chiefs' roles in other jurisdictions, See Griffith to Ripon, 8 July 1893, No.88 in 'Gold Coast Annual Report for 1892', *Parliamentary Papers, 1893, C. 6857–38* (hereafter C. 6857–38). See also Agbodeka, *African Politics*, pp.113–22.

25. On the jury system, see J.A. Jearey, 'Trial by Jury and Trial with the Aid of Assessors in the Superior Courts of British African Territories: I', *Journal of African Law*, 4 (1960), pp.141–3. Accounts in Gold Coast newspapers suggest that, the jury system had many problems. See *The Gold Coast Express* (Accra), 6 October 1897 (hereafter *Gold Coast Express*); and the *Gold Coast Express*, 7 December 1899.

26. See for example, General Correspondence of the Year 1880, Eisenschmid, 5 April 1880, No.4 in Paul Jenkins, *Abstracts of Basel Mission Gold Coast Correspondence* (Legon, 1970) (hereafter BMC); Gold Coast Despatches from Governor to Secretary of State, 1880–81, 25 May 1880, No.160, NAGA, ADM 1/2/24; and C. 6053, Redwar to Hughes, 27 August 1889, Encl. 17 in 59.

27. League of Nations, *Slavery: Report of the Advisory Committee of Experts*, Slavery 1938. VI.B. 1., pp.113–14.

28. League of Nations, *Slavery: Report of the Advisory Committee of Experts*, Slavery 1936. VI.B. 1., p.20.

29. Ibid.

30. League of Nations, *Slavery: Report of the Advisory Committee of Experts*, Slavery 1938. VI.B. 1., p.114.

31. Ibid.

32. C. 6354, Griffith to Knutsford, 26 January 1891, No.7.

33. BMC, Asante's Report for the Year 1874, 11 January 1875, No.218; BMC, Dieterle To Basel, Aburi, 22 June 1875; and BMC, Hermann Rottman to Basel, Accra, 30 June 1875.

34. BMC, Zimmerman, unaddressed, Abokobi, 26 July 1875.

35. C. 6053, Cole to Hughes, 17 September 1889, Encl. 8 in No.59. This was more so in the case of pawnship. See also BMC, Asante, Mohr, and Werner to the Slave Emancipation Commission (of the B.M. on the Gold Coast), 26 June 1875.

36. Dumett and Johnson, 'Gold Coast', pp.84–5 and pp.88–9.

37. Marion Johnson, 'Slaves of Salaga', *Journal of African History*, 27 (1986) pp.358–61; McSheffrey, 'Slavery', pp.350–3; and Robertson, 'Post-Proclamation Slavery', p.230; Dumett and Johnson, 'Gold Coast', pp.84–5.

38. Johnson, 'Slaves of Salaga', pp.358–60.

39. C. 1139 Strahan to Carnarvon, 19 September 1874, No.5; Lees to Hicks Beach, 5 July 1879, No.2 in 'Report by Sir David Chalmers on the Effect of the Steps Which Have Been Taken by the Colonial Government in Reference to the Abolition of Slavery Within the Protectorate', *Parliamentary Papers, 1878, C. 2148* (hereafter C. 2148); C. 6053, Hodgson to Knutsford, 17 February 1890, Encl. 1 in No.59; and C. 6354, Griffith to Knutsford, 26 January 1891, No.7.

40. See C. 6053, enclosures in No.59.

41. See for example, Employment of Women in Compulsory Labour, Case No. 11/1927, NAGA, ADM 11/967; Children of Non-European Origin Questionnaire 9, Case No. 14/1930, NAGA, ADM 11/1052; and *Gold Coast Colony: Memorandum on Forced Labour 1930* (Accra, 1930), pp.11–16 (hereafter *Memorandum on Forced Labour*).

42. This argument is made in Suzanne Miers, *Britain*, pp.158–9.

43. See for example, Gold Coast Despatches from Governor to Secretary of State, 1882, 6 March 1882, No.68, NAGA, ADM 1/2/26; C. 6053, Redwar to Hughes, 27 August 1889, Encl. 17 in No.59; and *The Times* (London), 1 September 1890 (hereafter *The Times*). For the period of the First World War, See Kwabena Opare-Akurang, 'Disaffection and

SLAVERY IN COLONIAL SOUTHERN GHANA

163

Opposition Against Chiefs: The Vortex of Indirect Rule and the First World war in the Gold Coast [Ghana], 1914–1918' (M.A. thesis, Wilfrid Laurier University, 1991), pp.51–5.

44. See for example, DC's Court Book No.6, August to September,1876, NAGA, ADM 17/1/3; Gold Coast Despatches from Governor to Secretary of State, 1882, 24 July 1882, No.336, NAGA, ADM 1/1/27; and Gold Coast Despatches from Secretary of State to Governor, 1883, Pt. 1, 20 April 1883, Encl. in No.142, NAGA, ADM 1/1/60.

45. See for example, C. 1139, Strahan to Carnarvon, 19 September 1874, No.5. See also McSheffrey, 'Slavery', p.353, mentions all excluding Captain Lees.

46. BMC, Asante, Mohr and Werner to the Slave Emancipation Commission (of the B.M. on the Gold Coast), 26 June 1875.

47. Gold Coast Despatches from Governor to Secretary of State, 1876–77, 13 March 1877, No.79, NAGA, ADM 1/1/21.

48. Gold Coast Despatches from Secretary of State to Governor, 1879 Pt. 2, 1 October 1879, No.377, NAGA, ADM 1/1/48.

49. Gold Coast Despatches from Governor to Secretary of State, 1882, 24 July 1882, No.336, NAGA, ADM 1/1/27. I have not found any report to this effect.

50. Gold Coast Despatches from Secretary of State to Governor, 1883, Pt. 1, 20 April 1883, Encl. in No.142, NAGA, ADM 1/1/60.

51. C. 6354, Griffith to Knutsford, 26 January 1891, No.7.

52. Ibid.

53. *Gold Coast Departmental Reports for 1905*, pp.7–8.

54. *The Gold Coast Nation* (Cape Coast) 30 December 1915 (hereafter *The Nation*).

55. David K. Patterson, 'The Influenza Epidemic of 1918–1919 in the Gold Coast', *Journal of African History*, Vol.24 (1983), pp.485–502.

56. Gold Coast Despatches from Governor to Secretary of State, 1875, 12 October 1875, No.198, NAGA, ADM 1/2/20; Gold Coast Despatches From Governor to Secretary of State, 1879–80, 12 February 1880, No.47, NAGA ADM 1/2/23; BMC, Buck's Report on the Akim Schools in 1878, 2 January 1879, No.223; BMC, Gold Coast Executive Committee of the Mission to Basel, 29 January 1878, No.7; C. 6053, Confidential Circular, Colonial Secretary's Office, 29 June 1889, Encl. 32 in No.59; and C. 6354, The APS to Colonial Office, 20 August 1890, No.1.

57. Gold Coast Despatches from Governor to Secretary of State, 1875/76, 15 February 1875, No.43, NAGA, ADM 1/2/20; and C. 6053, Heron to Hughes, 2 August 1889, Encl. 10 in No.59.

58. C. 1402, Strahan to Carnarvon, 14 August 1875, No.70; BMC, Asante's Report on the Boarding School in 1876, 5 January 1877, No.227; BMC, Asante's Last Quarter's Report from Akim, 15 April 1878, No.216; and BMC, Dieterle & Eisenschmid to Basel, 3 January 1878, No.1.

59. BMC, Dieterle and Eisenschmid to Basel, 3 January 1878, No.1, with copies of Freeling's letter to them, 26 December 1877, No.2, and their reply to him, 3 January 1877, No.3. See also BMC, Gold Coast Executive Committee of the Mission to Basel, 29 January 1878, No.7. On struggles between the Basel Mission and the Akyem Abuakwa state over the emancipation, see Noel Smith, *Presbyterian Church of Ghana 1835–1960* (Accra, 1966), pp.115–18; and Kofi Affrifah, 'The Impact of Christianity on Akyem Society, 1852–1887', *Transactions of the Historical Society of Ghana*, 16 (1975), pp.77–82.

60. Griffith to Granville, 27 May 1886, No.24 in 'Further Correspondence Respecting the Affairs of the Gold Coast', *Parliamentary Papers, 1885, C. 4906* (hereafter C. 4906); and C. 4906, Firminger to Governor, 15 May 1886, Encl. 1 in No.24.

61. Gold Coast Despatches from Governor to Secretary of State, 1880–81, 5 April 1880, No.100, NAGA, ADM 1/2/24; Young to Derby, 18 January 1885, No.61 in 'Further Correspondence Respecting the Affairs of the Gold Coast', *Parliamentary Papers, 1884, C. 4477* (hereafter C. 4477); C. 4477, Memo for the Honourable F. Evans in re Geraldo de Lima, 19 January 1885, Encl. 2 in No.65; C. 4906, Griffith to Carnarvon, 5 June 1885, No.1; Criminal Record Book, October 1886–June 1888, Case dd. 19/1/1888, NAGA SCT 17/5/9; C. 6053 Cole to Hughes, 7 August 1889, Encl. 6 in No.59; C. 6354, Griffith to Knutsford, 26 January 1891, No.7; Criminal Record Book, September 1891–November

164   SLAVERY AND COLONIAL RULE IN AFRICA

1892, Case dd. 13/4/1892, NAGA, SCT 17/5/12; *The Times*, 1 September 1890; and League of Nations, *Slavery: Report of the Advisory Committee of Experts* Slavery 1938. VI.B. 1. 1938., p.114.

62. See for example, C. 6354, From Peregrine, to Colonial Secretary, 7 October 1890, Encl. 1 in No.7; and *The Times*, 1 September 1890.

63. C. 6354, The APS to Colonial Office, 20 March 1891, No.8.

64. District Commissioner's Court, Book No.6, Case Number 88, August–September 1876, NAGA, ADM 17/4/3.

65. Gold Coast Despatches from Secretary of State to Governor, 1875, 16 April 1875, No.55, NAGA, ADM 1/1/39.

66. Gold Coast Despatches from Governor to Secretary of State, 1876–77, 13 March 1877, No.79, NAGA, ADM 1/1/21; and Gold Coast Despatches from Governor to Secretary of State, 1882, 6 March 1882, No.68, NAGA, ADM 1/2/26.

67. C. 6053, Hodgson to Knutsford, 17 February 1890, Encl. 1 in No.59.

68. See for example, C. 1159, Strahan to Carnarvon, 3 January 1875, Encl. in No.1; Case No.104, 3 November 1875, NAGA, SCT 17/4/2; Case dd. 31 August 1877, NAGA, SNA 11/1770; *The Times*, 1 September 1890; and C. 6354, Griffith to Knutsford, 26 January 1891, No.7.

69. C. 6354, The APS to Colonial Office No. 20 August 1890, No.1; and C. 6354, Griffith to Knutsford, 26 January 1891, No.7. See also Robertson, 'Post-Proclamation Slavery', pp.228–9.

70. C. 6354, APS to Colonial Office, 20 August 1890, No.1; and C. 6354, Griffith to Knutsford, 26 January 1891, No.7. See for example, C. 6053, Holmes to Hughes, 27 July 1889, Encl. 26 in No.59; C. 6053, Statement of J.A. Smith, 30 January 1890, Encl. 34 in No.59; Peregrine to Colonial Secretary, 7 October 1890, Encl. 1 in No.7; and C. 6354, Griffith to Knutsford, 26 January 1891, No.7.

71. See for example, C. 6053, Holmes to Hughes, 27 July 1889, Encl. 26 in No.59; C. 6053, Statement of J.A. Smith, 30 January 1890, Encl. 34 in No.59; Peregrine to Colonial Secretary, 7 October 1890, Encl. 1 in No.7; and C. 6354, Griffith to Knutsford, 26 January 1891, No.7.

72. C. 6354, Griffith to Knutsford, 26 January 1891, No.7.

73. C. 6354, The APS to Colonial Office, 20 August 1890, No.1.

74. Ibid; C. 6354, Griffith to Knutsford, 23 February 1891, No.7; C. 6351, APS to Colonial Office, 20 March 1891, No.8; C. 6354, Peregrine to Colonial Secretary, 7 October 1890, Encl. 1. No.7; and *The Times*, 1 September 1890.

75. C. 6053, Cole to Hughes, 17 September 1890, Encl. 8 in No.59; and NAGA, ADM 11/1096, 16 July 1904. Many forts and castles along the coast were turned into administrative units or prisons. See *Gold Coast Times*, 10 June 1882. In the interior,indigenous rulers operated what was known as the 'Native' or 'Chief's prison. See for example, Kpong Native Affairs, NAGA, ADM 11/1/604.

76. Case No. 104, 3 November 1875, NAGA, SCT 17/4/2; NAGA, SCT 17/5/10, 1890, p.43; C. 6354, APS to Colonial Office, 20 August 1890, No.1; and C. 6354, Griffith to Knutsford, 26 January 1891, No.7.

77. Robertson, 'Post-Proclamation Slavery', p.222.

78. C. 1343, Strahan to Carnarvon, 6 March 1875, Encl. 1 in No.42.

79. Ibid.

80. Ibid.

81. McSheffrey, 'Slavery', pp.355–6.

82. C. 1343, Strahan to Carnarvon, 6 March 1875, Encl. 1 in No.42.

83. See reports of various missionaries in BMC, Correspondence on the Slave Emancipation Proceedings in the Gold Coast 1874–75 (in a file called Gold Coast Slave Emancipation Commission, 1868–75).

84. Robertson, 'Post-Proclamation Slavery', p.222.

85. C. 6354, Griffith to Knutsford, 26 January 1891, No.7. See also, C. 6354, APS to Colonial Office, 20 August 1890, No.1.

86. The total figure is derived from C. 6354, Griffith to Knutsford, 26 January 1891, No.7;

SLAVERY IN COLONIAL SOUTHERN GHANA

Gold Coast Departmental Reports for 1899, NAGA ADM, 5/1/76; and C. 6053, Hodgson to Knutsford, 17 February 1890, Encl. 1 in No.59.

87. See C. 6053, all the enclosures in No. 59. The nine district centres in the Colony include Accra, Ada, Dixcove, Sekondi, Kwitta [Keta] Fort Prampram, Saltpond-Anomabu, Winneba. The ones in the Protectorate were Akyem, Aburi, and Tarkwa. Akyem was a centre of Basel missionary activity. See Affrifah, 'Impact of Christianity on Akyem.' Aburi, apart from being a centre of Christianity, was a place, where European officials went to convalesce because of its congenial climate. See 13<3, Strahan to Carnarvon, 5 March 1875, Encl. 1 in No.41. Tarkwa, an auriferous region, was important to colonial economic exploitation and development. Thus it had many European mining companies and a large colonial presence from the early 1870s. See Paul Rosenblum, 'Gold Mining in Ghana 1874–1900' (Ph.D. diss., Columbia University, 1972), pp.118–233.

88. See C. 6354, Griffith to Knutsford, 26 January 1891, No.7.

89. Dumett and Johnson, 'Gold Coast', pp.83–4.

90. *Gold Coast Departmental Reports for 1906*, p.9 and the *Gold Coast Departmental Report for 1908*, p.7.

91. Dumett and Johnson, 'Gold Coast', pp.83–4. In note 24, they write that 'These figures included about 100 arrests for each of these two years in Ashanti'. Thus, the figures for the Gold Coast were 151 cases in 1911 and 181 cases in 1912.

92. *Gold Coast Departmental Reports for 1918*, NAGA, ADM 5/1/95.

93. For a comparative examples, see Roberts and Miers, 'The End of Slavery', p.21.

94. Hammockmen & Carriers Increase of Wages, NAGA ADM 11/1/761, Case No. 44/1919; *Judgements of the Full Courts Held at Accra and Cape Cost in September, 1920, and March–April, 1921* (Government Printer, 1923), pp.134–50 (hereafter *JFC*, 1921); *Gold Coast Law Reports Full Court 1926–29* (Accra: The Government Printer, 1931), pp.241–5; Coloured Labour, NAGA, ADM 11/1/864, Case No. 9/1924; Employment of Women in Compulsory Labour, NAGA, ADM 11/1967, Case No. 11/1927; *Memorandum on Forced Labour*, pp.11–16; Forced Labour, NAGA, ADM 11/1/1058, Case No. 22/1930; *RCES*, CSO 41/33; and League of Nations, *Slavery: Report of the Advisory Committee of Experts*, Slavery 1936. VI.B. 1., p.20.

95. *JFC* (1921), 132–150; *Gold Coast Law Reports 1926–29*, pp.241–5; *Selected Judgements of the West African Court of Appeal for the Years 1930–33*, Volumes I–II (London, [1936–39], 1961), pp.12–14. (hereafter *WACA*); League of Nations *Slavery: Report of the Advisory Committee of Experts*, Slavery 1936. VI.B. 1.,p.20; M.J. Field, *Akim Kotoku* (Accra, 1948), p.20; *Civil Record Judgement Book, October 2, 1925–October 25, 1937*; and Suit No. L.73/1952, 28 February 1953, NAGA, SCT 23/4/89.

96. Field, *Akim Kotoku*, p.20; *Civil Record Judgement Book, October 2, 1925–October 25, 1937*; and Suit No. L.73/1952, 28 February 1953, NAGA, SCT 23/4/89

97. T. Elias, *Ghana and Sierra Leone: The Development of their Laws and Constitutions* (London, 1962), pp.119–20. For an account of the development of land laws and administration, see ibid.

98. C. 6053, Hodgson to Knutsford, 17 February 1890, Encl. 1 in No.59; C. 6053, Redwar to Hughes, 27 August 1889, Encl. 17 in No.59; and C. 6053, Vroom to Hughes, 5 August 1889, Encl. 19 in 59.

99. C. 6053, Vroom to. Hughes, 5 August 1889, Encl. in 19 in No.59.

100. C. 6053, Cole to Hughes, 7 August 1889, Encl. 6. in No.59. For a fuller account on scarification, see R.S. Rattray, *Ashanti Law and Consiitution* (Oxford, [1929] 1969), p.35 and note 2; and idem, *Religion and Art in Ashanti* (Oxford, [1927] 1979), p.65.

101. C. 6010, Firminger to Colonial Office, April 1889, Encl. 1 in No.47.

102. C. 6053, Vroom to Hughes, 5 August 1889, Encl. 19 in 59. See also, C. 6053, Heron to Hughes, 2 August 1889, Encl. 10 in 59. All those with scars were not slaves. As Acting Governor Hodgson noted, there was a large 'Mohemmedan population in Accra' including Hausas, Moshis [Mossis], and Grunshis, whose children born in the Colony sometimes were given 'tribal marks'. See C. 6053, Hodgson to Knutsford, 17 February 1889, Encl. 1 in No.59.

103. C. 6053, Cole to Hughes, 7 August 1889, Encl. 6 in No.59.

166   SLAVERY AND COLONIAL RULE IN AFRICA

104. Ibid.
105. C. 6010, Firminger to Colonial Office, 30 April 1889, Encl. in No.47.
106. C. 6053, Williams to Hughes, 30 January 1890, Encl. 22 in No.59.
107. Case No. 104, 3 November 1875, NAGA SCT 17/4/2; and BMC, Buck's Report for the Year 1879, 30/31 December 1879, No.150. See also Robertson, 'Post-Proclamation Slavery', p.228.
108. Case No. 104, 3 November 1875, NAGA SCT 17/4/2. For the influence of fetishes, see Gold Coast Despatches from Governor to Secretary of State, 1880–81, 25 March 1880, No.86, NAGA, ADM 1/2/24. See also Robertson, 'Post-Proclamation Slavery', p.228; and Henry Brackenbury, *The Ashanti War*, Vol II (London, [1874] 1968), p.325.
109. Dumett and Johnson, 'Gold Coast', p.85.
110. C. 6354, From Peregrine to Colonial Secretary, 7 October 1890, Encl. 1 in No.7. See also C. 6354, Griffith to Knutsford, 26 January 1891, No.7.
111. C. 6053, Redwar to Hughes, 27 August 1889, Encl. 17 in No.59.
112. See 6354, APS to Colonial Office, 20 August 1890, No.1; and *The Times*, 1 September 1890.
113. C. 6354, APS to Colonial Office, 20 August 1890, No.1.
114. Ibid; and *The Times*, 1 September 1890.
115. C. 6354, APS to Colonial Office, 20 August 1890, No.1; and C. 6354, Griffith to Colonial Office, 26 January 1891, No.7.
116. Rev. E. Sampson, *History of Aquapim and Akropong* (Accra, 1908), pp.12–13.
117. Gold Coast Despatches from Governor to Secretary of State, 1876–77, 5 April 1877, No.89, NAGA, ADM 1/2/21; *African Times*, 1 November 1879; and *The Western Echo* (Cape Coast), 14–28 February 1887.

'Amana' and 'Asiri':
Royal Slave Culture and the Colonial Regime in Kano, 1903–1926

SEAN STILWELL

After conquering the Sokoto Caliphate in 1903, the British were faced with the problem of administering a geographically vast region which contained a large, diverse population and a political system which had been evolving for well over seven centuries. Kano was one of the oldest, largest and most economically important cities in the Caliphate. The policy adopted by the British to administer northern Nigeria was 'indirect rule'.[1] Ideally, the British hoped to restructure Hausa/Fulani administration by making the system more amenable to British control. Accordingly, the British attempted to transform the indigenous rulers of northern Nigeria into a collaborating elite. In theory, colonial officials in Kano were supposed to work through and within the pre-colonial political structure. In practice, they endeavoured to place themselves at the head of the entire system: British officials made policy, advised 'native authorities' and intervened in local politics if their economic or political interests were threatened.

Traditionally, elements of cooperation and compromise between the British and the Hausa/Fulani have been stressed.[2] A. H. M. Kirk-Greene noted that 'the District Officer did not order, he advised, he did not rule, he administered'.[3] The relationship was far from being this simple. The British were forced to look for indigenous allies as they could neither bear the cost nor manpower to govern the region effectively. Sometimes rule was 'indirect' in name only: British officials deposed Emirs, altered the system of taxation and land-holding, and eliminated certain titles, positions and responsibilities of the Hausa/Fulani ruling elite.[4] While the 'native authorities' acquiesced in British rule, they chaffed under the restrictions and regulations imposed upon them by the colonial authorities. Occasionally their displeasure verged on rebellion.[5]

Indigenous rulers of northern Nigeria were not simply clients of the British. In Kano, Emir Abbas (1903–19) and Usman (1919–25) resisted the imposition of British control and reforms by relying on slave title-holders (Hausa: *Bayin Sarki*) who had served the state since the accession of *Sarkin* Muhammed Rumfa in c. 1463. Abbas and Usman used royal slaves to delay

168   SLAVERY AND COLONIAL RULE IN AFRICA

the implementation of colonial directives, supervise British officials in residence, and to subvert and control free title-holders whom some British officials planned to use as leverage against the Emir's own power and authority. Royal slaves guarded their own interests as well. As a group, they had a stake in maintaining pre-colonial patterns of government and administration. They too rebelled against certain British directives which were designed to reduce their status, position and influence in the court of Abbas and Usman. This article will explore the political and cultural interaction between the British colonial regime and the institution of royal slavery. While colonial officials in Kano generally despised individual royal slaves and condemned the institution of royal slavery, they were forced to work alongside and sometimes through royal slaves until 1926, when the institution was finally abolished by *Sarkin Kano* Abdullahi Bayero as a condition of his accession to the throne. The survival of the royal slave system demonstrates just how difficult it was for the British to impose their version of order and good governance on a dynamic elite slave system .

Political Competiton and Office-Holding in Pre-colonial Kano: The Genesis of a Royal Slave System

Competition for political power was a constant theme in the history of Kano between c. 999 and 1903. As Kano gradually incorporated, assimilated or conquered surrounding areas and then nearby kingdoms and peoples, an increasingly complex internal administrative hierarchy developed. The creation of political titles gave certain individuals access to wealth (through taxation, tribute, or control over resources) and command over people. Competition for titles and the benefits they offered was often a destabilizing force in Kano; indeed, the *Kano Chronicle* indicates that as a result of territorial and military expansion individual title-holders became more powerful over time.[6] For the *Sarki*, the central problem during this period was to establish ideological and institutional parameters that governed and regulated political competition, while also providing individual title-holders with rewards for service that did not destabilize the state and the kingship. A key element in this pattern of administration and kingship was the attempt to co-opt a variety of factions both in and outside of the court to the side of the *Sarki*. In effect, if one faction became too strong the *Sarki* had to ensure that he was able to balance their strength by securing a different faction's loyalty to the throne. Kingship became an exercise in balancing a set of interests in the court and harnessing them to the service of the throne. By 1781 royal slaves had emerged as the most effective representatives of this policy as they allowed the Kings of Kano to transcend lineage and family divisions that weakened their position and power relative to the free-born

ROYAL SLAVE CULTURE IN KANO

aristocracy. Creating slave titles and vesting power on individual slaves provided the *Sarki* with a group of office-holders he could control more effectively than free-born officials [Hausa: *masu sarauta*]. The *Sarki* could alter the responsibilities of slave-offices and replace individual slave-office holders more easily than he could change the offices of or replace the free-born aristocracy.

In 1807 Kano was conquered by Fulani clan leaders as part of Usman Dan Fodio's *jihad* or holy war against the primarily Hausa city-states of the region.[7] The victors were faced with a dilemma: how should Kano be governed? Initially, Usman Dan Fodio had criticized the Hausa regimes for giving authority to those who sought it: 'One of the ways of their government is succession to the emirate by hereditary right and by force and by exclusion of consultation'. The *jihad* was predicated upon the notion that it was incumbent upon Muslims to implement a pure form of Islamic government, in which most did not include the use of titled royal slaves or Hausa traditional titles: 'Therefore do not follow their way in government, and do not imitate them, not even in the titles of their king …Address your chief emir as "Commander of the Believers"…'.[8] There were only four approved administrative positions: a *wazir*, a judge, a chief of police, and a chief of the treasury. This ideal soon proved impossible to achieve.

In 1819, Ibrahim Dabo b. Mahmud (1819–46), of the Sullubawa clan, assumed the throne in Kano, and launched a policy designed to centralize the administration and boost revenue.[9] As part of this administrative centralization, royal slave titles were revived. Oral tradition records that it was a royal slave, *Dan Rimi* Barka, who advised Dabo to reinstate the slave titles, although Dabo wrote for permission from Sokoto before officially recreating the slave system.[10] Dabo realized it would be impossible to effectively govern Kano without the aid of royal slaves. As individuals and as a body royal slaves had become the repositories of political, military and economic knowledge that was vital to the administration of Kano Emirate. Like the previous Hausa rulers, Dabo used the distribution of titled offices to strengthen his own position by appointing his clients and supporters to important posts. In effect, the court of Ibrahim Dabo began to look very much like the Hausa court of previous times: 'At the court of the lord of Kano great pomp prevails. The original simplicity of the reigning Fulbe has disappeared and a strict code of protocol makes it difficult for subjects to approach their ruler'.[11] Dabo reinstated the high throne used by the Hausa rulers and all Emirate officials were required to prostrate themselves before it, a policy that was enforced by the royal slaves: 'The Emir sat on a throne guarded by slave officials while all the counsellors prostrated on the floor forming a line on either side of the throne'.[12] Although the responsibilities of some royal slave offices were altered by Dabo and his successors, they

170 SLAVERY AND COLONIAL RULE IN AFRICA

nonetheless played an increasingly influential role in the palace and administration of the Emirate as the nineteenth century progressed. Like the British after it, the Fulani machinery of government was unable to exist or even function independently of the Hausa system of administration, and eventually relied on offices and institutions established before the *jihad.*

The Royal Slave System in 1903

On the eve of British conquest royal slave power in Kano was based on four interwoven features: the political, military and economic duties attached to certain slave offices, their roles as 'gates' (Hausa: *kofofi*) for information and communication with the Emir, the *gidaje* system of household organization among royal slaves inside of the palace, and their unique personal relationship with the Emir which was governed by the concept of *Amana*, or reciprocal trust and loyalty. The paradigm most often used to explain the importance of the institution of royal slavery in Kano Emirate, especially in the nineteenth century, posits the evolution of centralized kingship supported by a slave bureaucracy and an elite cadre of slave musketeers.[13] However, while the duties royal slaves performed were integral to their political influence, the basis of their position and influence was not formalized or bureaucratized. Their position in the palace was generally determined by their individual relationship with the Emir based on *Amana*, as opposed to a codified, rigid system of promotion and power relations.

The four main spheres of male royal slave provenance in Kano Emirate were: (1) the supervision of palace custom and etiquette; (2) military service; (3) the administration of the Emirate and territorial supervision; and (4) household duties concerned with the distribution of food and palace upkeep. In general, royal slaves lived in the palace and served the Emir as administrators, personal retainers and guards. Three senior royal slaves were effectively senior military commanders and led bodies of slave horseman and musketeers. They were also responsible for the collection of taxes through their clients called *Jakadu* and supervised a number of royal plantations (Hausa: *gandu*) which supplied the palace with grains and other foodstuffs. As Imam Imoru noted, slave title-holders were also the Emir's informal councillors who advised him in matters of custom, politics and policy:

> In Kano one finds the following seven. The first is shamaki: he looks after the King's horses. He is also called jatau, 'overseer of the slaves'. The second is 'dan rimi who is the King's top slave official: there is a big family in his house and all the weapons are kept there.

ROYAL SLAVE CULTURE IN KANO

The third is salama, 'one who knocks at the door', and people call him aljifun sarki, the 'king's pocket' or 'half the king', or shashin sarki, the 'king's busom friend'. The fourth is kasheka: he shares out the household supplies to the king's wives. These last two officials are eunuchs and are among the slave officials. The fifth official is the 'guardian of the inner room', turakin soro. The sixth is abin fada, 'go-between': telling something to him is like telling it to the king. The seventh is kilishi: he is the one who prepares the sitting place with the hide mats for the king. These seven officials are called the 'slaves of the inner house', bayin cikin gida. When they greet the king in the morning, they sit and talk with him in a very attentive manner: one does not talk nonsense and there is no joking.[14]

By 1903 between three and ten royal slaves served on the 'yan majalisa (Hausa: children of the court) which had been recrafted as a state administrative council. This innovation was attributed to Ibrahim Dabo who was acting on the advice of the royal slave Dan Rimi Barka. The Emir, however, retained control over appointments to the senior slave positions, while the senior slaves were allowed to appoint their lesser subordinates as they wished.[15] Generally these subordinates had titles derivative of the senior slave in charge of them; for example, Ciroman Shamaki (the Ciroma of the Shamaki). Hausa-Fulani concepts of authority made it necessary that slaves occupy titles in order to formalize and legitimize their positions in the hierarchy. Titles served as designations of status, and generally defined the duties the title-holder performed. For example, the title Shamaki, which means stables, indicates that his primary responsibility was the supervision of the Emir's horses; the title Kilishi, which also means carpet, indicates that he was primarily responsible for laying out the Emir's carpet and maintaining the Emir's throne room; the Sarkin Hatsi, or 'King of Grains', was responsible for the collection and distribution of grains in the palace. Oral tradition indicates that generally Shamaki was first in order of importance and precedence, followed by Dan Rimi and Sallama. After these three, however, precedence was highly variable. This suggests that there was no permanent status order amongst royal slave title-holders. In addition, using the names of slave titles to extrapolate the functions and positions of offices, and individual office-holders, makes the institution appear too static and impervious to change. The entire system functioned to allow unique individuals to assume more influence and take on other responsibilities as their personalities and abilities dictated. Duties changed and evolved over time. Slave title-holders attempted to incorporate new functions into their offices in order to enhance their own positions and power.[16] The ability of a title-holder to expand his work also depended on

172   SLAVERY AND COLONIAL RULE IN AFRICA

the degree of trust between the title-holder in question and the person who appointed him. New title-holders were generally kept from extending their positions, as were those who seemed too powerful.[17] The royal slave system of nineteenth-century Kano was built upon a system of slave intermediaries[18] who were generally known as *Kofa* and *Kofofi* (door, gate; doors, gates).[19] In the *Kofa* system, the three most important royal slaves served as the channels of communication between free-born title-holders and the *Sarki*. This gave certain royal slaves secure access to sensitive political information. The system enabled royal slaves to become wealthy, as officials who wished to see the Emir normally had to provide financial compensation to the slave official who served as their 'gate'.[20] The system allowed the Emirs of Kano to play-off factions against one another, thereby centralizing their own power in the face of the rivalry between a variety of slave and free officials.

The *Dan Rimi* and *Shamaki* occupied compounds inside the northern section of the palace, while the *Sallama* had a compound just outside the palace. All the *Bayin Sarki* were placed under the control and supervision of one of the top three royal slaves: the *Shamaki*, *Dan Rimi*, or *Sallama*. It was within their households that slave labour was harnessed, apportioned and controlled for service to the state and the Emirship. Newly captured slaves brought into the *Gidan Sarki* would be placed among the *Shamakawa*, *Rimawa*, or *Sallamawa* (e.g. the people of *Shamaki*).[21] The organization of royal slaves into households or *gidaje* promoted competition and rivalry between slave title-holders. Members of the *Bayin Sarki* were not restricted to certain slave titles: a member of the *Sallamawa* could become *Shamaki*, for instance. Like political appointments made among the free-born aristocracy, the office-holding system encouraged rivalry for the highest offices and the rewards that they brought. While there were some restrictions over who could assume slave titles based on previous appointments and customary practice, the existence of these competing houses, and factions within houses, provided the Emir with political leverage that he used to control his royal slaves. Independent clients would also attach themselves to the households of influential slaves with the hope of gaining influence or positions as *Jakadu*. Indeed, beyond possession of important slave titles, status among royal slaves in the *Gidan Sarki* was governed by the number of clients a title-holder attracted, as indicated by the Hausa proverb, 'The chief of many exceeds the chief of strength'.[22] Other title-holders were also designated among one of the three main families, although they had their own households modelled along similar lines from which they drew their own slave subordinates. A fourth major family, the *Shettimawa*, became prominent in the *Gidan Sarki* after the title of *Shettima* was created in 1894.[24] Slave households were so important that

ROYAL SLAVE CULTURE IN KANO

after a slave title-holder was turbaned and paid homage the entire household went to the Emir to give their thanks for bestowing the title on the household.[24] These households were places where knowledge was acquired. Knowledge about the palace, its history and occupants, was transmitted from person to person informally. Specific skills were acquired, including knowledge about horses, grains, the military, building, plantation management and other economically and politically important activities. Sometimes, families were associated with a particular area of expertise, for example, the *Rimawa* with the preservation of palace and Emirate history.[25]

The *Bayin Sarki* were generally encouraged to marry other slaves in order to ensure a steady supply of second and third generation slaves in the *Gidan Sarki*.[26] Many royal slaves preferred to marry women of slave status, because the possibility then existed that one of their grandsons would succeed to the Emirship. The progeny of a slave-slave marriage, if female, could be given to the Emir as a concubine and might bear one of his sons. This would be a solid guarantee of favourable and privileged treatment.[27] There is a saying amongst the slaves that if the son of a wife of the Emir was to inherit his leadership instead of the son of a concubine, he would have no power.[28] This indicates the stress placed on ties between the Emir's household and the *Bayin Sarki*: 'That is why they can never do away with us, they must be patient with us and also we must be patient with them'.[29] This tie was also based on the patterns of male child-rearing inside of the palace. In the nineteenth century, Emirs and the free-born elite conducted a large number of wars outside of Kano and were frequently absent from the palace. As a result, their children were often brought up in the households of high ranking palace slaves.[30] This practice also stemmed from the fact that once children of the aristocracy and the royal family reached puberty they were forbidden to live amongst the concubines in the inner part of the *Gidan Sarki* and were thus raised in the houses of royal slaves.[31] This encouraged close relationships between individual slaves and prospective candidates to the throne, as well as providing sons of Emirs with the opportunity to benefit from knowledge found in slave households.[32] Most importantly, slaves close to a given Emir before his succession to the throne were usually given important slave titles afterwards.

Factions within slave houses sometimes developed based on descent relationships with particular slave office-holders. The descendants of *Dan Rimi* Barka and *Dan Rimi* Malam Barka were particularly successful in ensuring their relations acquired the position of *Dan Rimi*. Sometimes these smaller units attempted to dominate the wider households. On one level the system encouraged competition between distinct slave families, on the other, it served as a mechanism of integration. During the Kano Civil War (1893–95) royal slaves divided into two factions. Generally those who

174   SLAVERY AND COLONIAL RULE IN AFRICA

served under and supported Emir Abdullahi (1855–82) followed one pretender to the throne, Yusufu, while those who supported Mohammed Bello (1883–93) followed the other, Tukur.[33] While Barka's descendants among the *Rimawa* are said to have divided in two they did so in order to ensure one of them would retain the title of *Dan Rimi*: '(Yahaya) called Nuhu (his brother) and said to him 'you go follow Yusufawa at Takai. For me, I remain here with the Emir. If they come and win the war, then I know you will be there with them. If (Tukur) won the war, you know I am here'.[34]

Royal slaves were required to serve the Emirship as an institution. The relationship between the *Bayin Sarki* and the Emir was governed by the concept of *Amana*, or reciprocal trust.[35] *Amana* was renewed between the Emir and the palace slaves at each accession. Upon installing a new Emir, the *Waziri* of Sokoto summoned the senior royal slaves to meet their new master and announced: 'This is the man the Caliph has selected to govern Kano. Keep him well and obey him with good faith'.[36] This performance was designed to align royal slave interests with the new Emir, re-establish the palace hierarchy and in M. G. Smith's words 'ordain cohesion'.[37] Because the *Bayin Sarki* possessed the secrets (Hausa: *asiri*) of the Emir and the palace, they had to be trusted by the Emir before they were given high office.[38] However, as indicated above, their ability to gain access to delicate information in the palace gave them immense personal power among the title-holders, including the Emir. In theory an Emir had absolute power of life and death over each of his royal slaves. In practice, it was necessary an Emir be circumspect in his dealings with individual royal slaves.[39]

Second generation royal slaves were called *cucanawa* to distinguish them from those recently captured. The *cucanawa* valued their high status. The word *cucanawa* was likely derived from *cucananaci*, meaning 'impudent' or 'shameless effrontery and familiarity'.[40] Oral data suggests that *cucanawa* behaved in an off-hand or familiar way with the sons of royalty because they regarded themselves as the equals of the aristocracy (which they were not).[41] They considered themselves highly favoured because of the trust the Emir placed in them; a trust that many felt he was not able to vest on his own sons because they were competing with him for the throne. Status as a *cucanawa* existed independently of any particular slave-title. As such, it was an important component of royal slave identity, and served as a cultural resource from where they drew a significant amount of prestige and power. The physical manifestation of *cucanawa* status were the '*uku-uku*' or 'three-three' marks on the faces of eligible slaves. Palace tradition asserts that the *uku-uku* marks were first given by the Emir Ibrahim Dabo, who had no other way of telling his children apart from those of his royal slaves.[42]

Royal slaves generally identified their interests with those of the ruling

ROYAL SLAVE CULTURE IN KANO

elite, so much so that they came to represent the authority of the state and the Emir to commoners and regular slaves in Kano and beyond. The British conquest initially did little to change this relationship. The concepts of *Amana* and *Asiri* continued to govern the operation of the royal slave system well into the colonial period. After the conquest of Kano, royal slaves stayed in the palace and maintained their own positions in the hierarchy; they had no reason to run away: 'The Emir's slaves preferred to remain in slavery [rather] than gaining their freedom, because when they remained with the Emir, they wore expensive clothes, ate the food they liked, and confiscated property ... Those running away were our slaves, the common man's slaves'.[43]

Royal Slavery and Colonial Rule

The major policy aim of the British between 1903 and 1926 was to bureaucratize and regularize the nature and functions of the Emirate government. They aimed at routinizing and standardizing the form and conduct of what they regarded as a distinctly Fulani ruling class. This was accomplished by redefining pre-colonial official titles along what was basically a Western model of land administration and methods of governance. This is not to say that the British ignored what they termed 'traditional' practice, nor that they were not cognizant of the history of the region. Rather, their policy was directed at goals they found culturally understandable and laudable, and while sometimes modelled on British versions of Hausa-Fulani practice, the means for achieving their administrative goals were based on European models and history. Frederick Lugard noted: 'The British role here is to bring to the country all the gains of civilisation by applied science ... with as little interference as possible with Native customs and modes of thought'.[44] This Fulani political tradition was the tradition interpreted and approved by British officials and anthropologists. Indeed, it was part of the larger process of inventing and reinventing 'native traditions' which could then be used to service and protect colonial interests. This process was often contested, both by British officials and policy makers and by the Kano governing elite.

Between 1903 and 1926 the British attempted to eliminate the responsibilities and duties that royal slaves held in the Kano administrative hierarchy. By virtue of the conquest, the role of royal slaves in the military, including the control over the palace store of weapons, was eliminated. However, between 1903 and 1926 royal slavery not only persisted, but flourished. The royal slave community in the Emir's palace remained effective and independent precisely because it was not a formal bureaucracy along the model that the British were trying to impose. While royal slaves certainly played vital roles in the political and military administration of Kano Emirate, and were often agents of royal centralization, the institution was too fluid to be called a bureaucracy. There was no regular pattern of promotion, the duties and responsibilities of slave offices often shifted with the needs and abilities of individuals, and descent became an important qualification for certain slave titles. While these titles conferred prestige, status, power and authority on their holders, their flexibility and scope for change based on individual relationships and position was tremendous. In this respect, slave titles in and of themselves were less important than the individuals who occupied them. Royal slaves used their informal personal positions to maintain their influence in the face of repeated British attempts to curtail their power. Beyond their place in the hierarchy, royal slaves could draw on a wide variety of cultural resources[45] that both defined and established their place in the palace. Royal slaves were influential because they had close and secure access to the *Sarki* as his confidential advisers; in this case, personal power was more important than institutionalized power. Thus, the role of royal slaves as *kofofi* continued, and the British were unable to eliminate the cultural values that underlay the system.

While Sir Frederick Lugard advocated ruling 'indirectly' through indigenous institutions, he insisted that the Emirs must also obey 'the fundamental laws of humanity and justice'.[46] For Lugard and other British colonial officials, ruling through or with royal slave officials in Kano violated these laws of governance: 'This system-corresponding to the 'Palace Clique' in Constantinople-has been the curse of Nigeria ...it divorces power from responsibility, and places communities under the heel of a gang of low-class and avaricious retainers'.[47] Lugard claimed that the 'pernicious clique of head slaves and eunuchs' were 'the curse of every Emirate in this country', as they did not exercise 'any useful administrative functions [and] have been the greatest source of oppression and tyranny in the past, and to whose evil counsel most of the deposed Emir's owe their fall'.[48] His main criticisms were threefold: royal slaves were basically parasites who performed no worthwhile or important services, they oppressed the commoners, and they had a unique relationship with the Emir which was very difficult for the British to control or govern effectively. The ability of royal slaves to act outside what the British perceived to be the proper bounds of an efficient and progressive political culture troubled and infuriated them. The ideology of the British colonial administration was based on the importance of regularizing offices, making officials responsible for the territory they administered and curbing the 'despotic' power of the Emirs. Increasing revenue through development of regularized taxation was a central goal. In general, they sought to decentralize the administration. By 1909 when it was clear that territorial reorganization had

ROYAL SLAVE CULTURE IN KANO

failed to eliminate royal slavery, the British planned to curtail the power of the Emir and his court by creating a council of free-born title-holders that had distinct responsibilities, in which each counsellor had very precisely defined administrative duties. This policy was designed to replace the royal slave system with title-holders who were free-born and responsible to a wider body of interests than those of the Emir. Although this programme was carried out through approved 'traditional' institutions of governance, the broader aim was to transform and remake 'the other':

> We wish to substitute an ardour for progress and development for the former excitement of war and slave-raiding. Our object should be to give them an interest and an object beyond the routine performance of their duties, to interest them in the scheme of Government, to show them common interests, to engage sympathies in our efforts for secular education, and to promote a legitimate rivalry in civilised progress and even in sports.[49]

Lugard cautioned Residents to closely follow his general policy of standardizing and regularizing Hausa-Fulani political offices. If extended powers were indeed conferred upon an office simply because 'the particular holder happens to be an exceptionally able man' Lugard feared that the office-holder's 'less able successor [would] fail-perhaps with disastrous results'.[50] The use of official titles was also to be minimized if possible. The system of office-holding was certainly utilized to implement reforms; but its informal character, which gave the Emir access to advisers beyond the control of the British, and royal slaves the power to alter or shift the provenance of their offices based on personal relationships and the status of their household, was to be eliminated. In short, the British were trying to insert themselves between the Emir and the *Bayin Sarki*.

Despite their hostility, the colonial regime was forced to work alongside this 'palace clique'. Royal slaves continued to fulfil duties related to their titles, duties that the British were unable to eliminate immediately without making it impossible to govern Kano. In 1903 British officials in Kano were faced with an intransigent indigenous administration. Emir Abbas had the Residency under close supervision by his royal slaves and colonial officials had little room for manoeuvre: '...the Residency is watched the whole time by either the Dan Rimi or when he is not there by some other boy of his ...any act of friendship to us is blacklisted-in the case of a Seriki [*sic*] by dismissal from his post, in other cases by thieves being sent to plunder their houses, or if telekawi [*sic*, commoners] by simply ill-treating and taking their goods'.[51] Even as late as 1921 A. C. G. Hastings noted that it was 'easy to say that all the satellites must be got rid of, but I think it will probably be found that these much abused satellites are really doing useful work. It must

178

SLAVERY AND COLONIAL RULE IN AFRICA

be of great assistance to the Emir to have an intermediary between him and the D. [istrict] Heads'.[52]

After 1905, a series of British Residents attempted to reduce the power of leading royal slaves: '[Our Goal is to] adopt the natives own system but expend all the energy [we] possess in purifying them of what our more advanced civilisation knows to be abuses'.[53] However, royal slaves retained their place and influence in the court because they had a significant place in the palace. Most importantly, they served as the Emir's most trusted informal advisers. Because the *Tara ta Kano,* a council of the Emir's chief councillors,[54] was not reconstituted after the British conquest, the *Bayin Sarki* became even more central to the Emir. In keeping with pre-colonial patterns of office-holding, Abbas regarded the British as yet another faction at his court whose influence could be checked by relying more closely on his *Bayin Sarki.* Thus certain royal slaves became extremely powerful, especially during the reign of Usman, Abbas' successor, despite being gradually stripped of formal military and administrative roles by the British. Perhaps the most important of the official duties shared by the *Shamaki, Dan Rimi,* and *Sallama* was administration of so-called 'fiefs', located throughout the Emirate. Clan leaders appointed to titled positions by Ibrahim Dabo in c. 1819 retained as 'fiefs' the towns and villages they had conquered during the *jihad.* Members of the royal family also had fiefs, which were administered by a variety of free and slave titled officials. The fiefs were not contiguous; indeed, they were widely scattered throughout the Emirate: 'A Galadima might be found residing at [Kano] with perhaps two hundred towns and villages scattered all over the Emirate subject to his authority'.[55] As a result, fief-holders or state officials (*hakimai*) were not resident administrators, but delegated supervision of their territory to subordinates, who collected taxes from the inhabitants.[56] Royal slave messengers were sent to each fief to supervise the actual collection of taxes. They acted as spies for the absentee title-holders in Kano, but did not collect the taxes themselves.[57] Most of the *Jakadu* were under the control of one of the three top slave officials.[58] As more villages were established, some *Jakadu* expanded their offices by appointing clients to oversee tax collection in these villages: 'they have great power with the army of hanger's-on, principally slaves, who surround the emir, block progress, and rule many of the village chiefs'.[59]

Resident F. Cargill's solution to the royal slave 'problem' in Kano was to attempt to abolish the *Jakadu* and force the free-born *Hakimai* to live in the fiefs they administered, with the intention that they would eventually collect a regular salary.[60] The fiefs were also made contiguous. Cargill wanted to eliminate the extortion believed to be rampant throughout the Emirate by checking the 'multiplication of offices by the exaltation of

ROYAL SLAVE CULTURE IN KANO

179

favorite slaves ...for the Emir can no longer assign them to a district to squeeze dry by extortion'.[61] In 1907 Major Festing recommended that the 'personal followers' of the Emir, such as the *Dan Rimi*, not be allowed any 'landed interest' in Kano Emirate.[62] In short, the British wanted to eliminate the Emir's personal favourites from positions of authority over people and land. They hoped that by sending the *Hakimai* into the countryside they would eliminate the 'irresponsible' intermediaries and slaves whose political position would become untenable once they were unable to control collection of revenue. The British were convinced that the system needed to be reformed:

> I think that some of the more important *Hakimai* may turn out of real use to the government after some instruction and supervision. As a class they are men of refinement and understanding, and existing abuses can hardly be laid at their charge, as their offices have hitherto been merely nominal, and their functions usurped by the big slaves.[63]

However, the indigenous system was in no way 'feudal'. The fief-holders had not resided in the Districts because they had no reason to do so, their duty was to supervise tax collection and ensure they could provide a levy of soldiers if required by the Emir. They were territorial 'chiefs', in that they administered land and did not claim proprietary rights over the land they supervised. Likewise, they did not interfere in customary land rights and allocation of land at the local level.[64] Political life was conducted in Kano, and the attempt to move the high-ranking nobility to the new 'Districts' created by the British must have initally seemed troublesome to the governing class. Cargill argued that districts were difficult to reform because the Emir had in the past made 'arbitrary appointments' to official titles, transferring towns from title to title and ousting hereditary families in favour of his own relatives and royal slaves. He hoped to ensure that the Emir would be unable to do this in the future.[65] Likewise, in 1907 the slave districts controlled by the *Shamaki*, *Dan Rimi* and *Sallama* were abolished and incorporated into other districts. Abbas felt that this was a violation of Lugard's promise that the districts would remain under the control of his slaves.[66] However, according to Lugard and Cargill the districts were only allowed to remain under control of the *Bayin Sarki* as a 'temporary expedient' to 'conciliate the Emir and his slaves'. For Cargill, Festing and Palmer the time for conciliation was long past, and they next abolished the Emir's Judicial Council, which further damaged relations between the Emir and the Residency.[67] Festing claimed that the Judicial Council gave royal slaves too much influence in the districts.

Cargill's reforms met with resistance from the Emir, the *Bayin Sarki* and the *Hakimai*. Emir Abbas was concerned that his position and power would

180   SLAVERY AND COLONIAL RULE IN AFRICA

be diminished, making him into a mere 'figure-head'.[68] He also believed that the British were planning to replace him with the former Emir Aliyu.[69] Royal slaves were set against the reforms because they believed their influence would be diminished.[70] The *Hakimai* felt they were being banished from the court and that the direct collection of taxes was beneath them: 'The demand that the Hakimi should go out into the districts was met by sullen refusal ...undoubtedly a good deal of opposition came from the Palace Slaves who feared that if the Hakimi got out of Kano their power would diminish, while that of the Slaves of the Hakimi would be increased'.[71] Ideally, the British regime wanted to assign royal slaves some kind of useful agricultural work in order to increase the production of foodstuffs and boost tax revenue.[72] As the situation deteriorated, Cargill decided to work through certain *Hakimai* and to ignore the Emir's opinions if he considered them unreasonable. British Residents had placed Abbas in a position that made him politically vulnerable. Some of the *Hakimai* who were hostile to Abbas began to deal directly with the British, and used the state of affairs to embarrass the Emir publicly.[73] These officials had discovered that district reorganization could increase their power at the expense of the Emir and his slaves if the British cooperated. Cargill and Festing tried to explain away Abbas' intransigence by stating he lacked 'moral courage' and let himself 'be 'run' by slaves who oddly enough are almost invariably Habe of the lowest class ...[he is unable to] grasp a whiteman's idea of straight dealing and loyalty'.[74]

Essentially, Cargill, Festing and Palmer were advocating ' ...a more direct administration, and the destruction of the Giddan Seriki [*sic*]'.[75] The crisis came to a head after Cargill appointed *Dan Rimi* Allah bar Sarki to the position of *Waziri*. This appointment violated the custom, traditions and political culture of the palace. The post of *Waziri* was supposed to be held only by free-born men.[76] Moreover, the Emir's son and heir apparent, Abdullahi Bayero, was demoted from *Waziri* to *Ciroma* to make room for this slave official. Although Allah bar Sarki was supposedly emancipated before he took office, the appointment initiated a serious political crisis. Allah bar Sarki 'began to behave in an off hand manner to the Emir and Chiroma and encouraged his people to do the same'.[77] The new *Waziri* even became embroiled in a dispute over whether he or the *Chiroma* should pass through the town gate first. Allah bar Sarki was demoted in January 1909, but C. L. Temple believed that if he had remained in office six more months 'there would have been street fighting in Kano between the Emir's following and the Waziri's'.[78] Although Cargill believed that the Emir would not be 'jealous of a trusted slave':[79] 'the nobility of the country would not really accept an ex-slave as the deputy of the Emir'.[80] When he was deposed, Allah bar Sarki was forced to wear his slave loincloth in public

ROYAL SLAVE CULTURE IN KANO

181

and was publicly humiliated in order to make his slave status clear to the entire palace community.[81]

C. L. Temple replaced Cargill in 1909, and was a strong proponent of indirect rule. He criticized the previous administration for attempting to eliminate the Emir from the political life of the Emirate.[82] He repaired relations with Abbas, who in turn relied less on the *Bayin Sarki* once he felt his position was more secure. However, the Emir's authority was re-established, territorial and district reforms actually increased the power of the *Bayin Sarki*, effectively making them the only intermediaries between the *Hakimai* and the Emir. With important *Hakimai* and their retinues out in the districts, royal slaves were able to monopolize the information that travelled between the districts and the palace. Given the fact that the Emir trusted his *Bayin Sarki* their position was firmly entrenched. Furthermore, contrary to British expectations, royal plantations attached to the offices of royal slaves were still in existence in 1912 and appear to have retained their tax-exempt status.[83] Temple was initially more concerned with cultivating the good will of Abbas than in eliminating the royal slave system. However, he initiated the policy of attempting to substitute 'responsible' counsellors for the *Bayin Sarki*.[84] Soon a great deal of official correspondence was passing through *Waziri* Gidado. The native treasury was created to regulate finances, tax assessment was initiated to further regularize taxation, and in 1916 salaries were paid to district-heads, and villages were placed under responsible Village Headmen. In 1917 the reforms were extended to *Hakimai* living in rural areas.[85] After 1919, these tax and financial reforms lessened the ability of the Emir Usman to provide for his less important royal slaves.[86] However, the most important royal slave personalities had access to both informal resources and the beneficence of the Emir, rendering them immune for a time from the British financial restructuring. For instance, the ability of senior royal slaves to co-opt members of the 'native police-force' was *supposed* to be eliminated by carefully keeping records of domestic accounts. However, even in 1925 royal slaves were still able to give members of the palace establishment gifts, which even included horses purchased with 'public funds'.[87] For years royal slaves had developed networks of clientage by distributing material goods and rewards, and they continued to do so during the early colonial period.

While the British argued that they were working within the 'traditional' system, they had actually introduced some startling innovations based on their own conception of good government and administration. They were attempting to undermine the informal, personal and face-to-face methods of control often employed by royal slaves. No further action was taken until 1919, when Emir Abbas died and the British once again confronted an unstable political situation. The succession of *Sarkin Kano* Usman gave the

182 SLAVERY AND COLONIAL RULE IN AFRICA

Bayin Sarki an opportunity to reassert their control over the internal administration. Usman was quite old when he came to the throne, and was sick throughout his term of office. Key individuals among the *Bayin Sarki* began handling district administration without consulting the Emir, who was often too ill to give attention. Oral tradition is unanimous in stating that during the reign of Usman the *Bayin Sarki* became extremely powerful in their capacity as *Kofofi*.[88] In 1924 Arnett emphasized that messengers should not be the personal servants of the Emir but properly appointed officials. Otherwise, the 'veil of semi-secrecy' required by the *Bayin Sarki* to maintain their positions would never be lifted.[89] In 1921 Palmer claimed that the slaves were so influential that the *Waziri* was excluded from the Emir's counsel and recommended that the slave system be abolished.[90] The Governor agreed, but noted it was essential to determine who was necessary for the 'transaction of public business' and who were employed by the Emir 'for the purposes of his household'.[91] Once that decision was made, he recommended that those among the Emir's household who persisted in interfering in public affairs should be turned out of Kano. In short, he suggested that personalities had to be eliminated, not just the slave-titles.[92] Likewise, by insisting that the palace community be paid wages out of the Native Treasury he hoped to further drive a wedge between the Emir and his royal slaves and control the number and kind of 'servants' serving inside the palace. Oral tradition suggests that the free-born title-holders led by *Madaki* Mahmud engineered this palace coup to increase their own influence at the expense of the slaves.[93] However, the colonial regime was unable to make significant progress on any reforms until July 1925, when they forced Usman to accept the dispersal of his top royal slaves to their royal *gandu*. The *Madaki* and *Sarkin Bai* were brought in from their districts to serve along with the *Waziri* as the official and 'responsible' counsellors of the Emir.[94]

The British saw this as a revival of Hausa-Fulani political tradition: 'On the general question of the council and responsible advisors, the Resident Kano emphasized [that] it was ...a case of extricating the original functions of responsible advisors and themselves from the muck-heap into which they had fallen ...The Emir Usman ...heartily acquiesced in the accusation of having fallen from grace, and agreed that the true system was a chief with responsible advisors, and that such was the position of old as regards the constitution of Kano, though he was suspected of saying this with his tongue in cheek'.[95] Tongue in cheek indeed; the duties of each official were carefully and precisely apportioned. The messengers were now appointed by the colonial regime. The proper method of keeping records and neatness in the presentation of material was also emphasized.[96] In short, the way was now open to 'civilized' administration: 'The almost day-to-day direct

ROYAL SLAVE CULTURE IN KANO

contact of the senior members of the Council individually with the District Officers, the European departmental officers and the Resident should I believe lead to their learning the complicated art of administration on modern and civilised lines ...'.[97] Certainly, as indicated above, previous rulers had relied on councillors, and Mohammad Rumfa had even created the *Tara ta Kano* as an advisory body. However, the British envisioned a somewhat different organizational structure:

> ...the failure of the central administration to keep pace with the times and to function effectively as a controlling factor of the vast population had led the Governor in 1921 to consider seriously though reluctantly a suggestion for a closer direct control of the Emirate by the British staff. This was averted by the action taken in 1925 in reorganising the Council. The Council though the separate functions of its members are still in an evolutionary stage is composed of members who in an increasing degree carry out on behalf of and in the name of the Emir the responsible control of the departments of state with which they are entrusted. In short they are his ministers. All members of the Council have their separate departmental offices.[98]

The comment above is followed by a long list of functions that each Councillor had. The Council replaced the personal power of the *Bayin Sarki*: 'Irresponsible acts on the part of the ruler, mischievously elaborated through irresponsible channels, could now definitely be checked'.[99] Left unsaid by British officials was the fact that the Council also offered them closer control and supervision over the internal administration of Kano; indeed, service on the Council became a matter of 'consultation' between the Emir and Resident.[100] In order to ensure that the influence of royal slaves was eliminated, the most influential slaves were forced out of Kano along with their households. The system would otherwise still have been subject to their interference.[101] In 1929 British officials would comment that they had supervised the transition of Kano from a 'mediaeval city' into a 'modern one'.

The object was to ensure that the abolition of the *Bayin Sarki* was a fait accompli when the next Emir came to the throne.[102] Usman died on 23 April 1925, and his successor Abdullahi Bayero was installed in 1926. As a condition of his installation he agreed to manumit the rest of his household slaves. He also agreed to work through so-called 'Responsible Chiefs' on the 'Council'.[103] Even with the establishment of a formal, free council the legacy of certain royal slave personalities was not swept away. It was not easy for the new councillors to 'step into the shoes of powerful slaves whose self-confidence and greed were encouraged by temporary favour and whose attitude had to be schooled by ready subservience'.[104] According to oral

184 SLAVERY AND COLONIAL RULE IN AFRICA

tradition the royal slave system continued to operate inside the *Gidan Sarki*. Royal slaves who held little or no personal influence with the Emir continued to carry out their duties, including some title-holders. Others took positions with the Native Authority.[105] Abdullahi Bayero did not expect many of the royal slaves to leave the palace. He gave duties to remaining members of the *Shamakawa*, *Sallamawa* and *Rimawa* that were similar in scope to the duties that previous title-holders occupied. But times had changed. The duties of royal slaves living in the *Gidan Sarki* after 1926 were ceremonial or related to domestic activities.[106] The political culture that had sustained the royal slave system through the early period of colonial rule had now shifted to one that relied on free councillors and a more bureaucratic, formalized system of administration.[107] Symbolically, this was also the period when Western style public infrastructure projects and social services (electricity, schools and hospitals) were extended into the palace.[108] The role of royal slaves in the public sphere had been eliminated by the British. They no longer had military duties to perform or land to administer. Nor could they rely on their roles as advisers to the Emir or *Kofofi*. These positions had been seized by the Council members nominated by the British regime. It was by replacing key individuals and restricting the personal relationship between the Emir and the *Bayin Sarki* in the conduct of public affairs that the end of royal slavery as a state institution was brought about by the British colonial regime.

GLOSSARY

Amana	reciprocal loyalty, trust
Asiri	a secret
Bayin Sarki	slaves of the king
Cucanawa	those born into slavery of slave parents
Gandu	slave plantation or farm
Gidan Sarki	literally 'house of the king'. Refers specifically to the Emir's palace
Hakimi (plural Hakimai)	District-Head or Fief-Holder
Jakada (plural Jakadu)	royal messenger or servant
Kofa (plural Kofofi)	gate
Sarki	king or Emir

NOTES

I would like to thank Paul E. Lovejoy, Martin Klein and Suzanne Miers for their comments on a preliminary draft of this paper. Fieldwork in Kano was supported by grants from the Social Sciences and Humanities Research Council of Canada, the National Chapter of the IODE and York University.

1. For the conquest see R. A. Adeleye, *Power and Diplomacy in Northern Nigeria* (New York, 1971); Mahmud Modibbo Tukur, 'The Imposition of British Colonial Domination on the Sokoto Caliphate, Borno and Neighbouring States' (PhD Dissertation, unpublished,

ROYAL SLAVE CULTURE IN KANO

185

Ahmadu Bello University, 1979); Richard H. Dusgate, *The Conquest of Northern Nigeria* (London, 1985); D. J. M. Muffett, *Concerning Brave Captains* (London, 1964). On British administration see: Mary Bull, 'Indirect Rule in Northern Nigeria 1906–1911', in Kenneth Robinson and Frederick Manning (eds.), *Essays in Imperial Government* (Oxford, 1965), pp.47–87; C. N. Ubah, *Government and Administration of Kano Emirate* (Nsukka, Nigeria, 1985); P. K. Tibenderana, *Sokoto Province Under British Rule* (Zaria, Nigeria, 1988).

2. Michael Mason, 'The History of Mr. Johnson: Progress and Protest in Northern', *Canadian Journal of African Studies*, 27, 2 (1993), p.211. See also Brian Sharwood Smith, *"But Always As Friends": Recollections of British Administration in the Cameroons and Northern Nigeria 1921–1957* (Durham, 1969); Robert Huessler, *The British in Northern Nigeria* (London, 1968).

3. Cited in Mason, 'The History of Mr. Johnson', p.211. See Charles Allen, *Tales from the Dark Continent* (New York, 1983), xix.

4. See Philip J. Shea, 'How Indirect was Indirect Rule? A Documentary Approach to an Administrative Problem', *Kano Studies*, NS Vol.2, No.3 (1982/85), pp.154–62; C. N. Ubah, 'Colonial Adminstration and the Spread of Islam in Northern Nigeria', *The Muslim World*, 81, 2 (1991), pp.133–48; Anne Phillips, *The Enigma of Colonialism: British Policy in West Africa* (London, 1989).

5. See Paul E. Lovejoy and Jan S. Hogendorn, *Slow Death For Slavery: The Course of Abolition in Northen Nigeria, 1897–1936* (Cambridge, 1993) and Tukur, pp.248–333.

6. See *The Kano Chronicle* in H. R. Palmer, *Sudanese Memoirs* (London, 1967; originally published in 1928).

7. Murray Last, *The Sokoto Caliphate* (London, 1967); M. Hiskett, *The Sword of Truth: The Life and Times of Shehu Dan Fodio* (London, 1973); Ibraheem Sulaiman, *A Revolution in History: The Jihad of Usman Dan Fodio* (London, 1986).

8. M. Hiskett (ed.), 'Kitab Al Farq: A Work on the Habe Kingdoms Attributed to Uthman don Fodio', *Bulletin of the School of Oriental and African Studies*, XXIII, 3 (1960), p.567.

9. Adamu Mohammed Fika, *The Kano Civil War and British Overrule, 1882–1940* (Ibadan, 1978), pp.18–19.

10. Interviews with *Dan Masinin Kano*, 28 January 1996; Alhaji Muhktar Kwaru, 31 July 1996; *Dan Rimi*, 17 June 1996.

11. Paul Staudinger, *In the Heart of the Hausa States*, translated by Johanna E. Moody (Athens, 1990; originally published in 1889), I, pp.230–1.

12. A. A. Dokaji, *Kano ta Dabo Cigari*, cited by Halil Ibrahim Sa'id, 'Revolution and Reaction: the Fulani Jihad in Kano and its Aftermath, 1807–1919' (PhD dissertation, unpublished, University of Michigan, 1978), p.170.

13. Joseph Smalldone, *Warfare in the Sokoto Caliphate* (Cambridge, 1977), pp.110–33; Robin Law, *The Horse in West African History* (Oxford, 1980).

14. Douglas Edwin Ferguson, 'Nineteenth Century Hausaland Being a Description by Imam Imoru of the Land, Economy, and Society of his People' (PhD Dissertation, unpublished, University of California, Los Angeles, 1973), pp.209–10. On general duties see Interview with Alahji Abubukar Soron Dinki, 21 November 1996. See also interviews from the Yusufu Yunusa Collection, especially with *Dan Rimin Kano*, 30 December 1975, M. Isyaku, 17 September 1975, Muhammadu Rabi'u, 13 July 1975 and Muhammadu Sarkin Yaki, 29 September 1975. See also Yusufu Yunusa, 'Slavery in Nineteenth Century Kano' (BA Dissertation, unpublished, Abdullahi Bayero University, Kano, 1976).

15. Interviews with *Madakin Dan Rimi*, 18 August 1996; *Weziri*, 4 August 1996; *Sarkin Zage*, 13 August 1996.

16. Interviews with *Maja Sirdi*, 9 August 1996; *Maja Sirdi*, 20 August 1996; *Sarkin Ruwa*, 2 August 1996; Ilu Figini, 17 July 1996.

17. Interviews with *Sarkin Ruwa*, 2 August 1996; *Sarkin Dogarai*, 22 November 1995; Palmer, *Kano Chronicle*, p.131. See also: Interviews with Alhaji Muhktar Kwaru, 31 June 1996; *Jakadan Garko*, 3 December 1995.

18. M. Hiskett, 'The Song of Bagauda: A Hausa King List and Homily in Verse II', *Bulletin of the School of Oriental and African Studies*, 28, 2 (1965), p.118.

19. Abdullahi Mahadi, 'The State and Economy: The Sarauta System and its Role in Shaping

186 SLAVERY AND COLONIAL RULE IN AFRICA

the Society and Economy of Kano with Particular Reference to the Eighteenth and Nineteenth Centuries' (PhD Dissertation, unpublished, Ahmadu Bello University, 1982), p.271.

20. See SNP 10/9 120p/1921 for comments on royal slave wealth.
21. Interviews with *Dan Rimi*, 17 June 1996; Alhaji Muhktar Kwaru, 31 July 1996. See especially: Heidi J. Nast, 'Space, History and Power: Stories of Spatial and Social Change in the Palace of Kano, Northern Nigeria' (Ph.D. Dissertation, unpublished, McGill University, 1992).
22. R.C. Abraham, *An Introduction to Spoken Hausa and Hausa Reader for European Students* (London, 1940), p.952. On clientage, see Peter K. Tibenderana, 'British Administration and the Decline of the Patronage-Client System in Northwestern Nigeria, 1900–1934', *African Studies Review*, 32, 1 (1989), pp.71–95.
23. See Interviews with Alhaji Mohammad, 25 June 1996; *Kilishi*, 3 June 1996; *Madakin Dan Rimi*, 17 August 1996; *Sarkin Ruwa*, 2 August 1996. The first *Shettima* was appointed as a reward for his service in the Kano civil war.
24. Interview with Abba Tik, 14 November 1995.
25. Interviews with *Makaman Dan Rimi*, 28 Febuary 1996 and 26 July 1996; *Dan Rimi*, 17 July 1996.
26. Interview with *Babban Zagi*, 28 February 1996.There was a large excess of females over males (+6,379), which was explained by 'the large female households of the Emir, the Emir's chief slaves, the Waziri and other leading men ...'. SNP 9/5 3577/1921. On concubinage see Paul E. Lovejoy, 'Concubinage and the Status of Women in Early Colonial Northern Nigeria', *Journal of African History*, 29, 2 (1988), pp.245–66; Paul E. Lovejoy, 'Concubinage in the Sokoto Caliphate', in *Slavery and Abolition*, 11, 2 (1990), pp.159–89; Beverly Mack, 'Women and Slavery in Nineteenth-Century Hausaland' in Elizabeth Savage (ed.), *The Human Commodity: Perspectives on the Trans-Saharan Slave Trade* (London, 1992), pp.89–110. See also: Heidi J. Nast, 'The Impact of British Imperialism on the Landscape of Female Slavery in the Kano Palace, Northern Nigeria', *Africa*, 64, 1 (1994).
27. Interviews with *Babban Zagi*, 29 February 1996; *Dan Buram*, 3 September 1996. See also the family tree of M. Muhammadu Dikko, in the *Gwarzo District Notebook*. Dikko's father was brought from Borno to Kano as a boy after being enslaved in 'Rabeh's wars'. He grew up under the *Dan Rimi* and later married the niece of the 5th Emir Muhammad Bello. I should like to thank Professor Phil Shea for this reference.
28. Interview with Wada Dako, 27 January 1996.
29. Interviews with Wada Dako, 27 January 1996; Alhaji Umaru, 11 January 1996.
30. Interview with Alhaji Sadauki Panshekera, August 1977, conducted by Sai'd, 'Revolution and Reaction', p.353. The eldest son of Ibrahim Dabo, Usman Maje Ringim (Emir of Kano, 1819–1855) was brought up by Shamaki Nasamu and Abdullahi Maje Karofi (Emir of Kano, 1855–1882) was placed under under the care of Dan Rimi Barka. The *Shamaki* was required to discipline the Emir's children. See Interview with Wada Dako, 27 January 1996. Generally, only eunuchs were allowed in the female quarters. See also Heidi Nast, 'Space, History and Power'.
31. See Interview with Wada Dako, 27 January 1996.
32. Interviews with *Mabudi*, 1 November 1995; *Mabudi*, 9 February 1996; *Lifidi*, 24 November 1995. The current *Lifidi* stated that the current Emir used to play in the house of his family because of the relationship between his grandfather and Abdullahi Bayero's father. The *Lifidi*'s grandfather gave Ado Bayero one of his daughters as a concubine.Likewise, *Lifidi*'s elder sister was given to Ado Bayero as a concubine.
33. After the death of Emir Abdullahi, Mohammad Bello came to the throne. He purged Kano officialdom, dismissed a number of royal slaves, and made them divorce their free-born wives (Interview with *Mabudi*, 1 November 1995). After Bello's death Tukur succeeded to the throne against custom and the wishes of the many high title-holders. A civil war then broke out as Yusuf, a son of Abdullahi, tried to seize the Emirship. The disenfranchised slave community of Abdullahi supported Yusuf.
34. Interviews with *Sarkin Shanu*, 6 June 1996; *Waziri*, 12 August 1996.

ROYAL SLAVE CULTURE IN KANO

35. Interviews with *Lifidi*, 24 November 1995; *Shamaki*, 15 December 1995; *Mabudi*, 1 November 1995; Alhaji Muhktar Kwaru, 17 July 1996.
36. See Smith,*Government in Kano* (Boulder, 1997) p.293.
37. Smith, Ibid.
38. Interviews with *Makaman Dan Rimi*, 20 February 1996; Wada Dako, 27 January 1996.
39. See Palmer's comments in SNP 10/9 105p/1921. See also SNP 6/3 136/1907 and CSO 8/6/3 H.C. Gollan to Lugard, 24 June 1903.
40. G. P. Bargery, *A Hausa-English Dictionary* (Zaria, 1993; originally published in 1934).
41. Interview with *Makaman Dan Rimi*, 26 July 1996.
42. Interviews *Dan Rimi*, 15 December 1995; *Babban Zagi*, 28 February 1996; *Shamaki*, 17 December 1995.
43. Interview with M. Mumammadu, 9/10/75, Yusufu Yunusa Collection. See also *Northern Nigeria Annual Report*, No.594, 1907–1908.
44. Frederick Lugard, *Political Memoranda: Revision of Instructions to Political Officers* (London: Frank Cass, 1970), p.9.
45. See W. Arens and Ivan Karp (eds.), *Creativity of Power: Cosmology and Action in African Societies* (Washington: Smithsonian Institution Press, 1989), p.xiv and the previous section.
46. Lugard, *Political Memoranda* and *Annual Reports*, p.126. Cited by Ubah, *Government and Administration of Kano Emirate,* p.8.
47. *Northern Nigeria Annual Reports*, 1904. See also SNP 15/1 acc. 289.
48. *Northern Nigeria Annual Reports*, 1907–1908.
49. Lugard, *Political Memoranda*, p.317.
50. Lugard, *Political Memoranda*, p.300.
51. SNP 6/3 136/1907.
52. SNP 10/9 120p/1921. This situation was not unique to Kano. See SNP 7/8 3095/1907; SNP 7/9 1538/1908; SNP 7/8 2392/1907; SNP 7/10 5089/1909; SNP 10/1 631p/1913; SNP 7/13 6824/1912. See also M.G. Smith, *Affairs of Daura* (Berkeley, 1978).
53. SNP 7/8 3095/1907.
54. See also Paul E. Lovejoy *et al.*, 'C. L. Temple's "Notes on the History of Kano" [1909]: A Lost Chronicle of Political Office', *Sudanic Africa*, 4 (1993).
55. *Northern Nigeria Annual Report*, 1907–08, pp.25–6.
56. See *Northern Nigeria Annual Report*, 1904, 220; interview with Mallam Hamza, conducted by C. N. Ubah in Kano, August 1972.
57. See C. N. Ubah, 'Islamic Fiscal System and Colonial Innovations: The Kano Example', *Islamic Quarterly*, 23 (1979), p.176.
58. Interviews with Dan Rimin Kano, 30/12/75, Yusufu Yunusa Collection; Baba Jibir, 20/06/75, Musa Collection.
59. SNP 6/4 c.111/1908.
60. See SNP 7/10 472/1909.
61. *Northern Nigeria Annual Report*, 1904, pp.221–2. See also SNP 6/3 162/1907; SNP 7/8 3095/1907.
62. SNP 7/8 3095/1907.
63. *Northern Nigeria Annual Report*, 1904, p.227.
64. See Paul E. Lovejoy and Jan S. Hogendorn, *Slow Death for Slavery* and Tijani Garba, 'Taxation in some Hausa Emirates, c 1860–1939' (PhD Dissertation, unpublished, University of Birmingham, 1986).
65. SNP 7/9 1538/1908 and SNP 7/8 5112/1907.
66. Interview with *Madakin Kano*, 4 February 1996 and *Dan Iya*, 28 June 1996. See also SNP 7/9 2949/1908 and SNP 6/4 2/1908.
67. SNP 7/10 472/1909.
68. SNP 7/8 1543/1907;SNP 7/9 4992/1908; SNP 6/3 162/1907.
69. SNP 7/8 2392/1907.
70. Interview with *Sarkin Shanu*, 7 June 1996. SNP 7/8 2392/1907; SNP 7/9 2949/1908; SNP 6/4 c. 111/1908.
71. KANOPROF c. 111 and SNP 120p/1921. See also interviews with *Sarkin Shanu*, 7 June 1996 and *Dan Iya*, 28 June 1996.

188 SLAVERY AND COLONIAL RULE IN AFRICA

72. KANOPROF c. 111.
73. See SNP 15/3 A12, Palmer to Festing, 5 September 1907. See also: Ubah, *Government and Administration*, pp.54–5.
74. SNP 7/10 472/1909.
75. See SNP 6/3 136/1907.
76. See Interview with *Magajin Mallam*, 10 July 1996. See also: Ubah, *Governmental Administration*, pp.66–7 and Lovejoy *et al.*, 'Notes', pp.15–21.
77. SNP 7/10 6415/1909, Kano Annual Report.
78. Ibid.
79. SNP 7/9 5141/1908, cited in Lovejoy *et al.*, 'Notes', p.16.
80. SNP 6/4 c.111/1908.
81. Interviews with Wada Dako, 11 January 1996;*Dan Rimi*, 17 June 1996; Aliyu Waziri, 27 February 1996. See Palmer's comments dated 23 April 1921 in SNP 10/9 105p/1921.
82. KANOPROF c. 111.
83. SNP 7 4055/1912.
84. See SNP 7/10 6415/1909. See also Interview with the *Waziri*, 4 August 1996.
85. On Village re-organization see: SNP 7/10 3635/1909; SNP 10/4 170p/1916; KANOPROF 108/1916; SNP 10/5 518p/1916; KANOPROF 4/4 202/1917; SNP 10/9 120p/1921; SNP 9/12 635/1925; SNP 17/2 16687 Vol.I; on Taki see SNP 7/10 6415/1909; SNP 10/2 165p/1914; SNP 7/13 1114/1912; KANOPROF 5/1 1708A; SNP 10/6 491p/1918; SNP 10/2 165p/1914; SNP 10/8 316p/1920. On the *Bait al Mal* see: SNP 7/10 6415/1909; SNP 7/10 3635/1909; SNP 7/10 98p/1915; SNP 17/8 K. 105 Vol.I. See also Lovejoy and Hogendorn, *Slow Death for Slavery*; Tijani Garba, 'Taxation in some Hausa Emirates, c. 1860–1930'; and Sule Bello, 'State and Economy in Kano, 1894–1960' (PhD dissertation, unpublished, Ahmadu Bello University, 1982).
86. See Heidi Nast, 'Space, History and Power', 157.
87. SNP 9/12 635/1925 and Interview with Wada Dako, 27 January 1996.
88. Interviews with *Dan Rimi*, 17 June 1996; *Makaman Dan Rimi*, 20 February 1996. See also SNP 17/8 K. 105 vol. III; SNP 9/12 635/1925.
89. Arnett's handing over notes, *The Arnett Papers*, Mss Afr. s. 952, Rhodes House Library.
90. SNP 10/9 120p/1921.
91. SNP 10/9 120p/1921.
92. SNP 10/9 120p/1921.
93. See Interviews with *Makaman Dan Rimi*, 26 July 1996; *Madaki*, 13 December 1995.
94. KANOPROF 25/1926.
95. Cited by Smith, *Government in Kano*, p.259.
96. SNP 9/12 635/1925.
97. SNP 17/2 18956 Vol.II. See also SNP 17/3 21326 Vol.II.
98. SNP 17/2 16687 Vol.I.
99. SNP 17/2 16687 Vol.I.See Interviews with *Shamaki*, 15 December 1995; *Dan Rimi*, 17 December 1995.
100. SNP 17/2 16687 Vol.I; SNP 17/2 14686 Vol. I.
101. Interview with *Makaman Dan Rimi*, 20 February 1996.
102. See Arnett's handing over notes, *The Arnett Papers*, MSS Afr. s. 952.
103. SNP 17/8 K. 105 vol. III. See also Interview with *Dan Iya*, 28 June 1996.
104. SNP17/8 K. 6892. See also KANOPROF 24/1926.
105. See CSO 26/11799 Vol. IV, Secretary of the Northern Provinces to Chief Secretary, Lagos, 5 December 1936.
106. Interviews with *Makaman Dan Rimi*, 20 February 1996; *Sarkin Shanu*, 6 June 1996 *Dan Iya*, 28 June 1996.
107. SNP 17/2 12004, vol. I. See also SNP 17/2 18956, vol.II.
108. A point emphasized by Heidi Nast, 'Space, History and Power', p.177.

'When Slaves Left, Owners Wept': Entrepreneurs and Emancipation among the Igbo People

DON C. OHADIKE

Introduction

This chapter looks at the impact of British colonial rule on the institution of slavery among the Igbo people of southeastern Nigeria. It begins with examination of slavery in the region before 1900 and then goes on to look at British efforts to suppress it. Finally, it assesses the success or otherwise of these efforts. The purpose of the chapter is threefold. The first is to remedy the shortfall in African economic history that underestimates the importance of slave labour to relations of production in kinship-based economies. The second is to show that most slave owners, even within kinship structures, were entrepreneurs who used labour for economic production. The third is to demonstrate that the abolition of internal African slavery by European colonial rulers destroyed the pre-colonial entrepreneurial classes, eliminated a major source of labour, and altered the nature of dependency, power and authority for the Igbo people.

I focus my discussion on owners rather than on slaves to give the former a coverage they are often denied in African economic history texts. Most accounts of slavery within kinship-based African formations focus a great deal on slaves, but very little on owners. The result is that not enough is known about slave owners and the underlying economic factors that kept slavery working, century after century. Owners were the more active partners in slave-master relationships, albeit hostile, and slavery could never have functioned without their determination to make it work. They made the laws that regulated slavery, and most of the problems that the emancipation drive ran into were caused by their recalcitrance. In some parts of Africa, including Igboland, colonial armed forces had to be deployed against them. Slaves, on the other hand, whether they left or stayed and renegotiated their terms of service, merely took advantage of the conflict that raged between owners and colonial officers. Furthermore, in Igboland, as in some other areas, the stigma of slave status persisted, not because former slaves refused to forget their servile origins, but because former owners refused to forget that they formally were masters.

Although some Igbo slaves were secured for prestige and even strategic reasons, the vast majority was acquired for economic reasons. I believe that those writers who treat slavery within kinship structures as a non-economic institution are mistaken. The Igbo case confirms that there was a constant demand for labour for economic production – to grow crops, to produce palm oil and kernel, to carry loads, to paddle canoes, and to work as trading assistants. The demand for these forms of labour was satisfied, whenever possible, by enslavement. For in the absence of a well developed system of mobile wage labour, recourse to slave labour was an attractive choice. Moreover, since labour was a scarce commodity, owners exported slaves overseas only if internal supply outstripped demand, or when they reckoned that they would profit more by selling than by retaining them. We must, therefore, recognize that slave owners, whether acting as users or sellers of slaves, were enterprising men and women. The decisions they made were entrepreneurial in nature, and contributed to the astonishing increases in slave and palm oil exports from the Bights of Benin and Biafra.

The Atlantic Slave Trade and the Making of Igbo Entrepreneurs, 1650–1850

Slave exports from the Bights of Biafra and Benin began as early as the 1500s and increased over the years. In the eighteenth century, for example, Captain Adams stated that over a period of twenty years, 320, 000 Igbos were sold at Bonny, 50,000 at Calabar and Elem Kalabari.[1] Until well into the period of abolition, as Richard and John Lander testified, large fleets of canoes continued to bring slaves and provisions down the Niger River.[2] The trade created entrepreneurial classes and integrated Igboland into a world-wide economic system linked to spices, sugar, tobacco, cotton and industrial goods in the Americas, Europe and Asia. Unfortunately, like most African communities, the greatest contribution of the Igbo entrepreneurs to this global economic system was slaves. When the Atlantic slave trade was supplanted by 'legitimate' trade in the nineteenth century, Igbo entrepreneurs quickly entered the new business and emerged as the leading exporters of palm oil and kernel.

Pre-colonial Igbo entrepreneurs included traders, merchants, the heads of religious establishments, craftsmen and women, and the sole owners of cottage industries. Whatever line of enterprise they followed, most were household heads who accumulated their initial capital through hard work and thrift. The most successful were those who commanded the most wealth and dependants. Since status and wealth usually were achieved, not ascribed, parents socialized their young ones into understanding that hard work was the surest avenue to wealth and power. Thus every Igbo boy or

ENTREPRENEURS AND EMANCIPATION AMONG THE IGBO 191

girl began his or her life as an apprentice. From a very early age, a boy accompanied his father to the farm or on trading ventures. After a long period of apprenticeship, the boy would establish himself as an independent farmer or trader. He might receive assistance from his father, but there was a limit to how much assistance would be expected or given. One of the early lessons he would learn was that the success of any business depended on the number of reliable dependants. A dependant might be a wife, pawn, child, apprentice or slave. He would first aspire to secure a wife with whom he would start a household. In due course, and depending on how successful his household became, he might attract additional wives and acquire some slaves and pawns.

The same principles applied to women. From a very tender age, a girl regularly accompanied her mother to the farm and market place and in a few years would master the crafts. Like her male counterpart, she would realize that the success of any business depended on the number of reliable dependants or partners a person could secure. She therefore would endeavour to attract a husband with whom she would start a household. She might even decide to join an existing household as a junior wife or partner. Her status as a wife would not prevent her from setting up herself as an independent entrepreneur, operating from the very household to which she belonged. To increase the size of their labour force, some female entrepreneurs purchased their own slaves. In Atani and Osomari, for example, a female trader could purchase slaves to accompany her during her trading tours up and down the Niger river. The slaves paddled her trading canoe and helped her dispose of her merchandise. Also on the lower Niger, women acted as large-scale commercial farmers, utilizing slave labour. In 1841, MacGregor Laird, a British traveller, visited a woman of Aboh who had over two hundred slaves whom she used for the production of palm oil, yams and maize.[3]

Moreover, Igbo women were free to increase their labour force by taking other women as wives, thus becoming 'female husbands'. Ifi Amadiume reported that one Igbo woman had nine wives.[4] This enterprising 'female husband' lived in her husband's household and was herself one of several wives. She was reputed to command more wealth than her husband. A 'female husband' usually was an entrepreneur. By paying the customary bride price, she acquired the services usually associated with marriage and secured a female helper with whom she shared some of the work of the household. If she was a trader, 'her wife' would act as her trading assistant or partner. A woman who had more than one wife and engaged in different activities, like farming, trading, and weaving, would assign different responsibilities to her different wives. In short, in these Igbo communities, kinship idioms permitted successful women entrepreneurs to own as many

192   SLAVERY AND COLONIAL RULE IN AFRICA

slaves and wives as they wished or could afford, and to enjoy the same power, privilege, and prestige as male entrepreneurs.

I call these production units entrepreneurial households because they were strongly connected to enterprise. However, I will limit the terms entrepreneurs and entrepreneurial households to the more successful ones, recognizing that, before the introduction of a system of mobile wage labour into Igboland in the twentieth century, every household was potentially entrepreneurial. One major difference was that the more successful entrepreneurial households were under a constant pressure to admit outsiders because of their greater involvement in business and because their continued success depended on their size. As entrepreneurs, their economic survival was of primary importance.

The pressure to secure labour, both for export and for internal use, encouraged the expansion of several entrepreneurial groups, the most prominent among them being merchants who traded in slaves and imported European goods. Aro and Aboh merchants belonged to this group. Aro traders dominated the trade of regions lying to the east and west of the Cross River estuary, while Aboh merchants dominated the Lower Niger trade. Aboh traders were the major commercial intermediaries between coastal merchants and hinterland slave raiders and traders. This hinterland stretched to the Niger and Benue confluence and beyond, covering a distance of over five hundred miles.[5] During his visit to Aboh in 1841, MacGregor Laird called on several male traders of the town and found that some had over two hundred slaves.[6] Although kidnapping was rampant throughout Igboland and was well organized, Aboh entrepreneurs secured slaves mostly by purchase.

The Aro, on the other hand, acquired their slaves mostly from judicial incrimination and occasional warfare. Aro entrepreneurs were the most notorious Igbo slave dealers. Their oracles also acted as centres for divination and enslavement. The principal Aro oracle, *ibinoukpabi,* also known as the Long Juju, was only one of many Igbo oracles. Arochukwu was the home of the Long Juju and it was a court of appeal. Litigants came there from Igbo and non-Igbo towns to present their cases. The Aro, acting on behalf of the Long Juju, imposed heavy fines on the guilty and sold most of them into slavery, claiming that the oracle had 'eaten them'. Aro entrepreneurs often instigated wars between Igbo towns and used the confused political situation to impose themselves on the defeated groups from whom they extracted slaves. Those who did most of the fighting for the Aro were the people of Ohafia, Abam, Abiriba and Nkporo-Eda, sometimes loosely referred to as 'Abam mercenaries'. These warriors were not mercenaries but men who needed human heads as trophies, to demonstrate their courage in order to win the prized Ufiem Title.[7] Many

ENTREPRENEURS AND EMANCIPATION AMONG THE IGBO   193

other groups also availed themselves of the services of these fighters. Though motivated by diverse economic, social and political reasons, these wars resulted in enslavement.[8]

Next in order of success were entrepreneurs engaged in large-scale farming. They kept large stocks of slaves, depending on how wealthy they were and the amount of land they wished to cultivate. The Obi of Issele-Ukwu had several hundred slaves. In Oguta, the average holding was twenty, while in less affluent communities, some enterprising farmers owned no more than four slaves. These large-scale farmers contributed to the production of yams for the provisioning trade and also helped to sustain the Niger Delta communities that eventually gave up farming and salt making for the more lucrative European trade. An entrepreneurial household was thus a social and economic institution whose success and prestige depended on its size. Since labour was vital for entrepreneurial success, most Igbo households showed a tendency towards expansion rather than consolidation, that is to say, they tried to secure rather than part with labour. Moreover, since slaves were the best form of labour that could be acquired in the shortest possible time, and could be made to perform a wide range of services, they were an important source of wealth and power.

The third group of slave owners who deserve notice were religious priests. These men and women owned many slaves, some of them cult slaves or *osu,* dedicated to the services of the gods they served. Their methods of securing slaves were bizarre, however. A priest, believing that the deity he served needed some glorification, would demand a slave from the village. Money would be collected and a slave purchased and dedicated to the deity. The victim thus became an involuntary *osu* – a chattel dedicated to a deity. Some times, a freeborn man, fearing attack by his enemies, or a woman unwilling to marry a man chosen by her parents, might run to a *juju* (oracle) and place himself or herself under its protection.[9] *Osu* were not slaves in the ordinary sense of the word because they could neither be bought nor sold and could move about freely, yet they were discriminated against. Marriage between them and freeborn persons was taboo. Though well treated, the chief priests of the religious establishments to which they belonged exploited them by demanding labour.

The Golden Age of Pre-colonial Igbo Entrepreneurs, 1850–1900

Whatever success Igbo entrepreneurs might have achieved during the era of the Atlantic slave trade was dwarfed by the prosperity that they enjoyed in the second half of the nineteenth century, following the abolition of the Atlantic slave trade and its replacement by the palm oil trade. The palm oil trade was like manna from heaven. It provided new economic opportunities

194   SLAVERY AND COLONIAL RULE IN AFRICA

and created a new demand for labour. Igbo entrepreneurs experienced no problem securing all the labour they wanted at this time. Captives who would have been exported now were used locally either to produce profitable commodities, or as trading assistants, porters or canoe paddlers. Moreover, whereas slaves had transported themselves, now large amounts of labour, in the form of carriers, were required to transport produce. Before the arrival of trucks and trains, two vital problems that entrepreneurs had to face in Africa were transportation and labour. A carrier could carry a head-load of between 50 and 60 pounds, or 11 gallons of palm-oil between 15 and 25 miles a day. It took about 37 men to transport a ton of produce in one day,[10] whereas a lorry with two men could carry a ton four times the distance and 1,000 times this load could be carried by rail ten times the distance, employing about six men.[11]

The supply of slaves was also maintained by slave raiding activities of Muslim 'jihadists' to the north which created an unprecedented pool of captives in southeastern Nigeria.[12] Between 1804 and 1903, when the British completed their conquest of Sokoto Caliphate, thousands of captives were rounded up in the Middle Belt of Nigeria and driven south into the main palm oil and yam producing regions of Igboland and other places.[13] In the Igbo heartland, slaving also continued after the end of the Atlantic slave trade. Intergroup conflicts, kidnapping, judicial incrimination, and the demands of various Igbo oracles continued to generate slaves. The Aro expanded their activities and their trading network flourished. The slaving methods they had perfected remained undisturbed. Thus, between 1850 and 1900 the supply of slaves to Igbo communities matched and sometimes outstripped the demand.

The phenomenal increase in the demand for labour was created not only by the new demand for palm oil and kernel in Europe and America but also by the great demand for yams and other foodstuffs in Igboland itself. The closure of the overseas outlet for slaves had resulted in population growth. Slaves who would have been exported to the Americas were now retained and had to be fed. Entrepreneurs who engaged in food production and trade amassed wealth. The sudden rise in wealth and in the size of slave holdings was reflected in an increased number of entrepreneurs and the size of slave holding. There was also a noticeable shift in relations of power.

British Abolition Drive and the Revolt of Slave Owners

In the midst of this prosperity in the late 1880s the British began the conquest of southeastern Nigeria and decided to abolish slavery, thereby provoking a widespread revolt. That the British conquest of Nigeria was linked to the slavery issue is illustrated by the fact that the most violent

ENTREPRENEURS AND EMANCIPATION AMONG THE IGBO 195

encounters between the slave holding states of Nigeria and the British occurred during Joseph Chamberlain's tenure of office as British colonial Secretary (1895–1903). It was during this period that Benin, the Niger Delta city states, Western Igboland, Arochukwu and Sokoto Caliphate, including Ilorin and Nupe, were conquered. Before going into action, Chamberlain had warned that

> Sooner or later we shall have to fight some of the slave dealing tribes and we cannot have a better casus belli ... public opinion here requires that we shall justify control of these savage countries by some serious effort to put down slave dealing.[14]

But just as the British conquest of Nigeria was motivated by other economic, political, prestige and humanitarian considerations, so was Igbo resistance to British colonial rule motivated by factors other than slavery. Nonetheless, as we shall presently see, the slavery issue was central to the Anglo-Nigerian conflicts of this period.

British traders and imperial agents had begun to make war on Igbo towns before Chamberlain's tenure of office. In 1860 a British gunboat bombarded Aboh as a reprisal for its people's plundering of a British trading post.[15] In 1879, a British naval fleet attacked Onitsha, destroying much of it.[16] Again in 1883, on the charge that some Aboh citizens had attacked a British trader, three British warships, *Alecto*, *Flirt*, and *Sterling*, stood in mid-river and shelled and destroyed Aboh.[17] Then in 1888, the forces of the British Royal Niger Company[18] invaded Asaba, destroying half of it.[19] Most of these attacks were not linked to any desire to suppress slavery but to demonstrate British military might, to protect British commercial interests, and to subordinate Igbo entrepreneurs to European economic interests. However, they set the tone for subsequent Anglo-Igbo relations; military action had to be undertaken even as a first resort.

When the British finally embarked on actual conquest and began to attack slavery they hardly realized that they were touching the heart of an economic system that supported Igbo entrepreneurs. The most widespread wars of resistance against the British intrusion were financed and directed by these entrepreneurs who did not always form a united interest group but had an identifiable class interest. It was this that motivated the Aro traders to finance and unite several Igbo towns for a war against the British,[20] while on the west bank of the Niger, entrepreneurs organized and financed the Ekumeku movement.[21] The first battle of the Ekumeku was fought in Issele-Ukwu where the paramount chief, Obi Egbuna, influenced by the head of the Roman Catholic mission, freed his slaves and passed a decree abolishing human sacrifice in his chiefdom. Enraged by the action of the paramount chief, the slave owners of Issele-Ukwu rose in arms against him and a civil

196 SLAVERY AND COLONIAL RULE IN AFRICA

war broke out, dividing the town. One section, composed mainly of slave-owning chiefs, demanded the expulsion of the paramount chief and all people harboring European sympathies. In the opposing camp were the supporters of the royal cause, composed mainly of the personal friends of the paramount chief, a few Christian converts, and the bulk of the slave population. When slave owners in the neighbouring towns heard of the civil war in Issele-Ukwu, they sent their warriors to aid the rebels.

Realizing that the royal cause was hopeless without external assistance and that the royal cause was also the Catholic cause, Father Carlo Zappa appealed to the authorities of the Royal Niger Company for help. Early in January 1898, the soldiers of the Royal Niger Company left Lokoja and entered Western Igboland and found themselves embroiled in a running battle that lasted until December that year. Although the Royal Niger Company defeated the Ekumeku warriors, it was clear that the Niger territories were seething with discontent and that the company could not maintain law and order in the region. In December 1899 the British government withdrew the charter of the Royal Niger Company and took over its territories.

But neither the defeat of the Ekumeku nor the withdrawal of the company's charter brought peace to Western Igboland. Instead the British imperial government found itself locked into one of the most stubborn wars of resistance they encountered in Nigeria. Entrepreneurs recruited warriors, trained and armed them, and then dispatched them to engage the British in battles that ranged from minor skirmishes to full-scale wars. Warriors also carried out raids on British installations, court houses, trading establishments, and Christian missionary outposts. Using guerrilla tactics, they ambushed British soldiers and in many instances fought them to a stand off. Thus, what had started as a minor dispute over slavery and human sacrifice in Issele-Ukwu turned into a series of battles that lasted until 1911. The basic objectives of the Ekumeku movement were to resist British and Christian missionary interference with slavery and ward off European commercial and imperial penetration of the region.[22]

Entrepreneurs justified their resistance on the ground that incoming European traders threatened to strip them of the system of production and exchange they had striven so hard to develop and maintain. Between 1857 and 1875, European trading firms established over twenty trading posts on the Lower Niger, each located within twenty miles of the other, and trading directly with the interior. This threatened to deprive the Igbo of their middleman role and even undermine the traditional power structure of the societies. On top of this, between 1886 and 1899, the military forces of the Company and British imperial government attacked communities in the Niger territories and in the Niger Delta and Cross River estuary and were

ENTREPRENEURS AND EMANCIPATION AMONG THE IGBO

faced with the rebellions of over 50 towns in the Niger territories. The Niger Company destroyed Patani and Akassa in the Niger Delta, Gloria-Ibo and Oguta in the southeast and many towns further north.[23] These operations devastated the very communities with whom the Igbo entrepreneurs did business. The destruction of Niger Delta states was particularly painful. For example, Brass was destroyed as a reprisal for its people's raid on British trading posts in Akassa and was saddled with the military forces of the Niger Coast Protectorate and the Royal Niger Company.[24] Thereafter, starved of their traditional sources of wealth and power, the canoe houses and the merchant princes that owned them went into a period of decline from which they never recovered.[25]

There are direct relationships between British imperial penetration and the eclipse of the indigenous entrepreneurs in the Niger Delta and on the Lower Niger. However, the British probably did not have a predetermined plan to exterminate the indigenous entrepreneurial classes but wanted to subordinate them to European economic interests. European and African entrepreneurs often worked as partners, as happened in the Niger Delta during the era of the Atlantic slave trade, but Europeans always manipulated this partnership to their own advantage. In the late nineteenth and early twentieth centuries African entrepreneurs made bold attempts to free themselves from European commercial hegemony but found themselves in an economic strangle hold. King Jaja of Opobo, one of the wealthiest and most colourful entrepreneurs of the Niger Delta in the 1880s, tried to bypass British merchants and ship his palm oil directly to Europe, and consequently was disposed of as was the Oba of Benin, Ovonramwen. However, these Afro-European misunderstandings in southeastern Nigeria did not end domestic slavery.

Labour Crisis and the Last of the Pre-colonial Igbo Entrepreneurs

The British government finally declared Igboland a British protectorate in 1900,[26] and at once decided to abolish domestic slavery in the region by legal and military means. There were a number of proclamations intended to free slaves. Under The Master and Servant Proclamation, No. 12 of 1903, slaves were now called 'apprentices', and both they and their owners were bound by contracts laying down terms of service.[27] It was illegal for former slaves to wander around without an apparent source of subsistence. Another law authorized officials to call on chiefs or heads of houses to provide forced labour.[28] Officials explained that these enactments were necessary to accelerate suppression of slavery and establishment of a free labour market,[29] and that the restriction placed on the movement of freed slaves was necessary 'to preserve the masters' authority over the energies and movement of their slaves'. This was a ruse; officials did not want to ruin the economy or be saddled with a large population of fugitive slaves, although the Brussels Act bound signatories to repatriate or rehabilitate freed slaves in suitable locations near European stations.[30] The Native House Rule Proclamation of 1903, rather than free slaves, confined them to the houses to which they belonged.

As one would expect, the conflicts that ensued were largely over labour control, and because the principle enunciated in the House Rule Proclamation could not function properly,[31] the final say in matters relating to slavery and labour was generally left in the hands of warrant chiefs,[32] district officers, and native courts. Moreover, British officials were well aware that slavery in Igboland could not be suppressed by proclamations, particularly because the vast majority of the Igbo people had not even recognized British rule. Military subjugation was inevitable because, without complete control, the economic aims of the British could not be realized.

East of the Niger, the British attacked the Aro, determined to destroy their trading empire, even though they claimed that their objective was to destroy the Long Juju, which had served as a centre for enslavement. The British also attacked many other Igbo towns and villages, and were drawn into a running battle that lasted till after the First World War. As late as 1920 some Igbo communities in the Udi division of Onitsha province were still doing battle against the colonial government.[33] Nevertheless, with the Aro subdued in 1902 and impressive victories scored over the Ekumeku society in 1902 and 1904, the government felt able to recruit labour for the colonial exploitation of southeastern Nigeria.

Of special interest is the manner by which the Aro entrepreneurs tried to adjust to the new colonial situation and retain their long-standing economic dominance. According A. E. Afigbo,

> In the great days of the slave trade the Aro had been largely responsible for meeting the needs of the peoples of the hinterland of the Bight of Biafra for imported European goods. Their monopoly of this business had indeed been one of the main bases of the widespread influence and respect which they commanded among their neighbours. They did not abandon this trade with the imposition of colonial rule. What, however, they could not maintain, in spite of their attempts ... was the monopoly of it.[34]

After their defeat, the Aro tried but failed 'to refashion the basis of their ascendancy to suit the new situations that arose with the imposition of imperial rule'.[35] Also, fearing that their defeat and the destruction of the Long Juju would shut off their sources of prestige and wealth, Aro agents

ENTREPRENEURS AND EMANCIPATION AMONG THE IGBO 199

claimed that they had moved the seat of their oracle to a new site. They also deceived some communities into believing that they had employed the British to fight for them. They did this, first, by patching up their own differences with the British. Second, they used their new-found friendship with the British to extract bribes from unsuspecting communities who feared that the Aro might send the British against them just as they had previously sent Abam mercenaries.

Still determined to break the power of the Aro conclusively, the British decreed that wherever the Aro settled, they should be treated as guests and not as overlords. Colonial administrators also invited missionaries to work in Aro villages, to build churches and schools and provide the people with Western education. The vast majority of the first converts and school children were slaves who were anxious 'to identify themselves with the white man who in conquering them had also liberated them'.[36] The Aro were unrelenting, however. They followed their slaves to the worship of 'the white man's God'. Even the paramount chief of the Aro, Chief Kanu Okoro, who had been in hiding since the British invaded Arochukwu in 1901, reappeared in 1906 and converted to Christianity. In 1907 a colonial officer wrote:

> The head chief of the Aros, who was the chief formally in control of the Long Juju at Arochukwu, is one of those most favourable [to the missionaries]. He has already announced to the other chiefs his intention to rule in God's ways. He has been the most keen in asking the missionaries to come. A new church will be built and he offers to build a house for any missionary who comes.[37]

Chief Okoro's conversion, together with those of other chiefs and commoners who followed his example, may or may not have been genuine, but what is certain is that Aro traders were not ready to give up hopes of regaining their predominant economic position. After reviving their oracle, they relocated its seat, and until well into the 1930s dealt secretly in slaves. They forged new alliances with traders and oracles that served as secret centres for slave dealing. Thus, despite anti-slavery laws, slavery persisted well into the 1930s though on a steadily declining scale.

When the Slaves Left

Of equal importance are the specific modes of response of slaves to the new colonial order – how they contributed to their own 'emancipation', and how they adjusted to slave trading and the new political economy. Briefly stated, slaves took advantage of colonial laws and of conflicts that raged between indigenous entrepreneurs and incoming Europeans to assert their freedom.

200 SLAVERY AND COLONIAL RULE IN AFRICA

Not all slaves left. Many remained but worked for themselves. Some converted their slave villages into autonomous settlements. The colonial administration authorized newly created native courts to settle any disputes that might arise between owners and slaves. Although officials tried to discourage mass desertion and social unrest, thousands of slaves ignored these precautions and simply walked off. Some migrated into newly created urban centres, seaports, mining districts and cocoa and rubber plantations. Some joined nearby farming communities as labourers, and others, presumably, returned to their native homes. In some parts of Igboland, conflict broke out as owners tried to stop slaves from leaving, but colonial administrators intervened on behalf of former slaves. A few cases came before native courts later, but the decisions reached favored former slaves rather than owners. 'When the slaves left, their owners wept', recalled an Igbo chief.[38]

The response of former slaves to British rule depended on three inter-related factors. The first was the willingness of colonial administrators to support the freedmen's demand for complete autonomy. The available evidence confirms that until 1914, the administration's attitude towards emancipation was ambivalent. It was only after this period that it took bold steps to support ex-slaves' demand for freedom. For example, it was only in 1914 that the colonial administration decreed that the authority which heads of houses exercised over their members could no longer be recognized by the courts, and the police could no longer assist in recapturing those who left.[39] Thus, by the 1930s, all slaves were aware that they could not be forced to remain with their former owners and that if they left no court could compel them to return.

The second factor concerns the willingness or ability of owners to contest the actions of both former slaves and colonial administrators. In the Asaba hinterland, for example, after the final defeat of the Ekumeku in 1911 owners hardly contested the decision of slaves to either depart or establish their own autonomous settlements nearby, or even live among the communities that formerly owned them. It will be recalled that most Western Igbo slaves had been acquired during the palm oil boom of the nineteenth century. But the palm oil business collapsed in 1896 and all efforts by owners to extract whatever surplus they could from slaves were thwarted by the British wars of conquest, colonial laws, and Christian missionary interference with native laws and customs. Now, saddled with a hostile colonial military presence and an adverse economy, owners found out that they could no longer control their slaves.

The third factor concerns the options available to slaves and their determination to explore them. In this regard, one finds a remarkable difference between the attitudes of slaves (and owners) in the Western

ENTREPRENEURS AND EMANCIPATION AMONG THE IGBO 201

Igboland and in the Enugu district. In the latter place the coal industry, which opened in 1913, together with the construction of railway lines, motor roads and urban housing, created new economic opportunities which helped to prolong the period of conflict between former slaves and former owners. Owners took advantage of the new economy to assert themselves as labour-recruiters and commercial farmers providing food and provisions to Enugu. They invoked Proclamation No. 15 of 1903 – the Roads and Creeks Proclamation – which empowered officials and chiefs to 'regulate the compulsory labour existing under the tribal system' to exact labour from local communities with or without pay. Although they recruited both free and slave labour, they pocketed the wages of former slaves who, as they insisted, still belonged to them. Some former slaves responded by running away to Enugu and elsewhere and established themselves as independent wage earners. Others remained behind and tried to renegotiate their terms of service. By 1922 they had begun to contest the rights of former owners to confiscate all or part of their wages and deny them rights as full members of the society. The conflict that ensued climaxed in the Nkanu slave uprisings of the 1920s.[40]

It would appear that slave uprisings occurred only in Enugu area. This is understandable because no other part of Igboland was, at this time, provided with the type of economic opportunities that the coal and railway industries provided the people of Enugu and its environs. As the examples of emancipation in the various Igbo districts demonstrate, the fundamental reason for holding slaves and resisting emancipation was economic. Igbo slave owners gave up slavery only when they found it unprofitable or difficult to continue in the face of British colonial violence. By the mid-1920s, slavery in Igboland had suffered an irrecoverable setback and could no longer thrive in its old forms. In 1924 the government of Southern Nigeria observed with a mixed feeling that slavery had not been 'automatically and completely suppressed' but was gradually dying out.[41] A disturbing phenomenon was clandestine slave dealing, especially in small children.[42]

Another disturbing phenomenon was the persistence of *osu* or cult slavery. Although the chief priests of the juju houses suffered a tremendous loss of power in colonial society and could no longer obtain new supplies of chattels, and even though fewer and fewer people dedicated themselves voluntarily to these religious establishments, the number of *osu* continued to grow, largely because they could marry only each other, so all their offspring were *osu*. The *osu* remained bound to the deities to which they or their forebears had been dedicated, even if they never set eyes upon the shrines of these deities. Thus, while the other classes of unfree persons gained their freedom in the later colonial period, the *osu* remained a despised class.

202 SLAVERY AND COLONIAL RULE IN AFRICA

In May 1954, six years before Nigeria became an independent nation, the British Parliament had reason to query if *osu* slavery had been completely eradicated in southeastern Nigeria. This parliamentary question sparked off much discussion, and the colonial government in Nigeria was forced to admit that it still existed. It went on to explain, however, that

> the only remaining disability is reluctance of free born to inter marry with Osus. Even that is beginning to go. While there may be isolated cases of attempts to compel Osus to perform religious rites, complaints are seldom made and when they are complainants receive due protection of the law. Status of Osu is not legally recognised. ... Such disabilities as still remain are social and not legal.[43]

Two years later, in 1956, the question of *osu* slavery was raised in the Eastern House of Assembly (Nigeria) and was denounced. After a long debate, a law was passed abolishing it.[44] But *forty years later,* that is *to this day,* the *osu* phenomenon still exists in Igboland. Although these *osu* no longer work for the priests of the religious establishments, nor can the priests exercise any power over them, I believe that the silence of the *osu* themselves has contributed to the persistence of the phenomenon. The *osu* have allowed others to speak for them.

Meanwhile, as British colonial rule spread its benefits and hardships, entrepreneurs gradually gave up whatever hostility they might have had against former chattel slaves and their descendants. In areas where land was available, former slaves gained access to it. Today, however, the mention of slave origins still creates tension. Marriage between the descendants of freeborn and former slaves is still discouraged if the facts are disclosed. Some descendants of slaves are denied the right to officiate at ritual ceremonies or purchase higher titles although as money becomes more available, it is difficult to prevent prospective title seekers from purchasing them. Many Igbo still endure occasional painful insinuations about their slave origins but, as populations move forth and back, it is increasingly difficult to distinguish the descendants of former slaves from the freeborn. In fact, many Igbo who claim to be freeborn, and make the greatest noise about it, may not realize that their grandparents were slaves.

Also, as entrepreneurs recognized the benefits of Western education in the new colonial order, they began to send their children to school, but it took a whole generation to bridge the gap in educational attainment and wealth between them and those children of former slaves who had promptly embraced Christianity, Western education and wage labour. Finally, as part of their adjustment to the dislocations and uncertainties that characterized colonial rule, many entrepreneurs gave up polygyny also an important source of labour.

ENTREPRENEURS AND EMANCIPATION AMONG THE IGBO   203

By consciously giving land to former slaves and getting rid of parts of their labour force, entrepreneurs might be perceived as having engaged in a form of class suicide. That is not the case. Land is useful only if cheap labour can be found to cultivate it. Entrepreneurs were fully aware that whereas previously, large numbers of dependants produced wealth, they now ate up capital. Slaves were no longer a source of wealth; the rearing of children was becoming very expensive and polygyny was a major source of trouble as women increasingly petitioned successfully for divorce. Potential 'female husbands' would have a hard time finding 'wives'. Crippled by their own conservatism, as well as by political strife, trade competition, labour shortages, and the decline in the production of their main export crop, the old entrepreneurial classes limped into the First World War period with declining economic prospects. The adverse conditions of the First World War and the worldwide recessions of the 1920s and 1930s finally forced them to quit the shrinking stage of the colonial economy. The death of the old entrepreneurial classes also meant the death of slavery.

What we see in colonial Igboland is not a case in which the old entrepreneurial classes adjusted to a new economic system, but one in which their death occurred before a new one was born. Their slow and painful death contrasted with their spontaneous adjustment from slave trade to palm oil trade in the previous century. Until a new entrepreneurial class evolved and matured in the mid-twentieth century, the expatriate firms and the colonial government remained in total control of economic and political power. One can rightly speak of the total eclipse of the old entrepreneurial classes and slavery in Igboland.

Conclusions

This paper has demonstrated that the introduction of colonial rule into Nigeria destroyed both the pre-colonial Igbo entrepreneurs and slavery. Like slave owners in other parts of the world, Igbo slave owners resisted emancipation because slave labour was a source of wealth and power. Owners wept when slaves left because they now had to grow their own yams, carry their own loads, paddle their own canoes, and roof their own houses. It should be understood, however, that just as the desire to abolish internal African slavery was only one of the reasons behind the British conquest of Nigeria, so was the desire to maintain slavery only one of the reasons for the slave owners' resistance to British rule. Political, economic and cultural factors of the conflicts must also be considered. In accounting for the death of the old entrepreneurial classes, therefore, one must emphasize the following factors. First, the military conquest of southeastern Nigeria and the advance of British capital diminished the Igbo share of the

204 SLAVERY AND COLONIAL RULE IN AFRICA

available market. The system of direct trade that the Europeans introduced destroyed the pre-colonial pattern of commerce and undermined the traditional power base of pre-colonial entrepreneurial classes.

Second, the 1914 law, which abolished the House system, signified an effective break with the past, a parting of the ways between an entrepreneur's household and his or her employees. This sudden dissolution had called for a rapid readjustment, but entrepreneurs failed to respond promptly.

Third, changes in labour conditions adversely affected them because they had invested most of their assets in labour and chieftaincy titles rather than in tangible assets. Had they commercialized land and/or made use of hired labour, the labour transformations of the colonial period would have affected them less adversely. As a group they eventually collapsed because they could not effectively operate in an embryonic capitalist environment with their rigid pre-capitalist notions of production.

Fourth, and perhaps most important, pre-colonial Igbo entrepreneurs competed with foreign entrepreneurs who had not only official backing, but also worldwide connections, greater access to credit, and information about the market.

After a long period of experimentation a new generation of Igbo entrepreneurs emerged in the inter-war period. Many of these new entrepreneurs were former slaves or their descendants. To raise their initial capital, they served as wage labourers or petty trades. They also practiced thrift and joined local credit associations known as *isusu*. Although they retained some features of pre-capitalist relations of production, they were sufficiently sophisticated to take advantage of certain elements of the imported capitalist relations of production to advance themselves. They invested in land and real estate, and less in labour. They used the new transport infrastructure to move their goods around. They sought out new markets and invested in far away provinces. They also put their money in mass transportation and the distributive industry rather than in labour. Some engaged in trade or craft manufacture and the more adventurous went on to deal in imported materials, buying goods from the expatriate firms and retailing them in the local markets. One of their major difficulties was access to external loans. The banks, owned by expatriate firms, would not lend them working capital.[45] Unfortunately, they had virtually nothing to export; the expatriate firms, including the Lebanese firms, continued to serve as the major exporters of Nigerian produce until the indigenization decrees of the 1970s.

In sum, this article has demonstrated direct relationships between British rule and the eclipse of the pre-colonial indigenous entrepreneurial classes of Igboland whose operations depended on possession of slaves. Obviously,

ENTREPRENEURS AND EMANCIPATION AMONG THE IGBO

these historical events altered notions of power and authority. The number of people a person could hold no longer determined that person's power. Only success in modern business, higher education, and the professions conferred real power and authority. It is therefore accurate to say that some of the more important changes that British colonial rule introduced into Igboland were the emancipation of former slaves, the development of a mobile wage labour system, and the destruction of pre-colonial entrepreneurial classes who had made use of slave labour.

GLOSSARY

Juju	Deity; fetish; masquerade; oracle; talisman
Isusu	Credit association
Oba	Paramount chief among the Edo and Yoruba peoples
Obi	Paramount chief among the Igbo people: holder of ozo or eze title
Ohu	Slave
Osu	Cult slave

NOTES

Funding for this research was provided in 1994 by the Society for the Humanities, Cornell University, for which I am grateful.

1. Elizabeth Isichei, *A History of the Igbo People* (London: Macmillan, 1976), p.43.
2. Richard Lander and John Lander, *Journal of Expedition to Explore the Course and Termination of the Niger*, 2 vols. (New York, 1958).
3. MacGregor Laird and R.A.K. Oldfield, *Narrative of an Exploration into the Interior of Africa* (London, 1971), p.100.
4. Ifi Amadiume, *Male Daughters, Female Husbands, Gender and Sex in an African Society* (London: Zed Books, 1987), pp.48–9.
5. Chieka, C. Ifemesia, *South-eastern Nigeria in the Nineteenth Century: An Introductory Analysis* (New York: Nok Publishers, 1978), p.36.
6. Laird and Oldfield, *Narrative*, p.100.
7. N. Uka, 'A Note on the "Abam" Warriors of Igboland', *Ikenga: Journal of African Studies*, 1, 2 (1972), p.76.
8. J. N. Oriji, 'Slave Trade, Warfare and Aro Expansion in the Igbo Hinterland', *Geneve Afrique*, 24, 2 (1986), pp.102–18.
9. Don C. Ohadike, 'The Decline of Slavery Among the Igbo People', in Suzanne Miers and Richard Roberts (eds.), *The End of Slavery in Africa* (Madison: University of Wisconsin Press, 1988), p.439.
10. Bill Freund, *Capital and Labour in the Nigerian Tin Mines* (London: Routledge and Kegan Paul, 1981), p.58.
11. Allan McPhee, *The Economic Revolution in British West Africa* (New York, 1926), pp.54–5.
12. Mahdi Adamu, 'The Delivery of Slaves from the Central Sudan to the Bight of Benin in the Eighteenth and Nineteenth Centuries', in Henry A. Gemery and Jan S. Hogendorn (eds.), *The Uncommon Market: Essays in the History of the Atlantic Slave Trade* (New York: Random House, 1979), pp.171–2.
13. S.F. Nadel, *A Black Byzantium: The Kingdom of Nupe in Nigeria* (London, 1942).
14. Suzanne Miers, *Britain and the Ending of the Slave Trade* (London: Longmans, 1975), p.24.
15. Local Government Archives, Benin City File No. 26769. E.A. Miller, 'Aboh Intelligence Report', April 1931.

206   SLAVERY AND COLONIAL RULE IN AFRICA

16. Felix Ekechi, 'Traders, Missionaries, and the Bombardment of Onitsha, 1879–1880', *The Conch*, 5, nos 1 and 2 (1973), p.537.
17. Local Government Archives, Benin City File No. 26769. E.A. Miller, 'Aboh Intelligence Report', April 1931.
18. The Niger Company, a trading company, was granted a charter by the British government on 10 July 1886, thus becoming the Royal Niger Company. It was authorized to administer a strip of land on both sides of the Niger River running from the coast to undefined points in the interior. At the end of 1899 the company's charter was withdrawn and its territories transferred to the British government.
19. CMS, G3/A3/1888/50, Hugh S. Macaulay to Samuel Ajayi Crowther, 16 April 1888.
20. PRO, memorandum on Aro expedition, 1901.
21. Don C. Ohadike, *The Ekumeku Movement, Western Igbo Resistance to the British Conquest of Nigeria, 1883–1914* (Athens: Ohio University Press, 1991).
22. Ibid.
23. A.H.M. Kirk-Greene, 'Preliminary Notes on New Sources for Nigerian Military History', *Journal of the Historical Society of Nigeria*, 3, 1 (1964), pp.135–8.
24. Rhodes House Library, Oxford, 710. 17s4/6 Brass Inquiry 1899. Niger Territories Confidential 221. Sir J. Kirk to Marquees of Salisbury (received 30 August 1897).
25. The war between Brass and the Royal Niger Company at Akassa in 1895 sparked much discussion in official British circles concerning the position of the Royal Niger Company. Sir John Kirk's report on the Brass attack on company property was 'a very strong indictment against the administration of the Niger Coast Protectorate, besides throwing light on a condition of affairs prolific of disorder and discreditable to British prestige'. After the Akassa raid by Brass men, the British government had to pay 'a very large sum of money' as compensation for losses sustained in a war largely provoked by the company. A feeling emerged among British officials that the charter of the Royal Niger Company ought to be withdrawn not only to save the British administration from further embarrassments, but also to eliminate 'the awkward geographical location of the administrations', one of which was territory under the Crown and the other a narrow strip of riverbank under a Company, with both overlapping at certain points. For instance, Brass men whose lands lay outside the Company's territories could not reach their markets on the Niger without crossing the Company's frontiers and paying duties each time they did so. By 1897 it had become evident that dual administration was the source of much conflict in the area. Curtailment of the Company's privileges was suggested.
26. Before 1900 Igboland was generally regarded as a part of the Niger territories even though the authority of the Company did not extend beyond a few miles from the banks of the river.
27. PRO, CO 588/1, The Master and Servant Proclamation, No.12 of 1903.
28. PRO, CO 588/1, The Roads and Creeks Proclamation, No.15 of 1903.
29. PRO, CO520/13/83 of 26 February 1902, Ralph Moor to Colonial Office.
30. Miers, *Britain and the Ending of the Slave Trade*, p.252.
31. The Native House Rule Proclamation was originally intended for the Niger Delta communities, where corporate canoe houses were a principal feature of social and economic organization. As British influence spread into the hinterland, the law was extended to Igbo-speaking areas because of the wrong belief that all 'natives' in Southern Nigeria belonged to houses. As Igbo society was not organized like the Delta city states, the principle enunciated in the House Rule Proclamation could not function properly. In due course, final say in matters relating to slavery and labour was generally left in the hands of warrant chiefs, district officers, and native courts.
32. To enforce British laws, the colonial administration established Native courts in southeastern Nigeria and gave certificates of recognition, hence, warrants, to certain individuals, authorizing them to sit in those courts and try cases. Officials referred to these men as 'friendly chiefs', while the local people sometimes called them 'government chiefs'.
33. See for instance PRO, CO583/84, 25 February 1920.
34. A.E. Afigbo, 'The Eclipse of the Aro Slaving Oligarchy of South-eastern Nigeria, 1901–1927', *Journal of the Historical Society of Nigeria*, 6, 1 (1971), p.20.
35. Ibid., p.1.

ENTREPRENEURS AND EMANCIPATION AMONG THE IGBO

36. Ibid., p.6.
37. As quoted in ibid., p.7.
38. Chief Ijoma Esumai Ugboma, interviewed in Aboh on 23 December 1982.
39. NAE, CSE/1/85/2926, EP 5279, Vol.3. Governor's deputy to secretary of state for the colonies, 20 November 1939.
40. Carolyn A. Brown, 'Testing the Boundaries of Marginality: Twentieth-Century Slavery and Emancipation Struggles in Nkanu, Northern Igboland, 1920–29', *Journal of African History*, 37 (1996) pp.51–80.
41. NAE, CSE 1/85/2924, EP 5279, Vol.1 Chief Secretary for the government, 5 February 1924.
42. NAE, CSE 1/85/2924, EP 5279, Vol.1 Williams, acting secretary, Southern Provinces, to governor, 13 December 1939.
43. PRO, CO 554/1376 22 May 1954 From Acting Governor, Nigeria, to Secretary of State for the Colonies.
44. NAE, Eastern Nigeria Laws, 1956.
45. For the relationship between Expatriate banks and African businesses, see Hopkins, *An Economic History of West Africa* (London, 1973), pp.201–9.

'Do Dady nor Lef me Make dem Carry me': Slave Resistance and Emancipation in Sierra Leone, 1894–1928

ISMAIL RASHID

In January 1893, two boys being transported for sale at the Mellacourie River seized the opportunity to secure their freedom when their owner made a stop at Yelisanda, a town in Northwestern Sierra Leone. One of them saw a Colonial Frontier Police officer and pleaded in Mende: '*Dady, I am a slave from Meni – they are now taken me to the Susu country – Do dady nor lef me make dem carry me*'.[1] The policeman, Lance Corporal Alfred Coker, ignored the protest of the local headman, freed the boys and sent them to Freetown. In freeing the boys, Coker deprived the headman of his tribute from the trade and undermined his position as a host for slave traders. The action of the boys, on the other hand, supports the proposition in the literature on slavery in the Americas and Africa that resistance by slaves helped shape or destroy the conditions of their servitude. This essay builds on this theme and examines slave resistance in northwestern Sierra Leone.

The plea of the slave boys, their emancipation by the colonial policeman and the protest of the headman occurred at a significant moment in African history: the time of the European scramble for Africa. In Sierra Leone, the scramble culminated in Britain's declaration of a Protectorate over the hinterland in 1896. This was also a period of anti-slavery fervour in Britain.[2] Some colonial officials and local agents like Corporal Coker took the renewed abolitionist mood seriously and tried to terminate slavery on the ground. As demonstrated by the two boys, slaves gained their freedom by appealing to such colonial agents. Some of these local agents were themselves ex-slaves.[3] As in other parts of Africa, these ex-slaves had enlisted or had been forcibly recruited into the colonial armies which eventually subverted the power of their former masters.[4] The slave owners, who constituted most of the precolonial elite, struggled to reassert their authority against colonial agents, former slaves and the encroaching European imperialism. For slaves, the scramble represented a moment of opportunity and for the masters, a moment of crisis. The resistance of slaves against masters and of chiefs against colonialists placed European imperialists like the British in a quandary. They could not abolish slavery

MAP 8
SIERRA LEONE AND GUINEA

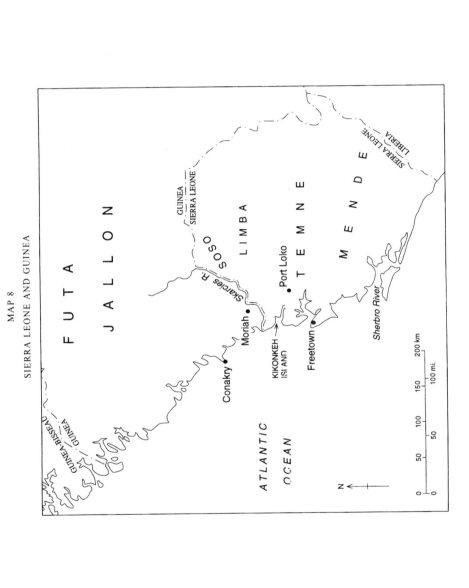

and, simultaneously, count on the collaboration of the pre-colonial elite in the colonial enterprise. Therefore, in Sierra Leone, the British resorted to legal and administrative mechanisms which concurrently ameliorated the conditions of slaves while strengthening the position of owners. It is within the context of interaction between slaves, masters and the colonial state in Sierra Leone that the process of resistance and abolition should be situated. The British sought to balance the interests of owners, slaves and the colonial state, and at the same time, to refurbish the moral economy of servitude. European social historians first fashioned the concept of moral economy to understand the actions and *mentalité* of pre-industrial protestors in Europe. They posited that in any society different social groups agree as to what are and what are not legitimate practices and behaviour and they argued that this consensus was based on shared social norms encompassing the functions, rights and obligations of each group. According to them, subaltern groups viewed any violation of this moral understanding as occasion for rebellious actions.[5] Social historians and anthropologists writing on Asia and Africa have elaborated on the concept of moral economy and have utilized it to analyze the actions of peasants, workers and other groups.[6] John Mason renovated it as the 'moral economy of the lash' to investigate the *mentalité* and actions of a single slave, 'Mey' and the reactions of his master and the Colonial Protector in the Cape Colony in the early eighteenth century.[7] Jonathon Glassman utilized the concept and Gramscian notions of hegemony to examine popular slave riots in the East African Coast.[8]

The concept of moral economy, while useful in understanding the mentality of slaves and masters, should not obscure the fact that their voices are inherently unequal. The concept should also not be read to imply that the actions and ideas of subordinate groups were fixed and incapable of innovation. The discursive elements of a moral economy, as Glassman and others have noted, are utilized in neither purely defensive nor offensive manners by subalterns. Rather they tend to be fluid in construction and usage over time. Equally the existence of a moral economy of servitude does not imply that slaves struggled primarily to define a 'moral consensus' rather than to destroy oppressive relations. A moral economy or consensus emerges as the result of a process of 'accommodation in resistance' in the confrontation between master and slave.[9]

The moral economy of servitude in pre-colonial Sierra Leone was manifested in the social differentiation and treatment of slaves, in their acquired 'rights', and the obligations expected of masters and other members of societies. In return, slaves were expected to provide labour, loyalty and other forms of support to their owners and host societies. The balance between the rights and obligations of masters and slaves emerged

SLAVE EMANCIPATION IN SIERRA LEONE   211

historically from the dynamic intersection of the pre-colonial mode of production, politics and customary laws, and slave resistance. This article concentrates primarily on the dynamics of slave resistance and emancipation in northwestern Sierra Leone.

The Pre-colonial Moral Economy of Servitude in Sierra Leone

The nature of the societies, polities and economy that emerged in northwestern Sierra Leone played a crucial role in shaping the usage and control mechanisms of servile labour. The culturally interrelated Bullom, Temne, Limba and Loko peoples comprised most of the population of the region. They lived in relatively small autonomous and semi-autonomous federated towns and villages ruled by competing lineage groups. The regional economy was largely based on the subsistence and petty commodity production of rice, kolanuts and palm products on upland savanna and patches of forest. Regional trade networks, extending from the Niger plains and Futa Jallon to the north to Freetown and the Atlantic Coast in the south, complemented agrarian production. Agricultural labour was largely organized around family and communal groups. Among Temne, Limba and Loko, servile labour complemented but never supplanted communal and kinship labour. The tendency to absorb slaves into kinship groups was greater among these peoples than the Mandingo and Fulbe. Throughout the eighteenth and nineteenth centuries, Temne, Limba and Loko groups and polities fought against and suffered from incursions from their more Islamicized and powerful Soso, Mandingo and Fulbe neighbours. Slaves, territorial claims, access to resources, control of regional trade networks and religious differences provided the fuel for these conflicts. The Mandingo, Soso and Fulbe controlled historically more powerful polities like Moriah and Futa Jallon. Their use of plantation slave labour tended to be more extensive and they were less inclined to absorb slaves into their societies.[10] The most violent slave protests in the region were usually directed against slave owners from these groups and states.

All groups in northwestern Sierra Leone differentiated among categories of slaves and provided for their absorption into their larger societies in the precolonial period. These distinctions and the processes of absorption varied with the mode of acquisition, the duration of servitude and the behaviour of the slaves. Ordinary slaves, consisting mainly of war captives, purchased persons and unredeemed pawns, stood at one end of the absorption grid. As people usually born outside the community, they had the least attachment to it and to their owners. Owners regarded them as disposable chattels and utilized them in arduous farm labour or porterage under close supervision.[11] They suffered from the greatest physical coercion

212 SLAVERY AND COLONIAL RULE IN AFRICA

and acquired the fewest rights and obligations from their masters. Their lot could be ameliorated over time if they became attached to their owners. Thus with time, 'well-behaved' and hard-working field slaves received wives, personal farm plots and incremental free days. Female slaves were 'married' by their masters or to male slaves. They were then relocated to slave villages where they became virtual 'serfs' and retainers of their owners.

At the other end of the absorption grid were the house slaves or *olisos* as they were known in Temne. Most were long-serving or second generation slaves. *Olisos* were more integrated into the owner's household and kinship group. They required less physical coercion and control. Considered as virtual kin of their owners, they had the most acquired 'rights' and obligations. They acted as domestic servants, and the males served their masters as squires during war. Although they could be hired out as wage labour or used as pawns, *olisos* could not be sold unless they committed grave offenses.[12] Indigenous laws and customs limited abuse and cruelty toward slaves among all groups. Kings, especially among the Temne and Soso, had an obligation to respond to the appeals of slaves and protect them against harsh owners. The are no indications of the degree to which social sanctions were enforced against cruel owners. Provisions were made for emancipation. Slaves could be freed by their own efforts or those of their kin by payment to their masters. How much was paid and how many slaves attained their freedom at different periods is unknown.

Rights and concessions acquired by slaves were not necessarily willingly granted. Sometimes they had to be won through resistance. Sierra Leone historical works contain cursory references to acts of escape, marronage and revolt by slaves in the northwestern region.[13] One of the most famous escapees in the precolonial period was Gumbu Smart, a Loko, who paradoxically became a slave trader and accumulated sufficient wealth to set up a powerful chieftaincy in Rokon. Many lesser known slaves eluded their masters, returned home or sought refuge in receptive communities.[14] Others had varying degrees of success. In 1785–96, a group of Temne, Baga and Bullom slaves rebelled against Soso masters in Moriah kingdom on the Guinea–Sierra Leone border.[15] For four decades starting from 1838, another slave, Bilali, battled Soso and Temne slave owners from his refuge in Tonko Limba Chiefdom.[16] In the mid-nineteenth century, a group of Koranko and Kono slaves led by Tamba killed their owners and other free people and fled to Tambakkha Chiefdom.[17]

The full range of contentious actions by slaves in pre-colonial Sierra Leone cannot be captured within the confines of this article. Historians of slavery elsewhere have demonstrated that slaves had an arsenal of strategies to resist servitude.[18] In Sierra Leone as elsewhere what emerges from the

SLAVE EMANCIPATION IN SIERRA LEONE   213

deployment of these strategies of resistance is a process of contestation, negotiation and accommodation with the freedom of the slave at one extreme and absolute domination by the master at the other. The accommodation that emerged between master and slave in northwestern Sierra Leone did not always depend solely on internal dynamics. External pressures were also crucial. The foundation of Freetown in northwestern Sierra Leone in 1787 as a settlement for freed slaves provided a bridgehead for European capitalist penetration of the hinterland and for abolitionist efforts to curtail the slave trade in West Africa. The British, who managed the Freetown settlement from 1808, consistently pushed the twin goals of anti-slavery and capitalist commerce in the hinterland. They despatched intermittent punitive military expeditions, signed numerous treaties and interfered incessantly in regional politics throughout the nineteenth century. Christian missionaries from Britain also made forays into the region to spread the gospel of anti-slavery and commerce. These efforts had mixed results. British efforts did not eliminate slavery, slave-trading or the participation of local elites in slave trading, but they did curtail it. Far more significant for slaves in the hinterland, however, was that by the end of the nineteenth century, Freetown provided a haven for them as it had done for its earlier colonists.

Slave Resistance and Colonial Consolidation 1894–98

The heightened role of Freetown as a refuge for freed slaves during this period can be understood within the context of the scramble for Africa and the fiscal crisis facing the coastal colonial administration. The long-running fiscal crisis faced by Sierra Leone Colony had been exacerbated by the worldwide depression and the contraction of commerce with the hinterland in the 1870s and 1880s. Endemic warfare had disrupted societies and trade networks between Freetown and the hinterland. The warfare stemmed from the decline of the Atlantic slave trade, lineage disputes, competition for servile labour and pressures from the Samorian Empire. Almami Samori Toure had carved out an empire in the upper Niger which by the late 1880s included parts of northern Sierra Leone. To safeguard the financial position of the colony and check the rapidly expanding French, the British despatched military expeditions which established a *Pax Britannica* in the hinterland. These actions lead to the incorporation of indigenous rulers into a Protectorate within a larger colonial territory that continued to be called Sierra Leone.[19] This process of territorial and political incorporation provides an important point of departure for understanding the reinvigorated attempt and subsequent failure of the British to abolish slavery.

214   SLAVERY AND COLONIAL RULE IN AFRICA

Governor Frederick Cardew, an impatient imperialist who took over the Freetown colonial administration in 1894, was a pivotal actor in this process. He accelerated and completed the incorporation of the hinterland into Sierra Leone. More than any preceding governor, he provided incentives to slaves from the hinterland who wanted to escape. Cardew committed government resources to resettle escaped slaves in Freetown. He gave wide latitude to government officials and the Frontier Police, established in 1891, to curtail slavery. They aggressively accosted slave-traders and released slaves from their captors and masters.[20] Masters who attempted to retrieve escaped slaves received no help from the colonial administration.[21] Before this period, although the government opposed internal slavery, it did not take vigorous actions to end it. With the support of the government, Kikonkeh Island became a beacon of freedom for escaped slaves in the last decade of the nineteenth century. Kikonkeh Island had been the site of factories for the lucrative timber trade in the eighteenth and nineteenth centuries. In 1876, Governor Rowe secured and converted it into a customs point for taxing the trade on the Skarcies River.[22] Slaves began fleeing to the island to seek protection against their owners around 1891. Initially, the reception of fugitive slaves was ill-organized and poorly monitored, but in 1894, Governor Cardew instituted a more systematic registration of the fugitives. Between 1894 and 1897, over 300 escapees registered at the post. During the peak period between 1894 and 1895, for which surviving records are most reliable, 262 persons sought refuge at Kikonkeh.[23]

John Grace has compiled and analysed the data on the fugitives, tabulating them by sex, age, ethnicity and geographical origin, and suggesting which areas and masters lost the most slaves.[24] The fugitives included male, female and children and were aged between four months and 55 years old. They came predominantly from chiefdoms around the Skarcies Rivers. Slaves gave three key reasons for escape – ill-treatment, fear of resale, and the desire for freedom. The first two – ill-treatment and fear of resale – indicate the harshness and insecurity of slave life; the third points to awareness by the fugitives of their disadvantaged status in the societies they were escaping. Many gave the 'desire to be free' as their main reason for fleeing slavery. What constitutes 'freedom' for slaves besides escape from the harshness and insecurity of servitude is difficult to fathom in the absence of detailed slave narratives.

Grace saw the escaped slaves as beneficiaries of a favourable anti-slavery British attitude. What he did not recognize and therefore did not emphasize was the importance of slave initiatives. Slaves escaped in groups ranging from three to twenty people, including males, females and children.[25] For example, on 2 March 1897, a group of 19 slaves including

SLAVE EMANCIPATION IN SIERRA LEONE
215

six men and 13 women escaped their masters, Amara and Murmodo of Mafallah village.[26] The active role of women challenges the notion they were less likely to escape servitude than men. Half of those who fled to Kikonkeh were women. Some came on their own; others came with children.[27] They included women of all ages and from different places in northwestern Sierra Leone. Nonetheless, Grace used the Kikonkeh data to rightly challenge and criticize colonial officials and Freetown Creole elites who insisted that the system was benign and the escapees were idlers and vagabonds.[28]

The Creole elite, who were ironically descendants of freed slaves, opposed the government's abolitionist efforts and the resettlement of escapees in Freetown. They feared abolition would disrupt trade and resettlement would create serious problems for the city. The Freetown press strongly argued that domestic slavery was inextricably interwoven into the economy of the hinterland and radical abolitionist actions would damage trade on which the colony depended.[29] It also maintained that resettlement of freed slaves in the city would lead to poor sanitation, disease and vagrancy.[30] The elite also feared the presence of a large freed slave population could create a labour glut in the city. The Krio press demanded stringent controls on 'immigration' to the city including the creation of a labour bureau to issue work visas and to monitor the movement and employment of rural immigrants.[31] Despite Creole concerns, government only adopted legislation to restrict the movement of rural labour in 1905 and 1908.

Objections by the Creole elite and the chiefs forced the government to end the official reception of escaped slaves at the Kikonkeh and resettlement in Freetown. Despite the government's retreat, chiefs in northwestern Sierra Leone, led by Bai Bureh, waged a nine-month war against the British in 1898. Although the catalyst for the war was an unpopular five shillings hut tax, the chiefs listed government efforts to dismantle domestic slavery as one of the most important of reasons for their taking up arms.[32] The British defeated the chiefs but could not compel them to accept the abolition of slavery. The colonial state lacked the money and the manpower necessary to end slavery, to transform labour relations, to economically exploit and to administer the colony without aid of the rural elite. The anti-slavery crusade gave way to pragmatic politics of accommodation. The precolonial elite were incorporated into the new dispensation. Economic and political necessity now forced the British to tolerate slavery. They tried, however, to ensure that the context within which servitude continued was transformed, by building a new moral consensus on slavery.

The Moral Economy of Servitude and Slave Resistance, 1899–1914

Within this new consensus, the government recognized the existence of slavery and the 'rights' of masters over slaves. It toned down its anti-slavery rhetoric, calling the system 'domestic' servitude and insisting on its mildness.[33] The government incorporated the precolonial parameters of servitude by relegating the responsibility for the treatment and the welfare of slaves to chiefs. As Colonial Attorney-General, P. Smyly, maintained, 'the status of native living in the protectorate is determined by native laws and customs'.[34] The colonial government drew a clear distinction between the coastal 'crown colony' and the hinterland 'Protectorate'. The Colony was administered under British laws which did not recognize slavery. The government administered the Protectorate under an ordinance passed in 1896 which implicitly recognized and tolerated slavery within certain limits. The government banned the slave trade, but it did not prevent owners from transporting their slaves. The government also did not provide guarantees against re-enslavement of escaped slaves who returned to their former chiefdoms.[35] It further refused to recognize the marriage of slave women to government soldiers without payment of redemption fees to owners.[36]

The government balanced the concessions and rights of masters by implicitly recognizing the 'right' of slaves to freedom. It made limited provisions for emancipation and for slaves to contest their masters' control. The amended Protectorate Ordinance of 1901 stipulated that adult and child slaves could be emancipated on payment of four pounds and two pounds sterling respectively to their owners. The same law protected slaves from being sold to another person and made it possible for slaves legally to contest attempts by their masters to sell them at the district commissioner's court. The right to contest an owner's actions, though limited, was the most important gain made by slaves within the colonial moral economy of servitude. The recognition by the colonial government of conflicting 'rights' of masters and slaves produced ambiguity and tensions in the implementation of its policies.[37] Thus the government neither ignored the complaints of masters nor vigorously assisted them in reclaiming escaped slaves.[38] In 1902 the government allowed 30 runaway slaves from French Guinea to return to Sierra Leone, some of whom resettled in Kaffu Bullom.[39] On the other hand, the District Commissioner of Karene, H.G. Warren expressed strong disapproval when Assistant Commissioner W. Addison freed 11 slaves at Rokon in 1903. The slaves, who had been ill-treated, appealed to Addison. Their owner, Sallu Karnu, however, protested to Warren about what Addison had done. The slaves were never returned, but Warren maintained Addison had no right to free them.[40] Many masters, like

SLAVE EMANCIPATION IN SIERRA LEONE 217

Sallu, made attempts to re-enslave freed and escaped slaves with mixed results.[41]

Government policies perpetuated rather than eliminated the ambiguity and tensions inherent in the government's position. This was vividly illustrated in a major policy directive from the Governor to the District Commissioners on domestic slavery in 1906. The Governor stated:

> You are aware that although the Government has not abolished existing slavery in the Protectorate, the policy has been to stand from the system: in other words, the power of the Government is never used to back up the system of slavery. The system of existing slavery is left to work itself out, and, in a decade or two, will probably cease to exist. [I]t is very difficult to distinguish between a freeman and a slave. This attitude of reserve will, of course, continue in the main to be the policy of the Government, but in the interest of the slave, I think it is better to insist that the native laws and customs respecting their treatment are to be rigidly observed by the natives.[42]

The government did not keep 'aloof' from the system. Its continued accommodation with, and support for the local elite shored up the system. The only significant official respite provided for slaves was to ensure that the government's chief representative in the protectorate, the District Commissioner, helped protect the rights of slaves. For slaves, this meant utilizing the District Commissioner's Court to contest actions of their owners.

Under the 1901 Amended Protectorate Ordinance, the District Commissioner's Court provided opportunities for slaves to regain their freedom and be protected from resale. Slave owners could be prosecuted and punished for selling or transferring slaves illegally. Through this loophole, a small number of slaves regained their freedom between 1900 and 1914.[43] Female, male and child slaves in northwestern Sierra Leone (constituted as Karene District after 1896 Protectorate Declaration) resourcefully used co-slaves, kith and kin as witnesses to challenge owners and gain their freedom.[44] Children in the process of being enslaved or sold eluded their captors and helped in prosecuting them.[45] Freedom usually came with a price. For female slaves, emancipation sometimes meant separation from their children. Masters retained the children, especially if they were the fathers or owners of the fathers.[46]

The opportunity for emancipation through the District Commissioner's Court should not be exaggerated. No guarantees existed that masters would be convicted or that slaves would be freed. Slaves and pawns had limited opportunity to bring up and successfully prosecute cases in the courts. Except in rare cases, slaves had little chance against men of 'some standing in their chiefdom'.[47] Getting cases brought to court largely depended on the vigilance of court messengers and the cooperation of local Chiefs, neither of whom had any interest in pursuing the matter. The courts sat in only a few locations, Batkanu, Samaya and Port Loko, which restricted their accessibility to slaves. Slave cases constituted a tiny proportion of total cases in the court, and it is difficult to extricate them from those of pawning and pledging which were different.[48]

Slaves usually had to depend on other methods of resistance. Many continued to escape and migrate to Freetown.[49] Desperation and harsh working conditions forced others to withhold their labour. This was the theme of an intelligence report to the British War Office in 1904 by Lieutenant Hart of the West African Regiment who was stationed at the headquarters of Karene District. He noted a 'certain amount of unrest among the owners who found it difficult to get their domestics to work'.[50] Many disputes erupted as a consequence. Hart remarked that any sweeping change was bound to produce 'some kind of rising'.[51] Discontent was not surprising since slaves worked harder and longer than other rural labourers. According to W. St. John Oswell, the Karene District Commissioner, '[t]hey work from sunrise till 6 p.m., whereas the freeman concludes work at 4. p.m'.[52] Continued slave resistance, especially by escape and migration, threatened the power of the chiefs and thus colonial order. Between 1905 and 1908, the government adopted stringent legislation to keep 'natives', including slaves, on the land, control their influx into Freetown and repatriate fugitives to their original chiefdoms.[53] Significantly, these measures came at the peak of mass slave desertions from their masters in French colonies and Northern Nigeria.[54]

The attempt to hold back this process was reflected in two incidents of slave resistance on the Guinea-Sierra Leone border. They involved large numbers of escaped slaves who fled from Guinea to the Sierra Leone side of the border. The District Commissioner of Karene and the French Commandant at Farana returned most of them to their masters.[55] Both administrators agreed to help chiefs recover 'domestics' who crossed the frontier. This contradicted an earlier assertion by the French Commandant that 'the mere fact of their crossing the Frontier, at once gave them [slaves] freedom'.[56] The administrators were attempting to curtail opportunities for cross-border escape and reduce conflicts among chiefs on different sides of the border.[57]

The government framed its actions in terms of the preservation of 'customary laws' and the maintenance of law and order. Colonialism had lessened the elite's control over slaves and peasants, and by extension their power and status.[58] The restriction and diversion of the centuries-old northern trade to Conakry by the French restricted the elite's access to

SLAVE EMANCIPATION IN SIERRA LEONE

219

alternate sources of wealth and power.[59] The colonial government also had to strengthen chiefs' control over slaves because it depended on them for cheap labour. Bai Forki, the Chief of Port Loko, for example, controlled a colonially designated labour reserve. He provided large quantities of requisitioned servile labour for the construction of military barracks at Wonkifu, and for railways and porters for the transportation of colonial officials.[60] The attempt to control slaves by legislation did not deter escape or migration. Indeed, the colonial government's treatment and remuneration of requisitioned labour sometimes undermined the intent of the legislation. Colonial officials paid and treated slaves badly. The labourers protested to chiefs who sometimes took up the matter with government. The Paramount Chief of Maforki, Bai Forki, warned the administration that 'if you do not lessen the burden on me the boys will all run away to another country so they are talking in my absence'.[61] The requisition process prevented peasants and slaves from carrying on their 'proper avocations'.[62]

By the end of the first decade of the twentieth century, colonialism had produced paradoxical consequences for slaves. The admonition of chiefs, the provisions for redemption and court challenges, and opportunities for migration to other areas compelled some owners to treat their slaves better. Colonial anthropological reports, written by W. St. John Oswell in 1906 and Northcote Thomas in 1916, refer to some of the gains and 'rights' acquired by slaves.[63] Both authors maintain that some slaves among the Temne and Soso had access to wives, agricultural plots and incremental free days. These slaves, however, held no title to the land they cultivated. They usually worked four days a week for their owners and three days for themselves. According to Thomas, no master could 'force a slave to work on his free day or days'. He also mentioned that slaves could freely dispose of products from their plots after payment of tribute to their masters.[64] On the other hand, the colonial administration's intolerance of the slave trade and its support for the owners may have prolonged slavery.[65] The inability of masters to purchase new slaves reduced their incentives to assimilate slaves as kin and fulfil the attendant social obligations.[66] Many masters refused to free slaves except for cash payment.[67] Colonial officials pointed to the low rate of redemptions as a sign of the slaves' contentment and improvement in servile conditions. They, however, failed to take into consideration the material reality of the slaves' position.[68] Some slaves may have secured additional 'rights' under colonial rule but not all witnessed improvement in their status and treatment. What in fact the colonial state sought to project to opponents of slavery was that the moral consensus it put in place was holding. It did hold tenuously until the outbreak of World War I.

220 SLAVERY AND COLONIAL RULE IN AFRICA

Resistance and Emancipation, 1914–28

The outbreak of the First World War challenged the moral consensus by providing new labour options and new opportunities for slaves to contest servitude. Some enlisted and served as carriers and soldiers with their owners' consent. Others served at the behest of chiefs who were mandated to mobilize them for the war effort. Although no firm figures exist, many of the over 8,000 carriers recruited from Karene District, who served in East Africa, were slaves.[69] Slaves also ran away and joined the army, usually under assumed identities. Masters pursued them, and in some cases were able to establish the true identity of the runaways and come to some settlement about their status.[70] Even though the colonial government accepted slaves into military service, it did not actively encourage their emancipation. In fact it instructed border chiefs not to harbour escaped slaves. Bai Sherbro, Paramount Chief of Samu, was told to deport all escapees and deserters from the French side of the border. Even slaves who had been redeemed were not exempt. Only slaves who had escaped and had been redeemed before the war received exemption.[71] Some slaves who joined the army were able to alleviate their condition. Wages earned in service and favourable inflationary economic conditions enabled some to redeem themselves. Redemption figures between 1917 and 1920 showed a steady increase; 1,950 slaves were redeemed in a 30-month period between 1920 and 1922. The estimated official average rate of redemption was about 800 persons per year. However, these numbers declined when recession and economic stagnation hit the colony in 1922.[72]

The second level at which the First World War challenged the colonial moral economy of servitude was through the economic and social crisis it generated in Sierra Leone. Government requisitioning of labour and food, coupled with variable weather, epidemics and food shortfalls, exacerbated the burden on slaves and peasants.[73] Slaves worked harder, and masters tended to feed them poorly. Many followed the footsteps of poor peasants by migrating to Freetown and other urban centres. One of the most spectacular protests against slavery, however, was mounted by the slave, Sedu. In response to his master's cruelty and his harsh working conditions, he brutally murdered three of his four children with an axe in 1919. Sedu's acceptance of responsibility for his actions and his testimony were unequivocal:

> My name is Sedu. I live at Roinkisa in the chiefdom of P.C. Bai Makari in the Karene District of the Protectorate of Sierra Leone. I am a slave to Almami Koroma. He gave me a slave girl, Musu, as wife. We had four children. Almami Koroma does not give us rice to eat, nor clothes to wear. When farm work begins, nobody rests. When I

SLAVE EMANCIPATION IN SIERRA LEONE

221

worked, my sores hurt me very badly. I got sick last August. Musu no longer cared for me when I fell ill. Almami Koroma sent to Musu to leave my house and go to his with my children Fatu, M'Balu, Derisa, Yeno. I got no medicine for sores. I rubbed cow dung on them. Almami Koroma gave orders for me to be prevented getting anything to eat from the farm and that my 'door mouth' should be closed so that I could not get out. Almami Koroma's son Amara cut all my rice. I had none of it. Almami Koroma said that the reason I lived was because I got something to eat, and that steps must be taken to prevent me eating so I would die. All this why I killed the children Fatu, M'Balu and Dambi. I killed them with this axe. My master took my wife, my children and my rice, and that is why I killed the children.[74]

The year 1919 had been punctuated by excruciating food shortages, influenza and economic retrenchment. Yet Sedu's crime was exceptional in twentieth-century Sierra Leone as was perhaps the cruelty of his master. His testimony spoke of inhuman conditions under which some slaves laboured during the war and the desperate actions it forced them to take. District Commissioner Addison of Karene, who presided over the case, recognized the legitimacy of Sedu's actions when he trenchantly remarked, 'If Sedu had not been a slave, he would not have murdered his three innocent children'.[75]

Sedu's actions and testimony raised many questions. Why did he kill his own children? Was he trying to save them from his fate? Why did he not strike the master? What do his actions and words reveal about slave consciousness? These questions cannot be answered with any precision. However, undeniably, the testimony and actions of Sedu were a powerful and poignant expression of the anguish and subjugation of generations of slaves. His discourse was about power and liberty. His master, Alimamy Koroma, had sharply underscored the disempowerment inherent in Sedu's servitude with his inhuman actions. Nowhere was the disempowerment more glaring than in Sedu's lack of control over his family. In his actions and statement, Sedu tried to reclaim some of that power and control. He insisted that his master had certain obligations to him. These included recognition of his humanity and rights to a tolerable existence – food, medical care, access to his family. By depriving him of these 'rights', and the empowerment contained in them, Sedu contended that his master had violated the 'moral consensus' around slavery. By his action, he indicated that his master had forfeited claims to either his labour or that of his progeny. In killing his children, Sedu struck at slavery in two ways. He destroyed his 'organic' relationship with his master. His crime meant certain death under the colonial system. Second, he deprived the servile system of a some of its next generation of slaves.

222   SLAVERY AND COLONIAL RULE IN AFRICA

A second contestation of the colonial moral economy of servitude involved the case of Mrs. Fibbian Williams, who attempted to redeem the slave woman Banja and her children in 1917. The case persisted until after the war. It became a prominent test of the degree to which owners were prepared to free slaves. Banja's mistress, Madam Kunna, refused to accept the redemption fee of £30. Supported by the chief and elders of Bendu Sherbro chiefdom, Kunna maintained that Banja, an old woman, had spent her entire life in servitude. Furthermore, Kunna had married Kanre, the ex-slave husband of Banja, making her the stepmother of Banja's children. Torn between keeping a 'family' unit together and backing the freedom of an old enslaved woman, W.B. Stanley, Commissioner of Sherbro District, sided with Madam Kunna. He agreed that Kunna treated Banja and her children well and questioned Fibbian Williams' supposed benevolence.[76] He blamed Mr. Cooper Williams, a relative of Mrs. Williams, who had allegedly 'cohabited' with one of the female slaves, for orchestrating the redemptions. Banja, however, escaped and eventually enticed her children to live with Mrs. Fibbian Williams.[77] Faced with the imminent return of Banja and her children to Madam Kunna, Mr. Cooper Williams appealed to the Anti-Slavery and Aborigines Protection Society (AAPS). The AAPS took the case to the Colonial Secretary, who drew the attention of the Sierra Leone Governor, R.J. Wilkinson, to the controversy and question of slavery in Sierra Leone. Wilkinson expressed interest in ending slavery but refused to reverse Stanley's decision to return the slaves to Madam Kunna.[78]

The cases described above coincided with a revival of international humanitarian and abolitionist sentiments. The Treaty of St. Germain-en-Laye in 1919 had called for the 'suppression of slavery in all its forms'. The League of Nations appointed the first of three commissions to collect evidence on slavery in 1924, and asked all countries to supply information on the concrete measures they had taken to eradicate slavery.[79] (See Miers in this collection.) For Sierra Leone, this international anti-slavery pressure came at a time when the colony was experiencing serious financial and economic distress. Production and export of the colony's main exports, palm oil and kernels, had stagnated. Proponents of free labour in Freetown and London blamed the post-war economic stagnation and depression in the colony on the persistence of slavery. They argued that slave labour was 'wasteful' and unproductive and held back economic expansion.[80] Thus the conjuncture of slave resistance, British abolitionism and domestic economic distress challenged the tenability of slavery as a viable labour system. Colonial administrators had to rethink the question of slavery in the colony.

The attempt by the colonial government to develop a new slavery policy had been marred up to this point by administrative indecision and lack of political will. Colonial officials expressed conflicting views on the nature of

SLAVE EMANCIPATION IN SIERRA LEONE   223

local slavery, the timetable for abolition, and the consequences of general emancipation. Many views put forward by officials were based on personal perceptions of the system rather than on concrete data. Governor R.J. Wilkinson, therefore, instructed district commissioners to collect information as a prelude to general registration of slaves.[81] He saw registration as essential to development of clear abolition strategies. Despite the support Wilkinson received from the Colonial Office, the project never materialized owning to the shortage of staff.[82] Governor A. R. Slater, a cautious abolitionist, succeeded Wilkinson in 1921. He continued the task of collecting information. The Governor also spent much time mediating the conflicting views of district commissioners, the interests of the Protectorate slave-holding elite and the vocal pro-slavery Krio public opinion.[83] The governor did eventually get a rough idea of the scale of servitude in Sierra Leone. From the figures submitted by the various district commissioners, it was estimated that slaves constituted between 15 to 30 percent of a Protectorate population of about 1.5 million.[84]

The colonial administration framed its anti-slavery legislative options around abolitionist precedents in Gambia and Nigeria. The Gambian Anti-Slavery Ordinances of 1895 and 1906 freed slaves born after the promulgation of the ordinances and all others on the death of their masters. Governor Slater, with the support of the Colonial Office, eventually put forth an amendment to the Protectorate Ordinance of 1901 along the same lines. The amendment did not arouse much debate but it did attract strong objection from the Protectorate elite. Bai Kompa, the Paramount Chief of Koya, who had been appointed to the Colonial Legislative Council in 1924, illustrated the stake of the masters:

> About the slave matter. We own slaves. We, all black men, are slaves, because Chiefs are the people Europeans tell not to do certain things. They gives us orders. They say we must set slaves free. Suppose, we set them free, will we be paid? We work for the people and our slaves work for us. Since we chiefs enter this council I have said nothing about anything, but as to this slave matter, we do not agree to it. If the slaves want freedom, they should redeem themselves so we can put money into the bank.
>
> They say when the master of a slave dies the slave must be set free. How can the master of slave die when he has got a child? He is only dead when he has no children ... In the case of the master and slave, the master bears children also, they grow together and live as brothers. When the master dies his son takes the slaves. If on the death of the master the slave is set free, who will work for the children of the master, who will support them.[85]

224 SLAVERY AND COLONIAL RULE IN AFRICA

In retrospect, Bai Kompa's dissent was futile since all slaves in Sierra Leone were emancipated in 1928 without compensation to owners. Yet his speech was important in its revelation of the mentality of masters and the discourse of slavery in Sierra Leone. It was a counterpoint to the statement seven years earlier of the slave Sedu. Like Sedu, Bai Kompa spoke within and appropriated discursive elements of the moral consensus of servitude to defend what he felt was a commonly understood and accepted relationship between masters and slaves.

While Sedu defended the rights of slaves, Kompa defended the rights of owners. He insisted on the role and function of slaves in producing wealth and perpetuating the status of his family. Kompa spoke like a true paternalist who viewed slaves as extensions of the family. He would never have supported the actions of Sedu or his master, Almamy Koroma. Almamy undermined the paternalism of the masters and violated social norms pertaining to the treatment of slaves. On the other hand, Sedu violated customary as well as colonial criminal laws with his murderous acts. Both transgressed the limits of tolerable social behaviour and threatened communal consensus on slavery. Kompa saw that same threat within the colonial attempt at emancipation. He was adamant that the children of owners needed the next generation of slaves to perpetuate themselves. On the proposition to free slaves on the death of their master, he asked, 'How can the master of a slave die when he has got child? ... who will work for the children of the master, who will support them?'[86] In other words, how would the slave owning class of Sierra Leone reproduce itself? Both Sedu and Bai Kompa spoke within the discourse of negotiated rights and obligations, and of the expected duties and roles of masters and slaves. What Bai Kompa refused to accept was that the 'moral consensus' at the centre of this discourse had been challenged by slaves like Sedu and the realities of post-war politics and economics. His colleague Paramount Chief Bai Comber had a more realistic grasp of the situation. Comber indicated the willingness of the Protectorate elite to cooperate with the colonial government on the issue of abolition.[87]

Bai Kompa's insistence on compensation received the support of the Krio political class and its press. A.E. Tobuku-Metzger, an elected representatives to the Legislative Council, maintained that slave owners should be compensated, as were slave owners in the Caribbean in 1834. The *Sierra Leone Weekly News*, while welcoming abolition of slavery as the 'removal of a cruel stain' on the reputation of Sierra Leone, nonetheless endorsed Tobuku-Metzger's views.[88] Krio upper-class opinions on abolition shocked external observers. A columnist in the *Daily Mail*, a newspaper in Britain, found it ironic that the 'descendants' of slaves would defend the institution of slavery.[89] Metzger and the *Sierra Leone Weekly News* insisted

SLAVE EMANCIPATION IN SIERRA LEONE   225

their views had been grossly misrepresented. They argued they had merely invoked British sense of 'fair play' and requested that slave-owners in Sierra Leone be treated like those in the Caribbean.[90] Creole views were definitely not misrepresented. Within the *Sierra Leone Weekly News*, a guest columnist writing the under the pseudonym, Modibo, strongly criticized Creole upper-class views. He argued that compensation to chiefs should be an 'act of grace and not to be expected of right'.[91] Pointing out the inherent oppression in the institution of slavery, Modibo asserted:

> No human being can ever have a right to the ownership of his fellow human. The liberty of man is an axiom that finds acceptance even among the most barbarous communities.[92]

He opined that slaves, not the masters, should be the ones getting reparations for the 'untold miseries they and ancestors have endured for generations'.[93]

Creole upper-class concerns about emancipation transcended questions of compensation. Members of that class had a longstanding antipathy towards rural migration to the city. They feared that sudden abolition would compound this trend and its resultant social ills, namely vagrancy, crime and unemployment. They wanted the state to discourage slaves from leaving their masters. In 1927, the *SLWN* repeated its call for a labour bureau to register and monitor all workers in the colony.[94]

The sentiments of the Creole upper class and the dissatisfaction of the slave-owning elite failed to sway the colonial administration. The Protectorate Amendment Ordinance No. 3 of 1926 passed easily in the Legislative Council.[95] The government instructed provincial and district commissioners 'to stop helping slave owners recover runaway slaves because it was now illegal for Government Officers, even in their executive position to recognize the legal status of slavery'.[96] The amendment was a half-measure since it did not emancipate slaves. However, it did provide an opportunity for slaves to seize the moment once more. Many slaves ran away with the expectation that their owners would not receive aid from the colonial government to recapture them. In Karene and Bombali districts, Loko and Limba slaves from Biriwa Limba left their Mandingo masters and returned home to Sanda Loko and Sella Limba Chiefdoms. Others refused to work for their masters.[97]

Slave owners attempted to reassert their crumbling authority by forcibly recapturing fugitive slaves and compelling them to work. The recaptured slaves appealed to the district commissioners. In Karene district, these appeals led to the arrest and conviction of Nfa Nonko, a Mandingo sub-chief, and several other slave owners for assault against former slaves. The convicted slave owners however took their case to the Court of Appeal in

226 SLAVERY AND COLONIAL RULE IN AFRICA

Freetown. The judges ruled in their favour. Three out of the five appeal judges decided Nfa Nonko and the other owners had used reasonable force in recovering their property.[98] The legal struggle between the fugitive slaves, Nfa Nonko and his colleagues, and the state exposed the limits of the anti-slavery amendment of 1926. Nfa Nonko and his colleagues effectively demonstrated that the colonial state had not abolished chattel slavery. They also exposed the limit to the possibility of recaptured slaves legally challenging their owners.

The masters, however, had merely achieved a Pyrrhic victory. The Appeal Court verdict in favour of Nfa Nonko and the other slave owners embarrassed the British Colonial Office. It exposed the unresolved ambivalence in the Colonial Office's policy on slavery in Sierra Leone. Conscious of British anti-slavery sentiment and the restive mood of slaves, the Colonial Office insisted that the Sierra Leone administration draft a new law abolishing slavery completely. It discounted arguments put forward by Governor Slater about compensation and postponing the abolition date. A Bill entitled 'Ordinance 24 of 1927 – Legal Status of Slavery (Abolition) Ordinance, 1927', was passed, abolishing slavery from the beginning of 1928.[99] The ordinance did not alter the social and material circumstances of slaves but it ensured that 'masters' and 'slaves' ceased to exist as legally recognized social classes.

Ex-slaves responded to the end of their servile relationship in a number of ways. Some left their masters and returned to their chiefdom of origin. Others stayed in the chiefdom of their enslavement but refused to work for their former owners. Still others joined the stream of migrants to Freetown and other urban centres. Between 1930 and 1931, many landless and destitute ex-slaves flocked to the millenarian movement of Idara Konthorfili, an itinerant Muslim cleric. Idara attacked religious laxity and corruption among the rural elite. He called for the revival of Islam and an end to taxation and British colonialism in Sierra Leone. Idara's movement dissipated when he was killed in a skirmish with British troops at Bubuya in Tonko Limba Chiefdom in February 1931.[100]

Many ex-slaves stayed with their former owners and worked out new relationships. Some became more fully integrated into their former masters' family. Others simply became tributary peasants and continued to till the land usually under circumstances not very different from those of servitude. Coercive labour continued as the colonial government and the local elite colluded to maintain control over rural labour in the post-slavery era. The Legislative Council passed the Forced Labour Ordinance in 1933 to enable chiefs and the rural elite to continue to draw on coerced and tribute labour. Coerced labour remained a contentious issue between the rural elite and the masses. It contributed greatly to the outbreak of anti-chief riots in 1955.[101]

SLAVE EMANCIPATION IN SIERRA LEONE 227

The history of servitude and its abolition in Sierra Leone conforms to Martin Klein's general observation in French West Africa that for many slaves 'emancipation involved a struggle that often lasted generations'.[102] Yet the experience and struggle of slaves in the hinterland of Sierra Leone contains an element of profound paradox, if not shock. Emancipation had come 141 years after the foundation of a colony on the coast of Sierra Leone as a haven for freed slaves, and 95 years after the famous Emancipation Act of 1833. In their prolonged and courageous struggle, slaves had constructed their resistance against servitude both within and against a moral consensus created around the system and recognized by the owners and the state. Their eventual refusal to accept this moral consensus and their challenge to its inherent immorality helped compel the state to abolish slavery in 1928.

NOTES

1. The Krio rendition of the statement is incorrect but the rough translation is 'Father, I am a slave from Mende Country. I am being taken to Susu Country. Please Father, do not let them transport me'. SLNA MP 45/1893, Sammar to Native Affairs Secretary 30 January 1893.
2. Suzanne Miers, *Britain and the Ending of the Slave Trade* (London, 1975), pp.201–9.
3. *Sierra Leone Times*, 18 May 1895; J. C. Mannah-Kpaka, an educated chief and trader echoed the same sentiments: '... Among the Frontiers were freed slaves who decided to lord it on their former masters'. Paramount Chief J.K. Mannah-Kpaka, 'Memoirs of 1898 Rising', *Sierra Leone Studies*, N.S. 1 (1953) pp.28–39.
4. Myron Echenberg, 'Slaves into Soldiers: Social Origins of the Tirailleurs', in Paul Lovejoy (ed.) *Africans in Bondage* (Madison, Wisconsin, 1986). pp.311–33; Myron Echenberg, *Colonial Conscripts: The Tirailleurs Senegalais in French West Africa, 1857–1960* (London, 1991), pp.7–24.
5. See E.P. Thompson, 'The Moral Economy of the English Crowd in the Eighteenth Century', *Past and Present*, 50 (1971), pp.76–136, & George Rudé, *The Crowd in History 1730–1848* (London, 1981).
6. James Scott, *The Moral Economy of the Peasant: Rebellion and Subsistence in South East Asia* (New Haven, 1976); Ibrahim Abdallah, 'Rethinking the Freetown Crowd: The Moral Economy of the 1919 Freetown Strikes and Riots', *Canadian Journal of African Studies*, 28 (1994), pp.202–13; T. Dunbar Moodie, 'The Moral Economy of the Black Miners Strike of 1946, *Journal of Southern African Studies*, 13 (1986), pp.1–35.
7. John Edwin Mason, 'Hendrick Albertus and his Ex-slave Mey: A Drama in Three Acts', *Journal of African History*, 31 (1990), pp.423–45.
8. Jonathon Glassman, *Feast and Riots: Revelry, Rebellion and Popular Consciousness on the Swahili Coast 1856–1888* (London, 1995).
9. Eugene Genovese, *Roll Jordan Roll: The World the Slaves Made* (New York, 1972). pp.597–9.
10. C. Magbaily Fyle, *The Solima Yalunka Kingdom: Precolonial Politics, Economics and Society* (Freetown, 1979), pp.49–73; James Steel Thayer, 'Religion and Social Organization among a West African Muslim People: The Susu of Sierra Leone, (PhD. Dissertation, University of Michigan, 1981), pp.71–4.
11. John Matthews, *A Voyage to the River Sierra Leone* (London, 1966 [First published in 1788]), p.150; F. Harrison Rankin, *The White Man's Grave: A Visit to Sierra Leone in 1834* (London, 1836), pp.76–7.
12. Ibid., pp.150–3.

228 SLAVERY AND COLONIAL RULE IN AFRICA

13. Frederick William Butt Thompson, *Sierra Leone in History* (London, 1926) pp.44–5; Peter Kup, *A History of Sierra Leone* (London, 1961), p.123; Christopher Fyfe, *History of Sierra Leone* (London, 1962) pp.53–4.
14. Fyfe, *A History of Sierra Leone*, pp.65–6; Kenneth Wylie, *Political Kingdoms of the Temne*, London, 1977) pp.80–2. Document from 'Journal of Zachary Macauley' in Christopher Fyfe, *The Sierra Leone Inheritance* (London, 1964), pp.107–8.
15. Bronislaw Nowak, 'The Slave Rebellion in Sierra Leone in 1785–1796', *Hemispheres* (Poland) 3 (1986), pp.151–69.
16. See CMS Archives CA1/024/25, Edward Blyden's letter to Arthur Kennedy, 10 January 1872; David Skinner, *Thomas George Lawson: African Historian and Administration in Sierra Leone* (Stanford, 1980), p.217.
17. F.W.H. Migeod, *A View of Sierra Leone* (London, 1926), pp.49–50.
18. Eugene Genovese, *Roll Jordan Roll*; C.L.R. James, *The Black Jacobins: Toussaint L'Ouverture and the San Domingo Revolution*, 2nd ed.,. rev. (New York, 1963); Michael Craton, *Testing the Chains: Resistance to Slavery in British West Indies, 1627–1838* (Ithaca, N.Y., 1982); Hilary Beckles, *Black Rebellion in Barbados: The Struggle against Slavery* (St Michael: Barbados, 1984); Jonathon Glassman, *Feasts and Riots*; Paul Lovejoy and Jan Hogendorn, 'Revolutionary Mahdism and Resistance to Colonial Rule in Sokoto', *Journal of African History*, 31 (1990), pp.217–44.
19. Fyfe, *A History of Sierra Leone*, pp.476, 501, 517–21.
20. For example, in October, 1893, the Frontier Police seized and freed 13 slaves at Robiss village. SLNA MP (Sierra Leone National Archive Minute Paper) 514/1893, Police Department, 13 Rescued Slaves, 19 October 1893; See also Fyfe, *A History of Sierra Leone*, pp.522–3.
21. SLNA MP 74/1894, Bocary Sesay, 1894; SLNA MP 49/1893, Alimamy Sourie, Kambia to Secretary of Natives. Letter trans. by M. Sanusi, Govt. Translator.
22. Government customs points at Tagreen, Mahela and Isles des Los close to Freetown also attracted escaped slaves, but the documents are fragmentary. See SLNA MP 195/1897, Escaped Slaves from Tagreen Point Forwarded, From Superintendent of Police to Secretary for Native Affairs, 12 June 1897; See also David E. Skinner, *Thomas George Lawson*, p.79.
23. John Grace, *Domestic Slavery in West Africa Particular Reference to the Sierra Leone Protectorate, 1896–1927* (London, 1975), pp.276–85.
24. Ibid., p.285.
25. SLNA MP 223/1896, List of Escaped slaves, from officer in Charge to Supt. of Police; See also SLNA MP 275/1896; SLNA MP 529/1896; SLNA MP 95/1897.
26. SLNA MP 95/1897, 20 Escaped Slaves from Kikonki. 17 March 1897, Superintendent of Police to Secretary of Native Affairs, 1897.
27. SLNA MP, 147/1897, 6 Escaped Slaves from Kikonki, Superintendent of Police, 29 April 1897.
28. Grace, *Domestic Slavery in West Africa*, pp.91–4.
29. The *Sierra Leone Times*, for example, argued that 'the suppression of the system of domestic slavery would strike an irreparable blow at and paralize[sic] the trade of the colony'. *Sierra Leone Times*, 18 May 1895; *Sierra Leone Times*, 9 June 1894.
30. An editorial of the Sierra Leone Times opined, 'We have our cities invaded by a countless army of aborigines, hailing from every quarter of the interior; a purposeless, wholly insanitary band or escaped slaves; drawn hither in their search after the hitherto unknown luxury of idleness, and freedom from restraint'. *Sierra Leone Times*, 15 December 1894, *Sierra Leone Times*, 27 April 1895; See also the paper's xenophobic opinions about Mende migrants to the city. *Sierra Leone Times*, *Sierra leone Times*, 23 Jan. 1897; 13 Feb. 1897; *Sierra Leone Times*, 7 Jan. 1898; *Sierra Leone Times*, 1 Oct. 1898, *Sierra Leone Times*, 8 Oct. 1898; Sierra Leone Times, 1 April 1899.
31. *Sierra Leone Times*, 27 April 1895; *Sierra Leone Times*, 16 May 1896; *Sierra Leone Times*, 15 April 1896; The *Sierra Leone Times*, 1 July 1899; *Sierra Leone Times*, 8 July 1899; *Sierra Leone Times*, 15 July 1899; *Sierra Leone Times*, 22 July 1899, *Sierra Leone Times*, 2 Sept. 1899.
32. See La Ray Denzer, 'Sierra Leone-Bai Bureh' in Michael Crowder (ed.), *West Africa Resistance* (New York, 1971), pp.233–67.

SLAVE EMANCIPATION IN SIERRA LEONE

229

33. SLNA MP 16/1901, Confidential, Acting Attorney-General to Governor, 1/3/1901.
34. Ibid.
35. SLNA MP 2731/1901, Maxwell, DC Karene to Colonial Secretary, 9/6/1901; SLNA MP 45/1901 Confidential Despatch, Governor to District Commissioner, Karene 8/5/1901.
36. SL CSO MP (Sierra Leone Colonial Secretary Office Minute Paper) 119/1911, Colonial Secretary, 3/12/1911; see also CSO MP 2332/1907 1/7/07. SLNA MP 36/1912, Magisterial Returns, March 1912.
37. SLNA MP 533/1901, D.C., Karene to C.S., 30/1/1901.
38. SLNA MP 1547/1905, W. St. John Oswell, District Commissioner, Karene to Colonial Secretary, 23/3/1905; SLNA MP 1189/1910, District Commissioner, Karene to Colonial Secretary. 11/3/1910.
39. SLNA MP 2264/1902, Acting Collector of Customs to Governor, 28/5/1902; See also the escape of six slaves from their masters, Surubali to Kaffu Bullom. SLNA MP 533/1901, District Commissioner, Karene to Colonial Secretary, 30/1/1901.
40. LM 152/1913, Sallu Karnu to District Commissioner: Complaint against Mr. Addison, Re: freeing of Slaves. 28/4/1913.
41. SLNA MP 4404/1901, District Commissioner, Karene to Colonial Secretary 28/9/1901; See the case of Baloo and her mother in Rex vs. Bai Samura, a sub-chief SLNA MP 3849/1903, cases #65/66, Return of Cases tried in District Commissioner Court, 1903; SLNA MP 1547/1905, District Commissioner, Karene to Colonial Secretary, 23/3/1905.
42. CSO MP/NA 2425/1906, Governor: Circular #80, Punishment of Slaves, 28/5/1906.
43. See SLNA MP 234/1901, Case 62, Returns of Cases, Karene District, 8/1/1901; SLNA MP 2797/1902, Case #41, Return of Cases, May 1902, 16/6/1902.
44. See for Example SL NAMP 234/1901, Case 64, Rex vs Gbella, Returns of Cases, Karene District, 8/1/1901.; SL NAMP 1735/190 Magisterial Returns, Karene District, March 1901. 10/4/1901; SL NAMP 3040/1901, Case #39, Magisterial Returns, Karene District, June 1901, 3/7/1901; SL NAMP 5193/1901. See also the case of Yenoh, who marshalled her co-slaves to testify and convict her master, Abdulai, for slave trading in SL NAMP 3040/1901, Case #36, Magisterial Returns, June 1901. 3/7/1901. The case of Gbinti, an escapee, whose son defended her against re-enslavement, is instructive of kinship support. SLNA MP 4377/1903, Criminal Cases, District Commissioner's Court, September 1903, 1/10/1903; S.L NAMP 276/1902, Case #90, Return of cases, December, 1901, Karene District, 1/1/02.
45. See for example, the case of Simebah, who prosecuted his guardians, Yeli Bockari and her husband, Umaru. SLNA MP 1039/1903, Case #1, Magisterial returns for January 1903.
46. See SL NAMP 1725/1905, DC Karene to Governor, 6/4/1905.
47. SL NAMP DC/K23/1912, Annual Report on the Karene, 1911, 29/2/1912.
48. See Allen M. Howard, 'Pawning in Coastal Northwest Sierra Leone, 1870–1910', in Toyin Falola and Paul Lovejoy (eds.), *Pawnship in Africa: Debt Bondage in Historical Perspective* (Boulder, Colorado, 1994), pp.267–84.
49. Michael Banton, *West African City: A Study of Tribal Life in Freetown* (London, 1957), p.15.
50. CO 267/474/15854, Confidential Despatch #3, Report by Hart in WO to CO May 3, 1904.
51. Ibid.
52. CO 267/501 XC/14263, Native Customs & Laws, Karene District, Sierra Leone Protectorate. 1906.
53. SL NAMP 4042/1904, Protectorate Native Law Ordinance 26/5/1905. See also Ordinance 19 of 1905 in PRO CO 269/6; See The Tribal Administration (Freetown) Ordinance 17 of 1908 in CO 269/6; SL NAMP 2238/1907 Attorney General's Memo, 27/6/1907; See also the Vagrancy Ordinance, 1908 and Manual Labour Regulation Ordinance 1908, *SLWN*, June 13, 1908; *SLG*, 15 May 1908; *SLWN*, 13 June 1908.
54. R. Roberts and M. Klein. 'The Banamba Slave Exodus and the Decline of Slavery in Western Sudan', *Journal of African History*, 21 (1980), pp.375–94; R. Roberts, 'The End of Slavery in French Soudan, 1905–1914', in S. Miers and R. Roberts (eds.), *The End of Slavery in Africa* (Madison, 1988), pp.282–307; Paul Lovejoy and Jan Hogendorn, *Slow Death for Slavery: The Course of Abolition in Northern Nigeria, 1897–1936* (Cambridge, 1993), pp.60–3.

230

SLAVERY AND COLONIAL RULE IN AFRICA

55. See the case between Almamy Bamba, a sub-chief, in Karene and Almamy Amara, sub chief in Kindia, Guinea in 1908 involving 25 escaped slaves. Eighteen were returned to Amarra. Only seven who were freed after payment of the requisite amount were allowed to stay in Sierra Leone. SLNA MP C189/1910, H.G. Warren, DC/Karene, 7/12/1910. See also the case involving the escape of Tennenbah, her three sons and a number of other Limba slaves from Brimiah Chiefdom, Guinea to Tonko Limba chiefdom, Karene District. See SL NAMP 4923/1908, W.St-John Oswell, D.C. Karene to Colonial Secretary, 11/2/08.
56. SLNA MP, Confidential 189/1910.
57. CS0 MP 2264/1902, Comptroller of Customs to Governor, 28/5/1902; SL NAMP 4259/1903, Secretary of State, Colonies to Governor, Sierra Leone, 16/7/1903.
58. PRO CO267/477/16954, 'Draft Ordinance: Protectorate Native Law Ordinance 1905', Probyn to Lyttleton, 4/5/1905.
59. Annual Report of the Colony of Sierra Leone, 1900; PRO CO 267/462/6282, Kingharman to Chamberlain, 29 January 1902.
60. SL NAMP 615/1909, District Commissioner, Karene District to Colonial Secretary, 1/2/1909.
61. SLNA MP 615/1909, District Commissioner, Karene to Colonial Secretary, 1/2/1909.
62. Ibid.
63. CO 267/501 XC/14263, Native Customs & Laws, Karene District, Sierra Leone Protectorate. 1906; Northcote W. Thomas, *Anthropological Report on Sierra Leone; Laws and Customs of the Timne and other Tribes* (London, 1916), p.159.
64. Ibid., p.159.
65. Mark R. Lipschutz, 'Northeast Sierra Leone since 1884: Responses to the Samorian Invasions and British Colonialism' (Ph.D. Thesis, University of California, Los Angeles, 1972), p.184.
66. Grace, *Domestic Slavery in West Africa*, pp.159–68.
67. CO 267/501 XC/14263, Native Customs & Laws, Karene District, Sierra Leone Protectorate, 1906.
68. See Despatch from Governor of Sierra Leone to Secretary of State, Colonies, 30 April, 1924, in CMD 3020, Correspondence Relating to Domestic Slavery in Sierra Leone, p.6.
69. N. A. Cox-George, *Finance and Development in West Africa* (London, 1961), pp.181–2.
70. SLNA MP 75/1917, District Commissioner, Karene, 7/8/1917.
71. SLNA DC/K 27/1916, Return of Deserters from French Territory, DC Port Loko, 10/2/1916.
72. SLNA Confidential CSO 107/22, Return of Persons redeemed from servitude in the Protectorate.
73. See PRO CO267/578/53257, W. Allan, Ag. Senior Sanitary, 'An Interim Report on the Epidemic of Influenza;' PRO CO267/572/52645, Report on Smallpox Epidemic', 8 June 1916; Karene District Reports 1914–1919.
74. Deposition in the Case Rex vs. Sedu in Batkanu, 1919 in secret file titled 'Domestic Slavery' n.d.
75. Addison, DC Karene to Evelyn, Colonial Secretary, 4 December 1919. Sierra Leone National Archives, Domestic Slavery. n.d
76. W.B.S. Stanley to J.A. Williams, J.P., 17 October 1917, in 'Domestic Slavery' n.d.
77. W.B.S. Stanley, District Commissioner, to Colonial Secretary, 17 November 1917, in 'Domestic Slavery' n.d.
78. Travers Buxton to Walter Long, November 11, 1918 & Walter Long to Wilkinson November 26, 1918 & Buxton to Secretary of State, Colonies, May 12, 1919, in Domestic Slavery. n.d.
79. Grace, *Domestic Slavery in West Africa*, p.233.
80. See Extract from the Despatch from the Governor of Sierra Leone to the Secretary of State, Colonies, 30 April, 1924 in Correspondence Relating to Slavery, pp.7–37.
81. Evelyn, Colonial Secretary to District Commissioners, 26 September 1919, in 'Domestic Slavery' n.d.
82. Secretary of State, Colonies to Governor of Sierra Leone, 24 November 1921, in Correspondence Relating to Slavery, p.12.

SLAVE EMANCIPATION IN SIERRA LEONE

83. Grace, *Domestic Slavery in West Africa*, pp.168–9, 238–9; SLNA MP 1300/1923, W.B. Stanley to the Colonial Secretary, 23 May 1923.
84. See Enclosure 4 in No.3. Numbers of Slaves redeemed in the Protectorate since the Formation of the Protectorate into Provinces (i.e. from 1 January 1920 to September 1922) in Extract from Despatch from the Governor to the Secretary of State for Colonies, 20 June 1924 in Correspondence relating to Slavery, p.38.
85. See Enclosure 2 in No. 6. Report on an Ordinance to Amend the Protectorate Ordinance, 1924 in Despatch from the Governor of Sierra Leone to the Secretary of State for Colonies, 12 April 1926 in Correspondence relating to Slavery, p.53.
86. Ibid.
87. Ibid.
88. *SLWN*, 17 September 1927; *SLWN*, October 1, 1927 & *SLWN*, 19 November 1927.
89. *Daily Mail* (London), 10 October 1927.
90. *SLWN*, 19 November 1927.
91. *SLWN*, 8 October 1927.
92. Ibid.
93. Ibid.
94. *SLWN*, 31 December 1927.
95. See *Annual Report of the Sierra Leone Colony*, 1926.
96. Grace, *Domestic Slavery in West Africa*, p.241.
97. Grace, *Domestic Slavery in West Africa*, p.224; *SLWN*, 17 Sept. 1927.
98. See enclosure 2 in No.9, Supreme Court Judgement in Rex v. Salla Silla and Rex v. M'fa Nonko and others, 1 July 1927, in Correspondence Relating to Slavery, p.67.
99. Ibid.
100. PRO CO267/633/5969, Petition, Chiefs to Governor. 6 April 1931. Enclosure 2 in Confidential Despatch. Acting Governor C.E. Cookson to Passfield April 17, 1931; David Moseray, 'Idara Konthorfili (1890–1931) and the 193. Insurrection in North-western Sierra Leone' (BA Thesis, Fourah Bay College, University of Sierra Leone, 1978).
101. *Report of Commission of Inquiry into the Disturbances in the Provinces (November, 1955 to March, 1956)* (Freetown: Sierra Leone Government, 1956).
102. Martin Klein, 'Slavery and Emancipation in French West Africa', in Martin Klein (ed.), *Breaking the Chains: Slavery, Bondage and Emancipation in Modern Africa and Asia*, (Madison, 1993), p.190.

The End of Slavery among the Yoruba

TOYIN FALOLA

There are many difficulties in the way of the total abolition of slavery in West Africa, but much can be done to insist upon [slaves] being treated with humanity and it has been found that the owners who treat their slaves with kindness and consideration are able to retain them without harsh and repressive measures.

Governor Carter of Lagos to Chamberlain, 1896[1]

I think before slaves should be free, there should be an interregnum – the slaves in their own interests as well as of their masters might serve a time, say five years.

Rev. James Johnson, 1898[2]

I had to hire people from Igboona or the north to work on my cocoa farm. In the past I could have had slaves.

Adeoye Agbaje, referring to the 1940s[3]

Slavery and the Foundations of Decline

This essay is concerned with the end of domestic slavery among the Yoruba.[4] It starts with changes in the nineteenth century which led just to its increase and then to its decline and then considers how colonial rule unleashed the conditions that terminated it in the first half of the twentieth century. The nineteenth century witnessed an extension in the use of slaves among the Yoruba of southwestern Nigeria. Yoruba political systems of the period witnessed both the continuation of powerful monarchies and the rise of military autocracy in a few places.[5] War lords such as *Are* Kurunmi of Ijaye, or wealthy merchants such as Efunsetan Aniwura of Ibadan, counted their holdings in hundreds. The large-scale use of slaves, especially among successful warriors and in such new states as Ibadan and Abeokuta, can be attributed to the abolition of the trans-Atlantic slave trade which made more slaves available for local use just at the time when the extensive development of the trade in palm produce created a demand for labour and protracted warfare required the building of large private armies and provided opportunities to capture slaves as booty. Slaves were also obtained

THE END OF SLAVERY AMONG THE YORUBA

through commercial transactions, by inheritance, as tribute to political overlords, and as gifts. As the majority of slaves were obtained by capture, the warriors and kings who organized wars owned far more slaves than ordinary people.

Slaves could be women and men, children and adults. They were used as farmers, as producers of a wide variety of industrial goods, as traders, domestics, and soldiers.[6] They enabled their owners to accrue economic profits – the cultivation of huge farms at Ibadan and Ilorin, for instance, was made possible by the use of slaves in large numbers.[7] They were also used in creative ways to expand the size of households and of private armies, and to maintain horses and weapons of war. They constituted a source of capital investment, far more enduring than other sources – pawns, goats, sheep and poultry.[8] From the point of view of the political class, they were far more reliable than the freeborn for building a dedicated and loyal following and developing resources for political and military power. At Ibadan, for instance, war chiefs used slaves to man their private armies, collect tolls, administer colonies, manage their farms and trade, negotiate diplomatic agreements and perform police duties.[9] So dependent did the war chiefs become on slaves that *Baale* Orowusi, the head of this city-state from 1870 to 1871, cautioned his colleagues against such reliance, but no one heeded him.[10]

By and large, slaves were integrated into the households and kinship groups of their masters. While they were denied some of the privileges enjoyed by the freeborn, opportunities were provided for redemption, marriage and mobility. As contemporary observers noted, there were slaves who owned slaves, had extensive farms and livestock, and also flaunted their status by possessing horses.[11] Slaves were neither passive nor docile – they reacted to their condition in creative ways, resisting when necessary, or seeking accommodation and privileges when this was profitable and feasible.[12] Writing at the turn of the century, six leading Yoruba writers declared that 'the slave was not regarded as a mere thing' but:

> Every opportunity was given him to obtain his freedom. If engaged in farming, a piece of land would be alloted to him to cultivate for his own benefit on certain stated days of the week. If engaged in trading, he was allowed to make profits for his own benefit, the goods being given to him to sell at a certain fixed price, and whatever he realized above the price was his own. With the money he obtained for the products of his farm and with his profits on sales he could purchase his freedom. If he distinguished himself in war, his master would reward him with his freedom. No master had the power to kill his slave.[13]

234 SLAVERY AND COLONIAL RULE IN AFRICA

In general, the condition of slaves was no worse than that of many ordinary free citizens, a comparison that deserves further investigation. Ann O'Hear has compared them at Ilorin:

> ... the practical differences between slaves and poor free farmers may well have also been relatively small. Both groups engaged in manual labour, although at least 'the freeborn worked for themselves'. But their freedom was curtailed. Free farmers were liable, for example, to be recruited into the Ilorin armies, and may well often have had no more choice in this than the slaves. And, as with the slaves, the fruits of their labour frequently ended up in other people's hands. They paid tribute, and might also be constrained to provide regular supplies of produce to the land agent or head tenant in their area. They could also be obliged to send their produce into Ilorin, instead of to other markets where they might obtain a better price.[14]

If the nineteenth century represented the peak of domestic slavery among the Yoruba, it was also the period when the foundations of its decline were laid. There were three principal anti-slavery forces, two 'external' to the Yoruba, and one 'internal', which gradually undermined slavery.The first force was the emergence of a tiny elite opposed to slavery. This was comprised mainly of Christian missionaries and many of their new converts. Opinions among this elite were sharply divided – not everybody agreed that slavery was bad or deserved to be abolished. Those opposed to it drew their inspiration from Christian principles and the abolition of the trans-Atlantic slave trade. Anti-slavery was part of the agenda and propaganda of missionary enterprise, broadly defined as the introduction of 'European civilization.'[15] Pioneer missionaries tried to recruit their first converts among slaves, while some like the Hinderers at Ibadan actually paid to redeem some slaves.[16] The impact of this anti-slavery Christian elite was minimal, but they did at least generate a discussion on the abolition of domestic slavery.[17]

The second force was the rapid expansion of British authority after 1885 which not only undermined the sovereignty of the various Yoruba states, but also that of many indigenous institutions. Earlier, in the mid-nineteenth century the British had established a base and a consulate in Lagos, but this had little or no impact on slavery in Yorubaland. The serious British impact came after Sir Gilbert Thomas Carter assumed the governorship of Lagos in 1891. The expansion of British control which followed was presented to the Lagos elite as a 'civilizing mission' – hostilities among the Yoruba would cease, slavery would be abolished, and many other so-called primitive vices would not be tolerated. This propaganda reached a crescendo when Carter attacked the Ijebu in May 1892 'in the interest of civilization'.[18] Long after

THE END OF SLAVERY AMONG THE YORUBA

the event, he continued to justify this attack as a war to end slavery and promote civilization. While his intentions were questionable, the expedition no doubt created panic among Yoruba authorities who anticipated a similar attack and feared an assault on other aspects of their culture. Anti-slavery missionaries also capitalized on it, linking British control with 'civilization'. Early in 1893, Carter travelled to many parts of Yorubaland, accompanied by soldiers, in an attempt to demonstrate the might of the British. This was interpreted by some chiefs as an attempt to liberate slaves, and they quickly sold off many of their slaves at reduced prices.

When the first British officers were posted to the Yoruba hinterland, many slaves exploited the situation. Thus, Captain Campbell, the first Resident at Ijebu-Ode, became a host to liberated slaves. When Captain R. L. Bower was posted to Ibadan as its first Resident and Travelling Commissioner in 1893, he ignored the promise made to the chiefs that slavery would not be tampered with, and asserted his power in the early months by offering refuge to hundreds of slaves escaping from their masters and in order to return to their original towns. The final force was the ending of the Yoruba wars after 1886. The peace treaty that ended the Sixteen Years' War between the Ibadan Empire and its arch rivals or former colonies (the Ekiti, Ijesa, Ijebu and Egba) was the last major one among the Yoruba.[19] The expansion of British power ensured that there would be no more wars and this ended the major source of slaves.

It also enabled recent captives and slaves to obtain their redemption through flight.[20] When the belligerents in the Sixteen Years' War agreed to disband in September 1886, the recently captured slaves of Ibadan warriors escaped, in a way that suggested a high degree of mobilizational skill and prior planning. Johnson, who is extremely reliable on this period, reported that:

> The Ibadan slaves who did not wish to return home with their masters took this opportunity to escape to their country. In order to effect this with safety, without drawing attention, they set fire to some houses, and during the confusion and bustle attending the conflagration hundreds of them made good their escape to the Ekiti camp which overlooked the Ibadan camp. The houses of the Maye of Ibadan, and the Timi of Ede and those of several men of lesser note, were consumed in this conflagration ... One chief alone...lost about 400 slaves. The Ibadan chiefs, fearing they would lose all their slaves in this manner, thought they ought rather to go at once and wait no longer.[21]

Similarly, when Carter invaded the Ijebu, many slaves seized the opportunity to escape and while Ijebu authorities were still grappling with

236   SLAVERY AND COLONIAL RULE IN AFRICA

this humiliation, more slaves took to flight between 1892 and 1895. No one knew the number involved, but Samuel Johnson, a contemporary, indicated that since the escape of slaves was now inevitable slavery as an institution was 'doomed to disappear'.[22] Some former slave masters complained of losing slaves by the hundred.[23] During the same decade, slaves also took to flight in Abeokuta where many headed for Lagos.[24]

In spite of these forces, however, slavery continued. There were still slaves in many towns and villages. Merchants, both local and foreign, wanted the trade in palm produce, rubber, cotton, and other goods to continue and they were aware that these were produced by slaves as well as freeborn farmers. They worried that an end to slavery would hurt them. Chiefs and wealthy slave holders in various parts of Yoruba country were also unwilling to support abolition. During Carter's 1893 trip among the Yoruba, the political elite expressed concern that the British were encouraging rebellion among slaves. Carter was also coldly received at Oyo, and was advised by Egba chiefs not to interfere with slavery.[25] At Ibadan, the chiefs said they were afraid that their slaves would 'assert their freedom by running to the Resident',[26] and partly for this reason they refused to sign a treaty with Carter that would impose a Resident on the city. When a treaty was eventually signed, a promise was extracted that the British would not encourage slaves to seek freedom by running to the Resident.

In all cities with slave-holding chiefs, the worry was similar and in a few instances, as in Ibadan, the British had to give an assurance that they would not interfere with domestic slavery and would not allow their officers to encourage slave rebellion.[27] However, what the British did insist upon was that slavery should be 'conducted on humane principles.'[28] Thus when the nineteenth century closed, slavery was still practised, but forces that would undermine it were already at work. Slaves could still be obtained, notably from the northwest of Yorubaland and northern Nigeria. Ilorin was a major supplier and its established trade links with the north at Jega on the Zamfara River – the market next to Kano in size – continued to be a major avenue for the slave trade.[29] The politics of Ilorin in the last years of the nineteenth century centred on how to benefit from the expanding trade with Lagos and the Royal Niger Company. What subsequently destroyed Ilorin's ability to supply slaves was partly the development of trade in new commodities. The process was gradual. During the nineteenth century, Ilorin remained more politically autonomous than most Yoruba cities, and the British found it difficult to police the region.[30] Within Yoruba society, many warriors turned inward, raiding around their own neighbourhoods, but indigenous authorities and the new British officers quickly put an end to this.

Slavery continued, however, because not all slaves escaped, either

THE END OF SLAVERY AMONG THE YORUBA 237

because they chose not to, if they were already fully integrated into their host societies, or because the opportunities were just not available. Indeed, some of those who escaped in 1886 at the Ibadan war camp were reported to have voluntarily returned to their masters because they found 'their old homes quite different from what they had expected, and conditions of life more arduous'.[31] As indicated below, those who escaped either returned to their original communities or chose refuge in barracks or in a city like Lagos where anti-slavery laws were probably easier to enforce. Those who remained behind probably continued to render services as before. Both slave-owners and slaves faced some problems in adapting to the post-war era. From the examples of Ogedemgbe and Fabunmi, two of the high profile generals of the Ekitiparapo alliance, it is clear that it was not easy to reallocate slave soldiers to other enterprises. In the case of Ogedemgbe, soldier slaves, enjoying similar privileges to free born soldiers, were known as the *ipaye*. In the early 1890s, they had so much time on their hands and so few opportunities for lucrative employment that they took to 'molestations of their country people, robberies, brigandage, and violence of every kind'.[32] However, the signals that slavery would not last for ever were beginning to appear in the last years of the century. It is to these that I now turn.

Slavery in Transition: From Force to Toleration, 1892–96

In the last years of the nineteenth century the Yoruba indigenous elite lost its power to the British who began to re-shape society in a number of ways and to assert dominance. We have seen how Carter bombarded the Ijebu in 1892 and how the first Residents showed generosity to slaves. Captain Bower, the first Resident of Ibadan, made it clear that he was in control, and was far superior to the chiefs and kings. His strategy was that the chiefs must either obey him or face trouble. In this face-off not only did the chiefs lose, but slaves were able to benefit by using the period of chaos and political uncertainty to obtain their freedom. A few examples of Bower's activities surprised the indigenous elite. For example, in 1894 he arrested Ogedemgbe, the hero of the Ekitiparapo alliance during the Sixteen Years' War, thereby disbanding his large army and followers including the slaves.[33] A year later, a similar fate befell Fabunmi, another Ekiti war hero. Captain Tucker, the Travelling Commissioner, arrested him and disbanded his private army.[34]

In 1895, Bower demonstrated very clearly to the Yoruba elite and the public that he was in control by bombarding Oyo because of the dispute over *Alaafin*'s judicial authority to impose capital punishment.[35] The bombardment had implications for slavery. The story would have spread to

238 SLAVERY AND COLONIAL RULE IN AFRICA

slaves and other marginalized people of how the *Alaafin* – the powerful king – had been humiliated and weakened by Bower and his Hausa soldiers. We cannot be sure of everything the slaves did with this information, but one thing is clear: a few seized the opportunity to escape. An eye-witness observer said that he freed 25 slaves the morning after the bombardment.[36] E. A. Ayandele states that over one thousand slaves escaped following the bombardment.[37]

If the activities of Bower and fellow Residents caused panic among the Yoruba political authorities, there was a simultaneous demonstration of power by the emerging indigenous colonial workers, notably the Hausa soldiers. Nigerians associated with the colonial authority exercised power 'illegally' to satisfy their own narrow interests. Adeniyi Oroge thinks that the actions of Hausa soldiers 'speeded the disintegration of domestic slavery'.[38] Hausa forces constituted the nucleus and majority of the Nigerian police and army, created by the British from 1862 onward originally to aid in the task of conquest and 'pacification'.[39] During and after an official mission, like the bombardment of Oyo, Hausa soldiers took the law into their own hands. Yoruba authorities complained bitterly that they engaged in extortion, looted property, seduced women and allowed slaves to escape,[40] particularly if they were fellow Hausa. According to Oroge, setting Hausa slaves free became the 'favourite pastime' of the soldiers.[41] Chief I. B. Akinyele reported they allowed slaves to desert in Ibadan, while Chief N. A. Oyerinde made a similar remark with respect to Ogbomoso.[42] It is easy to understand this attitude, as most of the soldiers had been fugitive slaves residing in Lagos. They were motivated by a desire to ridicule the Yoruba elite, to assist the slaves, and to gratify themselves, especially as they were also accused of abducting women. The number of slaves whose freedom was made possible by the Hausa soldiers may never be known. What is clear is that in such major cities as Ilorin, Ibadan, Ijebu-Ode and Lagos Hausa soldiers aided slave flights, leading Oroge to conclude that 'of the various factors that combined to undermine the institution of domestic slavery from the 1890's, the soldiers were probably the most potent.'[43]

Up until 1896, the governor's office in Lagos supported the use of force to free slaves, although it did not condone the excesses of its staff. 'Freedom to the masses', declared Governor Carter in 1895, as well as the 'endeavour to introduce civilized methods' would come not 'with the aid of a silk glove', but 'the iron gauntlet'.[44] While the Governor was thinking like this, his officers in the field had the means to use force and those lower in the hierarchy of power – the Hausa soldiers – did not need to fear punishment for their atrocities.

Force, however, had its own limitations. It could not be applied to every nook and cranny, and certainly not in the far-away villages where most

THE END OF SLAVERY AMONG THE YORUBA

239

slave-farmers were located. There was no official abolition of domestic slavery – in legal terms, the force being applied was illegal. It was effective to the extent that slave masters were afraid of the new power. More importantly, established economies that sustained slavery were still in place, and the leading beneficiaries were still positively in favour of slavery. Merchants in Lagos and key producers in various parts of Yorubaland were united in their concern for profit, and the new colonial government wanted greater trade and accelerated crop production. Slavery thus had to be tolerated, in spite of opposition from certain elements in power. According to Oroge, the use of force to promote slave desertion was having devastating consequences on the economy and society. It was alienating the indigenous elite and generating concerns that the Yoruba would rally under Ilorin to throw off the British yoke. The possibility of successful resistance was remote, but governance would have been far more difficult without the support of chiefs and kings. Secondly, there was a decline in the trade in palm produce, the leading export and the support of many Lagos merchants. Lastly Lagos was becoming a home for recidivists and idlers, a number of whom were former slaves without any regular occupation.[45]

Early in 1896, Governor Carter who had justified the use of force to free slaves began to soften his stand. He divided slaves into two categories – those who served under brutal conditions and those living under humane conditions. He only objected to the former. His previous support of the use of force was designed for those areas and people – such as the Ijebu – who were callous in their treatment of slaves. To him, the Egba and many other slave owners were generous in granting privileges which made slaves only so in name.[46] He began to justify slavery, repeating the arguments of merchants and indigenous slave owners. In January 1896 he informed the Colonial Office that he was not opposed to slavery in its entirety. Henceforth, he promised not to promote the desertion of slaves working under favourable conditions because such desertion would disorganize or 'extinguish' the industries of the country; and the 'rights of property' must be recognized.[47] A year later, he began to regard slave desertion as a problem bound to create rifts between his administration and indigenous chiefs. He warned his lieutenants in the field not only to discourage slaves from deserting, but to recover and return the runaways to their masters.[48] His position, he told his boss in London, might appear to contradict 'British traditions and methods', but a policy of abolishing slavery would render the ruling class powerless and make Yoruba country economically unproductive.[49] He added yet another reason: 'slaves seldom escape to complete freedom but only to some other form of bondage'.[50] This is an important remark, although Carter failed to elaborate on it. The alternative for many slaves, as it turned out, was to go back to the farms to work either

240   SLAVERY AND COLONIAL RULE IN AFRICA

as peasants or tenants, both of which subsequently created social and political problems during the twentieth century.[51]

Slavery in Transition: Fugitives and Redemption, 1897–1916

The major issue that dominated discussion as the nineteenth century came to a close was what to do with the escalating numbers of fugitives. Whether the colonial government and indigenous slave owners liked it or not, slaves knew that the best and fastest way for them to become free was to escape. Evidence is clear that this was a time when many slaves deserted, a trend similar to that described for some other societies in West Africa.[52] The power of the chiefs had weakened, indigenous empires such as Ibadan that could police their colonies had crumbled, the first generation of colonial officers had supported the bids of slaves to escape, there were emerging cities such as Lagos that could harbour refugees, and new farmlands were being opened up for the lucrative crop of cocoa offering jobs for tenant farmers. Everywhere, the talk was about escape, and the lament of slave owners was that they had lost slaves and suffered ruin. At Ibadan slaves of Ijesa origins continued to desert whenever there were opportunities to do so. Again, we are sure there was an escalation, but not of the numbers involved.

From the point of view of slave owners and the colonial authorities, there was a need to arrest the decline of slavery unleashed by escapes. Every new fugitive promoted the slow but sure disintegration of slavery. Slave owners were interested in halting the rate of desertion and reasserting control of recovered slaves and colonial officers were now faced with the task of helping slave owners and thus sustaining the practice of slavery. Residents and officers were warned not to encourage desertion and to return fugitives to their masters if possible. To justify this policy the old argument of a 'tolerant and humane system' was commonly used. Oroge cited the influential words of Governor H. E. McCallum who succeeded Carter:

> The problem of domestic slavery in states outside the pale of British law is a most delicate one and requires the exercise of much care and circumspection ...

> Speaking generally my instructions are that questions relative to domestic slaves are to be dealt with by the Native Authorities only and that we should interfere as little as possible in such matters provided that no complaint of cruelty or inhumanity is made to us ...

> It is when a slave however well treated does run away that the difficulties of our position come in. We will not allow the exercise of native custom which would mean a raid for recovery, or reprisals on members of the tribe to whom the slave has bolted. As we have to

THE END OF SLAVERY AMONG THE YORUBA

> passively tolerate domestic slavery in places outside our Protectorate (slavery which is of a patriarchal character and very mild in form) so we must endeavour to keep the peace ...[53]

Another excuse was that colonial officials were powerless to effect changes in Yoruba customs. The large area of Yorubaland, 50 miles away from Lagos, was regarded up until mid-1901 as only a 'sphere of British influence', meaning that British laws and so-called sense of justice did not have to apply to it. The British could fight slavery in the colony of Lagos, but not in Ibadan or Ilesa which were outside their direct control. This is a dubious interpretation which allowed officers to justify whatever they wanted to do – either to intervene or withdraw.

There was a third reason, even if official correspondence underplayed its significance. Foreign and local merchants in Lagos and a number of leading Yoruba elite were still in favour of slavery for economic reasons. Palm produce, still the major export, suffered a fall in prices in the 1880s and a fall in production in the 1890s. Many traders suffering a fall in profits began to take action to correct the situation.[54] To ensure that production did not fall – slavery, as a leading source of labour, had to be supported to achieve this. Members of the Lagos Chamber of Commerce and other Yoruba elite blamed economic decline on slave desertion and the weakening of the power of traditional authorities to compel their people to work hard.[55]

To sum up – the reality of the situation demanded that slavery had to continue and its abolition had to be gradual. After 1897, officers were told to ask deserting slaves to return to their owners. In one instance during that year, the British used force to recover slaves who had fled to Idoani from Ibokun and returned them to their owner.[56] As if to satisfy slaves and masters at the same time, an ordinance was passed late in 1897 to let slaves redeem themselves for a sum of £3.15s or 15 bags of cowries. Fugitive slaves did not have to return to their masters if they could raise the redemption fee. It is important to quote aspects of the rules, revised and propagated in subsequent years:

> The mere fact of a woman bearing children by her master renders her a free woman. All captured, homeborn or inherited slaves [are] redeemable for £3: 15/-

> All other slaves (bought) redeemable for the original price paid minus two bags (ten shillings), for every year of servitude. Cruelty on the part of the master or mistress constitutes sufficient grounds for the liberation of the slave in question.

> Children of a slave by a master not to be considered slaves, but children of slaves born in servitude as yet redeemable for £3: 15/-[57]

242 SLAVERY AND COLONIAL RULE IN AFRICA

The redemption fee was probably suggested to the British by the Yoruba elite based on the price of an able bodied slave at the time. To Oroge, this was a fair deal for masters, and perhaps 'attractive, as this was the highest price for which slaves were generally sold in the years immediately before the British penetration from 1892 ...'.[58] Unless slaves were willing to pay the redemption fee, Governor McCallum ordered that they should be returned to their owners. Without much evidence to support his assertion, he conveniently concluded that slaves who were fleeing were doing so not because they were badly treated but because of the nostalgia for their places of birth. To the Governor any interference in domestic slavery was to be deprecated until such a time that:

> ... we can by our influence and example show gradually how free labour can be substituted for serf labour without loss to the masters and without dislocation of industries, trade and agricultural enterprise.[59]

The Colonial Office endorsed the recommendations of its Governor.

Fixing a redemption fee was not without consequences. As the idea spread, it was not unlikely that it offered possibilities for slaves to gain their freedom and for owners to obtain compensation in form of cash. The trouble is that it relied too much on trust. Unless the money was paid in full and in the presence of a credible witness, a master could deny having received it. Yet another problem was that the colonial government assumed that all slaves, irrespective of age and gender, physical fitness and occupation, were worth the same. If the masters reckoned that they were worth more, they would not cooperate. In spite of all these difficulties, a register was established in some towns to record the payment of fees and issue of certificates of redemption.[60] The majority of slaves did not avail themselves of this opportunity, either because they were ignorant of it or because they lacked the means to pay. Desertion continued, for if the British officers could be told to accommodate slavery, it was difficult to obtain the cooperation of Hausa soldiers who continued to use their barracks as refugee centres for slaves in search of freedom.

Slavery in Transition: New Labour Demands and Forms

The death knell of slavery, however, was that wage labour was gradually being introduced to many places, with the result that the emerging formal sector did not have to be serviced by slaves. Wage labour was in fact becoming more lucrative than other forms of labour. At the turn of the century, the average daily rate of a labourer in Lagos was 9d, far more than people in other occupations could earn. Former slaves and others who made

THE END OF SLAVERY AMONG THE YORUBA

it to Lagos could obtain employment and make money. As wage labour expanded, opportunities opened for peasants and ex-slaves. Making it to Lagos became the dream of slaves of the Ijebu, Egba and Ibadan and possibly elsewhere. Not only were they likely to find employment in Lagos, they could also escape payment of the redemption fee and avoid being forced to return, as such laws did not operate there. Oroge has pointed to changes in currency and transport as additional forces which contributed to the decline of slavery in the early twentieth century by reducing the number of slaves necessary for exchange and human porterage. New currencies came with the British administration. After 1896, there was a major increase in the circulation of silver coinage, and later paper money became popular.[61] This reduced the number of slaves employed to carry large sums of cowries and also reduced the need to use slaves as barter for commodities as traders now used cash for their transactions.[62]

The British also built a railway through Yoruba country, and this together with road construction had a profound impact on many aspects of Nigerian society, including slavery. Construction began in 1896, reaching Ibadan in 1901. Later this line was extended to run northwards, passing through several Yoruba towns. At the same time, new roads had to be opened to link different towns and villages and connect with the railway lines. The roads and railway projects of the colonial government were top priority, in order to facilitate the movement of goods and people and allow the government to mobilize the army and police quickly.[63] The consequences of the railway were enormous. To start with, railway construction demanded many labourers. There was a need to tap into the existing pool of slave labour, either by recruiting fugitives as wage workers or demanding forced labour from chiefs who invariably included slaves among those sent to the government. Slaves and many freeborn looking for jobs after the war found great opportunities in railway employment. As the Governor noted in 1897, in the very early years of railway construction, the expanding job opportunities allowed former slaves or slaves running away from their masters to have immediate access to wage employment.[64] Slaves who negotiated monetary terms of redemption with their masters also had jobs which could provide them with the money to buy their freedom.[65] Early in the twentieth century, additional opportunity was also added when there was a major recruitment of 1,300 Yoruba to work in railway construction in Ghana.[66] Oyemakinde has also pointed out that the majority of the staff for the Nigerian railway was Yoruba for many years, until the Hausa and Gwari were recruited.[67] By 1899, over 10,000 had been recruited[68] – a very substantial number – which included many ex-slaves. Yet another impact was that construction increased the monetization of society. Thousands of people received wages for the first time, among them ex-slaves who

244   SLAVERY AND COLONIAL RULE IN AFRICA

probably used part of the money to buy goods previously denied them in addition to their freedom.

The Agency of Law: Anti-Slavery Ordinances, 1900–16

As monetization and railways were slowly eroding slavery, so too was the continued resistance of slaves. Whether officials were influenced by this trend is hard to tell, but a few began to call for abolition in the early decades of the twentieth century. Oroge referred to a growing 'public indictment' in Britain of officials who were tolerant of slavery,[69] thus instigating a more combative legal approach. In 1901 Governor William MacGregor received instructions to notify the people of Lagos Colony and the Protectorate that slavery had been abolished. This was published in July 1900, but it never extended beyond Lagos and its immediate environment. A year later, an ordinance made it illegal to use force or constraint to keep anyone in slavery. In practical terms, the ordinance encouraged officers not to cooperate with slave owners in recovering their fugitive slaves and not to discipline Hausa soldiers who promoted the liberation of slaves. In addition, MacGregor sought to raise money for slaves who did not want to desert their masters, to pay for their freedom. By 1910, there was evidence that the anti-slavery laws were becoming widely known, at least among the Yoruba educated elite.[70]

All the Protectorates in Nigeria were amalgamated in 1914 and the legislative attack on slavery took on a national dimension, led by Sir Frederick (later Lord) Lugard. He had been Governor of Northern Nigeria where he had pursued a policy of gradual abolition, partly to protect the rights of owners but also to ensure the survival of the economy.[71] His key ordinance in the fight against slavery as it affected the Yoruba was enacted in 1916. It emancipated all persons born into slavery or brought to the area as slaves with effect from 31 August 1916.[72] However, Lugard still insisted that this emancipation did not mean that a master could dismiss his slaves or that the law would interfere with their relationship, if it was harmonious. A slave could leave his owner, however, and could not be forced to return. In practical effect, what the ordinance did was to abolish the legal status of slavery rather than the institution itself.

Implementation of many of these legal measures fell on the administrators at the grassroots. Where chiefs were requested to use the agency of the Native Courts to implement them, laws were apparently interpreted to suit slave owners. Thus slaves had to pay redemption fees. British officers were not agreed as to how to proceed – a few were tough, others were liberal. Policing was easier in the cities where slaves could go to the British officers. Rural areas were a different story altogether. Official

THE END OF SLAVERY AMONG THE YORUBA

sources do not adequately reflect the circumstances of slaves in those areas. Legal abolition did not go with official compensation by way of money or jobs. The expanding economy and the new roads and railway projects served to absorb many ex-slaves. Many had to return to the villages to work as tenants, especially in the emerging lucrative cocoa farms. Those who returned to their original homelands and had access to family land were able to work as independent farm-holders. While the ordinances were important for stressing the illegal nature of slavery, it is important not to exaggerate their significance in bringing about the end of slavery.

Gradually large-scale slave holding became uncommon. Those who had slaves tried to keep them, but were aware that ill-treatment could encourage desertion. By the early 1920s, evidence was strong that slavery was on the decline. However, some exchange of children took place, imported from central Nigeria and Cameroon.[73] As the government itself continued to demand forced labour for public construction, indigenous chiefs resorted to demanding workers from different lineages who had to surrender their slaves and even free citizens to meet their quota. Although now illegal, the redemption fee was still demanded by masters, and many slaves assumed that they needed to buy their freedom for £3.15s. in order to change their status from slavery to freedom. Here expanding demands for wage labour, especially for railway construction, made the money available. Indeed, the colonial government encouraged slaves to work in the railway in order to use part of their monthly wages for redemption. Many relied on the Native Courts to make the payment, so that an official receipt would be issued and the new freedom sanctioned.

By the 1930s, we have evidence that slavery was nearing its end among the Yoruba. Not only had requests for redemption declined since the mid 1920s, but new slaves could not be recruited. There were no slave markets. Pawnship was on the rise, a strong indication that it had become the alternative to slavery in meeting growing labour demands. Even transactions in children in the 1920s gave way to the use of children within the framework of pawnship,[74] rather than slavery. The growth of cash crops for export, notably cocoa, had become firmly established and lucrative. Ex-slaves had jobs to do as peasants and large-scale farm owners turned to tenant labour.[75] There was a massive movement of former slaves and others from different Yoruba cities to the countryside where they participated in the booming agricultural activities.[76]

Yoruba economy and society were not devastated by the end of slavery. Some adjustments had been made in the late nineteenth century and early twentieth centuries especially by the chiefs and merchants who had to reconcile themselves to the loss of their slaves and, therefore, of their sources of labour and social prestige. It is important to bear in mind that

246

only a minority of Yoruba had ever owned slaves in any significant number; that except in the expanding military systems of the nineteenth century like Ibadan and Ijaye, large-scale slave holding was not possible and that production always depended mainly on freeborn smallholders. As slaves were liberated after the 1880s, many became farmers, thus ensuring the survival of the dominant economic sector. Warriors and merchants of the nineteenth century were quick to shift to cash crop production, notably cocoa. Even at Ibadan where militarism was long-established, it was not too difficult for warriors to return to their farms.[77] The majority of the population did the same. An emerging Christian and educated intelligentsia also realized the benefits of participation in the cocoa economy. The old and established pawnship system quickly replaced slavery, and wages were extended to farm labour. The construction of roads and railways diverted labour to a new sector. Recruitment into the army and police was also significant. At Ibadan in 1895, where the government recruited two battalions of men for its army in northern Nigeria, it removed from the city a number of restless people, including slaves. Rapid monetization of the economy enabled wealth to be accumulated in the new currencies rather than in slaves. Such things as corrugated iron sheets, bicycles, wrist watches, a variety of imported cloths replaced slaves as status symbol and money was needed to purchase them. The Yoruba also made substantial money from cocoa, enabling many of them to invest in modern education, thereby shifting some of the conditions of social mobility and stratification away from the traditional ones connected with warfare, power and slave holding.

Conclusion

The abolition of slavery among the Yoruba was not sudden, and its final end cannot be dated – no single colonial law or policy brought about the demise of slavery. Also, slavery did not end at the same time in all parts of the country. Where the forces of change occurred rapidly and colonial laws were easier to implement, slavery probably witnessed a faster rate of disintegration than in other areas. In the final analysis, slavery declined and ended over a period of four decades, beginning in the 1890s, owing to a combination of political, social and economic changes. New forms of dependency, notably pawnship, replaced it, while new methods of labour recruitment, notably wage labour, became important, especially in the formal sector. By 1960 when colonial rule came to an end, slavery was no longer found among the Yoruba. The economy had entered its modern phase. The formal sector relied primarily on wage labour. The informal sector relied partly on wage and family labour, pawnship and domestics.[78]

THE END OF SLAVERY AMONG THE YORUBA   247

Thus, within half a century, the established practice of slavery ended and new forms of labour relations were established.

NOTES

1. Public Record Office (PRO) CO 147/104, Carter to Chamberlain, 9 January 1896.
2. CO 147/133, Evidence of Rev. James Johnson, enclosed in Denton to Chamberlain (Confidential), 4 June 1898.
3. Oral Interview: Adeoye Agbaje of Ibadan, 87 years old in 1990 when I interviewed him. Igboona refers to the Igbomina in northern Yorubaland and the north is a broad use to refer to people around or beyond the rivers Niger or Benue.
4. The Yoruba occupy the area now known as western Nigeria, and can also be found in the Republic of Benin. During the nineteenth century, they were divided into many different sub-groups (e.g., Oyo, Egba, Ijesa, Ekiti, etc.). These groups shared many things in common, although they also had political reasons to engage in wars. In 1851, the British occupied Lagos, turning it into a colony in 1861. In the 1880s, Yoruba country was annexed to the Colony of Lagos as a British protectorate. In 1906, the Colony and Protectorate of Lagos was incorporated into the Protectorate of Southern Nigeria. In 1914, both the Northern Protectorate and Southern Protectorate were merged to become Nigeria. Until the Yoruba country became part of a protectorate, British laws were limited only to Lagos Colony.
5. Toyin Falola and Dare Oguntomisin, *The Military in Nineteenth Century Yoruba Politics* (Ile-Ife, 1984).
6. For contemporary accounts describing the role of slaves in society, see T. J. Bowen, *Adventures and Missionary Labours in Several Countries in the Interior of Africa* (London, 1968); W H Clarke, *Travels and Explorations in Yorubaland, 1854–1858*, J.A. Atanda (ed.) (Ibadan, 1972); R.H. Stone, *In Africa's Forest and Jungle or Six Years Among the Yoruba* (London, 1900); and A. Hinderer, *Seventeen Years in the Yoruba Country: Memorials of Anna Hinderer, wife of the Rev. David Hinderer, C.M.S. Missionary in Western Africa* (London, 1872) .
7. Rev. Samuel Johnson, *The History of the Yorubas*. Lagos: CMS, 1921, p.325; CMS, CA 2/049/104, Hinderer Account of Ibadan 1851. Hinderer also reported that Balogun Ali of Ilorin had about 26,000 slaves, a number that cannot be confirmed.
8. N.A. Fadipe, *The Sociology of the Yoruba*, O. Okediji and F. Okediji (eds.) (Ibadan, 1970). p.166.
9. B. Awe, 'The Rise of Ibadan as a Yoruba Power in the Nineteenth Century', DPhil thesis, Oxford, 1964; S.A. Akintoye, 'The Economic Foundations of Ibadan's Power in the Nineteenth Century' in I.A. Akinjogbin and S.O. Osoba (eds.), *Topics on Nigerian Economic and Social History* (Ile-Ife), 1980, pp.55–65; and Toyin Falola, *The Political Economy of a Pre-colonial African State: Ibadan, 1830–1900* (Ile-Ife, 1984).
10. Johnson, *The History of the Yorubas*, pp.386–7.
11. See for instance, J. Milum, 'Notes of a journey from Lagos up the Niger to Bida', *Proceedings of the Royal Geographical Society*, New Series, 3 (1881), p.36.
12. Toyin Falola, 'Power Relations and Interactions among Ibadan Slaves', *African Economic History*, 16 (1986), pp.95–114.
13. 'The Laws and Customs of the Yoruba Country', see original in C.O. 520/92 and printed version in A.G. Hopkins, 'A Report on the Yoruba, 1910', *Journal of the Historical Society of Nigeria*, V (1969), pp.67–100. The citation here is from the printed version, p.90.
14. Ann O'Hear, *Power Relations in Nigeria. Ilorin Slaves and their Successors* (Rochester, New York, 1997), p.45.
15. J.F.A. Ajayi, *Christian Missions in Nigeria, 1841–1891: The Making of a New Elite* (London, 1965), p.10.
16. Kemi Morgan, *Akinyeles' Outline History of Ibadan* (Ibadan, n.d.) Vol.11, pp.142–8.
17. Toyin Falola, 'Missionaries and Domestic Slavery in Yorubaland in the nineteenth century', *Journal of Religious History*, 14 (1986), pp.181–92.

18. PRO CO 149/3, Minutes of Legislative Council, 27 November 1891.
19. S.A. Akintoye, *Revolution and Power Politics in Yorubaland, 1840–1893* (London, 1973).
20. Johnson, *The History of the Yorubas,* p.517.
21. Ibid., pp.550–1.
22. Ibid., p.623.
23. For example, Chief Jasimi, the Balogun of Ikorodu, said that he lost four hundred slaves. CO 147/134, Denton to Chamberlain, 3 August 1898.
24. See for instance, CO 147/121, McCallum to Chamberlain, 20 December 1897.
25. Cd. 7227, Carter to Ripon, 11 October 1893.
26. Johnson, *The History of the Yorubas,* p.638.
27. Ibid., pp.639–40.
28. Ibid., p.639.
29. O'Hear, *Power Relations,* p.27.
30. Johnson,*The History of the Yorubas,* p.649.
31. Ibid., p.551.
32. Ibid., p.645.
33. Ibid.
34. Ibid., p.646.
35. E.A. Ayandele, 'The Mode of British Expansion in Yorubaland in the Second Half of the Nineteenth Century', *Tarikh,* 3 (1969), pp.23–37.
36. S.G. Pinnock, *The Romance of Missions in Nigeria.* Richmond, Virginia, 1918, p.35.
37. E.A. Ayandele, *The Missionary Impact on Modern Nigeria, 1842–1914: A Political Analysis* (London: Longman, 1966), p.167.
38. E.A. Oroge, 'The Institution of Slavery in Yorubaland with particular reference to the Nineteenth Century', PhD thesis, University of Birmingham, 1971, p.375.
39. S.C. Ukpabi, *The Origins of the Nigerian Army (A History of the West African Frontier Force 1897–1914)* (Zaria, 1987). Although called Hausa forces, not all the soldiers or police were Hausa in origin.
40. Oroge, 'The Institution of Slavery', p.375; Johnson, *The History of the Yombas,* p.622.
41. Oroge, 'The Institution of Slavery', p.375.
42. Akinyele, *Iwe Itan Ibadan* p.127; N.D. Oyerinde, *Iwe Itan Ogbomoso* (Jos, 1934), p.126.
43. Oroge, 'The Institution of Slavery', p.377.
44. C.O. 147/100, Carter to Secretary of State for the Colonies, 6 December 1895.
45. Oroge, 'The Institution of Slavery', p.380.
46. C.O. 147/104, Carter to Chamberlain, 6 February 1896.
47. C.O. 147/104, Carter to Chamberlain, 9 January 1896.
48. C.O. 147/104, Carter to Chamberlain, 20 April 1897.
49. Ibid.
50. Ibid.
51. O'Hear, *Power Relations,* chapters 5–8.
52. Martin A. Klein, 'Slave Resistance and Slave Emancipation in Coastal Guinea', in Suzanne Miers and Richard Roberts (eds.), *End of Slavery in Africa* (Madison, Wisconsin, 1988); R. Roberts, 'The End of Slavery in the French Sudan, 1905–1914', ibid.; and Martin A. Klein, 'Slavery and Emancipation in French West Africa', *Breaking the Chains: Slavery, Bondage, and Emancipation in Modern Africa and Asia* (Madison, Wisconsin, 1991).
53. Cited in Oroge, 'The Institution of Slavery', p.383 (CO 147/121, McCallum to Chamberlain, 8 December 1897).
54. See for instance, A.G. Hopkins, 'The Lagos Chamber of Commerce, 1888–1903', *Journal of the Historical Society of Nigeria,* 3 (1965).
55. See for instance CO 147/133, Evidence of John Bradley, enclosed in Denton to Chamberlain (Conf.), 4 June 1898.
56. C.O. 147/121, Scott to Fuller, 3 November 1897.
57. NAI, *Lagos Annual Reports,* 1899, pp.80–81.
58. Oroge, 'The Institution of Slavery', p.383.
59. Cited in Oroge, 'The Institution of Slavery', (p.387) CO 147/121, McCallum to Chamberlain, 20 December 1897.

THE END OF SLAVERY AMONG THE YORUBA

60. *Lagos Annual Reports*, 1899, p.81.
61. On the far-reaching implications of the new currencies, see Toyin Falola and A.G. Adebayo, *Owoseni: The Culture and Politics of Money among the Yoruba,* forthcoming.
62. Oroge, 'The Institution of Slavery', p.395.
63. See for instance, E.K. Hawkin, *Road Transportation in Nigeria* (London, 1958); and Gilbert Walker, *Traffic and Transport in Nigeria. The example of an underdeveloped tropical territory* (London, 1959).
64. National Archives, Ibadan (N.A.I.), C.S.O. 1/1, Vol. 20, Governor of Lagos to Secretary of State, December 1897.
65. N.A.I., Calprof 10/9 African (West) No. 647 – Correspondence relating to Railway Construction in Lagos and Nigeria between 11th August, 1897 and 31st December, 1901, pp.100–101.
66. N.A.I., Cd 2325, Papers relating to the construction of railways in Sierra Leone, Lagos and the Gold Coast, December 1904, p.19.
67. J. O. Oyemakinde, 'A History of Indigenous Labour on the Nigerian Railway, 1895–1945', Ph.D. thesis, University of Ibadan, 1970, p.25.
68. T. N. Tamuno, 'Genesis of the Nigerian Railway – 1', *Nigerian Magazine*, No.183, December 1963, pp.279–92.
69. Oroge, 'The Institution of Slavery', p.396.
70. 'The Laws and Customs of the Yoruba Country' .
71. Paul E. Lovejoy and Jan S. Hogendorn, *Slow Death for Slavery: The Course of Abolition in Northern Nigeria, 1897–1936* (Cambridge, 1993).
72. F.D. Lugard, *Political Memoranda*, p.220.
73. G.O. Olusanya, 'The Freed Slaves' Homes – An Unknown Aspect of Northern Nigerian Social History', *Journal of the Historical Society of Nigeria*, 3 (1966).
74. This was the use of labour as collateral and interest on loan. See Toyin Falola and Paul Lovejoy (eds.), *Pawnship in Africa: Debt Bondage in Historical and Perspective* (Boulder, Colorado, 1994).
75. Sara Berry, *Cocoa, Custom and Socio-Economic Change in Rural Western Nigeria* (Oxford, 1975).
76. The phenomenon of urban-rural migrations is one of the east studied aspects of Nigerian social history.
77. Johnson, *The History*, p.643.
78. Domestics, mainly teenagers, were paid labour, usually living in the households of their employers. Labour regulations varied from one family to another.

Festina Lente:
Slavery Policy and Practice in the Anglo-Egyptian Sudan

TAJ HARGEY

Equivocal Slavery Enforcement, 1898–1918

Following the British-led conquest of the Sudan on 2 September 1898, the new rulers were anxious to restore political and socio-economic equilibrium after the Turco-Egyptian devastation and Mahdist depopulation of the nineteenth century.[1] Though Egypt shared responsibility for governing the subjugated territory through the mechanism of the Anglo-Egyptian Condominium, the British were the real masters of the Upper Nile valley until the Sudan's independence in 1956. Given Britain's colonial experiences elsewhere in Africa, it proceeded prudently in dealing with the defeated populace while simultaneously introducing modern humanitarian values. This precarious balancing act was especially evident in the Condominium's incipient slavery policies. Confronted with the bleak realities of the post-Mahdist era, the infant regime accepted the vital role servile labour played in agriculture and in the wider economic sphere. Reliance on slaves, both male and female, to perform household chores, farm work, skilled labour, military duties – in addition to widespread concubinage – was an ingrained feature of Sudanese society and was viewed as divinely-ordained.[2] Moreover, the British, aware of the country's mass impoverishment, were faced with an invidious choice: not to abolish slavery would imperil Britain's anti-slavery commitment; but too rapid a transformation from a slave-based social system to a foreign-imposed wage labour economy would not only alienate influential Sudanese public opinion but diminish agrarian production, create social disharmony and exacerbate burgeoning urban tensions.

Faced with these dilemmas, the British-dominated administration tolerated customary slavery[3] but tried to cut off the supply of new slaves. In theory, slaves were now permitted to leave their owners (who had no legal or financial recourse against them), but in practice they were forced to remain in servitude, unless they were grossly maltreated. In 1901 a specific anti-slavery decree, supplemented by the new Sudan Penal Code, was promulgated.[4] Although the words 'slave' and 'slavery' were purposely

SLAVERY POLICY IN THE ANGLO-EGYPTIAN SUDAN

omitted, all forms of kidnapping, prostitution and forced labour were outlawed. To give teeth to these orders, the Egyptian Slavery Repression Department's operations were extended to Sudan by 1904.[5] In fact the slave trade was attacked while the question of existing, self-perpetuating domestic slavery was ignored. Children born to slaves under British rule, who should have been free, remained *de facto* in bondage. This was in keeping with a pragmatic policy designed to bring about the evolutionary extinction, rather than the sudden suppression, of servitude.

Within six months of the reconquest, Lord Kitchener, the first Governor-General of the Sudan, issued basic rules for this incremental eradication of chattel slavery.[6] The enslaved were now classified as 'volunteer slaves' and referred to in government correspondence as 'Sudanese', 'servants' or unpaid workers, giving credence to the official non-recognition of slavery. In private communication they were called 'crypto-servants' or 'indentured labourers'.[7] Such terminological inexactitudes were partly in response to one of the first petitions addressed to the new British leaders. In October, 1898 top Umm Durman notables requested Kitchener to restrain black (servile) troops from forcibly entering residences and seizing slaves on the dubious pretext of reuniting families.[8] Condominium administrators could not indefinitely ignore the resentment of the slave-holding class, who believed that the government should either preserve their servile labour force or compensate them for their losses. Speaking to an assembly of Umm Durman dignitaries in January 1899, Lord Cromer (the British Consul General in Egypt who was responsible for administering the Sudan), declared he was anxious to adopt the principle of *Quieta non movere* (or 'Let Sleeping Dogs Lie')[9] as far as slavery was concerned. He pledged that the Sudan Government would accept Islamic law *(shari'ah)* with regard to domestic servitude. This placated local opinion but evoked consternation in Britain. In Parliament, members with links to anti-slavery groups periodically pressured the Foreign Secretary to ensure that slavery would be suppressed in the Sudan.[10] Leading this campaign was the London-based anti-slavery society.[11] From the beginning of the Anglo-Egyptian Condominium, the colonial rulers were on guard against these vocal humanitarians whom they regarded as evangelizing zealots and uninformed agitators. In order to neutralize them, the Cairo and Khartoum authorities colluded with local Sudanese slave-holders to justify the slow but steady annihilation of slavery.[12]

The principal architect of Condominium slavery policy and chief defender of the servile dispensation until his premature retirement in 1914 was the Austrian, Rudolf von Slatin. Ever since his recruitment by General Gordon in 1879, Slatin's services first with the Turco-Egyptian regime, and then with the Mahdist theocracy (as a prisoner) and later with the Anglo-

252   SLAVERY AND COLONIAL RULE IN AFRICA

Egyptian expeditionary force had given him an unparallelled sensitivity to the Sudan. R.F. Wingate, the second Governor-General and supreme policy-maker of the early Condominium, named Slatin as his Inspector-General in 1899. Until the outbreak of World War I, Slatin's pro-slavery prejudices and priorities prevailed. Indeed, as he was Wingate's 'eyes and ears',[13] the Governor reckoned that the Inspector-General's 'understanding and knowledge of the slavery question [was] unsurpassed'.[14] Slatin's overt racism and forthright tolerance of slavery was evident even during the re-conquest. In the wake of the advancing Anglo-Egyptians in 1897–98, numerous Northern slaves either absconded or were drafted into the British army. Slatin privately sided with the embittered slave masters and railed against slaves: 'These godforsaken swine do not deserve to be treated like free and independent men... the blacks should be made to remain under the protection of their former masters who were forced to treat them well on the whole'.[15]

Slatin scorned the anti-slavery lobby and his pro-establishment policies remained unchallenged during his tenure in the Sudan. These ranged from sanctioning of public slave transactions in Umm Durman to returning runaways to their masters and eagerness in pandering to the wishes of the latter. Slatin believed that freed and fugitive slaves formed indolent, parasitic and crime-ridden ghettoes in Sudanese towns and that they construed ...'the abolition of slavery into meaning the abolition of work...'.[16] The Sudan's plight during the first decade of the twentieth century, according to Slatin, was largely due to indiscriminate slave liberation. Mounting discontent, economic impoverishment and social instability all hinged upon the thorny slavery dilemma. Slatin, therefore, advocated the preservation of the status quo. While former military slaves were given title deeds to arable land, other ex-slaves were sent to government farms or workhouses or returned to their erstwhile masters.[17] Such was Slatin's authority that his proposals were automatically implemented. His overriding concern was the slave-holding constituency.[18]

Throughout his time as Inspector General, Slatin recognized the perils of a public outcry in Britain. He ordered junior officials not to call servants 'slaves' and threatened 'to cut off the right hand finger of any who did so'.[19] His reports often contained blatant distortions or half truths. Typical of this duplicity was his declaration in 1906 that 'to my certain knowledge, no slave, male or female is obliged by force to stay with his so-called master'.[20] Most top officials, including Cromer[21] and Wingate,[22] shared Slatin's biases. In 1901 the Sudan rejected the anti-slavery society's offer of financial aid for freed females,[23] believing that acceptance would set a precedent for future intervention.[24] A similar pattern was also evident in the crude censorship of official documents.[25] Deliberate deletion of embarrassing

SLAVERY POLICY IN THE ANGLO-EGYPTIAN SUDAN

253

information became a Condominium practice. Thus the annual reports portrayed a favourable picture of anti-slavery enforcement before World War I.[26]

The most pressing problem facing the regime was the rehabilitation of demobilized troops of servile origin. Along with other emancipated and escaped slaves, they constituted a threat to law and order. Several state-sponsored schemes, such as 'battalion gardens' and colonization camps for liberated and unemployed troops were established with varying degrees of success. Although their transition to a self-supporting lifestyle was fraught with various vicissitudes, including a frenetic burst in urban crime,[27] most eventually evolved into productive cultivators, paid labourers or industrious civil employees.[28] Their success not only incited existing slaves to claim their freedom, but also was an initial step in changing a once servile sector into an independently viable one.

The Sudan Government's first ordinance on slavery was published in January 1902. It recognized the institution but provided for the registration of slaves to expedite their emancipation.[29] The administration, however, violated its own anti-slavery charter by drafting manumitted and absconded slaves into the army. This fostered fresh slave acquisition as owners sought to replace those conscripted. The endemic shortages of labour during the early Condominium – coupled with Arab disdain for manual work and the comparative cheapness of servile workers – induced Northern landowners to augment their slave stocks despite prevailing anti-slavery laws. While the administration maintained that it would 'gradually transform the status of slavery and substitute for it a system of paid labour', it acknowledged that existing vagrancy and slavery edicts were not uniformly enforced and that it would be 'a considerable time' before the Sudan would 'be able to show a clean bill of health as regards the plague of slavery'.[30] Government policy, irresolute as it was, provoked immense anger. Slave-holders resented the non-return of their runaways. This became a burning question and the Condominium's first decade was punctuated by several pro-slavery revolts such as the Tawlawdi uprising in 1904 and the Blue Nile insurrection in 1906. The ringleaders became public heroes for their defence of the traditional servile order,[31] forcing Wingate to confess that there could be no abrupt abolition of the system.[32]

In its report of 1908, the Condominium claimed that there was less reliance upon servile labour, but that no swift suppression of slavery was feasible without 'a liberal scheme of financial compensation' to slave-holders.[33] It admitted that fragmentary slave registration had not curbed the procurement of new domestic slaves. But no tightening of regulations was contemplated because 'slavery does not exist, politically speaking'.[34] As long as the regime was not prepared to confront the slave-holding class, no

254 SLAVERY AND COLONIAL RULE IN AFRICA

real progress in suppressing slavery was possible. Nevertheless, despite this calculated pusillanimity, both Cromer and Wingate commended themselves for what they considered efficient anti-slavery enforcement.[35]

By World War I, the Sudan's indecisive anti-slavery *modus operandi* had almost lapsed by default. Bureaucrats remained prejudiced against the servile population and routinely violated anti-slavery decrees. They found the hostility of their compatriots in Britain incomprehensible and misdirected. The policy of 'leaving the slaves quietly in the possession of their masters until they either disappear through death or are set free by manumission',[36] was considered the most prudent course. A few progressive British officials complained that 'decisions are given which are not only contrary to the British policy as regards slavery, but which cannot be justified by Mohammedan Law'.[37] To make matters worse, during the war, directives were issued to return all slave runaways using the "freedom railway" which connected the coast and the capital and was the most efficient means of escape for slaves. This new policy was in direct contravention of previous proclamations and provincial personnel became active agents in persuading people to remain in bondage. Only irreconcilable slaves prepared to purchase their liberty through a system of *fidyah* (ransom) payments were henceforth permitted to start life as freed individuals.[38] This official pro-slavery bias certainly helped secure the political loyalty of the key Northern Sudanese slave-holding constituency, most particularly during the dangerous years of World War I.[39] It also paid dividends in partly neutralizing Egypt's campaign to restore its exclusive sovereignty in the Sudan.[40]

World War I produced serious personnel changes, most noticeably the mandatory retirement of enemy aliens, including Slatin in 1914. Two years later Wingate, who 'was not worried about slave cases at all', became British High Commissioner in Egypt. The sudden departure of these two major figures marked the end of a distinctive era in Condominium politics and paved the way for a re-evaluation of slavery strategy. But this reappraisal was delayed by reactionary British officials. While new statutes were enacted in 1916 (regulating the wages and conditions of domestic servants; prohibiting the export of children to Egypt; and restricting Arab and *fallata*[41] access to the South),[42] these were rarely implemented. Such ambivalence and inconsistency were also evident in the recently annexed Western Sudan. Following the overthrow of Ali Dinar of Darfur in 1916, the new British rulers were given a free hand in slavery matters and provincial officials declared that 'the conditions of order and discipline cannot be maintained unless a slave class continues to exist.'[43]

Toward the end of World War I, the need for uniform and concerted anti-slavery action became imperative.[44] A coherent countrywide policy was

SLAVERY POLICY IN THE ANGLO-EGYPTIAN SUDAN

required since 'every Inspector has his own ideas and acts in accordance with them alone; one will go to any lengths to recover runaway [slaves], another is rabidly anti-slavery.'[45] Renewed plans for universal slave registration camouflaged a continued pro-slavery proclivity within the Condominium's hierarchy. Bureaucrats asserted that 'nothing would give the Arab population, who are seeing their slaves gradually disappearing, more satisfaction than to know that such [slaves] were being properly controlled and worked by the government.'[46] Senior administrators still defended the retention of the servile system, claiming that '... domestic service [slavery] suits both master and servant.'[47]

Powerful dissent, however, came from the Condominium's Legal Secretary, Wasey Sterry. Aware of a new British liberalism, he feared that the Sudan's unenlightened policies would trigger parliamentary interference and political embarrassment. In a damning dispatch he denounced toleration of servitude and the flagrant violation of anti-slavery laws. Citing horrific instances of recalcitrant slaves being forcibly tied to camels and carried back to their masters in defiance of both Islamic and English law, he described 'such proceedings as a disgrace to the British name'.[48] To assuage Sterry's concerns and prevent a parliamentary inquiry, a revised slavery manifesto was issued in March 1919.[49] This law, like its predecessors, was largely a sop to complaints from the Anti-Slavery and Aborigines Protection Society.[50] While holding out the prospect of freedom, this confidential circular ensured that most slaves retained their subordinate status because 'Sudanese servants who have lived with their masters are really happier and better off if they still remain part of their masters' families.'[51]

The lack of publicity and foreign pressure suited the Sudan Government perfectly. Regardless of its oft-repeated anti-slavery rhetoric, twenty years of vacillating action had neither altered the servile base of Sudanese society nor reconciled the chasm between stated objectives and actual practice. Financial constraints, inadequate administrative resources, the vastness of the country, the Sudan's permeable frontiers and the tenacity of this ingrained institution, could have been overcome with deliberate political will. Instead, the Condominium's catchphrase *Festina Lente* (hasten slowly) became the hallmark of its contradictory and ineffectual anti-slavery policy to the end of World War I.

Effective Anti-Slavery Enforcement, 1919–1939

After World War I, the country's expanding economy was underpinned by cotton production in the Gezira irrigation scheme between the Blue and White Niles, which generated opportunities for both free and slave.[52] Even before its completion during the mid-1920s, it attracted many emancipated

256 SLAVERY AND COLONIAL RULE IN AFRICA

and escaped slaves from all over the country. Here, the transition to autonomy was virtually assured and they became a model for others still enslaved. Given these employment prospects for ex-slaves and prodded by a resurgent Anti-Slavery Society, the regime in Khartoum began to reformulate a legal framework for ending slavery. The Anti-Slavery Society's renewed interest in the Sudan was the result of irrefutable evidence furnished by employees and evangelists working there in early 1919. They alleged that slavery with all its attendant ramifications (including the mortgaging and hiring of slaves; the wanton cruelty inflicted on females; the forceful return of runaways and the illegal subordinate status of children born since 1898) was still endemic.[53] While acknowledging that financial constraints, manpower shortages, corrupt native staff and British bias had inhibited anti-slavery enforcement, the Society criticized the Condominium's 'apathetic approach to the question'[54] and felt that 'it is a standing disgrace that [slavery] should be countenanced by British officials.'[55] The Society's indictment of the Sudan Government was submitted to the British Foreign Office in November 1919 and within a year was discussed by the cabinet. The Foreign Office avoided a full-scale inquiry by issuing placatory statements citing the latest directives.[56] Despite this, leading administrators in the Condominium continued to oppose any concessions to domestic slaves, arguing that socio-economic structures still relied upon servile labour. But to appease outside critics, the Condominium introduced new regulations, making it possible, in theory, for disaffected and ill-treated slaves to leave their owners[57] by voluntarily *fidyah* payments, and to become paid labourers and household servants.[58]

During the early 1920s, the Condominium extended its jurisdiction to the Southern Sudan and banned the long-standing practice of Northern Arab merchants taking local women and children back to the north in the guise of spouses and servants.[59] In 1922, these Arab traders were banned altogether from the southern provinces and the eastern borderlands with Ethiopia.[60] The exclusion of Northerners from these Closed Districts was intended to counteract growing Muslim influence in the South and to reinforce British supremacy over the upper Nile basin. The Egyptian-financed Slavery Repression Department was also terminated in 1922. Although statistical data revealed a decline in slave transactions within the Sudan,[61] the decision to disband the unit was taken in order to end *de facto* Egyptian co-sovereignty in the Sudan.[62] It proved premature, since slave-smuggling soon revived throughout the central Sudan and beyond.

The presence of new liberal-minded British recruits ended the Condominium's complacent anti-slavery practices. A train of events forced the Sudan into belated action. The catalyst was a Captain (later Major) P.G.W. Diggle, a young agricultural inspector in al-Bawgah district of

SLAVERY POLICY IN THE ANGLO-EGYPTIAN SUDAN   257

Berber Province in the northern Sudan, who awarded freedom certificates indiscriminately.[63] This provoked local slave-holders to demand immediate curbs on any further emancipation.[64] Diggle charged that 'the freeing of slaves is discouraged in this country both by secret circulars and also by the prevailing opinion among the senior administrative officials of the country …'.[65] He was supported by T.P. Creed, the Assistant District Commissioner at Berber, who complained that 'the present position of slavery is a standing disgrace to any British Administration'.[66] The Provincial Governor defended official policy and chastised his subordinates for discrediting the government.[67] This failed to pacify Creed who insisted that existing anti-slavery legislation was a sham. [68] Encouraged by Creed, Diggle persisted in freeing slaves despite vociferous local opposition.[69] In July 1924, he submitted a report highly critical of muddled anti-slavery enforcement. Creed was banished to far-off Dar Fur[70] and warned that 'there is no slavery to abolish either speedily or gradually'.[71] A frustrated Diggle now embarked on a personal crusade to expose this great evil: 'We abolished suttee in India; slavery is worse than suttee and less popular. If we dare not govern except by tolerating an abomination like slavery, we ought to get out [of the Sudan].'[72]

This provoked a rapid response. Modifications to slavery policy were enacted without allusion to Diggle. The new rules reinforced anti-slavery legislation and reaffirmed the freedom of all persons born since 1898. But this only antagonized slave-holders in Berber Province and, in June 1924, a futile assault on the Abu Hammad district office to repossess escaped slaves was followed by petitions to halt slave emancipation or provide tax relief.[73] A jittery Governor-General reassured labour-starved farmers of riverain Northern Sudan that their servile work force would not be freed without legitimate cause.[74] This promise was incompatible with that given to Diggle which reaffirmed the inalienable right of freedom for everyone.[75] Diggle could not be silenced and the upshot was a public inquiry.[76] The regime rejected Diggle's claims as unrepresentative of the general situation in the country,[77] It feared that disgruntled former employees would assert that the Sudan Government was encouraging slavery so that the Sudan Plantations Syndicate, which operated the Gezira scheme, could get cheap labour by employing slaves who then had to pay their owners' ransom.[78] Consternation about foreign interference was compounded by the turmoil which followed the 1924 assassination in Cairo of Sir Lee Stack, the Governor-General, an abortive army mutiny and the expulsion of Egyptian troops from the Sudan. These events preluded stringent enforcement of the anti-slavery laws which 'would be most unpopular with the Arab population of the country who have shown such loyalty in recent troubles'.[79]

However, persistent pressure from Britain resulted in more robust

258   SLAVERY AND COLONIAL RULE IN AFRICA

statutes being introduced in 1925. These were designed to prevent the misuse of Islamic law in custody cases involving the offspring of slave concubines.[80] Custodial disputes often arose over who would benefit from the labour of male or the bride price of female children.[81] The three most prominent politico-religious personalities in the Sudan (Sayyid Ali al-Mirghani, Sayyid Abd al-Rahman al-Mahdi and Sharif Yusuf al-Hindi), seeking to mitigate intensified anti-slavery enforcement, presented a secret manifesto in March 1925 to the authorities. They lamented the random freeing of slaves which they said generated increased prostitution, alcoholism and criminality, and declining agricultural productivity.[82] Their arguments were reinforced by the Grand *qadi* who objected to further dilution of the Islamic *shari'ah*.[83] While the Legal Secretary favoured immediate universal liberation, the Civil Secretary urged only gradual abolition.[84] After considerable debate, an English-only version[85] of a new slavery law took effect in May 1925 entitling disaffected slaves to impartial assistance and automatic manumission.[86]

Contrary to official predictions that British interest in the Sudan's anti-slavery progress would wane following the enactment of these measures, the anti-slavery society campaigned to put Sudanese slavery in the international spotlight, both at home[87] and at the League of Nations.[88] This prompted the Foreign Office to blame Islamic law and indigenous traditions rather than Condominium ineptitude and indifference for the persistence of slavery in the Sudan.[89] When the League of Nations crafted a new treaty to suppress global slavery in 1926, the British Government advised the Condominium to accede to it regardless of anticipated Egyptian opposition. The Sudan's swift and independent ratification was an attempt to deny any assertion of Egyptian sovereignty and to prevent '... the Moslems of Egypt and the Sudan from finding common cause against Great Britain'.[90] This was in response to Egypt's admission to the League and its desire to resume control over the Sudan.[91] The worldwide clamour for self-determination and national independence sparked by World War I was welcomed by Egyptian nationalists, who now saw the restoration of Egyptian suzerainty over the Nile valley as a distinct possibility. The Egyptians used the grievances of the Sudanese slave-holding class to promote their reunification agenda which now received considerable coverage in the Egyptian press.[92] Whereas at Geneva Egyptian propagandists Geneva could say, 'Of course slavery was abolished 50 years ago in Egypt and but for the Condominium would have been abolished long since in the Sudan', in the Sudan, the Egyptian agitator could take 'precisely the opposite tack' and say, 'now that the English have seized the Sudan they will destroy the sacred law and the Muslim religion and they will begin by making the Kadis give illegal decisions regarding slaves'.[93] As a matter of tactics, the British withheld all

SLAVERY POLICY IN THE ANGLO-EGYPTIAN SUDAN

259

information on slavery in the Sudan from Egypt and sent reports directly to the League of Nations to prevent the Egyptian government from reporting on the Sudan as a means of establishing its claims to sovereignty over the country.[94] Egypt protested[95] and despite lack of information sent slavery updates to Geneva every year. Egypt was further piqued by the Sudan's unilateral accession in 1927 to the Slavery Convention of 1926.

By this time, the Sudan Government, following the outcry fuelled by Diggle's revelations, was intensifying its anti-slavery measures. It cooperated with the British Legation in Jeddah to streamline the release and repatriation of Sudanese slaves in the Arabian peninsula; it coordinated the supervision of British naval patrols against the slave trade across the Red Sea; and it established an investigative commission on slavery.[96] These steps failed, however, to impress the anti-slavery society and its parliamentary supporters in Britain who were inflamed by reports of a thriving clandestine slave trade between Ethiopia and the Sudan. Their suspicions of Condominium policy were aroused when the offer of private British humanitarian funds for emancipated slaves[97] was summarily rejected.[98] This compelled the Anti-Slavery Society to call for a parliamentary debate on slavery in the Sudan in December 1925.[99] Under pressure from the opposition parties and from the Archbishop of Canterbury, the Foreign Office released confidential reports on Sudanese slavery.[100] In 1926, the British Government issued a White Paper on slavery in the Sudan, which eroded the hitherto hidden nature of the Condominium's anti-slavery programme.[101] Henceforth, its policies and practices were subject to public scrutiny.[102]

Simultaneously, the Sudan Government ordered a fact-finding mission and appointed C.A. Willis Slavery Commissioner with a brief to accelerate the abolition of slavery[103] and to construct a processing centre for manumitted slaves repatriated from the Hijaz. In conjunction with the British Consul in Jeddah, Willis implemented specific measures to stop surreptitious sale of children and to improve the security, quarantine and transport arrangements for pilgrims during this period of great internal upheaval in Arabia.[104] In the Sudan itself, Willis declassified all slavery regulations and harmonized the adjudication of secular and religious courts in cases of concubinage and the custody of servile children. He also forbade the hiring out of domestic slaves and banned the custom of slaves buying their freedom by paying compensatory ransom (fidyah) to their owners.[105] Willis rebutted Diggle's assertions (which had been the primary stimulus for his inquiry) and offered both a legislative blueprint to hasten the end of the slavery and precise steps to advance the transition to an independent wage-labour economy.[106]

260   SLAVERY AND COLONIAL RULE IN AFRICA

The Sudan Government remained wary of external criticism. There were numerous press reports on African slavery. This evoked increased anti-slavery lobbying in Britain with a corresponding nervousness in the Sudan. When a series of articles dealing with enslavement in West Africa appeared in the London *Times* in 1927, distraught officials in Khartoum inquired 'whether there are possibilities of trouble for us'.[107] The Condominium's heightened sensitivity was shown in its periodic reminders to all provincial governors that 'the Sudan Government has undertaken to eradicate slavery as soon as may be and must be prepared to face the very obvious difficulties entailed at the adoption of such a course'.[108]

The most singular exception to the progressive decline in slave-trafficking during the 1920s occurred along the eastern borders of the country. The disbanding of the Slavery Repression Department resulted in reduced surveillance of the Sudan's porous frontier with Ethiopia. By the mid-twenties, a clandestine trade in arms and slaves was at its zenith.[109] Sitt Amna and her Ethiopian husband, Shaykh Hassan Khojali, were the principal contraband merchants who supplied the central Sudan with weapons and slaves. Owing to her family's political status as Watawit chieftains in Beni Shangul in western Ethiopia, Sitt Amna enjoyed virtual diplomatic immunity in the Sudan. Since there was little firm evidence against her, the local Funj provincial administration was unable to stop her illicit activities.[110] However, in 1928, the situation changed overnight with the fortuitous discovery of recently imported slaves and firearms in the White Nile Province. During the next two years a concerted inter-provincial anti-slavery campaign culminated with the arrest of Sitt Amna and her associates and the retrieval of over a thousand slaves.[111]

This traffic prompted a reappraisal of anti-slavery methods. To ensure the death of the underground network along its long borders, the Sudan Government devised new strategies and tactics. Top priority was given to inducing tribal shaykhs and notables to liaise more effectively with local intelligence departments in detecting and detaining the purveyors of contraband from Ethiopia.[112] Amicable relations were cultivated with tribes in or near the frontier zone and these areas were patrolled to prevent non-domiciled Arabs from entering the borderlands under the Closed Districts Ordinance. This legislation supposedly had the dual purpose of containing Arab influence in the region and removing slave and arms dealers from the sources of their merchandise.[113]

A direct corollary to the 1928 White Nile anti-slavery campaign was the introduction, after prolonged discussions, of a three-tier classification of the servile population in the Sudan. Henceforth official parlance differentiated between 'slave', 'serf' and 'ex-serf'. The first category comprised those elements 'forcibly removed from their homes and subjected to illegal

SLAVERY POLICY IN THE ANGLO-EGYPTIAN SUDAN   261

restraint and compulsory labour, or liable to illegal sale or purchase'. The term 'serf' (or *muwallad*) denoted 'persons of Negroid origin living as dependents of an Arab master in a state of social inferiority but frequently treated as members of the family. The phrase 'ex-serf' referred to an individual of serf origin who had acquired freedom.[114] These designations were intended to speed up the mechanics of emancipation and the transition to an independent life. While every slave was entitled to freedom, local staff, especially in the Western Sudan persisted in arbitrarily returning runaways to their owners to preserve social stability.[115] Thus, while the Sudan Government publicly professed to be uprooting slavery, political irresolution hampered the liberation of slaves in distant Dar Fur and Kurdufan until the 1930s.

The anti-slavery society doubted Khartoum's declarations that servitude was in terminal decline. It harassed the Foreign Office for official documents relating to Sudano-Ethiopian slavery.[116] This annoyed the Sudan Government, but the discovery of White Nile slave-trafficking further undermined its credibility. As a direct consequence of the Diggle Affair, the Willis Commission, the White Nile campaign and League of Nations attention, the Condominium was forced to redouble anti-slavery enforcement. It instructed provincial governors to monitor the situation carefully and submit progress reports.[117] Provincial officials were told in March 1931 to be completely impartial in prosecuting slavery offenders. Five years later, the definitive policy statement that 'slavery is illegal in the Sudan, and has been so since the reoccupation' was transmitted to all provinces.[118] This announcement ended all ambiguity and redoubled action to end slavery. To facilitate this, religious and tribal courts were ordered to treat all people on the basis of complete legal parity and as free individuals.

In the light of this, the Condominium condemned as unfounded European press reports about the revival of Red Sea slave-smuggling during the early thirties.[119] Anglo-French rivalry in the region also complicated matters when allegations and counter-allegations were made regarding slavery in the Sudan. In 1932, accusations by a French national led the Foreign Office to order a full scale investigation.[120] The Sudan Government complained indignantly to the Foreign Office when it was given little credit for dismantling a centuries-old institution. Its annual reports to the League highlighted the steady progress in combating institutionalized servitude. The initial submission in 1927 dealt mainly with the effects of the Willis Commission and concluded that 'slavery in the Provinces north of Khartoum is moribund'.[121] There were ample opportunities for employment in the northern Sudan and the number of domestic slaves remaining with their masters was dwindling rapidly. In the extreme south, no sizeable slave-owning communities existed, but in the central provinces, most notably

262   SLAVERY AND COLONIAL RULE IN AFRICA

Kurdufan and Kassala, the manumission rate was low due to the nomadic lifestyle of the population, the vastness of the territory, the inadequacy of financial resources, and perpetual turmoil along the Ethiopian border.[122]

The reports in the late twenties focused on greater emancipation in the western regions while lamenting continued complicity of Ethiopians in the eastern frontier slave trade.[123] The imprisonment of Sitt Amna in 1929 produced a lull in slave smuggling, and extensive servile registration showed that only 10 per cent were considered chattel possessions or serfs of one kind or another.[124] The 1930 submission maintained that there had been no recurrence of the border contraband trade after local elders had been threatened with severe retribution. Not only were manumission papers issued freely but freed teenagers had obtained jobs on the Gezira cotton plantations. Moreover, while over 13,000 individuals had been registered in the White Nile province in some state of semi-independence, only a quarter wished to settle in government supervised villages. The rest preferred to remain with their former owners. The transition from servitude to a contractual labour system was proceeding without let or hindrance especially after the creation of tribally-based courts and the reform of the Sudan's judicial system and the Islamic courts.[125]

Further progress in ending organized slave trading was reported in 1931 when even the subservient Barta in the Eastern borderlands exercised their newly-acquired rights by rejecting the yoke of their Watawit masters. Escalating numbers of Ethiopian slave fugitives had entered the Sudan and lived unmolested in the midst of slave-holding tribes.[126] A reverse in this relatively smooth progression to a wage labour economy was evident in the 1933 report when armed Ethiopian slave-raiding gangs capitalized on frontier insecurity to seize local inhabitants. Otherwise, sustained anti-slavery enforcement diminished the number of pilgrims to Mecca engaging in illicit slave dealings, and a temporary lull along the turbulent eastern border contributed to fewer contraband transactions.[127] But in the west, a spate of child and female abductions in Dar Fur vividly reminded authorities that the institution had not been completely eradicated. Nevertheless, the 1934 submission noted with satisfaction that the implementation of the Islamic laws of inheritance which entitled slave offspring to a share of their master's estate 'will in future ensure that the descendants of the disappearing servile class automatically become owners of property, and that the seal is set on their status of equality'.[128]

From 1935 onwards, the Sudan Government's annual statements increasingly alluded to specific successes or intractable impediments in the fight against slavery. In that year the report again deplored Ethiopian slave raiding and the attendant influx of servile refugees into the country as well as frequent kidnapping in the western Sudan.[129] The Italian invasion of

SLAVERY POLICY IN THE ANGLO-EGYPTIAN SUDAN   263

Ethiopia in May 1935 precipitated a new influx of free and servile refugees into the Sudan, which inhibited progress towards final suppression.[130] Nevertheless, optimism peppered the Condominium's tenth annual report in 1936, which stressed phenomenal structural changes in the socioeconomic fabric of the country since 1898. Anti-slavery legislation had finally reduced slave trafficking to negligible levels. In 1937, the Condominium reiterated that slave raiding incidents along the Sudano-Ethiopian frontier hindered the end of the institution. Negotiations for the repatriation of kidnapped Beir tribesmen were aggravated by retaliatory raids as well as by the ongoing repercussions of the Italian conquest. Though it was difficult to distinguish between refugees displaced by war and slaves fleeing their masters, freedom papers were now handed out on demand. Elsewhere in the Sudan, there was no sign of contraband commerce.[131] Even in the west, kidnapping had dwindled owing to unprecedented cooperation from tribal elders. The report indicated 'evidence of the increasing realization by nomad Arabs that friendliness with their darker brethren is beneficial, and that slave labour is not economic'.[132]

In its penultimate submission in 1938, the Sudan Government informed the League that numerous refugees of slave descent had capitalized on the conflict in Ethiopia to desert their owners and establish themselves in the Sudan despite attempts to retrieve them forcibly. The deployment of a Sudan Defence Force detachment on the Ethiopian border, the Italian occupation of southwestern Ethiopia and the appointment of a frontier agent had improved peace and security in the region, stabilized inter-tribal relations and substantially reduced trans-border raiding and abductions. The report stressed that domestic servitude was disappearing fast except for isolated cases in the west.[133] The 1939 account was the Sudan's last because of World War II and the dissolution of the League of Nations. Around the country only a handful of relatively minor kidnappings had occurred, most of which were speedily resolved. One beneficial by-product of the Italian occupation of Ethiopia was the creation of military posts along the turbulent frontier, which prompted Khartoum to declare that 'the danger of slave raids from beyond our Eastern borders may be regarded as belonging to the past'. Equally prematurely, it maintained that concerted anti-slavery publicity, coupled with fearless demands for emancipation, was irrefutable proof that 'domestic serfdom as a factor in the economics and social life of the country is rapidly disappearing'.[134]

Accelerated anti-slavery enforcement earned the Condominium fulsome praise in London and Geneva. The British member of the League's Slavery Committee, Sir George Maxwell, noted approvingly[135] that the Condominium's gradualist policy had brought about a situation where 'Domestic Slavery as an institution has not been recognized for years, and

264 SLAVERY AND COLONIAL RULE IN AFRICA

where every "Domestic Slave" can obtain a "freedom paper" upon application'. This had been achieved, he emphasized, with minimal social upheaval mainly because the government was content to 'hasten slowly'.[136]

The Sudan and other states were also asked to provide data to the League of Nations Advisory Committee of Experts on Slavery to explain the mechanics of 'voluntary' slavery in the Sudan.[137] The Condominium described the limited *ad hoc* nature of its material assistance to freed slaves. Apart from the creation of state-supervised settlements (which always attracted runaways), there were few unexpected hurdles to overcome. No loans had been made to emancipated slaves, though free grain rations had been issued during the devastating 1929–30 famine. Most ex-slaves quickly evolved into self-sustaining peasant farmers and supplemented their income with casual labour, thereby assuring their economic self-sufficiency and social standing. In the central Sudan, as a consequence of the anti-slavery campaigns in White Nile province, liberated Barta slaves were placed in autonomous communes, but under the jurisdiction of the nearest tribal authority. Most were given cash grants, agricultural allotments, farming implements and dairy cattle to begin a free life. The government claimed that by the mid-thirties they were wholly self-supporting and even audacious enough to lay claim to the gum gardens of their erstwhile owners in Funj province.[138] On the eastern front, Ethiopian fugitive slaves arriving in Funj and Kassala provinces were housed in protective villages and given repayable grants to become independent cultivators. But these havens[139] also tended 'to attract a few nondescripts and ne'er-do-wells from among the servile class...' which added to spasmodic social tensions and criminality.

As late as the mid-thirties, the Condominium emphasized 'that the very name "slavery", is a misnomer, whose use is ... for lack of a suitable comprehensive term'.[140] This label, it suggested, referred to those of servile stock who, for various motives, were indisposed to avail themselves of their guaranteed right to freedom. The principal factors for this reluctance were the slow growth of sophistication amongst indigenous inhabitants and, despite official propaganda, the 'nervousness of facing Government which afflicts most primitives ...'[141] No mention was made of the brazen pro-slaving views of early Condominium officials. Another reason given for a decline in the number of freedom papers issued was the fact that many of the freed thought it an insult to be offered them since it emphasized a slave-origin they were anxious to forget.[142] By the 1930s, the authorities were convinced that prohibition of proxy marriages with servile women (often a potent instrument to retain control over them), combined with widespread miscegenation and the operation of the Islamic system of inheritance (which enabled all heirs to inherit regardless of status), would contribute to the elimination of, 'within the course of a generation or so, the name and the

SLAVERY POLICY IN THE ANGLO-EGYPTIAN SUDAN 265

implications of slavery alike'.[143] Moreover, there was also increasing recognition amongst slave-holders that service labour was inherently uneconomic. This was illustrated by the remarks of a prominent tribal shaykh that 'serfs nowadays demand sugar and tea, [and] will not stay without such cosseting and altogether are too expensive a luxury to be worth keeping'.[144] Even so, it was suggested that a tiny minority of slaves clung resolutely to their subordinate status because of a 'rooted conservatism and disinclination to desert the familiar for the strange, which is common to most of mankind but particularly dominates the uneducated native type.'[145]

Most liberated slaves were absorbed either by their former owners' clans or by their native tribal groups. Rather than migrating to the urban centres, the majority preferred to stay with their ex-masters.[146] Despite onerous socio-legal obstacles, many former slaves slowly gained customary rights over their ex-masters' cultivable allotments (which they eventually came to own), and also acquired livestock and other movable property. Thus, even landless ex-slaves (unlike their prewar predecessors who were entitled at best only to the usufruct of their masters' property) remained in contentment with their erstwhile owners and feared no re-enslavement, secure in the knowledge that they could revoke their vestigial subordinate links at will.[147] In the words of officialdom, 'it is no longer the master only who has the whip hand ...'.[148] Although prostitution, alcoholism, crime and other related issues plagued the servile sector as much as their freeborn counterparts, 'the Government has no fear of the growth of a class of Sudanese [slaves] without property, liable to become an economic problem or a menace to public order. Domestic slavery is dying by a euthanasia which, though necessarily gradual is speedier than might have been guessed two decades ago ...'.[149]

The Sudan Government forecast that 'sporadic and rare cases of slave acquisition would occur for a few years yet.[150] This assessment would prove to be remarkably prescient. Even after World War II and during the fifties, international news articles periodically alleged that a clandestine trade in slaves between the Sudan and the Hijaz continued. According to these reports,[151] Arabs, enriched by oil royalties, were paying double pre-war prices for slaves from Uganda, North Africa, Ethiopia, Eritrea and the Sudan. The Red Sea harbours of Port Sudan and Sawakin, they claimed, had again evolved into booming slave entrepots. Furthermore, pilgrims traveling by dhows smuggled and sold abducted children and other familial dependents in the Holy Places. Although the Condominium questioned these charges,[152] the Anti-Slavery Society persisted in seeking reassurances from the Foreign Office.[153] Reports regarding a slave trade from the Red Sea coast to the Arabian peninsula were examined by a committee of the United Nations, and upon attaining independence in 1956, the Democratic

266 SLAVERY AND COLONIAL RULE IN AFRICA

Republic of the Sudan promptly ratified the world forum's Supplementary Slavery Convention of that year.[154]

While these allegations were not verifiable, domestic slavery was on the verge of extinction by the eve of World War II in the Sudan. By adopting a cautious policy of *festina lente* (hasten slowly) the authorities had patiently and progressively undermined the supporting structures of the institution.[155] In this context, the Condominium reminded the League of Nations in 1939 that the cost of total emancipation had been minimal owing chiefly to the staggered, not sudden suppression of servitude in the Sudan. To the small farmer, the main effect had been that he had to do his own work. Large landowners were obliged to substitute contract labour for their servile workforce. In short 'it means that the Arab has got to find a place for the Dignity of Labour in his philosophy. To the ex-slave it means in some cases a new and independent existence, varying from the precarious to the assured'.[156]

By the late thirties, the transition to wage-labour seemed beyond doubt. There had been profound and phenomenal progress under the aegis of the Sudan Government after World War I. In two generations, it had moved from equivocal to earnest slavery suppression. In the process it transformed the Sudan from a slave-based society to a modern contractual labour state without precipitating a political convulsion or subjecting the population to a disruptive socioeconomic revolution. In view of its finite resources and the entrenched nature of the slave-system, this was indeed a tremendous triumph.

Postscript: The Contemporary Situation

Formal servitude and slave-trafficking had for practical purposes been stifled by World War II and was on the verge of extinction during the following decade. However, the country's independence in 1956 set into motion a train of events that led to the revival of the institution and the trade. A conflict between the predominant Arab North and the marginalized South started immediately after independence. These regional ethnic cleavages were aggravated both by historic antagonisms resulting from northern slaving in the south and by the deliberate decisions of the British. The denial of unrestricted mobility for Northerners (and *Fallata*) in the Southern Sudan was prescribed as a potent tool in fighting slavery but it also concealed the motives of the British in the Nile Valley. The result of their 'divide and rule' strategy, including the promotion of Christian proselytization, European education and Western values in the South at the expense of Islamic expansion, has been a prolonged civil war with calamitous consequences to the present day.

SLAVERY POLICY IN THE ANGLO-EGYPTIAN SUDAN

A distressing outcome was the resurgence of the slave trade and involuntary servitude during the 1980s. Acute economic and environmental degradation sparked by the devastating droughts that afflicted Sahelian Africa between 1983 and 1993 precipitated mass refugee migrations from the Southern Sudan to the North. The deployment by the Numayri regime in 1984 of heavily-armed tribal militias (*murahilin*) from Kurdufan and Dar Fur against the Southern rebels, together with the abduction of displaced refugees by Arab *jallaba,* provided a flow of slaves and servants from the south into the Northern Sudan by the late 1980s. The traditional enmity between the Arab militias and Southern tribes provided the motive, while modern weaponry furnished the means for recurrent raids in which men were systematically slaughtered while cattle, women and children were seized with impunity. The absorption of the ruthless *murahilin* into the Popular Defence Force in 1989 by General Omar Bashir, head of the Sudan's current military dictatorship, only served to accelerate and legitimize their extensive, brutal slave acquisitions. The plight of refugees in the Nile basin eventually exposed this resurrection of chattel slavery and prompted the United Nations Working Group on Contemporary Forms of Slavery to appoint a Special Rapporteur in 1993 to investigate the situation. This report corroborated the linkage between drought, displacement, destitution and the deprivation of human rights in the Sudan,[157] despite vehement official denials that 'slavery is not a practice of the government of the Sudan'.[158]

GLOSSARY

Fallata — West African itinerant immigrants en route to the Hajj in Mecca
Fidyah — Compensatory ransom payments by slaves to erstwhile owners
Murahilin — Arab tribal militias operating in the central and northern Sudan
Muwallad — Offspring borne to masters by female slaves
Qadi — Muslim judge assigned to interpret and enforce religious law
Shari'ah — The divine legislative code of Islam based on the Quran and Hadith (prophetic traditions)

NOTES

1. For variant statistical accounts and questionable figures on the ravages inflicted on the Sudan during the Mahdist epoch see the following: *Sudan Reports* 1903, p.xiii; PRO, FO 141/393: Wingate to Findlay, 12 October, 1905; SAD, Box 400/8: C.F. Ryder, Memoirs concerning the Sudan, 1905–1916: J. Stone, 'Sudan Economic Development, 1899–1913', Sudan Economic Institution (Khartoum, 1955), pp.59–60.
2. *Sudan Reports,* 1907, p.76.
3. H.C. Jackson, *Behind the Modern Sudan* (London, 1953), pp.93–4.
4. Civil Administrative Order No. 133, 5 December 1901; *Sudan Gazette,* no.63, 1 June 1904.
5. NRO, Intel 2/43/363: Civil Secretary to Assistant Director of Intelligence, 18 April, 1908 citing 'Memo on the position of the Slavery Department and the proposed rearrangement', 5 July 1904.

268   SLAVERY AND COLONIAL RULE IN AFRICA

6. SAD, Box 479/2: S.C.A. Confidential Memorandum No.1, March 1899.
7. NRO, Intel 4/1/6: C.A. Willis to Governor, Kassala Province, 2 February 1915.
8. SAD, Box 430/6: Petition by Omdurman notables to Lord Kitchener (Arabic text) October 1898.
9. SAD, Box 431/1: C.A. Willis: 'Sidelights on the Anglo-Egyptian Sudan', p.36. undated and unpublished.
10. NRO, Intel 2/43/363: Slatin to Wingate, Khartoum, 17 March 1908.
11. Called the British and Foreign Anti-Slavery Society until 1909 and thereafter the Anti-Slavery and Aborigines Protection Society.
12. PRO, FO 407/151: Muddathir Ibrahim to Wingate, 11 April 1899.
13. N.R. O., Cairint, 10/2/6: H.W. Jackson to Administrator, Suakin. Cairo, 16 October 1900.
14. SAD, Box 284/13: Wingate to Stack, Erkowit, 31 May 1908.
15. SAD, Box 438/653/3: Slating to Bigge, Merowe, 6 September, 1897.
16. E.A. Wallis Budge, *The Egyptian Sudan: Its History and Monuments* (London, 1907), vol.1, p.198.
17. SAD, Box 270/1/1: Slatin to Wingate, Cairo, 27 January 1900.
18. Ibid.
19. SAD, Box 183/3: Slatin to Wingate, 2 December 1912.
20. *Sudan Reports*, 1906, p.30.
21. PRO, FO 407/150: Report on the Finances, Administration and Condition of Egypt, 1899, p.118.
22. PRO, FO 407/157: Report on the Finances, Administration and the Condition of the Sudan, 1901.
23. RHO, A.S.S. Papers, Box G26: Cromer to Buxton, 26 June, 1901.
24. RHO, A.S.S. Papers, Mss. Br. Emp. G.26: Cromer to Secretary, Anti-Slavery Society, 24 February 1903 and 17 March 1904.
25. NRO, Cairint 10/2/6: Confidential Circular Memorandum, Khartoum, 30 March 1904.
26. SAD, Box 235/2: F.R. Wingate to G.W. Wingate, 20 May 1911.
27. In Kassala province ex-slaves were responsible for 80 per cent of petty theft and assault. *Sudan Reports*, 1903, p.35.
28. NRO, Publications 3/3/12: G.E. Matthews, Sudan Government Circular Memorandum, 1901, 1902.
29. NRO, Intel 2/43/363: Civil Secretary to Assistant Director of Intelligence, 18 April 1908.
30. NRO, Intel 4/4/29: Wingate to J. Batalha-Reis, 1 March 1910.
31. SAD, Box 272/4/2: C. Fergusson to Wingate, Khartoum, 16 June 1902.
32. *Sudan Reports*, 1907, p.76.
33. *Sudan Reports*, 1908, pp.137–8.
34. NRO, B.N.P 1/28210: Civil Secretary to Governor, Sennar Province, Khartoum, 6 January 1913.
35. SAD, Box 187/1/1: Cromer to Wingate, 25 July 1913.
36. SAD, Box 188/3/1: Bonham Carter to Wingate, 28 December 1913.
37. In some cases like those involving the custody of servile children, the *Shari'ah* was deliberately ignored or evaded. SAD Box 188/3/1: Bonham Carter to Wingate, 31 December, 1913.
38. NRO, Civsec 60/1/1: Governor, Red Sea Province to Civil Secretary, 15 March 1918.
39. SAD, Box 171/2: Wingate: Note [on impact of Egyptian Nationalism in the Sudan], December, 1918
40. SAD, Box 280/2: Wingate to Cromer, Khartoum, 30 January 1907
41. These West Africans making their way to and from Mecca were accused of child abduction and other forms of slave-trading.
42. *Sudan Gazette*, 5 January 1915, pp.201–2.
43. NRO, Civsec 60/2/7: Willis Report, 1925, p.19.
44. NRO, Civsec 60/1/1: Governor, Red Sea Province to Civil Secretary, 15 March 1918.
45. NRO, Civsec 60/1/1: W.P.D. Clarke, Medani District to Governor, Blue Nile Province, 24 April 1918.
46. NRO, Civsec 60/1/1: Governor, Blue Nile Province to Civil Secretary, Wad Medini, 3 July 1918.

SLAVERY POLICY IN THE ANGLO-EGYPTIAN SUDAN

269

47. NRO, Civsec 60/1/1: Draft of Sudan Government Confidential Circular Memorandum No.33 [1918].
48. NRO, Civsec 60/1/1: Wasey Sterry, Legal Secretary to Civil Secretary, 2 September 1918.
49. NRO, Intel 2/20/168: Sudan Government Confidential Circular, Memorandum No.33 – 'Regulations as to Sudanese Servants', Khartoum, 1 May 1919, signed by R.M. Feilden, Civil Secretary.
50. RHO, A.S.S. Papers, Mss. Br. Emp. 522 Box G282 "Memorandum from the Anti-Slavery and Aborigines' Protection Society upon the Existence of Slavery in the Sudan', 24 November 1919.
51. Ibid.
52. PRO, FO 407/192: F.T. Hopkinson, 'Gezirah Irrigation Scheme', 15 February 1922; H.M.S.O., Cmd. 2171: Correspondence respecting the Gezirah Irrigation Project, 1924; *Hansard*, 5th series, 1928, vol.214 and 1931–2, vol 267.
53. RHO, A.S.S. Papers, Mss. Br. Emp. 522 Box G282 "Memorandum from the Anti-Slavery and Aborigines', Protection Society upon the Existence of Slavery in the Sudan', 24 November 1919.
54. RHO, A.S.S. Papers, Mss. Br. Emp. S22, G282: H.S. Dumbell to W.E. Law, Khartoum, 3 December, 1918 and 6 March 1919.
55. RHO, A.S.S. Papers, Mss. Br. Emp. S22, G282: F.S. Le Mesurier to A. Shaw, Jersey, 22 June 1919.
56. RHO, A.S.S. Papers, Mss. Br. Emp. S22, G282: Anti-Slavery Society Memo, 24 November 1919.
57. NRO, Civsec 60/1/1: Private Secretary to Civil Secretary, 16 February and 5 March 1919.
58. *Sudan Government Gazette*, No.373, 15 April 1921; No, 530, 25 April, 1930, No.569, 15 July 1932.
59. NRO, Intel 2/31/254: C.A. Willis, Director of Intelligence to Private Secretary, 26 June 1920.
60. *Sudan Government Gazette*, No.363, 30 October 1920 and No.402, 15 October 1922; PRO, FO 407/222: C.H. Bateman to Viscount Halifax, 24 October 1938.
61. Between 1920 and 1922, the number of slavery convictions had dwindled from 54 to 14. PRO, FO 371/8988: Lee Stack, Governor General to Viscount Allenby, Erkowit, 6 May 1923.
62. PRO, FO 371/7767: Viscount Allenby to Curzon, Cairo, 20 May, 1922; E. Dawson, Egyptian Finance Ministry to Chancery, Cairo, 1 June, 1922.
63. NRO, Civsec 60/1/1: Governor, Kordofan Province to Civil Secretary, 3 December 1923.
64. NRO, Civsec 60/1/2: Petition by people of Bouga to Governor of Berber, 9 December 1923.
65. NRO, Civsec 60/1/2: T.P. Creed, Assistant District Commissioner to P.G.W. Diggle, 28 January 1924.
66. NRO, Civsec 60/1/2: T.P. Creed to Governor, Berber Province, 30 January 1924.
67. NRO, Civsec 60/1/2: T.A. Leach, Governor, Berber Province to District Commissioner, 3 February 1924
68. NRO, Civsec 60/1/2: T. P. Creed to Governor, Berber Province, 4 February 1924.
69. NRO, Civsec 60/1/2: P.G.W. Diggle to District Commissioner Berber, Bouga, 2 February 1924.
70. NRO, Civsec 60/1/2: T.A. Leach to T.P. Creed, 3 February 1924.
71. NRO, Civsec 60/1/2: T.A. Leach to T.P. Creed, 7 February,1924.
72. NRO, Civsec 60/1/2: P.G.W. Diggle to A.J.C. Huddleston, 8 February 1924.
73. NRO, Civsec 60/1/2: People of Darmali to Governor General, 3 April, 9 May and 10 July 1924.
74. NRO, Civsec 60/1/2: R.V. Bardsley, Private Secretary to Civil Secretary, 7 May 1924.
75. NRO, Civsec 60/1/2: C.E. Lyall to R.V. Bardsley, 12 June 1924.
76. PRO, FO 371/10901: Lord Cecil to Sir William Tyrrel, London, 26 February 1926.
77. PRO, FO 141/640/9976/77: G.F. Archer, Governor General to Viscount Allenby, 27 January 1925.
78. NRO, B.N.P. 1/28/211: A.J.C. Huddleston to Civil Secretary, 22 December 1924.
79. Ibid.

270 SLAVERY AND COLONIAL RULE IN AFRICA

80. NRO, Port Sudan 2/39/241: W. Sterry, 'Draft Circular', February 1925.
81. NRO, Civsec 60/1/3: W. Sterry to C.E. Lyall, Civil Secretary, 4 April 1925.
82. NRO, Civsec 60/1/3: Ali Mirghani, Yusuf Hindi and Abd al-Rahman al-Mahdi to C.A. Willis, Director of Intelligence, 6 March 1925.
83. NRO, Civsec 60/1/3: Legal Secretary to Civil Secretary, Khartoum, 4 April 1925; H.A. MacMichael to J. Murray, Khartoum, 2 July 1925.
84. NRO, Civsec 60/1/3: Civil Secretary, Inter-Office Memo, 7 April 1925.
85. NRO, D.P. 5/4/14: Civil Secretary to all Governors, 24 May 1925.
86. NRO, Civsec 60/2/5: C. Lyall, 'Sudan Government Circular Memorandum on Slavery', 6 May 1925.
87. NRO, Civsec 60/1/4: British press clippings of Diggle's allegations; PRO, FO 371/10901: Parliamentary Question, Mr. Johnson to Mr. A. Chamberlain, 6 July 1925.
88. PRO, FO 141/640/9976: F. Lugard to J. Murray, 26 May 1925.
89. NRO, Civsec 60/1/3: J. Murray, Foreign Office to F. Lugard, 4 June 1925.
90. NRO, Civsec 60/2/10: [Secret] Note by C.A. Willis, Khartoum, 19 December 1925.
91. SAD, Box 171/5: R. Wingate to Lord Hardinge, Cairo, 27 December 1918.
92. *al-Ahram*, 26 June, 1925; *The Egyptian Gazette*, 6 July 1925.
93. PRO, FO 371/10901: J. Murray, Inter-Foreign Office Memo, 3 June 1925.
94. NRO, Civsec 60/1/3: N. Henderson to Governor General, 19 June 1925.
95. NRO, Civsec 60/2/10: J. Murray for A. Chamberlain to Viscount Allenby, London, 26 May 1925.
96. NRO, D.P. 1/31/158: G.F. Archer, Governor General to Vice-Consul, Jeddah, 2 December 1925; Civsec 60/2/5: H.A. MacMichael to C.A. Willis, 16 January,1926.
97. PRO, FO 371/10901: J. Murray, Foreign Office to G. Archer, 21 November 1925.
98. NRO, Civsec 60/2/8: H.A. MacMichael to J.D. Matthew, 1 December 1926.
99. NRO, Civsec 60/2/5: Telegram, Lloyd (Cairo) to Archer (Khartoum), 6 December 1925.
100. NRO, Civsec 60/2/5: Lord Cecil to William Tyrell, 17 and 21 December 1925; F. Lugard to Lord Cecil, 18 December 1925; A. Chamberlain, Foreign Office to Lord Lloyd, 17 December 1925.
101. HMSO, Cmd. 2650: Sudan No.1 (1926), Papers relating to Slavery in the Sudan.
102 *London Daily Chronicle*, 21 May 1926.
103. NRO, D.P. 1/31/158: G.F. Archer, Governor General's Note, 30 November 1925.
104. *The Sudan Herald*, Khartoum, 28 November 1925; *Hadarat al-Sudan*, Khartoum, 19 January 1926.
105 NRO, Civsec 60/2/5: C.A. Willis to Legal Secretary, 31 January 1926.
106. NRO, Civsec 60/2/7: *Report on Slavery*, 1926.
107. NRO, Civsec 60/3/11: J.D. Craig, Civil Secretary to Legal Secretary, 21 September 1927.
108. NRO, Civsec 60/3/11: H.A. MacMichael to Governor, Dongola Province, 11 March, 1928.
109. NRO, Civsec 60/2/10: W. Tyrell, Foreign Office to Lord Cecil, London, 3 February 1926.
110. NRO, Civsec 60/5/16: N.E. Davidson to N. Henderson 7 August 1927.
111. NRO, Civsec 60/6/18: H.A. MacMichael, Civil Secretary to Sudan Agent, 15 May 1928; J. Maffey to High Commissioner, 24 May, 1928; A.J.C. Huddleston to High Commissioner, Egypt, 7 August 1928.
112. NRO, B.N.P. 1/29/214: J.D. Craig to White Nile Governor, 3 September 1928.
113. NRO, Civsec 60/6/19: N.G. Davidson, Legal Secretary to Civil Secretary, 16 October 1928.
114. NRO, K.N.P. 1/19/90: 'Slavery and Arms, Note of meeting held at Kosti, 2 January 1929.
115. NRO, K.N.P. 1/19/90: J.A. Gillan, Governor, Kordofan Province, 3 January 1929. 'Note of discussion held on 2 January with the Governor General, the Civil Secretary and Governor, White Nile'.
116. NRO, Civsec 60/5/16: Lord Lloyd to Governor General, Cairo, 24 December 1927.
117. NRO, Civsec 60/4/13: Civil Secretary to all Governors, 8 January 1931.
118. NRO, N.P. 2/93/1227: J.A. Gillan, Civil Secretary to all Governors, 8 May 1936.
119. *Le Matin*, Paris, 15 July 1932; *Daily Dispatch*, London, 13 April 1934.
120. PRO, 141/771/352/12/34: Foreign Office to High Commissioner, Cairo, 26 August 1932.
121. PRO, FO 141/571/9976/290: Sudan No. 1 (1927), Cmd. 2872: J.F. Maffey, Governor

SLAVERY POLICY IN THE ANGLO-EGYPTIAN SUDAN

General to Secretary General, League of Nations, 12 April 1927.
122. PRO, FO 141/571/9976/290: Sudan No. 1 (1927), Cmd. 2872: J.F. Maffey, Governor General to Secretary General, League of Nations, 12 April 1927.
123. NRO, Civsec 60/3/11: H.A. MacMichael to Secretary General, League of Nations, 29 May 1928.
124. PRO, FO 141/571/9976/399: J. Maffey to Secretary General, League of Nations, 15 April 1929.
125. NRO, Civsec 60/4/13: J.L. Maffey to Secretary General, League of Nations, 27 March 1930.
126. PRO, FO 141/571/9976/399: J. Maffey to Secretary General, League of Nations, 24 April 1931.
127. H.M.S.O., Cmd. Paper No. 4153 (1932) Papers concerning Raids from Ethiopian Territory into the Anglo-Egyptian Sudan; NRO, Civsec 60/4/13: H.A. MacMichael to Secretary General, League of Nations, 28 April 1933.
128. PRO, FO 141/497/173/4/34: M.W. Parr to Secretary General, League of Nations, 16 April 1934.
129. NRO, Civsec 60/4/14: R.D. Mayal, Civil Secretary to Secretary General, League of Nations [undated but 1935].
130. NRO, Civsec 60/4/14: J.A. Gillan, Civil Secretary to Secretary General, League of Nations, Khartoum, 7 March 1936.
131. NRO, Civsec 60/5/15: J.A. Gillan to Secretary General, League of Nations, 23 March 1937.
132. Ibid.
133. NRO, Civsec 60/5/15: J.A. Gillan to Secretary General. League of Nations, 15 February 1938.
134. NRO, Civsec 60/5/15: J.A. Gillan to Secretary Genera., League of Nations, 29 January 1939.
135. PRO, FO 371/19063: ' Précis of Information relating to Slavery in the Sudan', February 1935.
136. PRO, FO 371/19063: G. Maxwell, Memorandum, 8 January 1935. For a discussion of the League committees and Maxwell's impact see chapter by Miers.
137. PRO, FO 141/538/465/2/36: G. Maxwell to Stevenson, 3 July 1936.
138. NRO, Civsec 60/5/15: [Memo by] Secretariat, Khartoum, 5 December 1936.
139. Some ex-slaves used colourful and profane terms to name their villages, e.g. 'the master's bum'.
140. NRO, Civsec 60/5/15: Memo on Voluntary Slavery, Khartoum, 25 November 1936.
141. Ibid.
142. Ibid.
143. Ibid.
144. Ibid.
145. Ibid.
146. NRO, Civsec 60/5/15: Memo on Voluntary Slavery, Khartoum, 25 November 1936.
147. Ibid.
148. Ibid.
149. Ibid.
150. NRO, Civsec 60/5/15: J.A. Gillan to Governor, Blue Nile Province, 11 December 1938.
151 Evening News, London, 26 August, 1947; Sunday Dispatch, London, 7 December 1952.
152. NRO, 4 Kassala 2/72/297: B.M. El Deeb for Commissioner of Police to Governors, 5 March 1953; A. Paul, Governor, Kassala Province to Commissioner of Police, 9 March 1953.
153. NRO, 60/5/16: Acting Secretary, Anti-Slavery Society to Ernest Bevin, 17, October,1947.
154. NRO, Civsec 60/5/16: Civil Secretary to Legal Secretary, 27 December, 1955.
155. PRO, FO 141/713/309/1/35: J. Simon, Foreign Office to G. Briscoe, 15 January 1935.
156. NRO, Civsec 60/6/16: J.A. Gillan to League of Nations, 20 January 1939.
157. See amongst others, David Keen, The Benefits of Famine: A Political Economy of Famine and Relief in Southwestern Sudan, 1983–1993, (Princeton, 1994); A.W.L. de Waal, Famine

272 SLAVERY AND COLONIAL RULE IN AFRICA

that Kills: Darfur, Sudan, 1884–1995 (Oxford, 1989); U.A. Mahmud and S.A. Baldo, *The Diein Massacre: Slavery in the Sudan* (Khartoum, 1987); Amnesty International, *Sudan: Human Rights Violations in the Context of Civil War* (London, 1989); Anti-Slavery Society for the Protection of Human Rights, *Slavery in the Sudan* (London, 1989); M.J. Burr and R.O. Collins, *Requiem for the Sudan: War, Drought, and Disaster Relief on the Nile* (Boulder, Colorado, 1995).

158. Report of the Special Rapporteur Gaspar Biro, *Situation of Human Rights in the Sudan*, 1 February 1994, U.N. No. E/CN.4/1994/58; and also No. A/49/82, 21 February 1994.

Notes on Contributors

Dennis Cordell is Associate Dean and Professor of History at Southern Methodist University. He is the author of *Dar al-Kuti and the Last Years of the Trans-Saharan Slave Trade* (1985), co-editor with the late Joel Gregory of *African Population and Capitalism: Historical Perspectives* (1987 and 1994), and co-author with Victor Piché and Joel Gregory of *Hoe and Wage: A Social History of a Circular Migration System in West Africa* (1996). He is now working on a study of social reproduction and the trans-Saharan slave trade.

Andrew F. Clark is an Associate Professor of African and Global History at the University of North Carolina at Wilmington. He received his PhD from Michigan State University in 1990. He is co-author of the *Historical Dictionary of Senegal* (2nd edition, 1994). He has published numerous articles on the history of Senegal and Mali and is currently completing a full-length manuscript on slavery and its demise in eastern Senegambia.

Jan-Georg Deutsch is a Research Fellow at the Centre for Modern Oriental Studies, Berlin and teaches African history at Humboldt-Universität. He obtained his PhD from the School of Oriental and African Studies in 1990 with a thesis on the topic 'Educating the Middlemen: A Political and Economic History of Statutory Cocoa Marketing in Nigeria, 1936–1947', which was published in 1995. Currently, he is writing his post-doctoral *Habilitation* thesis on 'The End of Slavery in German East Africa', which will be published as a book.

Andreas Eckert is a Research Fellow at the Humboldt-Universität Berlin and currently teaches African history at Humboldt University and at the University of Bremen. He is the author of *Die Duala und die Kolonialmachte* (1991) and *Grundbesitz, Landkonflikte und Kolonialer Wandel: Douala, 1880–1998* (1998). He is currently working on a study of bureaucracy and African administrative elites in colonial Tanzania.

Taj Hargey is a South African historian and Professor of African Studies at Sarah Lawrence College, New York. A revised version of his Oxford University thesis will be coming out shortly as *Days of Freedom: The Suppression of Slavery in the Anglo-Egyptian Sudan*. He is also the editor of *The Rainbow Nation: Minority South Africa during the Rise and Fall of Apartheid*, which is due out in 1999.

Toyin Falola teaches history at the University of Texas in Austin. He is the author of *The Political Economy of a Pre-Colonial African State: Ibadan, c. 1830–1900* and *Politics and Economy in Ibadan 1893–1945*, and is co-editor of *African Economic History* and the Series Editor of Rochester Studies in African History and the Diaspora. He is now completing a book entitled *Yoruba Gurus: Intellectual Production in Africa*.

Martin Klein teaches African History at the University of Toronto. He is the editor of *Breaking the Chains: Slavery, Bondage and Emancipation in Modern Africa and Asia* and with Claire Robertson, of *Women and Slavery in Africa*. He is the author of *Slavery and Colonial Rule in French West Africa* (1998) and is now embarking on a study of slavery in comparative perspective.

Suzanne Miers recently retired from a position at Ohio University. She is the author of *Britain and the Ending of the Slave Trade* (1975) and is the editor with Igor Kopytoff of *Slavery in Africa: Historical and Anthropological Perspectives* (1977) and, with Richard Roberts, of *The End of Slavery in Africa* (1988) and, with Maria Jaschok, of *Women and Chinese Patriarchy: Submissions, Servitude and Escape* (1994). She is now working on a book entitled *The Anti-Slavery Game* on Britain and the suppression of slavery 1890 to 1990.

Don Ohadike teaches African History at Cornell University. He has written extensively on African social and medical history and is in particular the author of *The Ekumeku Movement: Western Igbo Resistance to the British Conquest of Nigeria, 1883–1914* (1991) and *Anioma: A Social History of the Western Igbo People* (1994).

Kwabena Opare-Akurang is a Ghanaian scholar and poet who is completing a thesis on the end of slavery in southern Ghana at York University in Toronto, Canada.

Ismail Rashid is a Sierra Leonian historian, who teaches History at Vassar College. He has recently completed a PhD thesis at McGill University entitled 'Patterns of Rural Protest: Chiefs, Slaves and Peasants in Northwestern Sierra Leone 1896–1956'.

NOTES ON CONTRIBUTORS

Ahmad Sikainga teaches African history at Ohio State University. He is the author of *The Western Bahr al-Ghazal under British Rule, 1898–1956* (1991) and *Slaves into Workers: Emancipation and Labor in Colonial Sudan* (1996). He is now doing research on the way the Muslim legal system in Morocco dealt with slavery.

Sean Stilwell is currently finishing a PhD Thesis entitled 'Royal Slavery in the Sokoto Caliphate, the Case of Kano, 1807–1956' at York University in Toronto, Canada.

Select Bibliography of Works Published in English, French and German

(This is not a comprehensive bibliography. It does not include primary sources, theses or official reports – for these see the endnotes for each chapter.)

Abdallah, Ibrahim, 'Rethinking the Freetown Crowd: The Moral Economy of the 1919 Freetown Strikes and Riots', *Canadian Journal of African Studies*, 28 (1994), pp.202–13.

Abun-Nasr, J., *The Tijaniyya*. London: 1962.

Abwa, Daniel, 'The French administrative system in the lamidate of Ngaoundéré, 1915–1945`, *Introduction to the History of Cameroon in the Nineteenth and Twentieth Centuries*, Martin Z. Njeuma (ed.). Basingstoke: Macmillan ,1989, pp.137–69.

Adamu, Mahdi, 'The Delivery of Slaves from the Central Sudan to the Bight of Benin in the Eighteenth and Nineteenth Centuries', in Henry A. Gemery and Jan S. Hogendorn (eds.), *The Uncommon Market: Essays in the History of the Atlantic Slave Trade*. New York: Random House, 1979.

Adeleye, R.A., *Power and Diplomacy in Northern Nigeria*. New York, 1971.

Afigbo, A.E., 'The Eclipse of the Aro Slaving Oligarchy of South-eastern Nigeria, 1901–1927', *Journal of the Historical Society of Nigeria*, 6 (1971), pp.3–24.

Affrifah, Kofi, 'The Impact of Christianity on Akyem Society, 1852–1887', *Transactions of the Historical Society of Ghana*, 16 (1975), pp.68–86.

Agbodeka, Francis, *African Politics and British Policy in the Gold Coast 1868–1900*. London: 1971.

Ajayi, J.F.A., *Christian Missions in Nigeria, 1841–1891: The Making of a New Elite*. London: Longman, 1965.

Akintoye, S.A., *Revolution and Power Politics in Yorubaland, 1840–1893*. London: Longman, 1973.

Akintoye, S.A., 'The Economic Foundations of Ibadan's Power in the Nineteenth Century' in I. A. Akinjogbin and S.O. Osoba (eds.), *Topics on Nigerian Economic and Social History*, Ile-Ife: University of Ife Press, 1980, pp.55–65.

Allen, Charles, *Tales from the Dark Continent*. New York, 1983.

Alpers, E.A., 'The Story of Swema: Female Vulnerability in Nineteenth Century East Africa', in C.C. Robertson and M. A. Klein (eds.), *Women and Slavery in Africa*. Madison, Wisconsin: University of Wisconsin Press 1983, pp.185–99.

Amadiume, Ifi, *Male Daughters, Female Husbands, Gender and Sex in an African Society*. London: Zed Books, 1987.

Amnesty International, *Sudan: Human Rights Violations in the Context of Civil War*. London, 1989.

BIBLIOGRAPHY

Anti-Slavery Society for the Protection of Human Rights, *Slavery in the Sudan*, London, 1989.

Arafat, Walid, 'The Attitude of Islam to Slavery', *The Islamic Quarterly*, 1966, pp.12–18.

Arens, W. and Ivan Karp (eds.), *Creativity of Power: Cosmology and Action in African Societies*. Washington: Smithsonian Institution Press, 1989.

Austen, Ralph A., 'Slavery among Coastal Middlemen: The Duala of Cameroon', *Slavery in Africa. Historical and Anthropological Perspectives*, Suzanne Miers and Igor Kopytoff (eds.), Madison, Wisconsin: University of Wisconsin Press, 1977, pp 305–33.

Austen, Ralph A., 'The Metamorphosis of Middlemen: The Duala, Europeans, and the Cameroon Hinterland, c.1800–c.1960', *International Journal of African Historical Studies*, 16 (1983), pp.1–24.

Austen, Ralph A., 'Slavery and Slave Trade on the Atlantic Coast: The Duala of the Littoral', *Paideuma*, 41 (1995), pp.127–50.

Austen, Ralph A. and Jonathan Derrick, *Middlemen of the Cameroon Rivers. The Duala and their Hinterland, c.1600–c.1960*, Cambridge: Cambridge University Press, forthcoming.

Ayandele, E.A., *The Missionary Impact on Modern Nigeria, 1842–1914: A Political Analysis*, London: Longman, 1966.

Ayandele, E.A., 'The Mode of British Expansion in Yorubaland in the Second Half of the Nineteenth Century', *Tarikh*, 3 (1969), pp.23–37.

Bade, Klaus J., 'Antisklavereibewegung in Deutschland und Kolonialkrieg in Deutsch-Ostafrika 1888–1890', *Geschichte und Gesellschaft*, 3 (1977), pp.31–58

Baier, Stephen, *An Economic History of Central Niger*, London: Oxford University Press, 1980.

Baier, Stephen and Paul Lovejoy, 'The Tuareg of the Central Sudan: Gradations in Servility at the Desert Edge (Niger and Nigeria)', in Suzanne Miers and Igor Kopytoff (eds.), *Slavery in Africa*, Madison, Wisconsin: University of Wisconsin Press, 1977.

Banton, Michael, *West African City: A Study of Tribal Life in Freetown*. London: Oxford University Press, 1957.

Bataillon, C. 'La tribu', 25–36. In UNESCO (ed.), *Nomades et nomadisme au Sahara*. Paris: UNESCO, 1963.

Bataillon, C. 'Modernisation du nomadisme pastoral', 165–173. In UNESCO (ed.), *Nomades et nomadisme au Sahara*, Paris: UNESCO, 1963.

Batran, Aziz Abdalla, 'The 'Ulama of Fas, M. Ismail, and the Issue of the Haratin of Fas', in J.R. Willis (ed.), *Slaves and Slavery in Muslim Africa*, vol. II, *The Servile Estate*. London and Totowa, New Jersey: Cass, 1985, pp.1–15.

Beckles, Hilary, *Black Rebellion in Barbados: The Struggle against Slavery*. St Michael, Barbados, 1984.

Bernus, Edmond. *Touaregs Nigeriens. Unité culturelle et diversité régionale d'un peuple pasteur*. Paris, 1981.

Bernus, Edmond and Suzanne. 'L'évolution de la condition servile chez les Touaregs sahéliens', in Claude Meillassoux (ed.), *L'esclavage en Afrique précoloniale*. Paris: Maspero, 1975.

278 SLAVERY AND COLONIAL RULE IN AFRICA

Bernus, Edmond, Pierre Boilley, Jean Clauzel, Jean-Louis Triaud (eds.), *Nomades et commandants: Administration et sociétés nomades dans l'ancienne A.O.F.* Paris: Karthala, 1993.

Berry, Sara, *Cocoa, Custom and Socio-Economic Change in Rural Western Nigeria.* Oxford: Oxford University Press 1975.

Blanckmeister, Barbara E., *'Di:n wa dawla!' Islam, Politk und Ethnizität im Hausaland und in Adamawa.* Emsdetten: Gehling, 1989.

Bley, Helmut, *Namibia under Colonial Rule.* Hamburg: LIT, 1996 (1968).

Boahen, Adu, *Ghana: Evolution and Change in the Nineteenth in the Twentieth Centuries.* London: 1975.

Bonte, Pierre. 'Esclavage et relations de dépendance chez les Touaregs Kel Gress', in C. Meillassoux (ed.), *Esclavage en Afrique précoloniale.* Paris: Maspero, 1975.

Bouche, Denise, *Les villages de liberté en Afrique noire française, 1887–1910.* Paris: Mouton, 1968.

Bourgeot, André, *Les sociétés touarègues: Nomadisme, identité, résistances.* Paris: Karthala, 1995.

Bourgeot, André, 'Rapports esclavagistes et conditions d'affranchissement chez les Imuhag', in C. Meillassoux (ed.), *Esclavage en Afrique précolonial.* Paris: Maspero, 1975.

Bowen, T. J., *Adventures and Missionary Labours in Several Countries in the Interior of Africa.* London, 1968.

Braukämper, Ulrich, *Der Einfluss des Islam auf die Geschichte und Kulturentwicklung Adamauas. Abriss eines afrikanischen Kulturwandels.* Wiesbaden: Steiner, 1970.

Briggs, Lloyd Cabot. *Tribes of the Sahara.* Cambridge, Massachusetts: Harvard University Press, 1960.

Brown, Carolyn A., 'Testing the Boundaries of Marginality: Twentieth-Century Slavery and Emancipation Struggles in Nkanu, Northern Igboland, 1920–29', *Journal of African History*, 37(1996), pp.51–80.

Brunot, Louis, *Textes Arabes de Rabat.* Paris: 1931.

Buell, Raymond Leslie, *The Native Problem in Africa*, 2 vols. New York: Macmillan, 1928.

Bull, Mary, 'Indirect Rule in Northern Nigeria 1906–1911' Kenneth Robinson and Frederick Madden (eds.), *Essays in Imperial Government Presented to Margery Perkam.* Oxford: Basil Blackwell, 1965, pp.47–87.

Burkett, Elinor, 'God Created Me to be a Slave', *New York Times Magazine*, 12 Oct. 1997.

Burnham, Philip, 'Raiders and Traders in Adamawa: Slavery as a Regional System', *Paideuma,* 41 (1995), pp.153–76.

Burnham, Philip, *The Politics of Cultural Difference in Northern Cameroon.* Edinburgh: University of Edinburgh Press, 1996.

Burnham, Philip and Murray Last, 'From Pastoralist to Politician: The Problem of a Fulbe "Aristocracy"', *Cahiers d'Etudes Africaines*, 34 (1994), pp.313–58.

BIBLIOGRAPHY

279

Burr, M.J. and Collins, R.O., *Requiem for the Sudan: War, Drought, and Disaster Relief on the Nile*. Boulder, Colorado: Westview Press, 1995.

Büttner, Thea, 'Die sozialökonomische Struktur Adamauas im 19.Jahrhundert', *Wissenschaftliche Zeitschrift der Karl-Marx-Universität Leipzig, Gesellschafts- und Sprachwissenschaftliche Reihe*, 15 (1966), pp.603–26.

Butt-Thompson, Frederick Williams, *Sierra Leone in History*. London: H.F. & G. Witherby, 1926.

Christelow, Allen, *Thus Ruled Emir Abbas*. East Lansing, Michigan: Michigan State University, 1994.

Christelow, Allen, *Muslim Law Courts and the French Colonial State in Algeria*. Princeton, New Jersey: Princeton University Press, 1984.

Clarence-Smith, William G., 'Plantation versus Smallholder Production of Cocoa: The Legacy of the German Period in Cameroon', in Peter Geschiere and Pieter Konings (eds.), *Itinéraires d'Accumulation au Cameroun*. Paris: Karthala, 1993, pp.187–216.

Clarence-Smith, William G., 'Cocoa Plantations and Coerced Labor in the Gulf of Guinea, 1870–1914', in Martin Klein (ed.), *Breaking the Chains. Slavery, Bondage, and Emancipation in Modern Africa and Asia*. Madison, Wisconsin: University of Wisconsin Press, 1993, pp.150–70.

Clark, Andrew F., 'The Challenges of Cross-Cultural Oral History: Collecting and Presenting Pulaar Traditions on Slavery from Bundu, Senegambia (West Africa)', *Oral History Review*, 20 (1992).

Clark, Andrew F., 'Slavery and its Demise in the Upper Senegal Valley, 1890–1920', *Slavery and Abolition* 15 (1994), pp.51–71.

Clark, Andrew F., 'Internal Migrations and Population Movements in the Upper Senegal Valley (West Africa), 1890–1920', *Canadian Journal of African Studies*, 28 (1994), pp.399–420.

Clark, Andrew F., 'Freedom Villages in the Upper Senegal Valley, 1890–1910: A Reassessment', *Slavery and Abolition* 16 (1995), pp.311–30.

Clark, Andrew F., 'Environmental Decline and Ecological Response in the Upper Senegal Valley, West Africa, from the Late Nineteenth Century to World War One', *Journal of African History*, 36 (1995), pp.197–218.

Clark, Andrew F., 'The Fulbe of Bundu: From Theocracy to Secularization', *International Journal of African Historical Studies*, 29 (1996), pp.1–23.

Clark, Andrew F., *The Ties that Bind: Servility and Dependency in the Upper Senegal Valley, 1890–1990* (forthcoming).

Clarke, W.H., *Travels and Explorations in Yorubaland, 1854–1858*, ed. J.A. Atanda. Ibadan: University of Ibadan Press, 1972.

Colin, G.S., 'Hartani', in *Encyclopedia of Islam*, new series, vol. III. Leiden, 1971, pp.231–2.

Conrad, David and Barbara Frank (eds.), *Status and Identity in West Africa*. Bloomington, Indiana: University of Indiana Press 1995.

Cooper, Frederick, *From Slaves to Squatters: Plantation Labour and Agriculture in Zanzibar and Coastal Kenya, 1890–1925*. New Haven, Connecticut and London: Yale University Press, 1980.

280 SLAVERY AND COLONIAL RULE IN AFRICA

Cooper, Frederick, 'Islam and Cultural Hegemony: the Ideology of slave owners on the East African Coast', in Paul Lovejoy (ed.), *The Ideology of Slavery in Africa*. Beverly Hills: Sage, 1981, pp.271–307.

Cordell, Dennis, 'The Delicate Balance of Force and Flight: the End of Slavery in Eastern Ubangi-Shari', in Suzanne Miers and Richard Roberts (eds.), *The End of Slavery in Africa*. Madison, Wisconsin: University of Wisconsin Press, 1988, pp.150–71.

Cox-George, N.A., *Finance and Development in West Africa*. London: Denis Dobson, 1961.

Craton, Michael, *Testing the Chains: Resistance to Slavery in British West Indies, 1627–1838*. Ithaca, New York: Cornell University Press, 1982.

Curtin, Philip, *Economic Change in Precolonial Africa*. Madison, Wisconsin: Wisconsin: University of Wisconsin Press 1975.

De Chassey, Francis, *Mauritanie 1900–1975: De l'ordre colonial à l'ordre néocolonial*. Paris: 1978.

Delancey, Mark W., 'Health and Diesease on the Plantations of Cameroon, 1884–1939', in Gerald W. Hartwig and K. David Patterson (eds.), *Disease in African History. An Introductory Survey and Case Studies*. Durham, North Carolina: University of North Carolina Press, 1978, pp.153–79.

Denzer, La Ray, 'Sierra Leone-Bai Bureh', in Michael Crowder (ed.), *West Africa Resistance*. New York: Africana Publishing Corp, 1971.

Désiré-Vuillemin, G. *Contribution à la Mauritanie*. Dakar: Clairafrique, 1962.

Deutsch, J.-G., 'What Happened to All the Slaves? Colonial Policy, Emancipation, and the Transformation of Slave Societies in German and British East Africa (Tanganyika), c.1890 – 1930', *Collected Papers of the 38th Annual Meeting of African Studies Association*, Orlando, Florida, 3–6 November 1995.

Deutsch, J.-G., 'Weidner's Slaves: A Misunderstanding in German Colonial Thought', *Working Papers*, 5 (1996), Institute of Development Studies, Helsinki.

De Waal, A.W.L., *Famine that Kills: Darfur, Sudan, 1884–1995*. Oxford: Oxford University Press, 1989.

Donham, D. and Wendy James, *The Southern Marches of Imperial Ethiopia*. Cambridge: Cambridge University Press, 1986.

Duffy, J., *A Question of Slavery*. Cambridge, Massachusetts: Harvard University Press, 1967.

Dumett, Raymond E., and Marion Johnson, 'Britain and the Suppression of Slavery in the Gold Coast Colony, Ashanti, and the Northern Territories', in Suzanne Miers and Richard Roberts (eds.), *The End of Slavery in Africa*. Madison, Wisconsin: University of Wisconsin Press, 1988, pp.71–116.

Dupeyron, G. 'Bintagoungou, Village de Faguibine: budgets et niveau de vie', *Cahiers d'Outre-mer*, 12 (1959), pp.26–55.

Dupire, M., *Organisation sociale des Peuples*. Paris, 1970.

Dusgate, Richard H., *The Conquest of Northern Nigeria*. London, 1985.

BIBLIOGRAPHY

Echenberg, Myron, *Colonial Conscripts: The Tirailleurs Sénégalais in French West Africa, 1857–1960*. London: Heinemann, 1991.

Echenberg, Myron, 'Slaves into Soldiers: Social Origins of the Tirailleurs', in Paul Lovejoy (ed.) *Africans in Bondage*. Madison, Wisconsin: African Studies Program, 1986, pp.7–24.

Eckert, Andreas, 'Cocoa farming in Cameroon, c.1914–c.1960', in William G. Clarence-Smith (ed.), *Cocoa Pioneer Fronts since 1800. The Role of Planters, Smallholders and Merchants*. Basingstoke: Macmillan, 1996, pp.137–53.

Eckert, Andreas, *Grundbesitz, Landkonflikte und Kolonialer Wandel. Douala, 1880–1960*, Stuttgart: Steiner, 1998.

Eckert, Andreas, 'African Entrepreneurs in the Cameroon Littoral, 1880s–1960s', *Journal of African History*, forthcoming.

Ekechi, Felix, 'Traders, Missionaries, and the bombardment of Onitsha,1879–1880', *The Conch*, 5, (1973), pp.61–81.

Eldridge, E. and F. Morton (eds.), *Slavery in South Africa: Captive Labor on the Dutch Frontier*. Boulder, Colorado: Westview, 1994.

Ellias, T.O., *Ghana and Sierra Leone: The Development of their Laws and Constitutions*. London, 1962.

Ennaji, Mohammed, *Soldats, domestiques et concubines: L'esclavage au Maroc au XIXe siècle*. Casablanca: EDDIF, 1994.

Fadipe, N.A., *The Sociology of the Yoruba*, ed. by O. Okedji and F. Okediji. Ibadan: Ibadan University Press, 1970.

Fall, Babacar, *Le travail forcé en Afrique occidentale française, 1900–1945*. Paris: Karthala, 1993.

Falola, Toyin, *The Political Economy of a Pre-colonial African State: Ibadan, 1830–1900*. Ile-Ife, Nigeria: University of Ife Press, 1984.

Falola, Toyin, 'Power Relations and Interactions among Ibadan Slaves', *African Economic History*, 16 (1986), pp.95–114.

Falola, Toyin, 'Missionaries and Domestic Slavery in Yorubaland in the 19th Century', *Journal of Religious History*, 14 (1986).

Falola, Toyin and A.G. Adebayo, *Owoseni: The Culture and Politics of Money Among the Yoruba* (forthcoming).

Falola, Toyin and Dare Oguntomisin, *The Military in Nineteenth Century Yoruba Politics*. Ile-Ife, Nigeria: University of Ife Press, 1984.

Falola, Toyin and Paul Lovejoy (eds.), *Pawnship in Africa: Debt Bondage in Historical and Perspective*. Boulder, Colorado: Westview 1994.

Field, M.J., *Akim Kotoku*. Accra, 1948.

Fika, Adamu Mohammed, *The Kano Civil War and British Overrule, 1882–1940*. Ibadan: Oxford University Press, 1978.

282 SLAVERY AND COLONIAL RULE IN AFRICA

Frémeaux, Jacques. *Les bureaux arabes dans l'Algérie de la conquête.* Paris: Denoël, 1993.

Freund, Bill, *Capital and Labour in the Nigerian Tin Mines.* London: Routledge and Kegan Paul, 1981.

Froelich, J.C., 'Le Commandement et l'Organisation Sociale chez les Foulbé de l'Adamawa', *Etudes Camerounaises*, 45–46 (1954), pp.5–90.

Fuglestad, Finn, *A History of Niger 1859–1960.* Cambridge: Cambridge University Press, 1983.

Fyfe, Christopher, *History of Sierra Leone.* London: Oxford University Press, 1962.

Fyfe, Christopher, *The Sierra Leone Inheritance.* London: Oxford University Press, 1964.

Fyle, C. Magbaily, *The Solima Yalunka Kingdom: Precolonial Politics, Economics and Society.* Freetown, Sierra Leone: Nyakon Publishers, 1979.

Gautier, E.F., *Le Sahara.* Paris: Payot, 1946.

Gemery, Henry A. and Jan S. Hogendorn (eds.), *The Uncommon Market: Essays in the History of the Atlantic Slave Trade.* New York: Random House, 1979.

Genovese, Eugene, *Roll Jordan Roll: The World the Slaves Made.* New York: Vintage Books, 1972.

Ghoraba, Hammouda, 'Islam and Slavery', *The Islamic Quarterly*, II (1955), pp.152–9.

Glassman, Jonathon, *Feast and Riots: Revelry, Rebellion and Popular Consciousness on the Swahili Coast 1856–1888.* London: James Currey, 1995.

Gomez, M., *Pragmatism in the Age of Jihad: The Precolonial State of Bundu.* Cambridge: Cambridge University, 1992.

Goodridge, Richard A., 'The Issue of Slavery in the establishment of British Rule in Northern Cameroon to 1927', *African Economic History*, 22 (1994), pp.19–36.

Goodridge, Richard A., 'Slavery, Abolition and Political Reform in Northern Cameroons to 1937', *Identifying Enslaved Africans. The 'Nigerian' Hinterland and the African Diaspora.* Proceedings of the UNESCO/SSHRCC Summer Institute, York University, Toronto, 14.7.–1.8.1997, pp.649–63.

Grace, John, *Domestic Slavery in West Africa with Particular Reference to the Sierra Leone Protectorate, 1896–1927.* London: Frederick Muller, 1975.

Harding, Leonhard, 'Die deutsche Diskussion um die Abschaffung der Sklaverei in Kamerun', in Peter Heine and Ulrich van der Heyden (eds.), *Studien zur Geschichte des deutschen Kolonialismus in Afrika.* Pfaffenweiler: Centaurus, 1995, pp.280–308.

Hargey, T., *Days of Freedom: The Suppression of Slavery in the Anglo-Egyptian Sudan.* London: James Currey, 1999.

Harrison, Christopher, *France and Islam in West Africa, 1860–1960.* Cambridge: Cambridge University Press, 1988.

Hausen, Karin, *Deutsche Kolonialherrschaft in Afrika. Wirtschaftsinteressen und Kolonialverwaltung in Kamerun vor 1914.* Zürich: Atlantis, 1970.

BIBLIOGRAPHY

283

Hawkin, E.K., *Road Transportation in Nigeria*. London: Oxford University Press, 1958.

Heywood, Linda M., 'Slavery and Forced Labor in the Changing Political Economy of Central Angola, 1850–1949', in Suzanne Miers and Richard Roberts (eds.), *The End of Slavery in Africa*. Madison, Wisconsin: University of Wisconsin Press, 1988, pp.415–36.

Hinderer, Anna, *Seventeen Years in the Yoruba Country: Memorials of Anna Hinderer, wife of the Rev. David Hinderer, C.M.S. Missionary in Western Africa*. Introduction by Richard B. Hone. London, 1872.

Hiskett, Mervyn, *The Sword of Truth: the Life and Times of Shehu Dan Fodio*. London, 1973.

Hiskett, M., 'The Song of Bagauda: A Hausa King List and Homily in Verse II' *Bulletin of the School of Oriental and African Studies*, 28 (1965).

Hopkins, A.G., *An Economic History of West Africa*. London: Longman, 1973.

Hopkins, A.G., 'The Lagos Chamber of Commerce, 1888–1903', *Journal of the Historical Society of Nigeria*, 3 (1965).

Hopkins, A.G., 'A Report on the Yoruba, 1910', *Journal of the Historical Society of Nigeria*, V (1969), pp.67–100.

Howard, Allen M., 'Pawning in Coastal Northwest Sierra Leone, 1870–1910', in Toyin Falola and Paul Lovejoy (eds.), *Pawnship in Africa: Debt Bondage in Historical Perspective*. Boulder, Colorado: Westview, 1994, pp.267–84.

Heussler, Robert, *The British in Northern Nigeria*. London, 1968.

Human Rights Watch, *Mauritania's Reign of Terror: State-Sponsored Repression of Black Africans*. New York, 1994.

Hunwick, John, 'Black Africans in the Islamic World: an Under-studied Dimension of the Black Diaspora', *Tarikh*, 5 (1978), pp.20–40.

Ifemesia, Cheika C., *South-eastern Nigeria in the Nineteenth Century: An Introductory Analysis*. New York: Nok, 1978.

Isichei, Elizabeth, *A History of the Igbo People*. London: Macmillan. 1976.

Jackson, H.C., *Behind the Modern Sudan*. London, 1953.

James, C.L.R., *The Black Jacobins: Toussaint L'Ouverture and the San Domingue Revolution*, 2nd ed,. Rev. New York: Vintage Books, 1963.

James, Wendy, 'Perceptions from an African Slaving Frontier', in Leonie J. Archer (ed.), *Slavery and Other Forms of Unfree Labour*. London: Routledge, 1988, pp.131–41.

Jearey, J.A., 'Trial by Jury and Trial with the Aid of Assessors in the Superior Courts of British African Territories: I', *Journal of African Law*, 4 (1960), pp.133–46.

Jenkins, Paul, *Abstracts of Basel Mission Gold Coast Correspondence*. Legon, Ghana, 1970.

Johnson, Marion, 'Slaves of Salaga', *Journal of African History*, 27 (1986) pp.341–62.

Johnson, Samuel, *The History of the Yorubas*. Lagos: Church Missionary Society, 1921.

Kaptué, Léon, *Travail et Main d'Oeuvre au Cameroun sous Régime Français, 1916–1952*. Paris: Karthala, 1986.

Karstedt, F. O., 'Zur Sklavenfrage in Deutsch Ostafrika', *Deutsch-Ostafrikanische Zeitung*, XVI (1914) 8, 24 Jan. 1914.

Kaiserliches Gouvernement von Deutsch-Ostafrika, *Die Landes-Gesetzgebung des Ostafrikanischen Schutzgebiets*. Tanga/Dar es Salaam, 1911.

Kambou-Ferrand, J.-M., *Peuples Voltaiques et Conqête Coloniale 1851–1914*. Paris,1993.

Keen, D., *The Benefits of Famine: A Political Economy of Famine and Relief in Southwestern Sudan, 1983–1993*. Princeton, New Jersey: Princeton University Press, 1994.

Kimble, David, *A Political History of Ghana*. Oxford: Clarendon, 1963.

Kirk-Greene, A.H.M., *Adamawa. Past and Present*, London: Oxford University Press, 1958.

Kirk-Greene, A. H. M., 'Preliminary Notes on New Sources for Nigerian Military History', *Journal of the Historical Society of Nigeria*, 3 (1964), pp.135–8.

Klein, Martin A., 'Slave Resistance and Slave Emancipation in Coastal Guinea', in Suzanne Miers and Richard Roberts (eds.), *The End of Slavery in Africa*. Madison, Wisconsin: University of Wisconsin Press, 1988, pp.203–19.

Klein, Martin A., *Slavery and Colonial Rule in Africa*. Cambridge: Cambridge University Press 1998.

Klein, Martin A. (ed.), *Breaking the Chains: Slavery, Bondage, and Emancipation in Modern Africa and Asia*. Madison, Wisconsin: University of Wisconsin Press, 1993.

Klein, Martin A., 'Slavery and Emancipation in French West Africa', in Martin A. Klein, *Breaking the Chains: Slavery, Bondage, and Emancipation in Modern Africa and Asia*. Madison, Wisconsin: University of Wisconsin Press, 1993, pp.171–96

Klein, Martin A. and R. Roberts, 'The Resurgence of Pawning in French West Africa during the Depression of the 1930s', *African Economic History*, 16 (1987), pp.23–37.

Kopytoff, Igor, 'The Cultural Context of African Abolition' Suzanne Miers and Richard Roberts, *The End of Slavery in Africa*. Madison, Wisconsin: University of Wisconsin Press, 1988, pp.485–503.

Kopytoff, Igor and Suzanne Miers, 'African 'Slavery' as an Institution of Marginality' Suzanne Miers and Igor Kopytoff (eds.), *Slavery in Africa: Historical and Anthropological Perspectives*. Madison, Wisconsin: University of Wisconsin Press, 1977, pp.3–81.

Kosack, Gudula, 'Aus der Zeit der Sklaverei (Nordkamerun). Alte Mafa erzählen', *Paideuma*, 38 (1992), pp.177–194.

Kup, Peter, *A History of Sierra Leone*. Cambridge: Cambridge University Press, 1962.

Laird, MacGregor and R.A.K. Oldfield, *Narrative of an Exploration into the Interior of Africa*. London, 1971.

Lander, Richard and John Lander, *Journal of Expedition to Explore the Course and Termination of the Niger*, 2 vols. New York, 1958.

BIBLIOGRAPHY

285

Last, Murray, *The Sokoto Caliphate*. London: Longman, 1967.

Law, Robin, *The Horse in West African History*. London: Oxford University Press, 1980.

Lefèvre-Witier, Philippe, *Idelès du Hoggar. Biologie et écologie d'une communauté saharienne*. Paris: CNRS Editions, 1996.

Lelong, M.-H. *Le Sahara aux cent visages*. Paris: Editions Alsatia, 1945.

Lethielleux, Jean. *Ouargla, cité saharienne des origines au début du XXè siècle*. Paris: Librairie Orientaliste Paul Geuthner, 1983.

Leue, A., 'Die Sklaverei in Ostafrika', *Beiträge zur Kolonialpolitik und Kolonialwirtschaft*, 1900/01, pp.606–8, 617–25.

Lewis, Bernard, *Race and Slavery in the Middle East*. Oxford: Oxford University Press, 1990.

Loiseau, Philippe,. 'L'administration et les rapports nomades/sédentaires', in Bernus *et al.*, *Nomades et commandants: Administration et sociétés nomades dans l'ancienne A.O.F.* Paris: Karthala, 1993.

Loti, Pierre, *Morocco*. Philadelphia, n.d.

Lovejoy, Paul, 'Slavery in the Sokoto Caliphate', in Paul Lovejoy (ed.), *The Ideology of Slavery in Africa*. Beverly Hills: Sage, 1981, pp.201–43.

Lovejoy, Paul, *Transformations in Slavery: A History of Slavery in Africa*. Cambridge: Cambridge University Press, 1991.

Lovejoy, Paul, 'Concubinage and the Status of Women in Early Colonial Northern Nigeria', *Journal of African History*, 29 (1988), pp.245–66.

Lovejoy, Paul, 'Concubinage in the Sokoto Caliphate' *Slavery and Abolition*, 11 (1990), pp.159–89.

Lovejoy, Paul (ed.), *The Ideology of Slavery in Africa*. Beverly Hills: Sage, 1981.

Lovejoy, Paul and Jan Hogendorn, 'Revolutionary Mahdism and Resistance to Colonial Rule in Sokoto', *Journal of African History*, 31 (1990), pp.217–44.

Lovejoy, Paul and Jan Hogendorn, *Slow Death for Slavery: The Course of Abolition in Northern Nigeria, 1897–1936*. Cambridge: Cambridge University Press, 1993.

Lovejoy, Paul *et al.*, 'C.L. Temple's 'Notes on the History of Kano (1909): A Lost Chronicle of Political Office', *Sudanic Africa*, 4 (1993).

Lugard, Frederick, *Political Memoranda: Revision of Instructions to Political Officers*. London: Frank Cass, 1970.

Mack, Beverley, 'Women and Slavery in Nineteenth Century Hausaland', Elizabeth Savage (ed.), *The Human Commodity: Perspectives on the Trans-Saharan Slave Trade*. London: Frank Cass, 1992, pp.89–110.

McPhee, Allan, *The Economic Revolution in British West Africa*. New York, 1926.

Mahmud, U.A. and Baldo, S.A., *The Diein Massacre: Slavery in the Sudan*. Khartoum: Khartoum University Press, 1987.

286 SLAVERY AND COLONIAL RULE IN AFRICA

Maier, Donna J.E., 'Slave Labor and Wage Labor in German Togo, 1885–1914', in Arthur J. Knoll and Lewis H. Gann (eds.), *Germans in the Tropics. Essays in German Colonial History.* New York: Greenwood, 1987, pp.73–91.

McDougall, E. Ann, 'A Topsy-Turvy World: Slaves and Freed Slaves in the Mauritanian Adrar, 1910–50', Suzanne Miers and Richard Roberts (eds.), *The End of Slavery in Africa.* Madiso, Wisconsin: University of Wisconsin Press, 1988, pp.362–88.

McSheffrey, Gerald, 'Slavery, Indentured Servitude, Legitimate Trade and the Impact of Abolition in the Gold Coast, 1874–1901: A Reappraisal', *Journal of African History*, 24 (1983), pp.349–68.

Manning, P., *Slavery and African Life.* Cambridge: Cambridge University Press, 1990.

Mariko, Kélétigui. 'L'attitude de l'administration face au servage', in Bernus *et al.*, *Nomades et commandants: Administration et sociétés nomades dans l'ancienne A.O.F.* Paris: Karthala, 1993.

Mason, John Edwin, 'Hendrick Albertus and his Ex-slave Mey: A Drama in Three Acts', *Journal of African History*, 31 (1990), pp.423–45.

Mason, Michael, 'The History of Mister Johnson: Progress and Protest in Northern Nigeria', *Canadian Journal of African Studies,* 27 (1993), pp.196–217.

Matthews, John, *A Voyage to the River Sierra Leone.* London: Frank Cass, 1966. First published 1788.

Maugham, Robin. *The Slaves of Timbuktu.* New York: Harper, 1961.

Mbodj, Mohammed, 'The Abolition of Slavery in Senegal, 1820–1890: Crisis or the Rise of a New Entrepenurial Class?', in Martin A. Klein (ed.), *Breaking the Chains:Slavery and Emancipation in Modern Africa and Asia.* Madison, Wisconsin: University of Wisconsin Press, 1993.

Mbodj Mohammed and Babacar Fall, 'Forced Labor and Migration in Senegal', in A. Zegeye and S. Ishemo (eds.), *Forced Labor and Migration: Patterns of Movement within Africa.* London, 1989.

Meillassoux, Claude, *L'esclavage en Afrique Pré-Coloniale.* Paris: Maspero, 1975.

Mercer, John. *Slavery in Mauritania Today.* Edinburgh: Human Rights Group, 1982.

Meyers, Allen A., 'Class, Ethnicity and Slavery: The Origin of the Moroccan *Abid*' *International Journal of African Historical Studies*, 10 (1977), pp.427–42.

Meyers, Allen A., 'Slave Soldiers and State Politics in Early Alawi Morocco, 1668–1727', *International Journal of African Historical Studies*, 16 (1983), pp.39–48.

Midel, Monika, *Fulbe und Deutsche in Adamaua (Nord-Kamerun) 1809–1916. Auswirkungen afrikanischer und kolonialer Eroberung.* Frankfurt-am-Main: Lang, 1990.

Miers, Suzanne, *Britain and the Ending of the Slave Trade.* London and New York: Longmans /Africana, 1975.

Miers, Suzanne 'Humanitarianism at Berlin: Myth or Reality', in S. Forster, W.J. Mommsen, R. Robinson (eds.), *Bismarck, Europe and Africa: The Berlin Africa Conference 1884–1885 and the Onset of Partition.* London: Oxford University Press, 1988, pp.333–45.

BIBLIOGRAPHY

Miers, Suzanne, 'Diplomacy versus Humanitarism: Britain and Consular Manumission in Hijaz 1921–36', *Slavery and Abolition*, 18 (1989), pp.102–28.

Miers, Suzanne 'Britain and the Suppression of Slavery in Ethiopia', *Slavery and Abolition*, 18 (1997), pp.257–88.

Miers, Suzanne and Igor Kopytoff (eds.), *Slavery in Africa: Historical and Anthropological Perspectives*. Madison, Wisconsin: University of Wisconsin Press, 1975.

Miers, Suzanne and Michael Crowder, 'The Politics of Slavery in Bechuanaland: Power Struggles in the Plight of the Basarwa in the Bamangwato Reserve, 1926–1940', in Suzanne Miers and Richard Roberts (eds.), *The End of Slavery in Africa*. Madison, Wisconsin: University of Wisconsin Press, 1988, pp.172–200.

Miers, Suzanne and Richard Roberts (eds.), *The End of Slavery in Africa*. Madison, Wisconsin: University of Wisconsin Press, 1988.

Migeod, F.W.H., *A View of Sierra Leone*. London: K. Paul, Trench and Truber, 1926.

Milum, J., 'Notes of a Journey from Lagos up the Niger to Bida', *Proceedings of the Royal Geographical Society*, New Series, 3 (1881).

Miner, Horace, *The Primitive City of Timbuktu*. Princeton, New Jersey: Princeton University Press, 1953.

Mohammadou, Eldridge, 'Les sources de l'exploration et de la conquete de l'Adamawa et du Bornou allemands (1893–1903): Passarge, Dominik, Bauer', *Paideuma*, 40 (1994), pp.37–66.

Moitt, B., 'Slavery and Emancipation in Senegal's Peanut Basin: The Nineteenth and Twentieth Centuries', *International Journal of African Historical Studies*, 22 (1989), pp.27–50.

Moitt, B., 'Slavery, Flight and Redemption in Senegal, 1819–1905', *Slavery and Abolition*, 14 (1993), pp.70–86.

Moodie, Dunbar T.',The Moral Economy of the Black Miners Strike of 1946, *Journal of Southern African Studies*, 13 (1986), pp.1–35.

Morgen, Curt von, *Durch Kamerun von Süd nach Nord. Reisen und Forschungen im Hinterlande, 1889–1891*. Leipzig: Brockhaus, 1893.

Morton, Fred, *Children of Ham: Freed Slaves and Fugitive Slaves on the Kenya Coast, 1873–1907*. Boulder, Colorado: Westview, 1990.

Muffett, D.J.M., *Concerning Brave Captains*. London, Andre Deutsch, 1964.

Nachtigal, Gustav, *Sahara and Sudan:Tripoli, the Fezzan and Tibesti*, Allan G. B. Fisher and Humphrey J. Fisher, trans. Vol. I and II. London: Christopher Hurst, 1974 and 1980.

Nadel, S.F., *A Black Byzantium: The Kingdom of Nupe in Nigeria*. London: Oxford University. Press, 1942.

Njeuma, Martin, *Fulani Hegemony in Yola (Old Adamawa) 1809–1902*. Yaoundé: Ceper, 1978.

Nowak, Bronislaw, 'The Slave Rebellion in Sierra Leone in 1785–1796', *Hemispheres* (Poland) 3 (1986), pp.151–69.

288 SLAVERY AND COLONIAL RULE IN AFRICA

Ohadike, Don C., *The Ekumeku Movement, Western Igbo Resistance to the British Conquest of Nigeria, 1883–1914*. Athens, Ohio: Ohio University Press, 1991.

Ohadike, Don C., 'The Decline of Slavery Among the Igbo People', in Suzanne Miers and Richard Roberts (eds.) *The End of Slavery in Africa*. Madison, Wisconsin: University of Wisconsin Press, 1988, pp.437–61.

O'Hear, Ann, *Power Relations in Nigeria. Ilorin Slaves and their Successors*. Rochester, New York: University of Rochester Press, 1997.

Olivier de Sardan, Jean-Pierre, *Quand nos pères étaient captifs*. Paris: Nubia, 1976.

Olivier de Sardan, Jean-Pierre, *Les Sociétés Songhay-Zarma (Niger-Mali)*.Paris: Karthala, 1984.

Olusanya, G.O., 'The Freed Slaves' Homes—An Unknown Aspect of Northern Nigerian Social History', *Journal of the Historical Society of Nigeria*, III (1966).

Oriji, J. N., 'Slave Trade, Warfare and Aro Expansion in the Igbo Hinterland', *Geneve Afrique*, 24 (1986), pp.102–18.

Ould Cheikh, Abdel Wedoud, 'L'évolution de l'esclavage dans la société maure', in Bernus *et al.*, *Nomades et Commandants*

Palmer, H.R., *Sudanese Memoirs*. London: Frank Cass, 1967, first published 1928.

Paramount Chief J.K. Mannah-Kpaka, 'Memoirs of 1898 Rising', *Sierra Leone Studies*, N.S. 1 (1953), pp.28–39.

Passarge, Siegfried, *Adamaua. Bericht über die Expedition des Deutschen Kamerun-Komitees in den Jahren 1893/94*, Berlin: Reimer, 1994.

Patterson, David K., 'The Influenza Epidemic of 1918–1919 in the Gold Coast', *Journal of African History*, 24 (1983), pp.485–502.

Perham, M., *Lugard: The Years of Adventure 1858–98*.London: Collins, 1956.

Perham, M., *Lugard: The Years of Authority 1898–1945*. London: Collins, 1960.

Person, Y., *Samori: une revolution dyula*. Dakar: Institut Français d'Afrique Noir, 1968–1975.

Phillips, Anne, *The Enigma of Colonialism: British Policy in West Africa*. London: James Currey, 1989.

Pinnock, S.G., *The Romance of Missions in Nigeria*. Richmond, Virginia, 1918.

Pipes, Daniel, 'Mawlas: Freed Slaves and Converts in Early Islam', *Slavery and Abolition*, 1 (1980), pp.132–77.

Rancon, A., *Le Boundou*. Bordeaux, 1894.

Rankin, F. Harrison, *The White Man's Grave: A Visit to Sierra Leone in 1834*. London: Richard Benthley, 1836.

Rattray, R.S. *Ashanti Law and Constitution*. Oxford: Oxford University Press, 1969 first published 1929.

BIBLIOGRAPHY

Rattray, R.S. *Religion and Art in Ashanti*. Oxford: Oxford University Press, 1979 first published 1927.

Redwar, H.W. Hayes, *Comments on Some Ordinances of the Gold Coast Colony with Notes on a few Decided Cases*. London: Sweet & Maxwell, 1909.

Renault, F., *Lavigerie, l'esclavage Africain, et l'Europe*. 2 Vols. Paris: E. De Boccard, 1971.

Renault, F., *L'abolition de l'esclavage au Senegal*. Paris: Société de l'Histoire de la France d'Outre-Mer, 1972.

Roberts, Richard and Suzanne Miers, 'The End of Slavery in Africa', in Suzanne Miers and Richard Roberts (eds.), *The End of Slavery in Africa*. Madison, Wisconsin: University of Wisconsin Press, 1988, pp.3–68.

Roberts, Richard, 'The End of Slavery in French Soudan, 1905–1914', in Suzanne Miers and Richard Roberts (eds.), *The End of Slavery in Africa*. Madison, Wisconsin: University of Wisconsin Press, 1988, pp.282–307.

Roberts, Richard and Martin A. Klein, 'The Banamba Slave Exodus and the Decline of Slavery in Western Sudan', *Journal of African History*, 21 (1980), pp.375–94

Robinson, D., *The Holy War of Umar Tal: The Western Sudan in the mid-Nineteenth Century* Oxford: Clarendon, 1985.

Robertson, Claire C., *Sharing the Same Bowl: A Socioeconomic History of Women and Class in Accra, Ghana*. Bloomington, Indiana: Indiana University Press, 1984.

Robertson, Claire C., 'Post-Proclamation Slavery in Accra: A Female Affair?' in Martin A. Klein and Claire C. Robertson (eds.), *Women and Slavery in Africa*. Madison, Wisconsin: University of Wisconsin Press, 1983, pp.220–45.

Robertson, Claire C. and Martin A. Klein (eds.), *Women and Slavery in Africa*. Madison, Wisconsin: University of Wisconsin Press, 1983.

Roux, E., *Notice historique sur le Boundou*. Saint-Louis-du Senegal, 1893.

Rude, George, *The Crowd in History 1730–1848*. London: Lawrence and Wishart, 1981.

Rudin, Harry R., *Germans in the Cameroons 1884–1914. A Case Study in Modern Imperialism*, New York: Greenwood, 1968 (1938).

Rüger, Adolf, 'Die Entstehung und Lage der Arbeiterklasse unter dem deutschen Kolonialregime in Kamerun (1895–1905)', in Stoecker (ed.), Vol.2, pp.149–242.

Salifou, André. *Histoire du Niger*. Paris, 1989.

Sampson, Rev. E., *History of Aquapim and Akropong*. Accra, 1908.

Schultz, Emily A., 'From Pagan to Pullo: Ethnic Identity Change in Northern Cameroon', *Africa* 54 (1984), pp.46–64.

Scott, James, *The Moral Economy of the Peasant: Rebellion and Subsistence in South East Asia*. New Haven: Yale University Press, 1976.

Seitz, Theodor, *Vom Aufstieg und Niederbruch deutscher Kolonialmacht*. 3 vols. Karlsruhe: Müller, 1927–29.

Shea, Philip J., 'How Indirect was Indirect Rule? A Documentary Approach to an Administrative Problem' *Kano Studies,* n.s. 2, 3 (1982/5), pp.154–62.

Shell, Robert, *The Children of Bondage: A Social History of Slave Society at the Cape of Good Hope, 1652–1838.* Hanover, New Hampshire: Wesleyan University Press, 1994.

Sikainga, Ahmad Alawad, *Slaves into Workers: Emancipation and Labor in Colonial Sudan.* Austin, Texas: University of Texas Press, 1996.

Skinner, David, *Thomas George Lawson: African Historian and Administration in Sierra Leone.* Stanford, California: Hoover Institution, 1980.

Smalldone, Joseph, *Warfare in the Sokoto Caliphate.* Cambridge: Cambridge University Press, 1977.

Smith, Brian Sharwood, *Recollections of British Administration in the Cameroons and Northern Nigeria 1921–57: 'But Always as Friends'.* Durham, North Carolina: Duke University Press, 1969.

Smith, M.G., *Affairs of Daura.* Berkely, California: University of California Press, 1978.

Smith, Noel, *Presbyterian Church of Ghana 1835–1960.* Accra, 1966.

Spaulding, J., 'The Business of Slavery in the Central Anglo-Egyptian Sudan, 1910–30', *African Economic History,* 17 (1988), pp.23–44.

Starrett, Priscilla, 'Tuareg Slavery and Slave Trade', *Slavery and Abolition,* 2 (1981), pp.83–113.

Staudinger, Paul, *In the Heart of the Hausa States.* Tr. From the German. Athens: Ohio University Press, 1990, originally published 1889.

Stoecker, Helmuth (ed.), *Kamerun unter deutscher Kolonialherrschaft,* 2 vols., Berlin: VEB Deutscher Verlag der Wissenschaften, 1960, 1968.

Stone, R.H., *Africa's Forest and Jungle or Six Years Among the Yoruba.* London, 1900.

Sulaiman, Ibrahim, *A Revolution in History: the Jihad of Usman Dan Fodio.* London, 1986.

Sundiata, I.K., *Black Scandal: The United States and the Liberian Labor Crises, 1929–1939.* Philadelphia, Pennsylvania: Institute for the Study of Human Issues, 1980.

Sundiata, I.K., *From Slaving to Neo-Slaving: the Bight of Biafra and Fernando Po in the Era of Abolition, 1927–1930.* Madison, Wisconsin: University of Wisconsin Press 1996.

Sunseri, Thaddeus, 'Slave Ransoming in German East Africa, 1885–1922', *International Journal of African Historical Studies,* 16 (1993), pp.1–18.

Tamuno, T.N., 'Genesis of the Nigerian Railway– 1', *Nigerian Magazine,* No.183, December 1963, pp.279–92.

Temperley, Howard, *British AntiSlavery 1833–70.* London: Longman, 1972.

Thomas, Northcote W., *Anthropological Report on Sierra Leone; Laws and Customs of the Timne and other Tribes.* London: Harrison and Sons, 1916.

Thompson, E.P., 'The Moral Economy of the English Crowd in the Eighteenth Century', *Past and Present,* 50 (1971), pp.76–136

BIBLIOGRAPHY

291

Tibenderana, P.K., *Sokoto Province Under British Rule*. Zaria, 1988.

Tibenderana, P.K., 'British Administration and the Decline of the Patronage-Client System in Northwestern Nigeria, 1900–1934', *African Studies Review*, 32 (1989), pp.71–95.

Tocqueville, Alexis de. 'Rapport sur l'Algérie (1847) – Extraits', pp.151–80, in Alexis de Tocqueville, *De la colonie en Algérie*. Paris: Editions Complexes 1988.

Toulmin, Camilla. *Cattle, Women and Wells. Managin Household Survival in the Sahel*. Oxford: Clarendon, 1992.

Ubah, C.N., *Government and Administration of Kano Emirate*. Nsukka, 1985.

Ubah, C.N., 'Colonial Administration and the Spread of Islam in Northern Nigeria' *The Muslim World*, 81 (1991), pp.133–48.

Ubah, C.N., 'Islamic Fiscal System and Colonial Innovations: the Kano Example' *Islamic Quarterly*, 23, (1979).

Uka, N., 'A Note on the 'Abam Warriors of Igbo Land', Ikenga: *Journal of African Studies*, 1 (1972), pp.76–82.

Ukpabi, S.C., *The Origins of the Nigerian Army (A History of the West African Frontier Force 1897–1914)*. Zaria: Gaskiya, 1987.

Van Hoven, E., 'Representing Social Hierarchy: Administrators and the Family in the French Soudan: Delafosse, Monteil, Labouret', *Cahiers d'Études Africaines*, 30 (1990), pp.179–98.

Vaughan, James and A.H.M. Kirk-Greene (eds.), *The Diary of Hamman Yaji – Chronicle of a West African Ruler*. Bloomington, Indiana: Indiana University Press, 1995.

Verecke, Catherine, 'The Slave Experience in Adamawa: Past and Present Perspectives from Yola (Nigeria), *Cahiers d'Etudes Africaines*, 34 (1994), pp.23–53

Walker, Gilbert, *Traffic and Transport in Nigeria. The example of an underdeveloped tropical territory*. London: HMSO, 1959.

Walz, Gotthilf, *Die Entwicklung der Strafrechtspflege in Kamerun unter deutscher Herrschaft, 1894 bis 1914*. Freiburg i.Br.: Klaus Schwarz, 1981.

Walz, Terence, 'Black Slavery in Egypt During the Nineteenth Century as Reflected in the Mahkama Archives of Cairo', J.R. Willis (ed.), *Slaves and Slavery in Muslim Africa*, vol.2, *The Servile Estate* (London: Frank Cass, 1985), pp.137–60.

Watson, James, *Asian and African Systems of Slavery*. Oxford: Basil Blackwell, 1980.

Watson, R.L., *The Slave Question: Liberty and Personal Property in South Africa*. Hanover, New Hampshire: Wesleyan University Press, 1990.

Webb, James. *Desert Frontier: Ecological and Economic Change along the Western Sahel*. Madison, Wisconsin: University of Wisconsin Press, 1995.

Webb, James. 'Trade in Gum Arabic: Prelude to French Conquest in Senegal, *Journal of African History*, 26 (1985), pp.149–68.

Wege, Arthur, 'Die rechtlichen Bestimmungen über die Sklaverei in den deutschen afrikanischen

Schutzgebieten', *Mitteilungen des Seminars für Orientalische Sprachen*, Vol. 18, No.3 (1915), pp.1–40.

Weidner, F., *Die Haussklaverei in Ostafrika*, Veröffentlichungen des Reichskolonialamts Nr. 7, Jena, 1915.

Willis, J.R., *Slaves and Slavery in Muslim Africa*. 2 Vols. London: Frank Cass, 1985.

Willis, Justin and Suzanne Miers, 'Becoming a Child of the House: Incorporation, Authority and Resistance in Giryama Society' *Journal of African History,* 35 (1997), pp.479–96.

Wirz, Albert, *Vom Sklavenhandel zum kolonialen Handel. Wirtschaftsräume und Wirtschaftsformen in Kamerun vor 1914*. Zürich: Atlantis, 1972.

Wooten, S., 'Colonial Administrators and the Ethnography of the Family in the French Soudan', *Cahiers d' Études Africaines*, 33 (1993), pp.419–46.

Worden, Nigel and Clifton Crais, *Breaking the Chains: Slavery and its Legacy in the Nineteenth Century Cape Colony*. Johannesburg: Witwatersrand University Press, 1994.

Wright, M., *Strategies of Slaves & Women. Life-Stories from East/Central Africa*. New York: Lilian Barber, 1993.

Wright, M., 'Bwanika: Consciousness and Protest Among Slave Women in Central Africa, 1886–1911', in Claire Robertson and Martin A. Klein (eds.), *Women and Slavery in Africa*. Madison, Wisconsin: University of Wisconsin Press, 1983.

Wylie, Kenneth, *Political Kingdoms of the Temne*. London: Holmes & Meier, 1977.

Index

Abbas, Emir, 167–8, 177–81
Abdullahi Bayero, 180, 183–4
Aboh, 192, 195
abolition: Algeria, 38–52; Cameroon, 133–44; German East Africa, 127–9; Gold Coast, 149–60; Igboland, 197–203; Mauritania, 85; Morocco, 65; Nigeria, 232–46; Sierra Leone, 208–27; Sudan, 250–67
abolition laws: French, 43, 65; Gold Coast, 150–1; Nigeria, 197–8, 201, 244–6; Sudan, 253, 255, 258
Adamawa: British rule, 143–4; Fulbe slave trade, 135–6, 142–4; German colonial rule, 141–3
Advisory Committee of Experts on Slavery (ACE), 32–4
Algeria: reluctance to abolish slavery, 38–52; slave trade, 45–6; slaves seeking asylum, 46–52
Allah bar Sarki, 180
Angoulvant, Gabriel, 30, 31
Anti-Slavery and Aborigines Protection Society, 23, 29, 83, 222; Sudan, 251, 252, 256, 258, 259, 261
anti-slavery campaigns, 16–35
'apprenticeship', 6, 155–6, 197
Aro, 192, 195, 198–9

Banja, 222
Bell, David Mandessi, 135, 138, 140
Bell, Manga, 137, 138
Bella, 75–86; revolt, 81–2
Bellegarde, L.D., 26
Beydan, 74–86
Bonnier, Étienne, 73
Bower, Captain R.L., 235, 237–8
British: Adamawa regime, 143–4; anti-slavery movement, 16–19; Gold Coast abolition, 149–60; Nigeria conquest, 194–7; Nigeria slavery policy, 167–8, 175–84, 197–8, 234–6, 237–46; *pax Britannica*, 21, 213; relationship with Germany, 142–3; Sierra Leone administration, 208–10, 213–27; Sudan conquest, 250
British and Foreign Anti-Slavery Society, 18

Brussels Act (1890), 19, 20, 21, 198
Bugeaud, Maréchal, 38–40
Bundu: Fulbe slaves, 91–106

Cameroon, 133–44; Adamawa, 135–6, 141–4; Duala, 134–5, 136–40; German colonial policy, 136–44; slave trade, 135, 142–4
Cardew, Frederick, 214
Cargill, F., 178–80
Carter, Sir Gilbert Thomas, 234–6, 239
Chamberlain, Joseph, 195
children: status, 67–8
Christian missionaries: anti-slavery, 234
cocoa plantations: slave labour, 137, 138–40
colonial officials: Gold Coast, 152–4
colonial regimes: Britain/Germany relationship, 142–3; labour needs, 6, 22; reluctance to abolish slavery, 1–2, 4–6, 20–2, *see also* British; French; Germans
Committee of Experts on Slavery (CES), 29–32
concubines: Fulbe, 105–6; German East Africa, 120–1; Kano, 173; Muslim law, 62, 67–8
contemporary slavery, 10–11, 266–7
Coppolani, Xavier, 77
Creed, T.P., 257
cult slaves: Ghana, 11; Nigeria, 193, 201–2
customary law, 6–7

Dabo, Ibrahim b. Mahmud, 169
D'Andrace, A. Freire, 26
de Tocqueville, Alexis, 38
Delafosse, Maurice, 26
Diggle, P.G.W., 257
domestic slaves: Fulbe, 91–106
Douala: German colonial regime, 136–40; slaves in society, 134–5

Egypt: Sudan relationship, 258–9
escaped slaves: colonial period, 7–8; Sierra Leone 212–18; Yorubaland, 235–6, 240
Ethiopia, 23–5, 30–1, 260, 263
export of slaves: prohibition, 19

Fabunmi, 237

294 SLAVERY AND COLONIAL RULE IN AFRICA

Festing, Major, 178–80
First World War: Bundu, 94; Nigeria, 203; post-war defections, 8; Sierra Leone, 8, 220–1; Sudan, 254–5
Forced Labour Convention (1930), 28–9
freed slaves: German east Africa, 109–30; jobs, 6, 10; servile ties, 91–106; Sierra Leone, 213, 214, 215
Freetown: freed slaves, 213, 214, 215
Freibriefe, 109–30; ages of slaves, 125–6, 127; district records (1893–96), 119–27; gender composition, 121–2, 127; numbers issued, 112–19, 125–6; reasons for issue, 111–12, 114, 115–19, 125–6
French: abolition law (1848), 43, 65; Algeria policy, 38–40, 43; Morocco policy, 65; Sahara conquest, 73–4, 76–7; West Africa policy, 76–8, 93–4
Fulani: Kano, 167–8, 169–70, 175
Fulbe: Adamawa slave trade, 135–6, 142–4; initiation, 104; Islam, 102–4; labour divisions, 100–1; *maccube* relationship, 91–106; marriage, 104–6; rights and obligations, 101–2; social divisions, 10–11, 96–9; trade slaves, 93

Gambia: abolition, 223
gender relations: slavery or marriage, 13, 50–2
German East Africa: abolition of slavery, 127–9; freeing of slaves, 109–30; plantation owners, 123; slave owners, 119–20
Germans: colonial legislation, 109–12, 127–9; relationship with Britain, 142–3; reluctance to abolish slavery, 127–8, 133–4, 136–44
Ghana *see* Gold Coast
Gold Coast: abolition laws, 150–1; administration of abolition, 151–6; 'apprenticeship', 6, 155–6; colonial officials, 152–4; Colony and Protectorate differences, 149–50, 154, 156–7, 160; evasion of abolition, 158–60; use of courts, 156–8
Grimshaw, Harold, 26, 27

Haratin: Algeria, 41–3; Mauritania, 11, 75–86; Morocco, 58–9, 63–4
Harris, John, 23–5
Hausa: colonial soldiers, 238; Kano, 167–8, 169–70

Ibadan, 232, 233, 234, 235, 237, 240, 246
Igbo: abolition of slavery, 197–203; Aro, 192, 195, 198–9; British conquest, 194–7;

descendants of slaves, 11; entrepreneurs, 190–4, 202–3, 204; palm oil trade, 193–4, 200; slave owners, 5, 189–205
Ilorin, 233, 234, 237
inheritance: Muslim law, 68–9
initiation: Fulbe, 104
International Labour Organization (ILO), 26
Islam: Fulbe, 102–4
Islamic law, 6–7; inheritance, 68–9; Morocco, 60–70
Issele-Ukwu: civil war, 195–6

Jasus, Sidi Al-Hajj `Abdel Salam, 63–4

Kano: British administration, 167–8, 175–84; Civil War (1893-95), 173–4; political competition, 168–70; royal slaves, 8–9, 167–84
Kikonkeh Island, 214–15
Kitchener, Lord, 251
Kompa, Bai, 223–4
Kunna, Madam, 222

labour: free slaves, 6, 10; German East Africa, 119–20; Igbo slaves, 192–4, 201; plantations, 123, 137, 138–40; wage labour, 10, 242–3
labour divisions: Fulbe, 100–1
labour needs: colonial regimes, 6, 22
Lagos, 234, 237, 239, 240, 241, 242–3, 244
Laird, MacGregor, 191, 192
laws, abolition: French, 43, 65; Gold Coast, 150–1; Nigeria, 197–8, 201, 244–6; Sudan, 253, 255, 258
laws, customary, 6–7
laws, Islamic, 6–7; Morocco, 60–70
League of Nations: Advisory Committee of Experts on Slavery (ACE), 32–4, 264; Committee of Experts on Slavery (CES), 29–32; Slavery Convention, 28–9, 258, 259; slavery suppression, 22–5, 34–5, 143, 222; Sudan, 258–9; Temporary Slavery Commission (TSC), 25–8
Letters of Freedom *see Freibriefe*
Lugard, Frederick: abolition of slavery, 26, 27, 30, 31, 244; Nigeria administration, 175, 176–7

McCallum, Governor H.E., 240, 242
maccube, 91–106
Mali: independence, 84
marriage: Fulbe, 104–6; royal slaves, 173; as slavery disguise, 13, 50–2
Maugham, Robin, 83
Mauritania: abolition of slavery, 11, 85; French colonialism, 77–8; independence,

84–5; Senegal relationship, 80, 85; slave status, 79–80; social organization, 75
mawla, 69
Maxwell, Sir George, 32–4, 263–4
Miner, Horace, 79
moral economy, 210
Morocco: abolition of slavery, 65; buying and selling slaves, 65–7; European law, 64–5; Muslim law, 60–70; slave army, 58–9, 63–4; status of slaves, 59–60; trans-Saharan slave trade, 57–8
Moulay Isma'il, 58–9, 63–4
Muslim law *see* Islamic law

N'Diaye, al-Hajj Mahamadou, 103–4
Nfa Nonko, 225–6
Ngaoundere, 135–6
Niger Delta: British conquest, 195–7
Nigeria: British conquest, 194–7; Cameroon relationship, 142; colonial slavery policy, 167–8, 175–84, 197–8, 234–6, 237–46; Igboland, 189–205; Kano, 8–9, 167–84; Yoruba, 232–46
Noel-Buxton, Lord, 30
nomads: Sahara, 74–5

Ogedemgbe, 237

palm oil trade, 193–4, 200
pawning, 12, 95
pax Britannica, 21, 213
plantations: Cameroon, 137, 138–40; German East Africa, 123
Ponty, Governor General William, 78

railway: Nigeria, 243
redemption price, 122, 123, 241–2, 245
redemption schemes, 6
Reguibat, 84
Royal Niger Company, 196, 197
royal slaves: British administration, 175–84; Kano, 8–9, 167–84; marriage, 173; relationship with Emir, 174; title-holding system, 170–3

Sahara: Algerian, 40–52; French conquest, 73–4; slave revolt, 81–2; slaves in society, 40–3, 75
scarification, 158
scramble for Africa, 1, 20, 208
Sedu, 220–1, 224
Selassie, Haile, 30–1
Senegal: independence, 96; Mauritania relationship, 80, 85
Senegambia: Bundu, 91–106
Sierra Leone: British administration, 208–10,

213–27; Colony/Protectorate distinction, 213–14, 216; compensation demands, 223–5; Creole elite, 215, 224–5; emancipation of slaves, 223–7; escaped slaves, 208, 212–18; Freetown, 213, 214, 215; pre-colonial servitude, 211–13; slave resistance, 208–27
Simon, Sir John, 29
Sitt Amna, 260, 262
Slatin, Rudolf von, 251–2
slave owners: German East Africa, 119–20; Igbo, 9, 189–205; redemption of slaves, 122–3; reluctance to free slaves, 9–10
slave resistance: Sierra Leone, 208–27
slave trade: Adamawa, 135, 142–4; Atlantic, 190, 192. East Africa, 124; Ethiopia to Sudan, 250, 263; trans-Saharan, 45–6, 57–8
Slavery Convention (1926), 28–9, 35, 258, 259
slaves: agricultural, 119–20; buying and selling of, 65–6, 83; cult slaves, 11, 193, 201–2; domestic, 91–106; escaped, 7–8, 212–18, 235–6, 240; origins, 124; present-day, 10–11, 266–7; royal, 8–9, 167–84; trade slaves, 93
Songhay: treatment of slaves, 81
Sterry, Wasey, 255
Stigl, Hermann, 120
Strahan, Governor, 150–1
Sudan: abolition of slavery, 256–66; Anglo-Egyptian Condominium, 250–67; contemporary situation, 11, 266–7; cotton production, 255–6; Egypt relationship, 258–9; First World War, 254–5; slave trade with Ethiopia, 260, 263; tolerance of slavery, 250–5

Temple, C.L., 131
Temporary Slavery Commission (TSC), 25–8, 34–5
Timbuktu, 73, 74, 79, 83
trade slaves: Fulbe, 93
Tuareg: resistance to French, 78–80; use of slaves, 41, 74–86
Tunisia: slaves fleeing to Algeria, 48–9

United Nations: Working Group on Contemporary Forms of Slavery, 35, 267
Usman Dan Fodio, 169
Usman, Emir, 167–8, 181–3

von Puttkamer, Governor, 141–2

wage labour, 10, 242–3
Williams, Fibbian, 222

Willis, C.A., 259
Wingate, R.F., 252, 254
women: concubines, 62, 67–8, 105–6, 120–1, 173; German East Africa, 121–2, 127; Igbo, 191–2; married into slavery, 13, 50–2; sexual exploitation, 67

World War I *see* First World War

Yoruba: colonial slavery policy, 234–6, 237–46; domestic slaves, 232–46; railway effects, 243; redemption fee, 241–2, 245; Sixteen Years' War, 235